Scott Thornbury

Natural Grammar

OXFORD

OXFORD
UNIVERSITY PRESS

Great Clarendon Street, Oxford OX2 6DP

Oxford University Press is a department of the University of Oxford.
It furthers the University's objective of excellence in research, scholarship,
and education by publishing worldwide in

Oxford New York

Auckland Bangkok Buenos Aires Cape Town Chennai
Dar es Salaam Delhi Hong Kong Istanbul Karachi Kolkata
Kuala Lumpur Madrid Melbourne Mexico City Mumbai Nairobi
São Paulo Shanghai Taipei Tokyo Toronto

Oxford and Oxford English are registered trade marks of
Oxford University Press in the UK and in certain other countries

The British National Corpus is a collaborative project involving Oxford
University Press, Longman, Chambers, the Universities of Oxford and
Lancaster, and the British Library.

Any websites referred to in this publication are in the public domain and
their addresses are provided by Oxford University Press for information
only. Oxford University Press disclaims any responsibility for the content

ISBN 0 19 438624 4

Illustrated by Roger Penwill

Printed in China

Symbols & Conventions

Symbols

' In the section called Set phrases, the phrases in speech marks
are more typical of spoken language than written language:

'… (and)/and that sort of thing' 'how do you do?'

▲ At the end of the Grammar patterns and Set phrases sections,
this symbol introduces an explanation of how a pattern works
or in which context an idiomatic phrase is used.

= This introduces an equivalent phrase or an explanatory gloss.

~ This indicates dialogue.

→ An arrow indicates a cross-reference to another keyword
(→ make) for comparison or more information; in the
Exercises section it also links an example question with an
example answer (What are you called? → *My name is Nigel*).

Conventions in the Grammar patterns:

1 **sort** | (+ of + NP)

This means that the pattern consists of the keyword *sort* on its
own, or *sort* followed by *of* and a noun phrase:

*I don't like jasmine tea. Do you have another **sort**?*
*What **sort of books** do you read?*

2 all/many/most | + **sorts** | (+ of + NP)

This means that the pattern consists of *all* or *many* or *most*
followed by *sorts,* or alternatively *all* or *many* or *most* followed by
sorts followed by *of* and a noun phrase:

*What sort of pizzas do they do? ~ **All sorts**.*
*I like **most sorts of music**.*

3 **sort** of | + […]

This means that the pattern consists of *sort of* followed by an
'open slot', that is, any part of speech, such as a noun, verb,
preposition, adjective, etc.:

*What's Janine like? ~ She's **sort of tall and pretty**.*
*What's the weather like? ~ It's **sort of raining**.*

Introduction
(for students and teachers)

This book is about grammar, but it is organized around words. Why? Very simply, words have grammar. That is to say, when you use a word, you are obliged to choose from the particular grammar patterns associated with that word. Take a word such as *for*, for example. The phrase *for students and teachers* is an example of the common pattern: **for** + NP. (If you are unsure about these grammar terms, look at the *Glossary*, p. iii.) But there are other patterns associated with *for*. For example:

- **for** | + -ing: *You can also use a compass **for telling** the time.*
- **for** | + NP | + to-infinitive: *I'm waiting **for him to call**.*

So, if you learn the grammar of *for*, you are learning at least three important grammar patterns in English. (Notice that there are no grammar patterns such as *for* + to-infinitive, or *for* + NP + -ing. So you cannot say: ~~I went to London for to see the Queen.~~ • ~~These pills are for me helping to sleep.~~)

These three patterns with *for* are also very frequent. This is because *for* is a very high-frequency word in English. In fact, it is the ninth most frequent word in written English (according to one study). It is not surprising that the grammar associated with high-frequency words – like *for, to, the, you, as, that,* etc. – is very high-frequency grammar and so, of course, very useful grammar. So, as Professor John Sinclair put it: 'Learners would do well to learn the common words of the language very thoroughly, because they carry the main patterns of the language.'

This book, then, is organized around one hundred of the most common words in English. The common grammar of each word is displayed in the form of patterns. These cover all the most important grammar structures in English. (On p. ii you will find a list of the common structures that are dealt with.) So, by learning these high-frequency words and their high-frequency patterns, the learner is getting traditional grammar 'for free', as it were.

For free, by the way, is a good example of a *collocation*. That is to say, *for* and *free* often go together – so often that they form a 'chunk', or 'set phrase' – such as *for example,* for example! Other collocations with *for* include the phrasal verbs *look for* and *long for,* and the 'noun + *for*' combinations: *time for, need for, room for, …* etc. This reminds us that, as the writer Virginia Woolf said: 'It is a very obvious but always mysterious fact that a word is not a single and separate entity: it is part of other words … words belong to each other.' So, as well as grammar information, this book displays useful collocations and set phrases derived from the hundred high-frequency words we have chosen. If nothing else, these 'chunks' may offer the learner a short-cut to the grammar of English.

The exercises that accompany each section explore the grammar and collocations of each word, with a view to helping fix these in the memory. There is a Key at the back of the book.

Some of the exercises include the use of *concordance lines*. These are examples of a word in its context, taken from a huge database (or *corpus*) of authentic texts, both spoken and written. The database we have used is the British National Corpus. Here, for example, are some concordance lines for *for*. Can you find examples of the three patterns mentioned in this introduction?

> I was able to arrange **for** him to do a project.
> He asked for the money **for** a cup of coffee.
> He blames himself **for** being naïve.

We hope you find this book useful, and that you will enjoy learning the grammar of English *naturally,* through its *words*.

Acknowledgements

The principles that inspired this book derive to a large extent from the insights of Michael Lewis, and of Jane and Dave Willis, and I wish to record my enormous debt and gratitude to them (without, of course, implying any direct responsibility on their part). For their hard work, professionalism, and encouragement, I am hugely grateful to the editorial, research, and design team at Oxford University Press, and, in particular, to my editor, Glynnis Chantrell.
Thanks | + to | + **you** | + all!

Contents

page	keyword	page	keyword	page	keyword
2	a/an	70	know	138	still
4	all	72	let	140	stop
6	am/is/are	74	like	142	take
8	and	76	little	144	tell
10	any	78	long	146	than
12	as	80	look	148	that
14	ask	82	make	150	the
16	at	84	may	152	then
18	back	86	mean	154	there
20	be	88	more	156	thing
22	been	90	most	158	think
24	being	92	much	160	this
26	but	94	my	162	time
28	by	96	need	164	to¹
30	can	98	never	166	to³
32	come	100	no	168	too
34	could	102	not	170	up
36	did	104	now	172	used
38	do/does	106	of	174	very
40	for	108	on	176	want
42	get	110	one	178	was/were
44	give	112	or	180	way
46	go	114	other	182	well
48	going	116	own	184	what
50	good	118	place	186	when
52	got	120	put	188	who
54	had	122	say	190	why
56	have/has	124	see	192	will
58	how	126	seem	194	with
60	if	128	should	196	work
62	in	130	so	198	would
64	it	132	some	200	you
66	just	134	sort		
68	keep	136	start		

Grammar index

Here are the keyword entries where you will find information about features of traditional grammar:

articles → a/an, → the

auxiliary verbs → am/is/are, → be, → been, → being, → did, → do/does, → had, → have, → was/were

comparatives → more, → than

conditionals → if; (**1st**) → will; (**2nd & 3rd**) → had, → was/were, → would

conjunctions → and, → but, → if, → or, → so, → then

determiners → a/an, → all, → any, → more, → most, → much, → (**also possessive**) → my, → no, → one, → other, → some, → that, → the, → this

discourse markers → and, → so, → then, → well

future tenses → going, → will
    future continuous → will   **future perfect** → will

infinitive → to¹

linking verbs → am/is/are, → be, → seem

modal verbs → can, → could, → may, → might, → need, → should, → used, → will, → would

negation → never, → no, → not

participle (past) → been; (**present**); → being, going

passive → by
    present passive → am/is/are   **past passive** → was/were
    present continuous passive → being
    present perfect passive → been

past continuous → was/were

past perfect → had

past perfect continuous → had

past simple → did

phrasal verbs → at, → back, → by, → come, → do, → for, → get, → give, → go, → in, → keep, → let, → look, → make, → on, → put, → see, → start, → stop, → take, → tell, → think, → up, → with, → work

prepositions → at, → by, → for, → in, → of, → on, → than, → to², → up, → with

present continuous → am/is/are, → still

present perfect → have, → just, → never

present perfect continuous → been, → have

present simple → do/does

pronouns → all, → any, → it, → more, → most, → much, → one, → other, → some, → that, → this, → you

questions → am/is/are, → did, → do/does, → had, → have, → how, → was/were, → what, → when, → who, → why
    indirect questions → how, → what, → when, → who, → why
    object questions → what, → who
    subject questions → what, → who

relative clauses → that, → who

reported speech → ask, → say, → tell, → that

superlatives → most

verb tenses → am/is/are, → be, → been, → being, → did, → do/does, → had, → have, → was/were

Glossary

adjective: a word like *short*, *red*, or *exciting*, that tells you about the qualities of a person or thing or event.

adverb: a word like *slowly*, *well*, *there*, etc. which tells you how, where, or when an event happens.

adverbial: a word or group of words that functions like an **adverb**. Adverbials can be adverb phrases like *very slowly*, or prepositional phrases like *in the corner*, or noun phrases like *yesterday afternoon*.

auxiliary verb: a word like *do*, *had*, *was*, etc. used with main verbs (*want*, *play*, etc.) to form tenses, questions, and negatives.

bare infinitive: the infinitive without *to* in front of it, as in constructions like *it helped me **decide***.

clause: a group of words containing a **verb**, forming the main structure of which sentences are built: [*I was working at home*], [*writing the report* [*my boss had asked for*]], [*when the phone rang*].

collocation: the way words typically combine with other words, as in *take a break*, *short hair*, or *get on with*.

conjunction: a word like *and*, *but*, *which*, *so*, that links two **clauses**, or phrases, or words.

countable noun: a **noun** that has both singular and plural forms, and which can be used with *a/an* and numbers: *a car*, *three cars*.

determiner: a word, like *the*, *some*, *my*, *many*, *no*, etc. that belongs to the class of words that can go at the beginning of a noun phrase: *the black taxi* • *my many friends*.

discourse marker: a word like *well*, *anyway*, *so*, *however*, that usually goes at the beginning of an **utterance** or **clause** and indicates a link between what has been said and what follows: *It was not a very good hotel. **Still**, it was cheap.*

idiom: an expression or **collocation** whose meaning is different from the literal meaning of the individual words that make it up: *out of the blue* (= unexpectedly); *take after* (= resemble).

if-clause: a clause starting with if, which tells us about possible or hypothetical situations. Also called a *conditional clause*. ➜ if

-ing: a word ending in -*ing*, such as *walking* or *seeing*, which is used 1. to form verb tenses (*I am **walking***) where it is also called the *present participle*, and 2. like a noun after certain verbs and prepositions: *I like **walking**.* • *I look forward to **seeing** you.*

irregular verb: see **regular verb**

lexical verb: a verb that is not an auxiliary verb or a modal verb, such as *make*, *understand*, *arrive*, etc. (Also called a *main verb*).

linking verb: a verb like *be* or *seem* that joins two ideas, giving more information about the subject: *She **is** a laboratory technician.* • *It **seemed** like a good idea.*

main verb: = **lexical verb**

modal verb: a verb such as *can*, *may*, *should*, *must*, etc. which is used to express possibility and to make offers, suggestions, commands, etc. Modal verbs function like **auxiliary verbs**.

noun: a word like *bus*, *driver*, *journey*, *fare*, *request*, etc. that can be used after a **determiner** as the **subject** or **object** of a sentence.

noun phrase (NP): a word or group of words consisting of at least a **noun** or a **pronoun** and which functions like a noun: *last night* • *your old car* • *I* • *those big red London buses*.

object: a **noun phrase** which refers to what or who is affected by the action described by the verb: *I caught **the bus**.* • *I paid **the driver*** (= indirect object) ***the fare*** (= direct object).

particle: an **adverb** or **preposition** which combines with a verb to form a **phrasal verb**: *Get **up*** • *I looked **for** the keys*, etc.

past participle: a verb form that is used to form the present perfect and the passive, for example: *I have **worked**.* • *The letter was **written**.* Regular past participles end in -*(e)d*.

phrasal verb: a verb and **particle** combination, often with idiomatic meaning (see **idiom**), e.g. *I **got up** at ten.* • *Does he **take after** his Dad?*

possessive: one of the **determiners** such as *my*, *your*, *their*, etc. which expresses possession.

preposition: a word, or group of words, like *in*, *on*, *behind*, *in front of*, which often indicate place or time, and are always followed by a **noun phrase**: *in the garden*; *on Sunday*; *behind the times*.

pronoun: a word like *she*, *me*, *it*, *you*, etc. that can be used in place of a **noun** as **subject** or **object** of a sentence.

regular verb: a **verb** such as *work*, *live*, etc. whose past tense and **past participle** are formed by adding -*(e)d* to the **bare infinitive**: *worked*, *lived*, etc. Irregular verbs do not follow this rule.

set phrase: a type of **collocation** which is fixed and functions as a complete unit, and is often used as a social formula or a **discourse marker**: *How are you?* • *So, to cut a long story short, … .*

subject: the **noun phrase** that typically comes before the verb and tells you who or what is the agent or topic of the clause: *I caught the bus.* ***The bus** was crowded.*

that-clause: a clause starting with *that*, often functioning as the object of a reporting verb: *I was told **that** he was busy.* Often the word *that* can be omitted: *I was told he was busy.* ➜ that

to-infinitive: the form of the verb that has no endings, tense, person, etc., and which is preceded by *to*: *'**To be** or not **to be**.'* ➜ to¹

uncountable noun: a **noun** which cannot be counted, and which therefore has no plural form and does not follow *a/an* or numbers: *some **bread*** • *a lot of **noise***.

utterance: something you say, consisting of one or more words, phrases, clauses, or sentences.

verb: a word or words such as *worked*, *has*, *costs*, *takes off*, that expresses what someone or something does or is (see **subject**).

wh-clause: a clause beginning with a **wh-word**: *I liked **what I saw**.*

wh-word (wh): a question word such as *where*, *when*, *who*, and *how*.

a / an

[indefinite article] used with singular nouns:
(1) to introduce a new person or thing into a text:
An Englishman, a Scotsman and an Australian were on a plane ....
(2) to show that a person or thing is a member of a group:
Fatima's a Muslim.
(3) to talk generally about a class of things: *An octopus has eight legs.*

NOTE: Use *a* in front of a word that starts with a consonant sound, and use *an* in front of a word that starts with a vowel sound:

a plane; a Muslim; a house; a university student
an octopus; an hour; an umbrella; an MA /ˌem'eɪ /

Grammar patterns

1 NP | + is/was | + **a/an** | + classifying noun

My flatmate is a Swede.
Jane Austen was an English writer.
The kangaroo is a marsupial.

▲ for classifying a person or thing, e.g. saying what their nationality or job is

2 there | + is/was etc. | + **a/an** | + NP | (+ adverbial)

There is a supermarket next to the station.
There was an immediate reaction.
There was a strange smell in the kitchen.

▲ for introducing a new topic, e.g. in a description
(→ there)

3 NP | + has/'s got | + **a/an** | (+ adjective) | + NP

Milan has a Gothic cathedral.
Jan's got a nice smile.
Has Vigo got an airport?

▲ for describing places, people, things

4 NP | + is/was | + such | + **a/an** | + NP

Kevin is such a hard worker.
It's such a shame.

▲ to emphasize how you feel about something or someone

Collocations

There are many 'verb + noun' combinations beginning *have a ...* or *take a ... .* For example:
have a drink, have a bite (to eat), have a laugh, have/take a look, have a go, have a talk, have a say, have a try, have a ride, have/take a walk, have/take a rest.

Can you take a look at my homework?
We stopped at a roadside café and had a bite to eat.
I had a go on Robin's new motorbike.
Everyone should have a say in the peace process.

Set phrases

- **a few / a little / a lot (of)** etc. → little

We had a few friends round for dinner.
There's a little salad left, if you'd like some.
How much time have we got? ~ A lot.
▲ for talking about quantities

- **a kilo / a metre / a dozen** etc.
Petrol costs 3 euros a litre.
How much are the eggs? ~ £1.50 a dozen.
▲ for talking about prices

- **a coffee / a fruit juice / a Coke** etc.
Would you like a coffee?
He bought me a tomato juice and ordered a Scotch for himself.
▲ to refer to a cup, glass, bottle, or can, of a certain drink

- **a hundred / a thousand / a million** etc.
A hundred and twenty people attended the meeting.
There were more than a million viewers.
▲ a less emphatic form of *one*

- **a year / a week / an hour** etc.
She checks her e-mail three or four times a day.
I go to the gym once a week.
They get paid less than ten dollars an hour.
▲ to talk about how often something happens, or the rate of something (Here *a/an* means 'every'.)

Exercises

❶ Classify the following animals, using these categories:

fish   bird   reptile   mammal   insect   amphibian

a   A horse is a mammal.
b   A frog is ....
c   A fly is ....
d   A snake is ....
e   A duck is ....
f   A whale is ....
g   A shark is ....
h   An ostrich is ....

❷ Choose a job from the list to complete each of the sentences below:

soldier   lawyer   mechanic   architect   cook
teacher   waiter   doctor   taxi-driver

a   She designs buildings. ~ Oh, so she's ....
b   Alan fixes cars. ~ So he's .... , is he?
c   My brother works in a school. ~ Is he............ ?
d   I have my own taxi. ~ Ah, you're .... , are you?
e   Jessica is studying medicine. ~ Oh, so she's going to be
    ....
f   Eric works with a law firm. ~ He's .... , is he?
g   My cousin's in the army. ~ How long has she been .... ?
h   Jack works in a restaurant. ~ Is he .... or .... ?

❸ Remember that *a/an* is used with countable nouns: that is, nouns like *book*, *person*, and *fact*. *A/an* is not usually used with nouns like *air*, *water*, *information*, that are masses, and therefore uncountable. However, many nouns can have both countable and uncountable senses, depending on whether we think of them as units or masses.

Complete these sentences with *a/an*, but only where necessary:

a   The houses made of .... stone survived the earthquake.
b   Hang on! I've got .... stone in my shoe.
c   You've got .... egg on your shirt.
d   Excuse me, waiter, there's .... hair in my soup.
e   Would you like .... lemon in your tea?
f   She's got .... long fair hair.
g   There's .... lemon in the fridge: can you cut it in half?
h   For breakfast I usually have .... boiled egg and a piece of toast.

❹ *To walk* refers to walking in general. *To have a walk* means to experience a single action of walking, from start to finish. Choose the best alternative to complete these sentences:

a   Shall we stop at the next café and .... ?
    (*drink/have a drink*)
b   My parents don't .... (*drink/have a drink*).
c   When you've got a moment, I'd like to .... It's about my salary. (*chat/have a chat*)
d   In the library you're not supposed to ....
    (*chat/have a chat*)
e   Don't .... ! I'm getting undressed. (*look/have a look*).
f   It's a nice day – let's go and .... (*swim/have a swim*)
g   My computer keeps crashing. ~ OK, I'll .... and see what the problem is. (*look/have a look*)
h   How do you keep so fit? ~ I .... (*swim/have a swim*).

❺ Match the two parts of the sentences.

a   I normally go to the dentist once   1   a dozen.
b   These roses cost $20   2   a litre.
c   The car was doing 150 kilometres   3   a year.
d   Lamb is selling at £7.50   4   a week.
e   The *Sunday Mail* is published once   5   a metre.
f   Electric cable costs 50 cents   6   a kilo.
g   How much is the oil? ~ €2.50   7   a day.
h   The mail is delivered twice   8   an hour.

all

[determiner] the whole number or amount of: *She ate all the chocolates.* • *The cat drank all the milk.*
[pronoun] everything; every single one: *All's well that ends well.* • *We can all go home.*
[adverb] completely: *Gavin was all alone.* • *The game is all over.*

Grammar patterns

1 **all** | + plural or uncountable noun

All birds have wings, but not all birds can fly.
All hotel guests must check out by 11pm.
All fruit is good for you.

▲ to talk in general about every person or thing in the world, or of a particular kind

2 **all** | + (of) | + the/these/my etc. | + plural or uncountable noun

All the marked items are half price.
We threw out all of the furniture.
All of our old schoolmates are coming to the reunion.
Thanks for all your advice.

▲ to say something about people or things viewed as a group or set

3 **all** | + (of) | + the/this/my etc. | + singular countable noun

Have you read all the newspaper?
The baby didn't eat all its dinner.
Nearly all of his body is tattooed.

▲ to say something about one thing in its entirety

4 **all** | + of | + object pronoun

Is there room in the car for all of us?
You'll have to share your sweets, because I haven't got enough for all of you.

▲ to include every person

5 NP | + **all**

We all live in a yellow submarine.
The children all stood in a line.

The meal was delicious: I enjoyed it all.

▲ to emphasize that everyone or everything is included

6 **all** | + relative clause | + is/was etc.

All I want is a room somewhere.
All you need is love.

▲ to say that only one thing exists or is necessary

7 **all** | + adjective/adverb/preposition

He sat all alone by the fire.
The party's all off – the landlord wouldn't give us permission.
I'd like to hear all about your wedding.

▲ to emphasize completeness

Collocations

Here are some frequent combinations of *all* + time expressions:

all day/night/morning/afternoon/evening etc.
all summer/winter etc.
all day long/all night long/all summer long etc.
all year round
all the time (= continually)
for all time (= for ever)
of all time

That bird sings all day long.
They live in their beach house all year round.
He was the greatest dramatist of all time.

Set phrases

(not) … at all = in any way
I liked the book but I didn't like the film at all.

' by all means '
Can I call you Jeffrey? ~ By all means.
▲ for giving permission

all in all
All in all, it was a very successful conference.
▲ for summing up

- **all of a sudden** = suddenly
  All of a sudden, a face appeared at the window …

- **for all** = despite
  For all his faults, he's still a nice guy.

- **'for all I/we know'**
  For all I know, he may be a hundred.
  ▲ to say that something may be true, but it's not important to you

- **first of all …**
  First of all, I want to thank the organizers …
  ▲ to emphasize what comes first

- **after all**
  You're coming after all! ~ Yes, I changed my mind.
  ▲ to say that something happens in spite of what has been said or planned

Exercises

① Note that in Grammar pattern 1 *of* is not possible, but in Grammar patterns 2 and 3, *of* is optional. In Grammar pattern 4, *of* is obligatory.

Decide if the following sentences are correct. Correct the ones that are not:

a All the women sat on one side and all the men sat on the other.
b All of tap water should be boiled.
c Thanks again for all your help.
d All of my cousins are married.
e All dinosaurs were cold-blooded.
f Dinosaurs are extinct. A meteor may have killed all them.
g All of babies cry at night.
h Climate change affects all of us.
i Have you done all of your homework?
j Sit down, all you!

② *All, every, whole,* and *both*. **Study how these words are used in these concordance lines:**

He's been bouncing about the office **all** day like a
  rubber ball.
Not **all** the information in electronic resources will
  be correct.

Every patient is treated according to his specific needs.
And because holism involves **every** aspect of
  the individual …
I work **every** day from 6.20 to 9.30 a.m.
It keeps the **whole** roof in position.
He brought the **whole** performance to life.
There is nowhere more beautiful than this in the
  whole world.
This account gives rise to two questions, **both** of them
  large and difficult.
She had loved **both** her parents.

Now choose the best word (*all, every, whole,* or *both*) to complete each of these sentences:

a .... child should learn to read and write.
b The .... town was flooded.
c I have two brothers. .... of them are married.
d They painted their .... house white.
e Someone has eaten .... the breakfast cereal.
f .... my parents were teachers.
g Not .... teachers are strict.
h .... teacher in our school is nice.
i The children spent the .... day playing.
j He takes the bus to work .... day.
k On Friday I worked .... day.

③ **Here are some more set phrases with *all*. Can you use them to complete the sentences below?**

all right	by all accounts	of all things	all along
all being well	all too soon	all the better	in all

a I knew .... that he wasn't a policeman. It was obvious.
b The traffic isn't too bad, so, ... , we should be home by midnight.
c I've never met her, but, ... , she's extremely nice.
d I love travelling, so, if my company sends me to China, ...
e At the funeral I counted over a hundred people, ...
f The concert ended .... : I was just starting to enjoy myself.
g I can't understand my sister. Now she wants to work in a circus, ...
h Don't cry. Everything's going to be ....

am / is / are

[present of irregular verb → be] (1) a lexical verb, linking two ideas: *Emma is a teacher.* • *The eggs are in the fridge.*
(2) auxiliary verb: *I'm doing my homework.* • *Coffee is produced in Colombia.*

NOTE: The forms of the verb *be* in the present are:

	singular	plural
1st person	I am (I'm)	we are (we're)
2nd person	you are (you're)	
3rd person	he is (he's) she is (she's) it is (it's)	they are (they're)

→ be
→ being
→ was/were
→ been

Grammar patterns
(main verb)

1 NP | + **am/is/are** | + NP/adjective/preposition/adverb

Warsaw is the capital of Poland.
Are you well?
I'm in the shower.
The neighbour's lights aren't on.

▲ to give more information about the subject, such as who, or what, or where, or when, or how

(auxiliary verb)

2 NP | + **am/is/are** | + -ing

Kate is watching TV.
The nights are getting colder, aren't they?
 Whenever we go to Bilbao it is raining.

▲ to talk about things in progress in the present – either now, or these days, or very generally (This pattern is called the present continuous.)

I am flying to Athens next week.
When are you seeing Aurelio?

▲ to talk about future arrangements

3 NP | + **am/is/are** | + to-infinitive

Talks are to begin next week in Washington.

▲ a more formal way of talking about future arrangements, emphasizing their certainty

4 NP | + **am/is/are** | + past participle

Where is Catalan spoken?
Towels are not provided.
I'm often asked that question.

▲ to talk about things that happen in the present, without needing to say who or what causes them (This is called the simple present passive. → by)

Collocations

Some of the most frequent verbs that occur in Grammar pattern 4 (the passive) in spoken language are: *do, make, call, put, give, take, use,* and *tell.*

The laundry is done on Fridays.
What is a cash-dispenser called in French?

Some of the most frequent verbs that occur in the passive (in all tenses) in technical and academic writing are: *make, give, use, find, see, take, do, call,* and *say.*

Most light switches are made from white plastic.
A Petri dish is used for cultivating bacteria.

Adverbs that most frequently occur with Grammar pattern 4 (the passive) are: *now, also, well, still, actually,* and *often.*

Rhodesia is now called Zimbabwe.
Alligators are also found in China.
The kitchen sink is still blocked.

Set phrases

 • '**are you (still) there?**'
… and so I was saying to Brenda … Are you there? ~

Yes, yes, I'm listening. Go on.

▲ when you are speaking on the telephone

- ‘ **Where are you?** ’

  Hi. ~ Where are you? ~ I'm on the train.

  ▲ frequently asked question when speaking on a mobile (or cell) phone

- ‘ **Where are you from?** ’

  Where are you from? ~ Well, I was born in England, but I grew up in Australia.

  ▲ to ask someone's nationality, or home town

- ‘ **What's it called in Spanish/English/Chinese?** etc. ’

  What's an artichoke called in Spanish? ~ Una alcachofa.

  ▲ to ask for a translation

Exercises

❶ Put the word in brackets in the correct place in the sentence:

a (is) What your brother doing these days?
b (not) The price of oil is going up.
c (are) You're not Canadian, you?
d (you) Where are from?
e (always) Alessandro is late for class.
f (playing) Our team is not on Saturday.
g (am) Are you making lunch or I?
h (is) It's not snowing but it raining.
i (to) The conference is start on Saturday.
j (is) What a scanner used for?
k (still) Some chopsticks are made of wood.
l (is) Chinese also spoken in Singapore.

❷ Use the verbs below to complete the text, using the present continuous. With pronouns use short forms (*I'm, you're*, etc.):

stay   watch   do (x2)   make   have
read   write   play   go

Hi Ali, how are things? I (a) .... this e-mail while Chris (b) .... dinner. It's unusually quiet here at the moment. The boys (c) .... TV and the girls (d) .... computer games in their room. Mum (e) .... the newspaper, and Dad (f) .... a bath. Gran (g) .... with us at the moment: she (h) .... into hospital next week for her operation. She (i) .... a crossword right now. Well, that's about it. And you, what (j) .... ?
Bye for now,
Rosie.

❸ Choose from these verbs to complete the sentences:

~~get~~   spread   improve   get   rise
fall   expand   disappear   increase

a The climate in many countries is getting warmer.
b Because of this global warming, the level of the sea ....
c The population of the world .... steadily, …
d … although in some developed countries it ....
e The standard of living in many 'northern' countries .... ,
f … while in the 'south' it .... worse.
g Unfortunately, many traditional cultures and languages .... , …
h … while the use of English .... to all parts of the world, …
i … and the global marketplace .... relentlessly.

❹ Match the two parts of these questions:

a Where is tea …		1 now called?
b Where is Farsi …		2 made from?
c What is an axe …		3 manufactured?
d What is Leningrad …		4 played?
e Where are koala bears …		5 spoken?
f What is spaghetti …		6 produced?
g Where are Toyota cars…		7 used for?
h Where is cricket …		8 found?

Now, write answers for the questions.

Farsi is spoken in Iran.

and

[conjunction] joins two words, word groups, clauses, and sentences: *There's hot and cold water.* • *The match finished and we all left.* • *'The bus is fast. And it's not expensive.'*

Grammar patterns

1   phrase | + **and** | + phrase
    phrase, phrase | + **and** | + phrase

We bought some apples and bananas.
Everyone was waving and cheering madly.
You and I are both Scorpios.
The apartment was small, dark and very uninviting.

▲ to join two or more ideas

2   clause | + **and** | + clause

Jack did the dishes and Jill watched the news.

▲ to say that two (or more) things happen at the same time

Jack washed the clothes and Jill ironed them.

▲ to say that one action follows another

Jack was tired and went to bed.

▲ to show that one thing causes another

3   (you) | + imperative | + **and** | + clause with *will*

You do that again and I'll call the police!
Keep practising and you'll get better.

▲ to say that, if something happens, something will result

4   try | + **and** | + verb
    come/go | + **and** | + verb
    wait | + **and** | + see

Try and relax.
Come and see the penguins.
Shall we phone for a doctor? ~ No, let's wait and see.

▲ to join two actions by saying what the purpose of the first one is

5   word | + **and** | + same word
    lots/loads/tons etc. | + **and** | + lots/loads/tons etc.

I laughed and laughed.
The speeches went on and on.
It got colder and colder.
There were loads and loads of presents.

▲ to emphasize the fact that something is repeated, or continues for a long time, or increases, or is a lot

6   both | + phrase | + **and** | + phrase

Both my brother and my sister are fair-haired.
He can both speak and write Chinese.

▲ to emphasize that two things exist or share the same characteristics

Collocations

The following verbs frequently follow 'go + and':
see, get, have, do, make, buy, tell, ask.

Let's go and have a pizza.
Can you go and see who's at the door?

The following verbs frequently follow 'come + and':
get, see, sit, say, have, help, stay.

Come and help with the cleaning.
Why don't you come and sit next to me?

The following verbs frequently follow 'try + and':
get, find, remember, do, make, put.

Try and remember: where did you last put the keys?

Many adjectives can follow *nice and …* or *good and …* to add positive emphasis:

The shops are nice and handy.
It makes your teeth nice and white.
Tie it up good and tight.

And follows *hundred*:

a hundred and ten; six hundred and twenty-five

Set phrases

- '**and so on / and stuff / and everything**' = etc.

  They asked me for my driving licence, my passport and so on.
  She does all kinds of dangerous sports, like hang-gliding and stuff.

  ▲ for expanding a category, or finishing an utterance, in a vague way

- **and / or …**

  Come round for a drink and/or a meal.

  ▲ to say that two things, or only one of them, can exist or may happen

Exercises

❶ Put *and* in the correct place (one only) in each of these sentences:

a   Can you get a dozen large eggs, some green cooking apples, some carrots?

b   It's a lovely modern house it has a garage.

c   The children were shouting at each other throwing things.

d   Tim came home, hung up his coat, sat down, turned on the TV.

e   They charge ten pounds fifty for a hundred fifty copies.

f   You can come have some chocolate cake if you like.

g   These big leather armchairs are nice comfortable.

h   Try remember where you left my blue plastic folder.

❷ Many word pairs are joined by *and* to make a set phrase:

I'm going somewhere where there's a bit of peace and quiet.
I don't like it when the boat goes up and down.

These word pairs are often formed from synonyms (*peace and quiet*) or opposites (*up and down*), or words that sound similar: *part and parcel*, *spick and span*, *high and dry*.

Make word pairs by matching words in the two columns, and then use them to complete the sentences below.

off		then
here		foremost
back	**+ and +**	out
in		there
there		on
first		forth

a   I seem to spend the entire day driving the kids ………… to school.

b   They liked him so much they offered him the job ………… .

c   ………… , I would like to thank the organizers of this conference.

d   I've worked here, ………… , for about two years.

e   It's been very busy in the office: there've been people ………… all morning.

f   The island is very unspoilt – with just a few holiday homes ………… .

❸ Now for some noun and adjective word pairs. Choose words from the list to complete each pair:

sweet   bounds   knees   ends   sound   dry   early   tired

a   You can find some nice odds and ………… in the second-hand shops.

b   I hope you got home safe and ………… .

c   Time to go to bed if we want to get up bright and ………… in the morning.

d   I'm sick and ………… of listening to him complaining about work.

e   I know you're tired, so I'll try and keep my speech short and ………… .

f   The bosses ran off and left a hundred workers high and ………… .

g   Since he moved to Italy, his Italian has improved in leaps and ………… .

h   He was on the floor on his hands and ………… .

❹ Other ways of linking ideas and expressing addition. Use the words or expressions below to rewrite the sentence six ways, without *and*, but so that the meaning is more or less the same:

what's more   also   too   moreover   as well   in addition

Klean-Kat is fast. And it's safe.

any +

[determiner and pronoun] indicates an indefinite quantity of something: *Have you got any change?* • *Any fool knows that.* • *I don't like any of these shoes.*
[adverb] to any extent or degree: *None of us are getting any younger.*

→ some
→ no

Grammar patterns

1 **any** | + /plural noun | + ?

Is there any milk?
Do you have any brothers or sisters?

▲ to ask about a quantity without being exact

2 not | + **any** | + plural or uncountable noun

She hasn't got any experience. ~ None at all?
There weren't any cucumbers in the market. Not a single one.

▲ to say that not one thing of a particular type exists

3 if | + **any** | + plural or uncountable noun

If you have any questions, you can ask them at the end.
I'd be surprised if she has any savings.

▲ to talk about a hypothetical quantity without being exact

4 **any** | + NP

Use any towel – take your pick.
Any green vegetables can be stir-fried.

▲ to mean one of a kind but it doesn't matter which

5 **any** | + of | + NP

Have you read any of her books?
I don't like any of his music.
Do any of you speak German?

▲ to refer to one or several people or things, or to part of something

6 (not) | + **any** | + comparative

The two-star hotel wasn't any cheaper than the three-star one.
Do you feel any better?

▲ to emphasize a comparison

Collocations

Any occurs in 'non-assertive' contexts, such as negative statements, questions, and *if*-clauses. It also occurs with adverbs that have a negative meaning, like *never, hardly, seldom, rarely*, and with verbs that have a negative meaning, like *refuse, doubt*; it also follows *without*:

They never have any nice things in this shop.
There's seldom any traffic here, except in the weekends.
I doubt that there will be any papers left.
She left for the shops without any money.

Set phrases

· **not any good/use**
It isn't any use complaining: they won't listen.
A big car isn't any good in the city.
▲ to say something is not good, or useful, or effective

· **in any case / in any event** = whatever the situation is, or may be
We may be late, but, in any case, they never start on time.
Mrs Thomas hasn't arrived yet. In any event, she has our phone number.

· '**at any rate**'
The bus is packed! ~ Well, we won't be lonely, at any rate.
▲ to say that at least one thing about the situation is true or all right

· **by any chance**
Are you and Julie related, by any chance?
▲ to find out if something is true

· **any longer** → long

Exercises

❶ Put *any* in the correct place in each sentence.

a   Ask policeman and they will tell you the way.
b   I love stuffed vine leaves, but they didn't have.
c   I can't wait longer: let's start dinner without them.
d   There wasn't bottled water, and I can't drink tap water.
e   You can cash travellers cheques at branch of our bank.
f   My mobile doesn't work because there isn't coverage.
g   It isn't use learning Latin: no one speaks it more.
h   I forgot to buy the paper. In case, the news is always the same.

These sentences are already correct but *any* adds emphasis. Where can you put *any* in each one?

i   If you see melons in the market, can you buy one?
j   He survived ten days without food, just drinking salt water.
k   She refused to take money so I gave her flowers.
l   If Eva grows taller she's going to need new clothes.

❷ Change these sentences with *no* into sentences with *any*:

We have no bananas → *We haven't any bananas.*

a   There's no coffee left.
b   There were no parents at the meeting.
c   Is there no sugar?
d   They have won no games this season.
e   I have no cousins.
f   Do you have no money at all?
g   They gave us no information.
h   I've heard no news from Paul.

❸ *Some, any, no* and *none*. Study these sentences:

I've got *some* money. I've got *some*.
Have you got *any* money? Have you got *any*?
I haven't got *any* money. I haven't got *any*.
I've got *no* money. I've got *none*.

Complete these sentences with *any, some, no,* or *none*:

a   We gave her .... money, but she didn't spend ....
b   Were there .... students there? ~ Not many, but there were ....
c   Do you have .... coins? ~ No, ...
d   There are .... clean glasses, not one.
e   We tried to get tickets but there weren't .... left.
f   I need a stamp. ~ There are .... in that drawer.
g   Give me a banana. ~ There aren't ....
h   Pour me some coffee. ~ There's .... left.
i   She has .... brothers or sisters that I have know of.
j   I searched everywhere for .... cucumbers, but there were ....

❹ *Any* combines with *-thing, -one*, etc., to form indefinite pronouns. The difference between *something* and *anything*, etc. is the same as between *some* and *any*. Complete these sentences by choosing indefinite pronouns from the list:

anything	anywhere	anyone/anybody
something	somewhere	someone/somebody

a   I left my keys .... and I can't find them.
b   We passed by but there wasn't .... at home.
c   There is .... wrong with the TV: I can't get Channel Five.
d   Do you know .... about computers?
e   She never travels – she hasn't been ....
f   I know .... who works in the Co-op.
g   Did .... go to the lecture last night?
h   I don't have .... to wear to the wedding.

as

[preposition] in the role of, in the form of: *He worked for a while as a logger.* • *The news came as a shock.*
[adverb] used with adjectives and adverbs to make comparisons: *It's not as hot today.* • *I can type almost as fast as you.*
[conjunction] (1) when, while: *The phone rang just as I was leaving.*
(2) because: *As you're new here, I'll give you a hand.*
(3) in the way which: *We'd better leave things as they were when we arrived.*

Grammar patterns

1 clause | + **as** | + clause
   as | + clause, | + clause

   The people cheered the soldiers as they marched past.
   As we were leaving, the sun came out.

   ▲ to say that something happened while something else was happening

   You go first, as you know the way.
   As Friday is a holiday, the banks will be closed.

   ▲ to give a reason for doing something

   I prefer the office as it was, with the desk opposite the door.
   Fasten the seat belt, as shown.

   ▲ to talk about the way something is, or the way it is done

2 **as** | + adjective/adverb | + **as** | + NP/clause/adjective

   Terry is nearly as tall as her brother.
   She swims well, but not as well as you (do).
   Your exam results were not as bad as you think.
   I'll do it as soon as I can (OR: *as soon as possible*).

   ▲ to compare the qualities or abilities of two things or people, or to compare something against some standard

3 NP | + verb | + **as** | + if/though | + clause

   It looks as if it's going to rain.
   You sound as though you've got a cold.

   ▲ to talk about appearances

Collocations

Common verb phrases with *as* (preposition) are: *serve as, use something as, be known as, be regarded as, be seen as, be considered as, be defined as.*

   The carrying case also serves as a convenient work surface when travelling.
   Beethoven's Third Symphony (also known as the Eroica) *was composed in 1805.*
   Motivation is sometimes defined as goal-oriented effort.

As often introduces clauses which point forward or back, in written reports and explanations:

   As we have seen, the best method of preventing …
   As shown in diagram 6.1 …
   As we shall see in Chapter 5 …

Adverbials that often precede *as … as* (Grammar pattern 2) are: *almost, nearly, at least,* and *just,* plus expressions like *twice, three times, half.*

   That giraffe is almost as tall as the tree.
   This restaurant is just as expensive as the other one.
   Dave works twice as hard as Cameron.

Set phrases

· **as well as** → well

· **just as well** → well

· **as for …**
  As for the postal strike, I think that …
  ▲ to change to another subject

· **such as …** = for example
  Many tropical fruits, such as mangos and papayas, are available in your local supermarket nowadays.

as yet = until now
I don't have any news as yet, but we expect to hear from them soon.

・ **as it is / as it was …**
The plane was meant to arrive at 5.30, but as it was, we didn't get there till midnight.
▲ to say what the real situation is or was

・ **as long as** →long

Exercises

❶ Put *as* in the correct place in these sentences. (Sometimes it is used twice.)

a   You sit next to Nigel you are both Canadians.
b   I felt a sharp pain in my back just I got up.
c   The exercise wasn't difficult I thought.
d   This pullover is the same yours.
e   Tom looks if he's seen a ghost.
f   What does Manel do? ~ He works an air-traffic controller.
g   I'm quitting my job next month, you probably know.
h   This computer is at least twice expensive that one.
i   Some sports, such hang-gliding, are known 'adventure sports'.
j   It's too early to say, yet, if there have been any survivors.

❷ Change these sentences according to the model:

Kris is taller than Jan. → *Jan is not as tall as Kris.*

a   Steel is harder than iron.
b   Cairo is hotter than Alexandria.
c   March was worse than April.
d   The train leaves more often than the bus.
e   Glasgow has more people than Edinburgh.
f   Liverpool is further away than Manchester.
g   Lilian earns more than Gary.
h   Toni is better-looking than Hugo.

❸ Rewrite these sentences, using *as*, so that the meaning is more or less the same:

a   Because it was Sunday, I got up late.
b   I was getting out of my car when I heard the explosion.
c   The Indian elephant is smaller than the African elephant.
d   It is less windy today, compared to yesterday.
e   You weren't home so I left a note.
f   Woody Allen is funny, but Groucho Marx is funnier.
g   Since you are not busy, can you set the table?
h   Our sunglasses are the same.

❹ Expressions with *as … as*. Choose a word from both list A and list B to complete the idioms in each of these sentences, adding *as*:

A: warm   sick   old   flat   good   hard   white   thin

B: a dog   toast   the hills   gold
a rake   nails   a pancake   a sheet

a   You're still using that ancient computer! It's as ………… .
b   When she heard the dreadful news, she turned as ………… .
c   It's as ………… in here. Have you got the central heating on?
d   How were the children? ~ They were little angels: as ………… .
e   You look awful! ~ Yes, I drank too much last night and I feel as ………… .
f   Nothing seems to affect her: she's as ………… .
g   I'm worried about Joanne. She never eats and she looks as ………… .
h   Benny sat on my sunhat and left it as ………… .

ask

[regular verb: *ask, asked, asked*]: to make a question, request, or invitation: *'Do you live round here?' she asked.* • *Let's ask someone the way.* • *I asked Bronwyn to dinner.*

Grammar patterns

1 **ask** | (+ NP) | + NP

A man asked me the time.
Can I ask you a few questions?
I need to ask a favour.

▲ to talk about getting information, permission, help, etc.

2 **ask** | (+ NP) | + for/about | + NP

The landlady has asked for the rent.
I'd like to ask you about your work.

▲ to talk about, or report, requests and inquiries

3 **ask** | (+ NP) | (+ not) | + to-infinitive

A client was asking to see the manager.
I was asked to take off my shoes.
Can you ask the children not to touch the paintings?

▲ to talk about requests and orders to do things

4 **ask** | (+ NP) | + wh-clause

She asked the school when the Italian course started.
I'll ask where the bus leaves from.

▲ to talk about or report wh-questions

5 **ask** | (+ NP) | + if-clause

Ask him if he knows the Prescotts.

▲ to talk about or report yes/no questions

6 **ask** | (+ NP) | + wh | + to-infinitive

I asked how to get to the airport.
Ask the teacher what to do next.

▲ to talk about or report procedures

7 'quote' | + NP | + **ask** | (+ NP)

'What's the matter?' she asked him.
'Have you got the right time', I asked.

▲ to report questions and requests in direct speech

Collocations

These noun phrases frequently occur with *ask* in Grammar patterns 1 and 2: *a question, questions, permission, my opinion, the way, a favour, the time, some advice, the price.*

Do you mind if I ask you a question?
To see the rare books you have to ask permission.
Can I ask a favour?

These adverb particles occur with 'ask + someone' to make phrasal verbs meaning 'invite': *out, along, over, up, back.*

Michael asked me out, but I told him I was too busy.
Let's ask Nigel and Alfonso over.
Elena is downstairs. ~ Ask her up.

Set phrases

• **' … if you ask me '**
  The plan won't work, if you ask me.

  ▲ to show that you are stating a strong opinion

• **' may I ask? '**
  Who's calling, may I ask?

  ▲ a polite, even formal, way of asking a question

• **' if you don't mind my/me asking '**
  How old are you now, if you don't mind my asking?

  ▲ to ask about something which might be a sensitive topic

• **' Don't ask '**
  How much did you pay for your nose job? ~ Don't ask!

  ▲ to say, informally, that you don't want to answer the question

• **' Don't ask me '**
  Where's Joey? ~ Don't ask me.

  ▲ to say, often with irritation, that you don't know the answer

Exercises

1 Classify these concordance lines with *ask* into Grammar patterns 1 to 7. (There are two examples of each.)

a 'How was your evening?' **asked** Alex.
b Don't **ask** a babysitter to look after a sick child.
c I went to see Valeria to **ask** if she could help.
d I was going to **ask** Mr Hogan for a loan of the car.
e Doctors can **ask** us all sorts of intimate questions.
f Don't forget to **ask** how much energy an appliance uses in a year.
g The girl **asked** me where to get a bus ticket.
h He didn't **ask** us our names.
i **Ask** him where this Irena is now.
j You better **ask** Joey Bonanza about that.
k Then one day she rang to **ask** if I would go to see her.
l I had to **ask** my tutor how to make them.
m After the meal Gerald **asked** his daughter to sing for them.
n 'Can I have a little time to think it over?' Paula **asked** boldly.

2 Put the word in brackets into the correct place in the sentence:

a (you) I'd like to ask your opinion about UFOs.
b (to) A policeman asked Jason move his car.
c (not) I asked you to shut down the computer.
d (were) We asked if we had packed our bags ourselves.
e (for) Chuck asked his boss a day off to take his driving test.
f (if) Why don't you ask a policeman he knows the way?
g (was) A tourist asked Anna where the station.
h (do) Ask the waiter if they takeaways.
i (to) We should write and ask what do.
j (I) 'Where are you going?' asked her.

3 Collocations.
Use one of the following words to complete each of these sentences:

favour	permission	advice	time
opinion	question	price	way

a Can I ask your .... : do you think TV violence is harmful?
b I need to ask you a .... : can I borrow your car this weekend?
c Someone stopped me and asked me the .... to Muswell Hill.
d If you want to take photos of the exhibits, you will need to ask ....
e She phoned the airline and asked the .... of a one-way ticket.
f I don't have a watch so I am always asking the ....
g I'll stop now, in case anyone wants to ask a ....
h He wrote to a magazine and asked for .... about his relationship.

4 Change the direct speech into reported speech, using *ask*:

'Angeles, can you clean the board?' said the teacher.
→ *The teacher asked Angeles to clean the board*.

'Alan, where is the nearest cashpoint?' I said.
→ *I asked Alan where the nearest cashpoint was.*

a 'Are you taking a taxi, Matt?' Roger asked.
b 'Please follow me,' the waiter said to us.
c 'Is this Reading?' I asked the man sitting next to me.
d 'Marry me, Rita,' said Harry.
e 'What is your first name, Mr Vázquez?' asked the customs officer.
f The teacher said, 'Be quiet, children.'
g 'Do you take credit cards?' I asked the shop assistant.
h 'Can you bring me a fork?' said Mrs Hill-Smith to the waiter.

at

[preposition] (1) used to indicate the place or event where something happens: *I'll drop you at the station.* • *They met at a conference.*
(2) used to indicate the time something happens: *The train leaves at 6.00.* • *Will you be home at lunchtime?*

Grammar patterns

1 **at** | + NP

At one end of the beach there is a restaurant.
We have just landed at Gatwick Airport where the local time is 11.25.
I left my wallet at home.
The Prime Minister lives at 10 Downing Street.
Let's meet at the cinema.

▲ to talk about places as points in space, points on a journey, addresses, or places where you do certain activities

The meeting finished at 9.00.
The trains stop running at midnight.
I only ever see my family at Christmas.
Dad retired at 65, and took up gardening.

▲ to talk about clock times, or time as points in the day or calendar or a person's life

2 verb | + **at** | + NP

Look at the moon!
Don't shout at the dog: it can't understand you.
The children waved at the train as it passed.
I pointed at my glass and the waiter refilled it.

▲ to talk about directing your attention, voice, or gesture, to someone or something

3 adjective | + **at** | + NP

Isobel is good at maths.
At school I was terrible at sports.

▲ to talk about doing things well or badly

Collocations

Common phrases with *at* which indicate a place or event include:

at the beginning, at the end, at the top, at the bottom.
at home, at work, at school, at university, etc.
at Stuart's (place), at Lorna's, etc.
at the doctor's, at the hairdresser's, at the drycleaner's, etc.
at the bank, at the station, at the post office, etc.
at a party, at a meeting, at a concert, at a wedding, etc.
at breakfast, at lunch, at dinner

Time expressions that frequently combine with *at* include: *dawn, sunrise, sunset, noon, night, midnight, the weekend.*

Verbs that frequently form combinations with *at* (Grammar pattern 2) are: *look at, stare at, smile at, laugh at, get at,* and *be aimed at.*

Don't stare at the nuns. It's rude.
Can you get at the jar on the top shelf? I'm not tall enough.
I don't understand you. What are you getting at?
The publicity is aimed at teenagers.

Set phrases

· **at (long) last** = eventually
At long last the food arrived, but we were too tired to enjoy it.

· **at once** = immediately, or, at the same time
Serve it at once, while it is still hot.
You shouldn't try and do so many things at once.

· **at least …**
There were at least a hundred people at the funeral.
If you do nothing else, you could at least tidy your room.
▲ to say that something is the minimum number, or the minimum that can be done

· **at the moment / at present** = now
I'm sorry, I'm rather busy at the moment. Can you call back?

· **at its/his/her** etc. **best** = in its/his/her etc. best state
I'm sorry, I'm not at my best before breakfast.

·

* ' **while you're at it** '

I'm going to get some bread. ~ Can you get some croissants while you're at it?

▲ to tell someone to do something at the same time they are doing something else

* **at all** → all

Exercises

❶ Put *at* in the correct place in each of these sentences. (Sometimes it appears twice.)

a   On your way home can you stop the chemist's?
b   There's a train that arrives Stansted Airport every half hour.
c   I'll meet you tomorrow morning the corner of Queen and Market Streets.
d   Is Melanie here the moment? ~ No, I think she's lunch.
e   The concert started eight o'clock and finished midnight.
f   What are you staring? ~ Nothing. I was just looking myself in the mirror.
g   Let Jane draw it because she's clever drawing.
h   Can you iron my shirt while you're it? ~ I'll do it once.

❷ Match the two parts of these exchanges:

a   Where did you study Chinese?
b   When do you spend time with the family?
c   Where do you spend time with the family?
d   Sam's car must have cost $10,000.
e   Where do I sign the contract?
f   When did you wake up?
g   Here comes the bus.
h   Where can I get a train ticket?

1   ~ At last.
2   ~ At home.
3   ~ At the bottom.
4   ~ At the weekend.
5   ~ At the station.
6   ~ At dawn.
7   ~ At university.
8   ~ At least.

❸ Choose a word from the list to complete each sentence, adding *the* or *a* if necessary:

wedding   work   dentist's   bottom
home   top   breakfast   airport

a   I can't talk now. I'm at .... , having a check-up.
b   There was a crowd of fans at .... , awaiting the band's arrival.
c   There's a restaurant at .... of the tower, with a fabulous view.
d   Let's go to sleep now. We can talk about it tomorrow morning at ....
e   When Joe and Alice got married there were two hundred people at ....
f   On Sunday's we usually stay at .... and catch up with the housework.
g   He fell in love with someone he met at .... They were sharing an office.
h   It's easier if you start at .... and work up.

❹ *At, in, on.*
Very generally, we can say that things are *in* containers, *on* surfaces or lines, and *at* a point (→ in, on). Choose the correct preposition to complete these sentences:

a   Can you answer the phone? I'm .... the bath.
b   Where is the key? ~ I left it .... the kitchen table.
c   The car didn't stop .... the traffic lights.
d   Hang the picture .... the wall.
e   Their house is the big one .... the end of the street.
f   We live .... 55 Gumnut Drive.
g   I have an aunt who lives .... Valencia.
h   Valencia is .... eastern Spain, ... the coast.
i   The flight to Valencia stops briefly .... Barcelona.
j   You can get a taxi .... the airport.
k   I'll meet you .... the meeting-point .... the airport building.

back

[adverb] (1) away from here or now; behind here or before now: *Please move back: you're in the way.* • *When I look back on my days in the army … .*
(2) home, in the original place: *When did you get back?* • *Put the books back on the shelf.*
[noun] rear, area to the rear: *There is a garden at the back of the house.* • *I've hurt my back.*
[adjective] rear: *Sit in the back seat and I'll sit in the front.*
[regular verb: back, backed, backed] (1) move backwards: *Back the car into the garage.*
(2) support: *Which team are you going to back?*

Grammar patterns

1 verb | + **back**

I looked back and saw someone following me.
Stand back, and let the doctor through.
I often think back to my school days.

▲ to talk about reverse movement, that is, in a direction behind you, or into the past

Are the neighbours back?
We leave on Thursday and get back on Sunday night.
He flew there and back in the same day.

▲ to talk about return movement, that is, to home, to the original place, or to some other starting point

2 verb | + NP | + **back**
verb | + **back** | + NP

What government has ever cut back spending on defence?
I'll run the tape back, and we'll listen to it again.

▲ to talk about reversing things

I'm busy right now. Can you phone me back?
Mrs Jeffries brought back that pan she borrowed.
Don't lend money to George: he never pays it back.

▲ to talk about returning things

3 verb | + **back** | + preposition | + NP

The government promised to raise pensions but it went back on its word.
The ruins date back to the tenth century.

▲ to talk about returning or reversing

Collocations

Phrasal verbs that belong to Grammar pattern 1 include:
(reverse movement): *fall back, hang back, lean back, lie back, stand back, step back, turn back, look back.*
(return movement): *arrive back, be back, bounce back, come back, drive back, fly back, get back, fight back.*

Don't hang back: go and ask Fiona for a dance.
The market experienced sharp falls last week, but it has bounced back in the last few days.

Phrasal verbs that belong to Grammar pattern 2 include:
(reverse movement): *cut back, keep back, set back.*
(return movement): *answer back, call/phone back, bring back, get back, give back, hand back, pay back, play back, put back, take back, win back.*

The spending cuts have set back research several years.
I take back what I said about Jim: he's proved me completely wrong.
Did you get your money back?

Phrasal verbs that belong to Grammar pattern 3 include: *cut back on, date back to, go back on.*

My doctor told me I had to cut back on sugar and fat.

There are also phrasal verbs formed from the verb *back*:

If you *back down* from something you said earlier, you change your mind. (*The government refuses to back down.*)
If you *back into*, or *out of*, a parking space, you reverse your car into, or out of, that space.
If you *back out* of something that you agreed to do, you no longer agree to do it. (*Hania offered to design my web page, but she's had to back out.*)
If you *back* someone *up*, you support them. (*I'm sure Anita would back me up if she was here.*)

Set phrases

- **at the back / in the back** = in the rear part of something
  There is an index at the back of the book.
  You sit in the back with the kids.

- **back and forth** = going and returning
  With mum in hospital, I've been back and forth all week.

- **back to front** = with the back part at the front
  You've got your sweater on back to front.

- **behind my/his** etc. **back** = without my/his etc. knowing
  When I was on holiday, the architect changed the plans behind my back.

Exercises

❶ **Ten examples of *back* (or *backed*) have been taken out of this text. Can you put them back?**

The journey from the beach was a nightmare. We had to take the roads because of the traffic on the main roads. By the time we got, it was midnight and the kids were asleep on the seat. I the car into the garage, and went to open the front door. It was then that I realized I didn't have the key. I must have left it at the hotel. I went round to the of the house and tried to force open the door. Then I felt a terrible pain in my. I haven't been able to go to work for a week.

❷ **There are many compound words formed with *back* such as *backbone, playback*, etc. Choose words from the list to make compounds that complete these sentences:**

log   set   ground   cut   full
pack   up   paper   drop   lash

a I'll start by giving you some of the back .... to the present situation.
b The scandal was a huge .... back to the government's anti-corruption campaign.
c The generator provides a back .... if there is a power failure.
d Because I was away, I have a huge back .... of work to catch up on.
e The government's .... backs have caused shortages in the health service.
f I travel light: just a back .... with a change of clothes in it.

g The government's liberal policies prompted an angry back .... in the right-wing press.
h The waterfall provides a delightful back .... for your wedding photos.
i Stephen's book has just been published in .... back.
j He plays .... back on the local football team.

❸ **Choose words from the list to complete these sentences:**

pay   turn   call   lie   bring   come   put   take

a Barry phoned while you were out. He said he would .... back later.
b Is the government serious when it says it wants to .... back capital punishment?
c It started snowing halfway up the mountain so we decided to .... back.
d When you've finished with those tools, can you .... them back in the garage?
e Has the electricity .... back? ~ No, it's still off.
f Here's ten dollars. ~ Thanks. I'll .... you back tomorrow.
g I'm sorry I said you were wrong. I .... it back. You were right.
h Just .... back and relax. You won't feel a thing.

❹ **There are a number of idioms with *back*. Can you match the two parts of each exchange?**

a Those awful neighbours are leaving at last.
b Their marriage broke up after his business went bust?
c If they know you're a theatre critic, they give you the best seats.
d Shouting at the children didn't seem to have much effect.
e The new boss seems to be giving you a hard time.
f Are you sure we won't get lost?
g That was clever of Terry, scoring the winning goal.
h His partner left and started a rival business.

1 ~ A case of: you scratch my back and I'll scratch yours.
2 ~ Yes, I wish he would get off my back.
3 ~ Wow, she really stabbed him in the back.
4 ~ Good. I'll be glad to see the back of them.
5 ~ No, it was like water off a duck's back.
6 ~ Yes. It was the straw that broke the camel's back.
7 ~ Look, I know this place like the back of my hand.
8 ~ Yes, he deserves a pat on the back.

be

[irregular verb: → am/is/are]
(1) a lexical verb: *You must be Quentin.* • *It will be sunny tomorrow.*
(2) auxiliary verb: *Will you be using your computer?* • *This report needs to be filed.*

→ am/is/are
→ was/were
→ being
→ been

Grammar patterns

1 (don't) **be** | + adjective/NP

Be quiet! I'm watching the news.
Be careful. You'll fall.
Don't be sad. Don't be an idiot.

▲ to tell people how to behave or feel

2 modal | + **be**

It should be a nice day tomorrow.
Adrian must be in his forties.
There's someone at the door. ~ Who could that be?

▲ to talk about the possibility, or uncertainty, of a present or future state (→ should, could, will, etc.)

Can you please be quiet?
You must be over 18.

▲ to talk about present states that are obligatory or necessary

3 modal | + **be** | + -ing

I'll be staying at the Plaza Hotel.
It may be raining when we get there.
Where's Tony? ~ He might be watching TV.

▲ to talk about the possibility of present or future activity being in progress (→ should, could, will, etc.)

4 modal | + **be** | + past participle

New students will be interviewed on Monday.
These glasses should be washed.
Mobile phones must be turned off.

▲ to talk about possible, necessary, or desirable actions, in the present or future, without needing to say who performs them (This is a form of the passive.)

5 verb | + to **be**

When she grows up, she wants to be an architect.
For once, he managed to be on time.
You need to be a member.

▲ to follow verbs that take to-infinitives, such as *want, hope, try, manage,* etc.

Collocations

Participles that frequently occur in Grammar pattern 4 are: *bothered, done, allowed, finished.*

Are you going to basketball practice? ~ No, I can't be bothered.
This assignment must be done before Friday.
You won't be allowed into the club without a tie.
When will your house be finished?

Set phrases

· **let […] be**
  Do you think it's time to wake the girls?
  ~ I would just let them be.
  ▲ to advise someone not to try to change a situation

· '**to be fair / to be honest / to be frank** etc.'
  Danny never offers to help with the housework.
  ~ Yes, but to be fair, he does all the shopping.
  ▲ to indicate how you feel about what you are going to say next

· **… as can be / … as could be** = as much as possible
  Now that she has her own home, she's as happy as can be.

· **[…]-to-be** = future.
  The bride-to-be was wearing pink.
  ▲ added to nouns such as *husband, father,* etc.

Exercises

1 **There are twelve instances of *be* missing from this text. Can you put them back?**

A home can improved by removing a wall between two small rooms, to create one big room. Removing a wall needn't a big job. It can done easily and quickly. But before you go ahead, ask yourself the following questions:

Will the loss of a room inconvenient? If you have a growing family, for example, you may needing extra bedrooms in the future. And, will the shape of the new room suitable for your needs? What family activities will carried out there? Will it used both for having meals and for watching TV? Will children doing their homework, while others are listening to music? And, careful! If the wall is structural, it could dangerous to remove it. To sure, consult an architect first.

2 **Read these short descriptions of animals and decide what each one could be, choosing words from the two boxes:**

might	must
could	may
can't	

elephant	giraffe
kangaroo	ostrich
whale	albatross
gorilla	rhino
shark	penguin

a   This one lives in the sea. It could be a shark. It can't be a gorilla.
b   This one has two legs, two arms and lives in trees.
c   This one is a very big bird.
d   This one is a big bird: it can't fly, but it can run fast.
e   This one is a large African mammal.
f   This one can swim but it can't fly.
g   This one can move quickly using its two legs.
h   This one is very dangerous.
i   This one has sharp teeth and is very dangerous.
j   This one is found only in Australia.

3 **Choose nouns from list A and verbs from list B and write sentences to match the signs below, using the pattern 'modal + be + past participle':**

A:	young children	seatbelts	~~mobile phones~~	cars
	smokers	hard hats	arms and legs	goods

B:	fasten	~~turn off~~	wear	cover
	carry	tow away	declare	fine

Mobile phones must be turned off.

been

[past participle of be] (1) lexical verb: *It has been a nice day.*
• *It must have been terrible.*
(2) auxiliary verb: *Have you been waiting long?*
• *The photocopier hasn't been fixed.*

→ am/is/are
→ be
→ being

Grammar patterns

1 NP | + have/has | + **been**

I've been really busy lately.
Has Eric been a good boy?

▲ to talk about states in a period from the past to the present (This is an example of the present perfect.)

1a NP | + have/has | + **been** | + to | + NP

Why are you late? ~ I've been to the dentist.
This week the Prime Minister has been to Brussels and Rome, and next week he is going to Moscow.

▲ to say that a person has visited a place and come back (→ go)

1b there | + have/has | + **been** | + NP

There have been reports of an accident on the M5.
I can't issue your ticket yet. There has been a problem with the computer.
Has there been any news from home?

▲ to announce (or ask about) an event that took place in a period from the past to the present, and hasn't been mentioned yet

2 have/has | + **been** | + -ing

The boys have been playing all morning.
What have you been doing lately?
The phone hasn't been working since last week.

▲ to talk about activities or situations that have been in progress from a time in the past up to now, or recently. (This is called the present perfect continuous. → have)

3 had | + **been** | + -ing

It had been raining and the roads were slippery …
When she arrived, we had been waiting nearly an hour.

▲ to talk about activities or situations that were in progress up to a point in the past. (This is called the past perfect continuous. → had)

4 have/has | + **been** | + past participle

A man and a woman have been arrested.
The old post office has been pulled down.
Have my shirts been washed?

▲ to talk about things that have happened at some time in a period from the past until now, without saying who caused the things to happen. (This is called the present perfect passive.)

5 modal | + have | + **been**

Who ate all the plums? ~ I don't know. It might have been Sara. Or it could have been Leo.
You should have been at the meeting. It was really interesting.
My dad would have been furious, if he'd known.

▲ to talk about what was possible, probable, or desirable in the past (→ could, might, would, etc.)

Collocations

Time expressions that are commonly associated with the perfect continuous (past and present) include the words: *all, for, lately, since,* and *just.*

He said, 'What have you been doing **all** this time?
They had been trying to contact her **for** several days.
She's been getting terribly restless **lately**.
Tom has been training people in the use of business software **since** 1983.
I've **just** been speaking to him on the phone.

(→ for, → just)

Set phrases

· ‘ **it's been one of those days** ’
  You look tired. ~ Yes, it's been one of those days.
  ▲ to say you've had a busy and tiring day

· ‘ **it's been ages since …** ’
  It's been ages since I saw a good film.
  ▲ to emphasize the length of time since something last
  happened

Exercises

❶ **Put the word in brackets in the correct place in the
   sentence:**

a (you) How long have been waiting?
b (not) My father-in-law has been feeling well lately.
c (have) I'm feeling sick. ~ It must been the fish you ate.
d (to) Have you ever been Brazil? ~ Yes, I've been once.
e (been) I see that the classrooms have repainted at last.
f (been) Where have you lately? I haven't seen you around.
g (may) Who phoned? ~ I don't know. It have been Martin.
h (been) The sheets have washed and ironed.
i (had) He been drinking and he had a headache.

❷ **Write responses to these statements, in the form of a
   question with *How long …?* Use the words in brackets.**

  I'm working for the ABC. (them)
  → *How long have you been working for them?*

a I'm staying with Bob. (him)
b She's living with Pat. (her)
c I'm working on a new book. (it)
d Ted and Todd are studying Chinese. (it)
e We're looking for a new apartment. (one)
f I'm waiting for my work permit. (it)

❸ The present perfect continuous is often used to say how
   long an activity has been continuing. It is frequently used
   with either '*for* + period of time', or '*since* + a specific time in
   the past':

   I've been living here for three months.
   They've been manufacturing software since 1998.

   → for

Complete these sentences with either *for* or *since*:

a We've been waiting ………… hours.
b She's not been feeling well ………… Saturday.
c The baby has been sleeping ………… nine o'clock.
d I've been living on my own ………… I finished college.
e Artur has been editing the magazine ………… two years now.
f What have you been doing ………… I last saw you?
g It's been raining ………… a long time.
h They've been digging up the road ………… months now.

❹ **Respond to these sentences using a passive structure
   (Grammar pattern 4):**

   Their house needed painting.
   ~ It's been painted.

a The door needed repairing.
b The windows needed cleaning.
c The TV aerial needed fixing.
d The plants needed watering.
e The grass needed cutting.
f The garden needed looking after.
g The whole place needed tidying up.
h Their car needed washing, too.

being

[present participle of be]: (1) a lexical verb: *She loves being a student again.* • *Being single has its advantages.*
(2) auxiliary verb: *The lift is being repaired.* • *I don't like being corrected.*

→ am/is/are
→ was/were
→ be
→ been

Grammar patterns

1 **being** | + adjective/NP

I don't like being ill.
Stop being so irritable.
The worst thing about being a waiter is the hours.
Being single again has its advantages.

▲ to talk about states as ongoing, as if they were processes

2 am/is/was, etc. | + **being** | + adjective/NP

The children are being silly.
Were the neighbours being noisy?
Tony was being a bore, so I left and came home.

▲ to talk about temporary ways of behaving or feeling

3 am/is/was, etc. | + **being** | + past participle

Those old apartment blocks are being pulled down.
I can't give you a lift: the car is being serviced.

▲ to talk about things that are happening in the present, without needing to say who is the cause. (This is a form of the passive: the present continuous passive.)

4 like/love/hate, etc. | + **being** | + past participle

The politician didn't like being interrupted.
The dog loves being taken for a walk.

▲ to talk about things you like or don't like happening to you, without needing to say who is the cause

5 (it) **being** | + adjective/NP | + main clause

It being Sunday, I didn't need to go to work.
He offered me a cigarette but, being a non-smoker, I refused.

▲ to give the reason for something

Collocations

Adjectives that frequently go with Grammar pattern 1 are: *silly, unfair, rude, stupid, honest, good, naughty, ridiculous, careful, serious, selfish,* and *unreasonable.*

I think you're being a bit unfair on me. I never said …
I hope you're not being serious: do you really think …?

Set phrases

· **for the time being** = temporarily
You can leave your luggage in reception for the time being.

· **all things being equal** = if there are no other factors that will affect the situation
All things being equal, women are better language learners than men.

"JUST FOR THE TIME BEING …"

Exercises

1 **Find examples of Grammar patterns 1–5 in these concordance lines:**

a She didn't like **being** called Linda at all.
b Both players are **being** paid by Preston until July.
c They trust no one, and hate **being** questioned about their lives.
d **Being** the youngest in a family of six meant I never got to choose my own clothes.
e I'm afraid I'm **being** a bit of a nuisance.
f He has now been located and is **being** cared for by relatives.
g After dinner, it **being** light at the time, we took our friend into the hotel garden.
h You are just not **being** realistic.
i New promotional materials are **being** developed.
j John has a calming influence on the team, **being** older than most of the lads.
k I hope you're **being** a good girl today.
l The evidence is there. The damage is **being** done.
m It felt strange **being** the only man amongst so many women.

2 **Use verbs from the list to answer these questions, using the present continuous passive.**

repair	question	iron	~~dryclean~~	restore
feed	paint	print	interview	defrost

a Where's my suit? It's being drycleaned.
b Where's my white shirt?
c Why is our doctor on TV?
d Why is Room 101 not in use?
e What's happening to the suspects?
f Where's the TV?
g Where's that report I wrote?
h Why is the fridge empty?
i Where is the Rembrandt self-portrait?
j Where are the pandas?

3 **Match the two parts of these sentences:**

a Cats like
b Dogs like
c Plants don't like
d Cats don't like

1 being washed.
2 being over-watered.
3 being stroked.
4 being taken for walks.

Do the same for these sentences:

e Babies love
f Young children like
g Teenagers hate
h Nobody likes

5 being asked lots of questions.
6 being ignored.
7 being tickled.
8 being read to.

4 *Be, being,* or *been?* **Complete these song titles by choosing the best word:**

a 'You must have .... a beautiful baby.' (Bobby Darin)
b 'You'll .... a woman soon.' (Neil Diamond)
c 'Baby I've .... missing you.' (The Independents)
d 'Let it ....' (The Beatles)
e 'It should have .... me.' (Gladys Knight and the Pips)
f '............ anything (but .... mine).' (Connie Francis)
g 'Tired of .... alone.' (Al Green)
h 'Reach out – I'll .... there.' (The Four Tops)
i 'I've .... loving you too long to stop now.' (Otis Redding)
j 'How sweet it is to .... loved by you.' (James Taylor)
k 'I feel like .... like a sex machine.' (James Brown)
l 'I've .... lonely too long.' (The Rascals)
m 'When will I .... loved?' (The Everly Brothers)

but

[conjunction] indicates a contrast between two words, word groups, clauses, and sentences: *It was cold but sunny.* • *She ate the vegetables but not the meat.* • *I liked her first book but the second was very disappointing.* • *I have to go. ~ But it's only ten o'clock.*
[preposition] except: *There was no one on the late-night bus but me.* • *I can't give you anything but love.*

Grammar patterns

1 word/phrase | + **but** | (+ not) | + word/phrase

I got the bread but not the milk.
We returned home tired but happy.
They played well but not well enough.

▲ to link two ideas when the second is different from the first

2 clause | + **but** | + clause
sentence. | + **But** | + sentence

She threw a party but only two people came.
On Monday the storm was still raging. But when we woke on Tuesday morning the wind had dropped …

▲ to link two ideas by presenting extra information where this contrasts or surprises in the context

I would've been on time but the bus was late.
I'd love to come to dinner, but I'll be away.

▲ to explain why something doesn't or can't happen

3 utterance. | + **But** | + utterance

It's your turn to do the dishes. ~ But I did them last night!
I won't be able to help you move. ~ But you promised!

▲ to express surprise, annoyance, or disagreement

4 not only | + word/phrase | + **but** | (+ also) | + word/phrase

The computer is not only slow, but it crashes all the time.
He's not only a brilliant musician, but he's also a talented cook.

▲ to emphasize additional information

Collocations

As a conjunction, *but* is often followed by emphatic *do* (→ do) in spoken language:

I don't like mussels but I do like oysters.
We didn't go to Florence but we did go to Siena.

As a preposition, *but* often follows words like *nothing, no one, anything, anyone,* etc.:

He does nothing but complain about his salary.
I'll eat anything but cucumbers.

Set phrases

• **' yes, but … '**
The movie was good, wasn't it? ~ Yes, but it was too long.
▲ to signal a difference of opinion in conversation

• **' I'm sorry, but … / I'd love to, but … '**
Would you like to come with us? ~ I'd love to but I'm just far too busy.
▲ to introduce an apology or excuse

• **but for …** = except for / if it hadn't been for …
Everyone's ready but for Helmut.
But for Josie, I don't know what I would have done.

• **but then (again) …**
She speaks fluent Arabic. But then, she did live in Egypt for ten years.
▲ to show that what you have just said is not surprising

• **all but …** = almost completely
They had all but given up hope of rescue.

• **the last but one** = not the last one but the one before the last one
Our house is the last but one on the left-hand side.

Exercises

1 **Match the two parts of each sentence and link them with *but*:**

a It was a lovely day
b She was not waving
c I've been to Glasgow
d I like olives
e We had planned to take the train
f It was cold at first
g The theatre was full
h I've not only been to Glasgow

1 ... not to Edinburgh.
2 ... the weather improved.
3 ... someone sold us two tickets.
4 ... drowning.
5 ... I married a Glaswegian.
6 ... there weren't any seats.
7 ... only the green ones.
8 ... windy.

2 **In the following dialogue the word *but* appeared ten times, but it has been removed. Can you put it back?**

A: How about a game of tennis tomorrow?
B: I'd love to, I've got a lot to do.
A: You promised!
B: I know, I'm just so busy. I thought I'd finish everything today I haven't.
A: You do nothing work. For tennis you'd get no exercise at all. Remember, Tom, I'm not only your friend, I'm also your doctor. You need to take it easy.
B: Yes, don't forget I actually enjoy work, Ed. You're right: let's play tennis tomorrow.
A: Great.
B: Just one game.

3 **Other conjunctions.**
And, so, because, and *but* are ways of joining parts of sentences (→ and, so, why). **Complete these sentences by choosing one of these conjunctions in each case:**

a They got married .... they were so in love.
b They were in love .... they decided to get married.
c They were married for ten years .... they had three children.
d They had a lot in common .... their marriage was a disaster.
e They were always fighting .... they decided to live apart.
f At first they were happy .... they soon got lonely.
g They got lonely .... they missed each other.
h They missed each other .... they decided to get back together.
i They stopped fighting .... started doing things together again.
j Their marriage finally succeeded .... they had so much in common.

4 **Other ways of expressing contrast.**

But is the most common way of linking contrasting ideas, especially in spoken language: *They played well but they lost.* *Though* is also common in spoken language: *They played well. They lost, though.*

The following contrastive linkers are more common in writing:

Although they played well, they lost.
They played well. *However*, they lost.
They played well. *Nevertheless*, they lost.
They played well. *And yet/Yet* they lost.
They played well. *Even so*, they lost.

Rewrite each of the following sentences in at least four different ways, substituting *but* with other linkers, and making any necessary changes:

a Wind power is a viable energy source. But it is still underused.
b It is very difficult, but not impossible, to breed pandas in captivity.
c The fight against malaria continues but a cure is still a long way off.

by

[preposition] (1) near or beside, or movement past (a place): *They sat by the fire.* • *I drove by the new hotel.*
(2) on or before (a time): *I have to be home by 11 o'clock.*
(3) to say who or what did something, or how: *Has he read anything by Janet Frame?* • *The tiles were painted by hand.*
[adverb]: near, past: *We heard a train go by.*

Grammar patterns

1 by | + -ing

They live by fishing and hunting.
By reading a lot you can improve your vocabulary.
They escaped by climbing a wall.

▲ to say how someone does or achieves something

2 by | + NP

I usually go to work by train, but sometimes I go by bus.
Please send the documents by e-mail.
Can I pay by credit card?

▲ to say how people travel, or communicate, or how things are processed

I used your toothbrush by mistake.
The dentist sees clients by appointment only.
By chance, she ran into Marcel in the bank.

▲ to say whether an event is planned or not

3 am/is/was etc. | + past participle | + by | + NP

Jessica was bitten by a dog.
Her next film will be directed by Lars von Trier.
The beaches are being cleaned by groups of volunteers.

▲ to say who or what did something (This construction is called the passive.)

4 by | + himself/herself/themselves etc.

The train goes by itself.

▲ to say that someone or something does something without help

He was sitting by himself

▲ to say that someone is alone

5 by | + time adverbial

The photos will be ready by Friday.
Dinner's at seven. Will you be home by then?

▲ to talk about things happening no later than a certain time

6 by the time | + clause, | + clause

By the time we arrived, the restaurant was closed.
By the time you get this, I will have left.

▲ to say what happened or will happen before a certain time

Collocations

By (as preposition) is followed by nouns belonging to these groups:

transport: *by car, by train, by bike,* etc.
communications: *by e-mail, by phone, by word of mouth,* etc.

By (as adverb and preposition) occurs with lots of verbs of movement, such as *go, pass, run, fly, rush, walk,* etc.:

We watched the soldiers march by.
Time flew by.
A mysterious figure passed by the window.

By (as adverb particle) forms a number of phrasal verbs:

If you *get by* you manage to live or survive with minimal resources. (*Without a job, how does he get by?*)
If you *put* money *by*, you save it for later use. (*If I were you I'd put some money by for your retirement.*)
Drop by is an informal way of saying *visit*. (*I'll drop by and see how you are.*)

By (as preposition) forms these phrasal verbs with idiomatic meaning:

If you *come by* something, you obtain it. (*How did you come by this first edition of* Nineteen Eighty-Four*?*)
If you *stand by* or *stick by* someone, you give them your support. (*'Stand by your man!'*)
If you *swear by* something, you believe it is reliable or effective. (*I swear by these new ski boots: they're fantastic!*)

By is often found after these words: *followed, caused, surrounded,* and also: *surprised, worried, pleased, impressed.*

The house is surrounded by trees.
Were you surprised by the news?

Set phrases

- **by and large …**
  By and large, AIDS is an economic issue.
  ▲ to talk generally about something

- **bit by bit / little by little / step by step** etc. **…**
  Jane's Spanish is improving bit by bit.
  ▲ to say that something happens gradually

- **' by the way … '**
  By the way, is it true that you've been promoted?
  I'd love to come to dinner. I'm a vegetarian, by the way.
  ▲ to introduce a new topic or comment into the conversation

Exercises

❶ **Here are some concordance lines with *by*. Can you identify the Grammar pattern (1–6) in each case?**

a It would heal quickly **by** itself.
b My brother was murdered **by** poison.
c My father tried to stop her **by** standing in her way.
d Holmes will hastily travel there **by** cab.
e **By** the time the demo was over, I was really nauseous.
f I solved this problem **by** connecting the printer.
g These changes are influenced **by** human actions.
h She loved to walk **by** herself.
i All work should be completed **by** February.
j We will show our thanks **by** sending you a free copy.
k He must have ordered them **by** telephone.
l **By** seven o' clock he was ready to walk the dog.
m They are out of date **by** the time they appear.

❷ **Put the words in the box into four groups of four, so that the words in each group all complete one of these sentences:**

Please send it by ………… .
They sell them by ………… .
She became an actor by ………… .
Can I pay by ………… ?

air	credit card	the dozen	accident
cash	the kilo	bank draft	luck
sea	the box	road	choice
rail	cheque	necessity	the pound

❸ **Choose the best preposition (*by, at, on,* or *in*) to complete these sentences:**

a Phone me ………… seven and not before.
b Can you dry-clean this suit ………… Friday at the latest?
c ………… this time next week, I will have finished my exams.
d The bus usually arrives ………… eleven but today it arrived at quarter to.
e Try to be at the station ………… six, because the train leaves ………… six sharp.
f My parents are arriving ………… Friday afternoon.
g ………… 2050 the population of Caracas will have doubled.
h They finish work ………… five and ………… five-thirty they've usually all left.
i My drivers licence expires ………… 2015.
j This book is due back at the library ………… 12th June.

❹ **Here are some short encyclopedia entries about famous people. Can you rewrite them so that they are about famous achievements?**

Cervantes, Miguel de. He wrote *Don Quixote* in 1605.
Curie, Marie and Pierre. They discovered radium in 1898.
Gates, Bill. He started Microsoft in 1975.
Fender, Leo. He invented the electric guitar in 1948.
Fleming, Alexander. He discovered penicillin in 1928.
Hill, Mildred and Patty. They wrote 'Happy Birthday' in 1893.
Queen Zenobia. She ruled Palmyra in the third century.
Roddick, Anita. She started *The Body Shop* in 1976.

Don Quixote: Don Quixote *was written by Cervantes in 1605.*
a **electric guitar**
b **'Happy Birthday'**
c **Microsoft**
d **Palmyra**
e **Penicillin**
f **Radium**
g ***The Body Shop***

can

[modal verb] to be able to, or free to, do something:
Most birds can fly, but some can't. • *You can stay the night, if you like* • *Chocolate can be addictive.*

NOTE: The negative form *cannot* is always spelt as one word. Its contraction is *can't*.

Grammar patterns

1 **can/can't** | + bare infinitive

Eric can speak five languages.
Can you ski? ~ No, I can't.

▲ to talk about your ability to do something

Doing grammar exercises can be boring.
Madrid can be very cold in winter.

▲ to talk about what sometimes happens, i.e. possibility

It can't be five o'clock already, surely?
He can't be French: he hasn't got a French accent.

▲ to say that you think something is unlikely or impossible

Can I use your hairdryer?
You can go into the mosque but you can't take photos.

▲ to request, give, or refuse permission

Can I help you with that?
I can do the shopping, if you like.

▲ to make offers

2 **can't** | + have | + past participle

Andrew can't have left: his coat's still here.
Judging by her Italian, she can't have lived in Italy very long.

▲ to say that it is not possible that something happened

Collocations

Can/can't are frequently combined with verbs of perception, like *see, hear, smell, feel,* etc., to say that you are aware of something happening now, through your senses:

> *I can hear someone playing music in the next apartment.*
> *Can you see that bird? It looks like a finch.*
> *Does that hurt? ~ No, I can't feel a thing.*

Can/can't are also combined with verbs of cognition, like *imagine, believe, understand*:

> *I can't imagine what's happened to Ted.*
> *Can you believe it? Mary wants to go back to New Zealand.*

Set phrases

· ' **I can't tell you how …** '
I can't tell you how relieved I was when they all left.
▲ to express strong feelings

· ' **I can't believe (it)!** '
Cathy! I can't believe it. What are you doing here?
I can't believe how much the boys have grown.
▲ to express surprise

· ' **Who can that be?** '
There's the phone. ~ Who can that be, at this time of night?
▲ to ask about an unexpected guest, phone call, etc.

Exercises

1 Study these concordance lines with *can* and classify them according to whether they relate to:
1 ability
2 possibility
3 permission
(There are three of each.)

a I **can** cook anything because I'm a Cordon Bleu chef.
b You **can** also reach the museum by train from any station on the suburban line.
c Now follow me, Piper, and you **can** join me in a bit of supper.
d Chimps **can** create artworks, use tools in a quite sophisticated fashion, and understand the concept of language.
e Anyone who turns up on the day **can** join in the fun.
f Many paddling pools **can** also be used as sandpits.
g Tropical fish **can** live without food for six weeks.
h Many credit cards **can** now be used to draw cash from ATMs around the world.
i You **can** keep it. I've got others.

2 Which of these sentences are true and which are false? Can you correct the false sentences?

a Cats can't see in the dark.
b Some tortoises can live up to 150 years.
c Most bats can't fly.
d Some fish can fly short distances.
e Chameleons can change colour.
f Kangaroos can't jump long distances.
g Penguins can fly.
h Some snakes can swim.
i Horses can sleep on their feet.
j Elephants can lift heavy weights.

3 Say what these signs mean, using *can't*:

You can't smoke here.

a
b
c
d
e Keep off the grass
f
g
h No Admittance

4 Other ways of expressing ability.

Look at these sentences that express ability:

Francesca *knows how to* design web pages.
Kangaroos *are capable of* jumping 12 metres.
I regret not *being able to* play a musical instrument.
James *has the ability to* pick up languages quickly.
Our technical support team *is equipped to* provide fast, speedy service.

Rewrite these sentences, using the word in brackets, so that the meaning is the same or similar:

a Camels can travel long distances without water. (equipped)
b Can Matthew talk yet? (able)
c I think Robin can do much better at school. (capable)
d Can you write in Arabic script? (know how)
e We are looking for someone who can inspire confidence. (ability)
f Some people can't teach. (incapable)
g We regret that we cannot accept your offer. (unable)
h Can anyone here change a tyre? (know how)

come

[irregular verb: *come, came, come*] expresses movement to or towards the speaker (or writer): *My brother came to visit.*
• *There's a storm coming.* • *Here comes the train.*
The movement can also be by the speaker towards the listener: *I'll come down and open the door for you.* • *We are coming on the ten o'clock bus.*

NOTE: *come* contrasts with *go*, which usually expresses movement away from the speaker: *Come here. Now, go over there.*

→ go

Grammar patterns

1 come | + adverbial

When are you coming home?
Marco came into the room.
She comes to work by train.

▲ to talk about people or things moving towards the speaker

2 come | + to-infinitive

My parents came to stay.
Someone's come to fix the photocopier.

▲ to talk about the reason for the movement towards the speaker

How did you come to learn Turkish?
That's how I came to know Kim.

▲ to talk about a process and its outcomes

3 come | + and | + verb

Come and see what I've found.
A couple came and looked at the flat.

▲ to talk about two closely related actions, where the second is the reason for the first

4 come | + -ing

The walls came tumbling down.
The dogs came running and barking across the field.

▲ to describe actions that are often fast and sudden

Collocations

Come combines with many adverb and preposition particles to form phrasal verbs:

If you *come across* something or someone, you find it, or meet them, by chance. (*I came across Ed's book in a second-hand bookshop.*)
If someone *comes at* you, they move towards you threateningly. (*The man came at him with a knife.*)
If something *comes back,* it returns.
If something *comes down,* it crashes or collapses.
If you *come down with* an illness, you catch that illness. (*I came down with a terrible cold when I was on holiday.*)
If you *come into* money, you inherit it.
If something *comes off* something, it becomes detached.
If something *comes out,* it emerges.
If someone *comes round,* they become convinced. (*They are not convinced by our offer, but I think they'll come round.*)
If someone *comes to,* they regain consciousness. If a bill *comes to* a certain amount, it adds up to that amount. If you say 'What are things *coming to?*', you are showing surprise or shock about a situation.
If something like a document *comes through,* it is sent to you; if someone *comes through* an experience, they survive it.
If a job *comes up,* it becomes available. If someone *comes up with* a plan or an idea, they suggest it. If something like a problem *comes up,* it happens. (*I'll be late home: something unexpected has come up.*)

Set phrases

· ⁶Come in!⁹
Come in and make yourself at home!
▲ for inviting

· ⁶Where do you come from?⁹
Where do you come from? ~ Peru.
▲ to ask about someone's country or place of origin

- **coming and going**
  The square was full of people coming and going.
  There's been a lot of coming and going in the office this morning.
  ▲ to describe a lot of movement

- **… come as a shock/surprise/disappointment** etc.
  This may come as a surprise to you, but I'm married.
  ▲ to talk about news and events

- **come what may** = in spite of any difficulties
  I promise I won't leave you, come what may.

- **'How come?'**
  The window's broken. ~ How come?
  How come you're not at work today?
  ▲ to ask for the reasons for something

Exercises

❶ *Come or go?* **Decide which verb is best in each case:**

A telephone conversation

A: Hello?
B: Hello, Anna. This is Brian.
A: Hi, Brian. How are you?
B: Fine, thanks. Listen, I was just wondering if you'd like to (a. *come/go*) over to my place and have dinner? I'm (b. *coming/going*) on holiday next month, so I thought we could get together …
A: That'd be nice. But my piano teacher is (c. *coming/going*) shortly. And my car is at the garage.
B: That's all right. I'll (d. *come/go*) and get you. When does your piano lesson finish?
A: She usually (e. *comes/goes*) at seven-thirty. And then I have to (f. *come/go*) and do some shopping. Why don't you (g. *come/go*) and meet me in town, and we can (h. *come/go*) to a restaurant?
B: OK …

❷ **Look at these concordance lines for *come*. With reference to the Grammar patterns 1–4, identify the pattern in each case:**

a The White Cliffs of Dover **came** into sight.
b Phillip **came** to depend on his housekeeper.
c My brother will **come** to keep me company.
d The sunshine **came** flooding in.
e **Come** and look at the books any time.
f I only **came** to say goodbye.
g The word villa **came** to mean both 'town' and 'village'.
h Please **come** and get me.
i I wondered if you'd like to **come** over to dinner sometime?
j She only needed to **come** and see me one more time.
k Elinor **came** running up the garden path.
l The hotel manager **came** to investigate.

❸ **Rewrite each sentence, substituting the underlined phrases with verbs formed by *come* and one of these particles, so that the meaning is the same:**

into   out   up   back   down   to   through   off

a When he <u>recovered consciousness,</u> he realized he was in hospital.
b Several buildings <u>collapsed</u> in the earthquake.
c We couldn't see anything until the moon <u>emerged</u> from behind the clouds.
d My application for a work permit still hasn't <u>been processed.</u>
e There are no jobs at the moment, but if something <u>becomes available</u> I will let you know.
f When her grandparents died, she <u>inherited</u> a lot of money.
g When I picked up the coffee pot, the handle <u>detached itself.</u>
h When do you <u>return</u> from Italy?

❹ **The following words and expressions form set phrases with *come*. Can you complete the sentences, choosing the best word from the list:**

to an end   along   first   here
into view   again   true   right

a The holiday's over. All good things come ………… , I'm afraid.
b Don't go away. Come ………… : I want to speak to you.
c Jan came ………… in the school's speech competition and won a prize.
d Come ………… , we'll miss the bus if you don't hurry.
e His dream of owning his own yacht finally came ………… .
f Come ………… ? I didn't hear you. Can you repeat it?
g We turned a corner and the sea came ………… .
h Your ankle is sprained. Don't walk on it and it should come ………… .

could

[auxiliary verb, the past of can] (1) to be able to, or allowed to, do something: *I could hear voices in the next room.* • *She couldn't understand what I was saying.* • *Could I look at your photos?*
(2) to be possible: *It could be an allergy.* • *Where could I have put my keys?*

NOTE: The contracted form of 'could + not' is *couldn't*; 'could + have' = *could've*.

→ can

Grammar patterns

1 could/couldn't | + bare infinitive

Mozart could read music when he was only three.
Before they cut down those trees, you couldn't see the neighbours. Now you can.

▲ to talk about a general ability in the past

There's someone at the door. ~ Who could that be?
It could rain: you'd better take your umbrella.

▲ to talk about the possibility of something in the present or future

Could we leave our bags in reception?
Could you turn the music down just a little?
The director asked if she could observe my class.

▲ to ask permission and make requests

What you could do is hire a car for the day.
Your mother could stay with us, if she likes.

▲ to make suggestions and offers

2 could | + have | + past participle

We lost, but we could've won, if we'd played a bit better.
I locked myself out and had to climb in the window. ~ That was dangerous. You could've fallen.

▲ to talk about what was possible in the past, but didn't happen

Why didn't Alice come to the meeting? ~ I don't know. She could've forgotten. Or maybe she was busy.

▲ to make deductions about what caused past situations

3 could | + not | + have | + past participle

Who phoned Sweden last month and talked for an hour? ~ It couldn't have been Mike because he was on holiday.

▲ to make conclusions about what didn't cause past situations

Collocations

These adverbials often go with *could* and *couldn't*:
easily, hardly, only, never, possibly, maybe, perhaps, and *well*.

It could easily be stress that's causing the sleep disorder.
It was so dark I could hardly see the shore.
I couldn't possibly agree to those terms.
You could maybe get a watch dog.
This subject could well come up again.

The verbs that most commonly go with *could* and *couldn't* are:
be, see, do, get, and *hear*.

They could be Irish, judging by their accent.
I couldn't see the point of learning Latin.
Could you get some chicken livers?

Set phrases

· ' **I couldn't care less** '
What do you want to watch? ~ I couldn't care less. You choose.
▲ to emphasize that something is of no importance to you

· ' **I couldn't agree more/less** '
If you ask me, caviar is over-rated . ~ I couldn't agree more. It's just fishy black stuff.
▲ to show strong (dis)agreement

· **... couldn't be better/worse**
What are your neighbours like? ~ Really nice. Couldn't be better.
▲ to emphasize how good (or bad) things are

· ' **could do with ...** '
I could do with a drink. What's in the fridge?
▲ to say that you need something

Exercises

1 Rewrite the underlined sentences using *could*:

a Who's at the door? ~ I don't know. <u>Perhaps it's the postman</u>.
b What's happened to Brian? ~ <u>Maybe he got lost</u>.
c Who ate the steak? ~ <u>It's highly unlikely it was Karl</u>. He's a vegetarian.
d We're going to the coast for the weekend. ~Take your swimsuits. <u>It may be hot</u>.
e Don't stand on the chair. <u>It's possible it will break</u>.
f Who turned the lights on? ~ <u>Perhaps it was Sheila</u>. She's got a key.
g Who's been using my computer? ~ <u>It certainly wasn't the children</u>, because they're still at school.
h I can't find my sunglasses. ~ <u>Perhaps you left them in the car</u>.

2 Read the text about Jill and Jack. What questions with *could* did they ask at each stage in the story?

My friends Jill and Jack are quite demanding. When they were on holiday last year, they were looking for a hotel. They (a) asked for a double room, but they (b) wanted to see the room first. After looking at the room, they then (c) asked for a room with a view. Once in their new room, they phoned and (d) ordered some sandwiches and soft drinks in their room. Then they went down to reception and (e) asked the receptionist to recommend a good local restaurant. When they got back later that evening, they (f) asked the receptionist to give them a wake-up call at eight the next morning. They also (g) ordered breakfast for two in their room. Finally, back in their room, they phoned to ask reception (h) to tell the people in room 102 to be quiet.

a *Could we have a double room, please?*

3 *Could* for past ability.

Note that you use *could* to talk about general abilities in the past:

I could speak a bit of Arabic once, but I've forgotten it now.

You can also use *could* with verbs of perception (*hear, see,* etc.) to talk about particular situations:

When I woke up, I could hear people shouting.

However, you do not use *could* to say that you succeeded in doing something in a particular situation. In that case, you have to use *was/were able to* or *managed to*:

The car engine was cold, but after one or two tries, I managed to start it.

But you can use *couldn't* to say someone didn't succeed in doing something in a particular situation:

When we got to the car, I couldn't find my car keys.

Choose the correct verbs to fill the gaps in this story:

The weather was perfect that morning, and we got up very early and took the boat out. We put our lines out, and (a. *managed to/could*) catch one or two nice-sized fish. Grandpa told me that when he was young, you (b. *managed to/could*) catch a dozen fish in as many minutes. By midday, it was starting to get windy, and dark clouds were looming. So we decided to head back. But we (c. *didn't manage to/couldn't*) get the motor to start. I was getting nervous. I (d. *managed to/could*) see the shore, only half a mile away. But I knew that grandpa (e. *didn't manage to/couldn't*) swim, even though I (f. *managed to/could*). But in the end he (g. *managed to/could*) get it started, and we (h. *were able to/could*) get back before the storm really started.

did

[auxiliary and main verb, past of do] used for past time reference: *What did you do yesterday?* • *We did some sightseeing.*

→ do/does

NOTE: 'did + not' is contracted to *didn't*.

Grammar patterns

(main verb: → do)

(auxiliary verb)

1 (wh) | + **did** | + NP | + verb | + ?

Did you like the film?
Why didn't you phone?
When you were in Ibiza, did you go out a lot?

▲ for asking questions in the past simple, about past states, events, and habits

2 negative clause | + **did** | + pronoun | + ?
positive clause | + **didn't** | + pronoun | + ?

Gary didn't phone, did he?
They seemed very happy together, didn't they?

▲ for checking facts, opinions, etc., about the past, when you are not sure (in which case you use a rising intonation), or for seeking agreement for something you already know (in which case, you use a falling intonation)

3 NP | + **did** | + not | + verb

The Aztecs didn't have horses.
The concert didn't finish until after midnight.

▲ to say that something was not the case in the past (→ not)

4 NP | + **did** | (+ not)

Did you get some butter? ~ No, I didn't, but I think Jo did.
Kristina always played a lot of sport but Angela didn't.

▲ for referring back to (and avoiding the repetition of) a previous clause

5 NP | + **did** | + verb

We did enjoy the dinner. Thanks ever so much.
I really did think it was Friday.
Bernard has a beard … or, he did have one.

▲ to add emphasis, or to make a contrast or correction.

Collocations

These time expressions often go with did: *yesterday, last night/week/month/summer/year, last Monday/Tuesday etc., at the weekend, this morning.*

Did you get paid last month?
Where did you go last summer?
Did you see that programme on TV yesterday?

Set phrases

- **so did I/he/she/Diane** etc.
  I liked the movie. ~ So did I.
  Hania used to live in Egypt and so did Barbara.
  ▲ to say that some affirmative past state, event, or habit was also true for someone else

- **neither/nor did I/he/she** etc.
  I didn't enjoy the concert very much. ~ Neither did I.
  Gary didn't attend the meeting and nor did Julie.
  ▲ to say that some negative past state, event, or habit was also true for someone else

- '**did she/he/you?** etc.'
  Howard phoned. ~ Did he? What did he want?
  ▲ to respond with interest, surprise, etc. to an affirmative statement about the past

- '**didn't she/he/you?** etc.'
  He didn't say. ~ Didn't he? How strange.
  ▲ to respond with interest, surprise, etc. to a negative statement about the past

- '**what did you·do (then)? / what did you/he/she** etc. **say?**'
  … so then the car stopped completely.
  ~ Oh no! What did you do then?
  … and she walked in and we all shouted 'Surprise!'
  ~ Oh, wow! What did she say?
  ▲ to get more information when someone is telling you about something that happened to them

' **I/We didn't know/realize/think** etc. '
I'm sorry, I didn't realise you were waiting.
I didn't know it was your birthday. I'm really sorry.
▲ to give an excuse when you are apologizing

' **I'm sorry I didn't …** '
I'm sorry I didn't phone but I was really busy.
I'm sorry I didn't get back to you, but …
▲ to apologize

Exercises

❶ Auxiliary or main verb? In the following dialogue, there are 13 examples of *did*. Decide in each case if *did* is acting as an auxiliary verb or a main verb:

A: (a) Did you have a nice weekend?
B: Yes, I (b) did. Very nice. (c) Did you?
A: Not bad. What (d) did you do?
B: I (e) did some things around the house. Fixed a tap, put some shelves up, (f) did some gardening, that sort of thing. What about you?
A: I (g) didn't do anything quite as constructive! Although I (h) did do some ironing on Sunday night. No, all we (i) did was eat, drink and watch TV. And after Sunday lunch I (j) did the *Times* crossword …
B: While Chris (k) did the washing up, I bet.
A: How (l) did you guess! But otherwise we (m) did nothing, really …

❷ Past simple.

Note that in the pattern 'did + verb' (e.g. Grammar patterns 2, 3, and 5) the verb form is the infinitive: *did you go?* (NOT ~~did you went~~?) and *I didn't know* (NOT ~~I didn't knew~~).

Write the correct form of the verb in the spaces in these sentences:

a Where did you .... that lamp? ~ I bought it in an antique shop.
b She ate the meat but she didn't .... the vegetables.
c Did you .... anything? ~ I felt some pain, yes.
d I met her father but I didn't .... her mother.
e How much money did you .... ? ~ I spent it all.

f I didn't .... the dog. I only fed the cat.
g We saw the Pyramids but we didn't .... the Sphinx.
h Did your team .... ? ~ Yes, we won three-nil.

❸ *Did* or *have done*?

Did is a past tense form. It refers to states or events which happened in the past, and which are not connected to the present. It is often used with time expressions that ask or say when something happened, such as *when, last week, yesterday.* To talk about situations that started in the past and continue to the present, use the present perfect (*have done* → have), and expressions like *how long, for,* and *since.*

Choose the correct verb form in each sentence:

a How long (*did you live/have you lived*) here now?
b (*Did you see/Have you seen*) the news last night?
c What (*did you do/have you done*) on Sunday?
d When (*did you buy/have you bought*) that hat?
e (after midday) (*Has the doctor called/Did the doctor call*) this morning?
f (before midday) (*Has the doctor called/Did the doctor call*) this morning?
g What books (*did you read/have you read*) lately?
h What books (*did you read/have you read*) when you were on holiday?

❹ Match the apologies with the excuse:

a I'm sorry I didn't e-mail …
b I'm sorry I didn't call …
c I'm sorry I didn't meet you …
d I'm sorry I didn't bring anything …
e I'm sorry I didn't recognize you …
f I'm sorry I didn't offer to pay …

1 but I left my wallet at home.
2 but the shops were all closed.
3 but my computer was down.
4 but I wasn't wearing my glasses.
5 but I mislaid your phone number.
6 but I was held up at work.

do / does

[irregular verb: *do, did, done*] a common verb which mainly refers to activity: *What are you doing?* • *I'll do the dishes.*
[auxiliary verb] (1) for forming questions and negatives in the present simple: *Where do you live?* • *Sue doesn't drive.*
(2) for referring back: *So does Andy*
(3) for adding emphasis: *I do like oysters.*

→ did → make

NOTE: 'do + not' is contracted to *don't*. 'Does + not' is contracted to *doesn't*.

Grammar patterns
(auxiliary verb)

1 (wh) | + **do/does** | + NP | + verb | + ?

Where do you live? Do you drive?
Do Steven and Sarah arrive tomorrow?

▲ for asking questions in the present simple, about present states, habits, and about future plans

2 negative clause | + **do/does** | + pronoun | + ?
positive clause | + **don't/doesn't** | + pronoun | + ?

You don't take milk, do you?
Ben and Danny arrive next week, don't they?

▲ for checking facts, opinions, etc. about the present, when you are not sure, or to seek confirmation

3 NP | + **do/does** | + not | + verb

Max doesn't ski.
We don't have any children.

▲ to say that something is not the case in the present (→ not)

4 **don't** | + verb | (+ NP/adjective/adverbial)

Don't be silly. Don't walk on the grass.

▲ to tell someone not to do something, or not to behave in a particular way

5 NP | + **do/does** | (+ not)

Who usually takes the kids to school? ~ I don't. Jon does.

Dan hardly ever plays chess, but when he does, he always wins.

▲ for referring back to (and avoiding the repetition of) a previous clause

6 NP | + **do/does** | + verb

I do like these curtains. Are they new?
Do have some more pudding.

▲ to add emphasis, often in order to be more polite

The train's comfortable, but it does take much longer.
I thought you liked broccoli? ~ I do like it but I'm not hungry.

▲ to add emphasis in order to make a contrast, or a correction

(main verb)

7 NP | + **do/does** | + NP

I do yoga and Anita does aerobics.
I'm going to do English Literature at college.

▲ to talk about activities, jobs, or studies that you perform

8 **do** | + determiner | + -ing

James does the shopping and I do the cooking.
Make sure you have time to do some sightseeing.

▲ to talk about work and free-time activities

Collocations

The following phrasal verbs are formed with *do*:

If you *do* something *to* something, you affect it, or change it in some way. (*What have you done to your hair?*)
If you *do up* something like a shirt, you fasten it.
If you *do up* a building or an apartment, you improve it.
If you *do without* something, you manage to live or work without it

Set phrases

• **'how do you do?'**
Jean, this is Mr Brennan. ~ How do you do? ~ How do you do.
▲ for greeting someone formally

- **'what are you doing …? / what's it doing …? etc. '**
  What are you doing in my room?
  What's this sock doing here?
  - ▲ to show surprise, at finding someone or something where you didn't expect it

- **'so do we / so does Jenny etc. '**
  I like this wine. ~ So do I.
  Ahmed comes from Egypt and so does Hoda.
  - ▲ to say that some affirmative present state, event, or habit is also true for someone else

- **neither do I / nor does Ellen etc.**
  We never watch that programme. ~ Neither do we.
  I don't speak French and nor does Tom.
  - ▲ to say that some negative present state, event, or habit is also true for someone else

- **'… will do '** = will be sufficient:
  How much shall I leave for a tip? ~ Five dollars will do.

- **could do with …**
  This soup could do with more salt.
  I could do with a cold drink.
  - ▲ to say that something is needed

- **'… has nothing to do with me '** = is not my responsibility
  We need more ink. ~ Ask Fina. It has nothing to do with me.

Exercises

❶ Read this short text about an athlete. What were the *do/does* questions that the interviewer asked him in order to get the information numbered a–i? Use the correct form of the verbs that are underlined:

  a. Where do you live, Dennis?

Dennis Newson is a keen triathlete, and (a) <u>lives</u> in Stockport. (b) He <u>works</u> in an insurance company. But (c) every morning he <u>gets up</u> at seven and (d) <u>runs</u> 15 miles before breakfast. After work (e) he <u>spends</u> three to four hours in the gym. And (f) at the weekends he <u>swims</u> 1,500 metres and (g) <u>cycles</u> up to 100 kilometres. (h) Dennis <u>eats and drinks</u> a special high-protein diet. (i) He <u>hopes</u> to win next year's Iron Man contest in New Mexico.

❷ *Do* and *is*, *have*, *can*, etc.

Note that, as an auxiliary, *do* is not used with the verb *to be*, or with other auxiliary verbs (such as *can*, *may*, *will*, etc.).
Do you drive? Can you drive? Are you driving?

When *have* or *do* are main verbs they take auxiliary *do*:
Do you have a driving licence? (more usual than *Have you a driving licence?*)
When do you do your driving test?

Change the following sentences into *yes/no* questions:

He works in a fitness centre.
→ *Does he work in a fitness centre?*

a	Ana is single.	e	Monica has arrived.
b	Gregor has a new job.	f	She likes world music.
c	Miriam can sing well.	g	She has a lot of CDs.
d	You will be busy.	h	Jo does up old cars.

❸ Complete these sentences with the correct form of the auxiliary *do*:

a I like country and western music. ~ So ………… I.
b Maria works for an NGO, and so ………… her friend, Matt.
c Does anyone want a lift? ~ Yes, Tom and I ………… .
d I don't usually buy a newspaper but my flatmate ………… .
e I don't speak a foreign language but it's important that my children ………… .
f Iannis doesn't eat meat and neither ………… his friend.
g The next bus leaves at nine. At least, I think it ………… .
h Sometimes my uncle visits us, and, when he ………… , he always brings a trout.

❹ Choose the best word from the list to complete each of these sentences:

shopping	140 miles per hour	economics	hair
homework	sandwiches		kung-fu	dishes

a Do you do ………… ? ~ Yes, what filling would you like?
b The boys do ………… and the girls do yoga.
c I'm going to do the ………… . Do we need more onions?
d Jenny, please do your ………… . It's so untidy.
e Joshua wants to do ………… at university.
f The new Audi can do ………… .
g You can watch TV but first you have to do your ………… .
h Whose turn is it to do the ………… ? Come on, I cooked.

for

[preposition] (1) indicates the person who receives something: *This package is for you.*
(2) indicates purpose or reason: *What is this cupboard for?*
• *Thanks for the flowers.*
(3) indicates a destination or distance: *The bus leaves for the city centre.* • *We walked for miles.*
(4) indicates a period of time: *How long have you been waiting for? ~ Not long. For about five minutes.*

Grammar patterns

1 **for** | + NP

This book is for students of English.
The green bin is for glass.
They left for the beach half an hour ago.

▲ to talk about recipients, purposes, reasons, and destinations

1a **for** | + NP (period of time)

We stayed there for a couple of nights.

▲ to talk about periods of time

2 **for** | + -ing

You can also use a compass for telling the time.
This little bell was for summoning the servants.

▲ to say what the purpose of something is

2a verb | (+ NP) | + **for** | + -ing

I don't blame you for losing your temper.
Forgive me for not paying attention.
She apologised for losing the book.

▲ to say what the reason is for doing or saying something

3 **for** | + NP | + to-infinitive

I'm waiting for Doug to phone.
They arranged for the neighbour to collect the mail.

▲ to talk about someone else doing something

3a it | + is/was etc. | + adjective | + **for** | + NP | + to-infinitive

It was difficult for me to understand his accent.
It's not normal for the shops to be closed.

▲ to describe the ease, likelihood, value, etc., of someone doing something, or of a situation

3b NP | + **for** | + NP | + to-infinitive

There's no need for you to wait.
Is there any reason for us to stay?

▲ to talk about the reasons or opportunities of people doing things

Collocations

Verbs that are followed by *for* to form phrasal verbs include: *account for* (= give a reason for), *arrange for, ask for, bargain for, care for, fall for, long for* (= want very much), *look for, plan for, prepare for, provide for* (= look after financially), *settle for* (= agree to have), and *wait for*.

There were extra expenses I hadn't bargained for.
It's an old trick but I fall for it every time.

Nouns that are frequently followed by *for* include: *time, room, space, need, desire, hope, chance, opportunity, reason, purpose, case, argument, plan, arrangement, search, cure,* and *use*.

Adjectives often followed by *for* include: *good, bad, suitable, ready, famous, responsible, sorry, thankful, useful,* and *late*.

Adjectives that are common in Grammar pattern 3a include: *right, wrong, hard, difficult, easy, dangerous, common, normal, usual, unusual, important, necessary, possible,* and *impossible*.

Set phrases

• **for ages** = for a long time
  I've known Jo for ages: since we were at school together, in fact.

• **for now / for the time being**
  You can share books for the time being, until new ones arrive.
  ▲ to suggest something as a temporary solution

- ' **what for?** ' = why?
  Put you shoes on. ~ What for? ~ We're going for a walk.

- **if it weren't for / if it hadn't been for …**
  If it hadn't been for Tom, I would never have got that job.
  ▲ to say that someone or something is solely responsible for a situation

- **be all for** = approve of
  I'm all for a bit of fun, but this is ridiculous.

- **for all …** → all   • **for one thing** → thing

- **but for …** → but   • **for a start** → start

- **as for …** → as

Exercises

1 **In this text fifteen examples of *for* have been taken out. Can you put them back in?**

Have you planned your retirement and old age? It is common people to postpone these important life decisions, to put them off another day. But you should be preparing your future now. A start, will you have enough money your needs? If you don't, who will provide you, and care you if you are ill? Even if you have been working a long time, your pension may not pay a comfortable life style, nor be enough emergencies. What are you waiting? Sign up our Lifesaver Guaranteed Capital Growth Fund now! If not you, do it your loved ones.

2 *For*, *since*, and *during*:

> *For* and *since* answer the question *how long*? You use *for* to talk about the length of time, and *since* to say when the time period began:
>
> *I've been living in this house for twelve years.*
> *They've been together since last summer.*
>
> *During* answers the question *when*?:
>
> *They met during their summer holidays.*

Complete each sentence with *for*, *since*, or *during*:

a She lived overseas .... several years.
b I've been feeling ill .... last Saturday.
c My mother and father met .... the war.
d I haven't been to Brighton .... I was a child.
e I usually read the newspaper .... breakfast.
f She's been living on her own .... a long time now.
g My mother has been staying with us .... last January.
h I fell asleep .... the movie and missed most of it.
i It rained once or twice .... the night.
j I'd like to stay .... three nights, please.
k Have you heard from Steve .... his accident?
l I've been waiting for you .... an hour.

3 **Choose phrases from the list to answer these questions, making full sentences. Put the verbs into the correct form:**

What's a bread knife used for?
→ *A bread knife is used for slicing bread.*

chop wood	relieve burns	remove stains
repair torn paper	bang nails in	keep stamps in
put candles in	keep herbs in	

a What's a hammer used for?
b What's a glass jar useful for?
c What's ice good for?
d What are wine bottles useful for?
e What's an axe used for?
f What's salt good for?
g What's sticky tape useful for?
h What's a cigar box good for?

4 **Rewrite these sentences, using the word in brackets, so that the meaning is more or less the same:**

Wolves commonly hunt in packs. (common)
→ *It is common for wolves to hunt in packs.*

a Bats usually sleep upside-down. (usual)
b Bears normally sleep through the winter. (normal)
c Cats can easily see in the dark. (easy)
d Seals run fast with difficulty. (difficult)
e Owls commonly hunt at night. (common)
f Chimpanzees don't usually eat meat. (usual)

get

[irregular verb: *get got got* (or US: *gotten*)] receive, obtain, become, etc.: *I got some new sunglasses.* • *How did you get that burn?* • *They got married three years ago.* • *It's getting late.*

→ got

Grammar patterns

1 **get** | + NP

I'm going to get some milk. Is there anything else we need?
How much did you get for that job?
I think we should get a taxi: it will be quicker.
I got food poisoning when I was on holiday.

▲ to talk about obtaining and buying things, about earning money, about taking transport, catching illnesses, etc.

2 **get** | + adjective

It's getting late and I'm getting tired.

▲ to talk about things changing, becoming different

3 have | + **got**
(→ got)

4 **get** | + adverbial

When you get to the traffic lights, turn left.
What time did you get home?

▲ to talk about arriving at places

5 **get** | + NP | + NP

I got Damien a DVD for his birthday.
Can you get me a coffee?

▲ to talk about giving things to people, or fetching things for people

6 **get** | + past participle

I got robbed last night.
When did you get married?

▲ to talk about things that happen to you, caused by someone else

7 **get** | + NP | + past participle

We're getting the kitchen repainted.
Did you get that report finished?

▲ to talk about causing things to change, improve, become completed

8 **get** | (+ NP) | + -ing

We'd better get moving.
It took ages to get the car going.

▲ to talk about causing things to work, or move

9 **get** | + to-infinitive

Did you get to see the ruins?
She always gets to meet interesting people.

▲ to talk about managing to achieve things

10 **get** | + NP | + to-infinitive

Can you get Tim to tidy his room?

▲ to talk about causing people to do things

Collocations

'get + past participle' (Grammar pattern 6).
Some of the most frequent past participles in this pattern are:
rid (of), involved (in/with), married, started, dressed, stuck, lost.

'get + to-infinitive' (Grammar pattern 9).
Some of the most frequent infinitives in this pattern are:
to know, to hear, to see.

get combines with adverb particles to form phrasal verbs.
Some of the most frequent of these are: *get away, get back, get in, get on, get out, get over, get up.*

Set phrases

• **get it** = understand
I don't get it. Why has the traffic stopped?
He told me a joke but I didn't get it.

• '**it gets me/what gets me is …**'
I hate it when people correct my Spanish. It really gets me.
What gets me about Bruce is the way he treats Sarah.
  ▲ for saying that something annoys you

• **to get there** = to achieve your goal
It's not perfect, but we are getting there.

Exercises

① **Identify the Grammar patterns (1–10) in these concordance lines:**

a The symptoms will **get** worse.
b But certainly I wouldn't **get** mad with her.
c We've got to **get** moving.
d He was eager to **get** back to work.
e One of the doctors managed to **get** the laundry going.
f It is now possible to make a booking or **get** a ticket printed in your office or hotel.
g You can't **get** a train home after about 10 pm.
h When I **get** to be President, we're going to shut that place down.
i This might persuade his mother to **get** him a new bike.
j I could always **get** Fenella or somebody to answer the phone.
k He has said he won't **get** divorced.
l The principal concern is to **get** the job done.
m My parents just **get** me things I need.
n The bus failed to **get** up the first steep hill.
o Why don't you **get** Hamid to run you over.
p So I went out to **get** some fish and chips.
q I would expect things to develop quickly once they **get** going.
r She thought that he might **get** killed.
s He is all right when you **get** to know him.

② **Phrasal verbs with *get*. Can you match the verb with its definition or synonym?**

a get up	1 have a friendly relationship
b get over (sth)	2 finally start (doing sth)
c get back	3 avoid (doing sth)
d get on with someone	4 recover (e.g. from an illness)
e get away	5 return (e.g. from a journey)
f get in	6 wake up and get out of bed
g get out of (doing sth)	7 escape
h get down to	8 enter

③ **Now, use the phrasal verbs from exercise 2 to complete these sentences:**

a When did you .... from Greece?
b The prisoners managed to .... in a stolen car.
c Don't you think you should turn the TV off and .... work?
d What time do you usually .... in the morning?
e Don't try to .... doing the shopping: it's your turn.
f It took him years to .... the death of his son.
g How well do you .... with Alistair?
h The thieves managed to .... by breaking a window when no one was at home.

④ **Complete these situations with *getting* followed by one of these adjectives:**

warmer   tired   older   late   crowded   fat

a When we arrived there weren't many people here, but now there are more and more. It's ....
b Jeff's showing the signs of age. He's ....
c Look at the time! We'd better go. It's ....
d The weather's been so cold, but at last it's ....
e You should really get more exercise. You're ....
f Can you take over the driving. I'm ....

⑤ **The words *get* and *got* are often overused in writing. Can you either replace the underlined words in this text with synonyms, or delete them if they are unnecessary?**

I got up, got dressed and got the children their breakfast. I got a paper and got the bus early, but it got held up in the traffic, so I got to the meeting late and I got shouted at by the boss. Things got worse when I got a call on my phone in the middle of the meeting. Then I spilt my coffee and had to get a rag to clean it up. After the meeting I got an angry note from the boss, saying my behaviour had got to get better, or I'd get fired.

give

[irregular verb: *give, gave, given*] to provide or supply someone with something: *What shall we give Mum for her birthday?*
• *They gave me flowers.* • *Luke was given a standing ovation.*

Grammar patterns

1 **give** | + NP | + NP

Give the dog a bone.
I gave the woman directions.
We were given a tour of the palace.

▲ to express handing something over, offering, and receiving

2 **give** | + NP | + to | + NP

What shall I do with this old coat? ~ Give it to Oxfam.
She gave a speech to the World Health Organisation.
This ring was given to me by my grandmother.

▲ to say that something is transferred or transmitted to a person or a group

3 **give** | + NP

She gave a scream and rushed from the room.
The painting gives a sense of peace.

▲ to talk about performing certain actions or conveying certain sensations

Collocations

Give commonly combines with nouns in these categories:

human expressions: *a shout, a cry, a sigh, a smile*
physical actions: *a kick, a punch, a push*
communication events: *some advice, an answer, a (phone) call, a clue, an example, some information, an interview, a lecture, the news, a report, a speech, a talk, a warning*:

She gave a sigh and turned on the TV.
I saw her give the dog a kick.
I'll give you an answer tomorrow.
This exercise is too difficult: give me a clue.
Dr Fisher was given an interview by the BBC.

Give also combines with particles to form these phrasal verbs:

If you *give* something *away*, you give something you no longer need.
If you *give* something *back*, you return something.
If you *give in*, you surrender, or agree unwillingly.
If you *give* something *out*, you distribute it.
If you *give up* doing something, you stop doing it.

He gave all his money away to charity.
Can you give out these questionnaires?
When did you give up smoking?

Set phrases

· **'I'd give anything to …'**
I'd give anything to have a view of the sea.
▲ to say that you are very keen to do or have something

· **given …** = considering
It's not surprising, given her age.
Given the circumstances, you can hardly blame him.

· **'give or take …'** (verb phrase)
It will take three weeks to have the flat painted, give or take a day or two.
▲ to be vague about the exact amount of time

· **give and take** (noun phrase) = compromise, flexibility
There has to be a bit of give and take in any marriage.

Exercises

❶ Transform these sentences from Grammar pattern 2 to Grammar pattern 1, using a pronoun for the first noun phrase:

I gave a copy of my book to all my friends.
→ *I gave them a copy of my book.*

a Natalia has given her car to her brother.
b The children are giving bread to the ducks.
c I'm going to give my books to my daughter.
d The government gave a pension to me and my wife.
e What did the teacher give to the students?
f Do you think the committee will give the prize to you?
g Someone gave milk to the cat.
h Who will give my money back to me?

❷ Use this diagram to make three sentences of each of these types (nine sentences in all):

Jenny gave Bill a book.
Bill was given a book.
The book was given to Bill.

❸ Choose words from the list to complete these sentences with *give*:

some advice	a call	an example	a talk
an interview	a shout	a big smile	a push

a Can you give me .... tomorrow morning? My number is 301 22 68.
b The baby stopped crying and gave me ....
c Can you help give the car .... : it won't start.
d Before you do this exercise, I'll give you .... : *gave* is the past of *give*.
e The Youth Club asked me to give .... about my experiences in the Congo.
f Let me give you .... : never drink and drive.
g I've applied for a teaching job and they're giving me .... next week.
h If you need some help with the gardening, give me ....

❹ There are a number of idioms with *give*. Match the two parts. If you don't know the idiom, try and make an intelligent guess:

a I've never been skiing before, but I'm prepared to give …
b Ed's getting a new car. His old one gave …
c Doctor, tell me the worst. Give …
d I need help pushing the car. Can you give …
e Patrick was furious with me. He really gave …
f Promise me you won't tell Jan. Give …
g I tried to keep the party a secret, but Terry gave …
h Never try arguing with Jenny. She always gives …

1 … me a hand?
2 … as good as she gets.
3 … it a go.
4 … me hell.
5 … me your word.
6 … the game away.
7 … up the ghost.
8 … it to me straight.

go

[irregular verb: *go, went, gone*] (1) to move or travel (away from speaker or writer): *A bus goes from here into town.* • *The boys went to the beach.* • *Have the guests all gone?*
(2) to progress, become: *How did your talk go?* • *The milk has gone off.*

NOTE: *go* contrasts with *come*, which usually expresses movement towards the speaker: *Don't go! Come back.*

→ come
→ going

Grammar patterns

1 **go** | (+ preposition | + NP)

It's late. Let's go. ~ You go. I'll stay.
First I went to the bank and then I went to the supermarket.
We're going for a swim. Do you want to come?

▲ to talk about movement away from where you are now

2 **go** | + and | + verb

Go and get your coat. I'll wait for you here.
Let's go and have a cup of coffee.
Last night we went and saw The Lord of the Rings.

▲ to talk about two closely related actions, where the second is the reason for the first

3 **go** | + -ing

We often go walking in the Lake Districts.
Helmut's gone diving in the Red Sea.
I'm going shopping. Do we need anything?

▲ to talk about leisure activities and shopping

4 **be** | + going | + to-infinitive

They're going to open a restaurant.
What are you going to do this weekend?
(→ going)

5 **go** | + adverb

The dinner went well, didn't it?
How did the interview go?

▲ to talk about events and processes and how they happen

6 **go** | + adjective

My toes have gone numb.
We should eat the fish before it goes bad.

▲ to talk about things changing their state or condition

Collocations

Go combines with many adverb and prepositional particles to form phrasal verbs:

If something *goes ahead,* it starts or progresses. (*The meeting went ahead as planned.*)
If you *go away,* you leave your place of work, or home, e.g. for a holiday.
If you *go back* to a place, you return there.
If something like a ship *goes down,* it sinks. If prices *go down,* they decrease; if they *go up,* they increase.
You can *go in(to)* or *go out of* a place, or you can *go over* it, or *go round* it.
If something *goes on,* it continues. (*How long will the strike go on, do you think?*)
If you *go on* doing something, you continue doing it.
If someone *goes on* about something, they talk about it continually.
If something like a bomb or an alarm *goes off,* it is activated.
If a light *goes off,* it stops working. If food or drink *goes off,* it is no longer fresh.
If you *go over* something, you check it carefully. (*Let's go over the details one more time.*)

Set phrases

• ❝ **go on!** ❞
Go on, try one. They're delicious.
… so then this man sits down next to me … ~ Go on. ~ … and he says to me …

▲ for encouraging someone to do something, or to continue telling you something

• **'go away!'**
Go away! I'm busy.
▲ to tell someone to stop bothering you

• **have a go** = attempt to do something
Would you like to have a go on the scooter?
If you don't get all the answers correct, have another go.

Exercises

❶ All the examples of *go* in this text have been taken out. Can you put them back? (There are ten.)

Every summer, when we on holiday, we to a place in the mountains called Blue Lakes. There are lakes, mountains and forest, so it's perfect for the kids. The boys like to fishing while me and the girls hiking and bird watching. Sometimes we all sailing together and you can also hire kayaks and kayaking on the lake. There's a local store where we and buy basic stuff, and there's a village a few miles away where we once a week to do the shopping or to the cinema if the weather is not good and where you can and have a meal in the one or two restaurants.

❷ *Been* or *gone*? Look at the difference between these two sentences:

Lin has gone to Hong Kong. (= He went and he is still there.)
Lin has been to Hong Kong. (= He went and came back.)

Choose either *been* (→ been) or *gone* to complete these sentences:

a It's very quiet: where have the children .... ?
b Have you ever .... to China? ~Yes, three years ago.
c Carl is not here this week: he's .... to look after his father.
d My Kylie Minogue CD has .... Has anyone seen it?
e You look well. ~ Yes, I've .... skiing.
f My parents have never .... overseas.
g Where is David? ~ He's .... rock climbing.
h Did you remember to tell the postman that we've .... away?

❸ Complete these sentences, choosing the correct word from the list:

on   back   up   away   off   ahead   together   out

a The price of petrol has gone .... from 85 cents to 90 cents a litre.
b I've been at home all day. Let's go .... this evening.
c Take some painkillers and the pain will go ....
d Harold was going .... about his holiday in Tunisia and I nearly went to sleep.
e I don't think the pink tie and the green shirt go .... How about the brown tie?
f We've come the wrong way. I think we should go .... and start again.
g Don't wait for us: go .... and start eating.
h The power went .... while I was working on the computer.

❹ Here are some more set phrases with *go*. Can you match the two parts of each sentence?

a She's studying for her final exams: there's only three weeks	1 goes to show.
b There's one sandwich left so let's	2 here goes!
c You see what you can do if you try! It just	3 in one go.
d She's so active – she's always	4 anything goes.
e Terry and Chris liked each other	5 to go.
f I've never ridden a horse before, but	6 on the go.
g Don't worry about dressing formally –	7 from the word go.
h See if you can drink it all	8 go halves.

going

[present participle of go] *Where are you going?* • *Keep going – we're not finished yet.*
[modal verb: *going to*] to make predictions or talk about plans and intentions: *You're going to fall.* • *Aren't they going to get married?* • *I was going to e-mail you.*

→ go

Grammar patterns

1 be | + **going** | + adverbial

I'm going to the shops. Is there anything we need?
We're going home: do you want a lift?

▲ to talk about present or future movement. (This is an example of the present continuous. → go)

2 be | + **going**

My eyesight is going.
I think the batteries are going.

▲ to say that something is getting weak. (This is an example of the present continuous.)

3 be | + **going** | + to-infinitive

They're going to adopt a child.
What are you going to have? ~ I'm going to have the squid.

▲ to talk and ask about future plans, arrangements, intentions

House prices are going to level off.
The weather's going to get better, they say.

▲ to make predictions, and to talk about predictions

I was going to phone you, but I've been busy.
Weren't you going to join a gym?
He said that things were going to change.
I thought I was going to die of embarrassment.

▲ to talk about past intentions, plans, etc. and past predictions

4 be | + **going** | + to have | + to-infinitive

We're going to have to hurry, or we'll miss the start.
You're just going to have to work harder.

▲ to talk about future necessity and obligations

Collocations

The verbs that most commonly follow *going to* (Grammar pattern 3) are: *be, have, do, get, go, say, take* and *ask*.

It's going to be fine tomorrow.
I'm going to go shopping.

The adverbs that most frequently go between *be* and *going to* are: *just, never, always, only, actually*, and *probably*.

It's just going to take a second
I'm only going to be away for a day or two.
I think I'm actually going to have the lasagne.

Set phrases

· **keep going** = continue
Keep going, don't stop, you're nearly finished!

· **get going** = start going (somewhere), or start leaving (a place)
It's getting late. We'd better get going.

· **going on** = happening
What's going on here? ~ Nothing. Just watching TV.

· **'How's it going?'**
How's it going? ~ Not bad. Yourself?
▲ to greet someone informally

Exercises

1 Put the word in brackets in the correct place in the sentence:

a (are) What you going to do this weekend?
b (to) I'm going the supermarket: can I get you anything?
c (was) I going to come to the party but I got lost.
d (never) You're going to get into college if you don't study.
e (to) I'm going to have get a new computer.
f (probably) Jakob is going to hand in his resignation.
g (be) It looks like it's going to wet again tomorrow.
h (keep) I think we should going until it gets dark.
i (not) We are going to stay with your mother.
j (you) How long are going to be?

2 Here are some other – rather more formal – ways of talking about plans and arrangements. Rewrite the following sentences using *going to*:

a They are planning to build a new bridge.
b We intend to discuss this at the next meeting.
c I won't be flying. I'll be taking the train.
d What do you plan to say to the lawyer?
e It's our intention to sign the agreement.
f We have decided not to take any action.

3 Now, rewrite these sentences, using the word in brackets, so that the meaning is more or less the same:

a Are you going to place a large order? (intend)
b I'm going to discuss this with Jean-Pierre. (will be)
c They are not going to reconsider our offer. (decided)
d Our lawyers are going to keep you informed. (plan)
e We are not going to pursue the matter. (intention)
f I'm going to spend a week in Brazil. (planning)

4 Here are some set phrases with *going*. Can you put each one into its context?

he's going on 40
he's got a lot going for him
if I'm coming or going
the way things are going
while the going is good
it was tough going
which was good going
to be going on with

a I think Sergio will be an excellent team leader: ....
b We got to Birmingham in just two hours, ... considering the time of day.
c Our boss is not that old: I'd say ....
d I don't think we can afford to raise your salary, ...
e We finally managed to persuade them to sign the deal, but ....
f The share market is very buoyant, so buy now ....
g I won't give you more reports to edit. You've got plenty ....
h I've been so busy these last few days: I don't know ....

IT WAS TOUGH GOING.

good

[adjective; comparative: *better*; superlative: *best*] pleasant, of a high standard, suitable, of the right kind, well-behaved, etc.
Did you have a good weekend? • *Your English is very good.* • *Is this a good time to call?* • *That's a good idea.* • *If you're good, I'll take you to the zoo.*
[noun] benefit: *No good will come of this.* • *Drink this soup: it will do you good.*

Grammar patterns

1 NP | + is/was etc. | + **good**
   NP | + is/was etc. | + **good** | + NP

   The film was very good. Much better than his last one.
   Terry is a good swimmer. He swims well.

   ▲ to say that something or someone is pleasing, of a high standard, etc.

2 it | + is/was etc. | + **good** | + that-clause
   it | + is/was etc. | + a **good** thing | + that-clause

   It's good that you phoned.
   It was a good thing someone had remembered to bring a torch.

   ▲ to say that some action is suitable or appropriate

3 it | + is/was etc. | + no | + **good** | + -ing

   It's no good complaining: no one's going to pay any attention.

   ▲ to say that an action or behaviour is pointless

Collocations

Verbs that frequently precede *good* are: *be, feel, look, seem, smell, sound, taste,* and *get, become.*

   That smells good. What is it?
   He's getting good at diving, isn't he?

Do and *make* also occur with *good*:

   A holiday in the sun will do you good.
   It will cost a lot of money to make good the damage caused by the storm.

Prepositions that follow *good* include *at, for, to,* and *with*:

   She's good at languages: she speaks about four or five.
   Are you good at maths?
   Fresh fruit and vegetables are good for you.
   Lots of fat and sugar isn't good for you.
   The neighbours were very good to me when I was ill.
   Elizabeth is a brilliant teacher: she is so good with children.

Set phrases

· **good morning / good afternoon / good evening**
  Good morning, John. ~ Hi, Susan.
  ▲ for greeting people when you or they arrive

· **goodbye / good night**
  Good night. See you tomorrow.
  ▲ said when people are going away

· **for good** = for ever
  The days of cheap oysters have gone for good.

· **what good …?**
  What good is money if you can't enjoy it?
  ▲ to suggest that something has no benefit

· **… any good?** = of any value? of any interest?
  Was the party any good? ~ It was a bit boring, actually.

· **that's no good**
  I'll phone you at work. ~ That's no good. I'm in a meeting all day.
  ▲ to say that something is not suitable

· **a good deal** = a lot
  That swimming pool must have cost them a good deal.
  She's a good deal older than him.

· **good for him/her/Albert** etc.
  Albert passed his driving test at last. ~ Good for him!
  ▲ to say that you are pleased about something good that has happened to someone

· **for your own good** → own

· **this/it** etc. **will do you good**
  You need a rest. A holiday will do you good.
  ▲ to recommend something to someone

Exercises

❶ Put the word in brackets in the correct place in each sentence:

a (good) You can stay up and watch TV, but only if you are.
b (good) That soup smells. Can I try some?
c (thing) It's a good that we booked a table.
d (at) Do you want a game of pool? ~ OK, but I'm not very good it.
e (no) It's good shouting at them: they don't speak English.
f (with) Did you make that? You're so good your hands.
g (you) You need some exercise. A walk will do good.
h (good) What is a degree if you can't get a job?
i (any) Is this book good? ~ Yes, but it's not as good as her first one.
j (good) They say they will make any damage that they cause.

❷ Twelve examples of the word *good* have been taken out of this conversation. Can you put them back?

A: Morning, Jeff.
B: Hi, Natalie. How are you?
A: Thanks. Did you have a weekend?
B: Not bad. We went to that exhibition.
A: Any?
B: Not really. It's a thing you didn't go. What about you?
A: Yeah, I won a medal, playing chess.
B: For you! You must be at it.
A: Well, I practise a deal. But what is it, if you can't make any money out of it?
B: Yeah, well. Hey, feel like a drink later on?
A: That's a idea. How about six?
B: That's no. I'm busy. Seven?
A: Fine. See you then.
B: Bye.

❸ *Good, better, best,* and *well.* (→ well)
Complete these sentences by choosing the best word from the above list:

a Which is .... ? White sugar or brown sugar?
b It was the .... holiday I've ever had.
c You play the guitar very .... : where did you learn it?
d Our team played .... than the other team.
e What was the weather like? ~ Very .... It didn't rain once.
f Eat your broccoli: it's .... for you.
g Which one is .... for a holiday: Ibiza, Madeira, or the Canaries?
h How do you feel? ~ .... than yesterday, thanks.
i His teacher says he's the .... in the class.
j How .... is your French? ~ I can speak it, but I can't write it very ....

❹ More set phrases with *good*. Choose from these words to complete the idioms:

thing   time   books   far   news   new   true   turn

a Well, we're nearly halfway there. ~ So .... , so good.
b We didn't win the free TV. It was a mistake. ~ I thought it was too good to be ....
c I fixed your umbrella for you. Look, it's as good as ....
d After two weeks at the beach, I started getting bored. ~ Yes, you can have too much of a good ....
e You didn't have to offer to babysit. ~ Well, you took the kids to the pool, and one good .... deserves another.
f The boss has asked me out for lunch. ~ Mm. You must be in her good ....
g I'm worried about Barry. I haven't heard from him since he left. ~ Well, no news is good ....
h When can we open our presents? ~ Be patient. All in good ....

got

[past and past participle of *get*] *I got some fish at the market.*
• *Have they got back yet?*
Combined with *have: have got:*
(1) possess, own (in the present): *I've got a new laptop.* • *Have you got a coin?* • *She's got a nice smile.*
(2) to express obligation: *I've got to go now.* • *What have you got to do today?*

→ get
→ have

NOTE: *have got* (for possession, etc.) is more common in spoken and informal English than in written and formal English. It is also more common in British English than in American English. In American English the form *have/has* is more commonly used to express possession: *I have a new laptop. Do you have a coin?*. In spoken language *have got* is sometimes reduced to *got*: *I got a new laptop*. And *have got to = gotta*: *I gotta go*. Also, in American English, *gotten* is sometimes used for the past participle of *get*: *Have they gotten back already?*

Grammar patterns

1 have/has | + **got** | + NP

The neighbours have got a new car.
Have you got the right time?
I haven't got any brothers or sisters.
How many legs has a spider got?
Has this soup got meat in it?

▲ for talking about things people presently possess, or are holding, about relationships, and about what things consist of

I've got a meeting on Thursday.
The doctor's got two more patients to see.

▲ to talk about future plans and arrangements

2 had | + **got** | + NP

Last time I saw him, he'd got a beard.
She said she'd got a cold, so she wasn't coming to class.

▲ to talk about things people possessed or had obtained in the past. 'Had + noun' is the more usual pattern in writing (… *he had a beard;* … *she had a cold*).

3 have/has | + **got** | + to-infinitive

They say I've got to get a work permit.
What have you got to do this afternoon?
You've got to study hard if you want to pass.

▲ to say what is necessary, obligatory

Collocations

Got is frequently followed by quantifiers like: *lots of, a few, many*, etc.

Gary's got more money than the rest of us.
We haven't got much time.
They haven't got many choices open to them.
She's got a lot of talent.
They'd all got loads of money.
We've got masses of food for a picnic.
Have you got a few minutes?
We've got enough troubles of our own.
I've got another meeting tomorrow.

Set phrases

- **have you got a […] on you?**
  Have you got a pen on you? ~ Here you are. ~ Thanks.
  ▲ for asking to borrow something

- **I've got no idea / I haven't got a clue**
  How do you change the toner in the photocopier? ~ I've got no idea.
  ▲ for saying you don't know the answer

- **you've got me there**
  What's the capital of Bahrain? ~ You've got me there.
  ▲ for saying you don't know the answer

- **you've got to be joking/kidding**
  Billy wants to be a ballet dancer. ~ You've got to be joking!
  ▲ for expressing disbelief

- **what've you got against …?**
  What've you got against hunting? ~ Well, for a start, it's cruel.
  ▲ to ask why someone opposes or rejects something or someone

' where has/have […] got to? '
Where have the children got to? ~ I think they're in the shed.
▲ for asking where someone or something is

' what's got into …? '
What's got into Gavin? He's in a terrible mood.
▲ for asking what's the matter with someone

Exercises

❶ *Got* appears in the following patterns:

1 past of *get*: *I got the fish.*
2 present perfect of *get*: *Have they got back yet?*
3 *have got* for possession: *Have you got a pen?*
4 *have got to* for obligation: *I've got to go now.*

Look at the following concordance lines and identify the different uses of *got*.

a I've **got** to put it down to experience.
b I **got** engaged to a girl called Jane Wilde.
c There are many other things they haven't **got** right.
d People here have not **got** the result yet.
e Now everyone's **got** a car.
f In 1918 women over 30 **got** the vote in Britain.
g He's **got** a long way to go.
h You'll know if you've **got** it because it is very painful.
i We have **got** to use less and conserve more.
j We've **got** through all this just by being ourselves.
k The technique has **got** to be perfect.
l I've **got** an album full of new music.

❷ *Have* and *have* got are interchangeable when you mean possession, or when talking about relationships, or the qualities of things:

Sue has a digital camera. (= Sue's got a digital camera.)
I have a cousin in the States. (= I've got a cousin in the States.)
Most ants don't have wings. (= Most ants haven't got wings.)

But you can't use *have got* for events or actions that are expressed with *have*:

We usually have breakfast in the kitchen. (NOT ~~We usually have got breakfast …~~)
Have a nice weekend. (NOT ~~Have got a nice weekend.~~)
etc.

Rewrite the following sentences using *have got,* but only those where *have got* is possible:

a How many children do you have?
b Sam has blue eyes and fair hair.
c Don't kiss me: I have a terrible cold.
d I hope you have a good time in Berlin.
e Does your flat have central heating?
f I always have a shower at the gym.
g Do you tip the hairdresser when you have a haircut?
h I don't have any change, I'm sorry.

❸ Put *got* in the correct places in this dialogue. (There are 12 places it can go.)

A: Excuse me, can I ask you some questions?
B: Well, I haven't much time. But … OK.
A: Have you a mobile phone?
B: Yes, I have. I've two in fact.
A: Why have you two?
B: One's for work and one's for family and friends.
A: Have you a big family?
B: No, I haven't. Look …
A: Have you seen the new Magifone?
B: No, I haven't.
A: Here, I've one here. It's lots of exciting new features. It's a hundred different ring tones. And it's an integrated digital camera and colour display. And …
B: Look, really, I've to go. I've an important meeting.
A: OK. But take one of these brochures. It's all the details of our special offer.
B: Thanks.

❹ *Have got to.*
This is what is required for a work permit in a certain country. Rewrite the list, so that it is less formal, using *You've got to …* :

a A work contract must be provided.
b Applicants must be in possession of a valid passport.
c Applicants are required to provide photocopies of the above items.
d Three passport-size photographs are necessary.
e It is essential that a valid medical certificate be provided.
f Applicants are obliged to prove they have no criminal record.
g Form WP100 must be completed by all applicants.
h Payment of $US 75 is obligatory.

had

[past and past participle of *have*, main verb, auxiliary verb and modal verb (*had to*)]
main verb: *Have you had lunch?* • *It had rained all night.* • *I had to see the doctor.*

The patterns of *had* as main verb are the same as for *have*:
They had no friends. • *We had a nice chat.*

→ have

NOTE: 'had + not' is contracted to *hadn't*

Grammar patterns

1 **had** | + past participle

The film had already started when we got there.
At the airport I realized I had left my passport at home.
Until last week, it hadn't rained in the region for several years.

▲ to look back from a point in the past, and talk about something that happened before then (This is called the past perfect.)

Stephen told me he had found a new agent.
The doctor asked him if he had ever had hepatitis.

▲ to report what people said, or asked, about the past

2 **had** | + been | + -ing

It had been raining heavily all morning, and the roads were still slippery.
Before he moved to Toronto he had been living in Vancouver.

▲ to look back from a point in the past, and talk about something that was in progress up to that point (This is called the past perfect continuous.)

3 **had** | + been | + past participle

They told me that the house had just been sold.
Before I bought it, the car had been owned by a retired professor.

▲ to look back from a point in the past, and talk about something that was affected by an action before then (This is called the past perfect passive.)

4 if | + **had**-clause (past perfect tense), | + clause (would have/could have etc.)

If we had booked, we would have got a table.
(→ if, Grammar pattern 1c)

5 **had** | + NP | + past participle, | + clause (would have/could have etc.)

Had we been informed of the situation, we would have acted accordingly.

▲ a more formal way of saying Grammar pattern 4

6 **had** | + to-infinitive
did | + not | + **have** | + to-infinitive

I'm sorry I'm late but I had to take the kids home.
It snowed so much they had to close the airport.
Because it was a holiday, Emma didn't have to work on Monday.

▲ to talk about what was necessary or obligatory, (or what is not necessary or obligatory)

7 **had** | + better | (+ not) | + infinitive

Look at you! You're soaking wet. You had better come in and dry off.
We'd better not tell Rob, or he'll want to come too.

▲ to say what you think should (or should not) happen; to give advice

Collocations

Some of the most frequent verbs in the past perfect are:
be, make, go, come, take, see, have, say, and *leave.*

It had been ages since I had last seen Felicity.
We'd made good progress by the time the snow started.

The adverbs that most commonly go with the past perfect are:
never, already, ever, always, just, once.

Before I went to Finland, I'd never had a sauna.
Although we'd already eaten, we accepted their offer of a snack.
It was the first time I had ever seen a yak.
This was not my first visit. I had been there once before.

Set phrases

· '**have had it**' = be in a bad condition, be in serious trouble
The TV has had it. It's time we got a new one.
I lost Jim's digital camera. ~ Now, you've had it.

Exercises

❶ Twelve instances of the word *had* have been taken out of this text. Can you put them back?

Tom sat down to dinner and reflected on his day. It begun badly. He been worrying about things the night before, so he a bad night, and he overslept. Consequently he arrived late for his class. What's more, he forgotten there was an exam. If he known, he would have stayed in bed. He his dinner in silence. He to do his homework, but he didn't feel like it. He a cup of coffee and turned on the TV. He asked himself what he done to deserve a life like this.

❷ The past perfect is often used to provide background information for a narrative.

The following events happened in this order:

Otto took a train from Berlin the night before.
He arrived in the town early in the morning.
He found a hotel, and checked in.
He took a walk around the town and ate in a cheap restaurant.
He spoke to nobody. Nobody spoke to him.
He wrote a couple of postcards.
He went back to his hotel.
He opened the door and entered his room.
It was then that he knew that the game was up.

Rewrite the story so that it begins:

As he entered his room Otto knew that the game was up. He had taken a train …

❸ Change the direct speech into reported speech:

'I've run out of petrol,' he said.
→ *He said he had run out of petrol.*

a 'We've had an accident,' she said.
b 'Have you eaten yet?' he asked Derek.
c 'I spoke to the boss,' he told me.
d 'I broke the fax machine,' she admitted.
e 'They didn't ring me,' he complained.
f 'Why didn't you write?' she asked me.

❹ Here is a list of things Karen had to do yesterday. Make sentences using *She had to …* and verbs from the list:

go to   make   take (x 3)   buy   pick up (x 2)

- kids to playschool
- dog to vet
- car to garage
- 1 kilo beef, ½ kilo tomatoes

- dentist
- car from garage

- kids
- dinner

have / has

[irregular verb: *have, had, had*] (1) a lexical verb meaning: to own, possess, be holding, etc.: *She has 16 cats.* • *Do you have your keys?*
[auxiliary verb] used to form the present perfect: *I have been on holiday.*
(2) combines with *got* to form *have got.*
[modal auxiliary (+ *to*)] expressing necessity: *I have to work.*
→ had → got

NOTE: 'have + not' is contracted to *haven't;* 'has + not' = *hasn't.*

Grammar patterns

(auxiliary verb)

1 **have/has** | + past participle

Irena has climbed the Matterhorn.
Have you ever been on TV?
Our taxi has arrived.

▲ to talk about things that happened sometime in a period from the past up to now, often with present results (This is called the present perfect.)

They have always lived in this building.
How long have you been together?

▲ to talk about a situation that started in the past and is still continuing (→ long, never, ever, just)

2 **modal** | + **have** | + past participle

I must have left my umbrella on the train.
You could have hurt yourself.
I saw you with someone. ~ That would've been my brother.

▲ to talk about the possibility, or desirability, of situations in the past → could, would, will, should, etc.

3 **have/has** | + been | + -ing
(→ been)

4 **have/has** | + to-infinitive
doesn't/don't | + **have** | + to-infinitive

In the UK you have to drive on the left.
You don't have to wear a tie: it's an informal dinner.

▲ to talk about what is (not) necessary or obligatory (→ got)

5 **have/has** | + NP | + past participle

I'd like to have this photo enlarged.
How often do you have your hair cut?

▲ to talk about causing things to be done

(main verb)

6 **have/has** | + NP

He has an apartment in the city.
I have an uncle who has Parkinsons.
Sylvia doesn't have a job.

▲ to talk about possessing or owning things, including relationships, illnesses, etc. (Note that you can also use *have got.* → got)

Can you have a look at the dishwasher?
I didn't have a very good time in Oxford.

▲ to talk about actions and experiences, where the meaning is mainly carried by the noun. (Note that you can't use *have got* in this case. → had)

Collocations

The most frequent adverbs that go before the past participle in Grammar pattern 1 are: *already, never, always, just, also, now, ever, only, recently,* and *actually.*

Adverbials that frequently follow Grammar pattern 1 are: *yet, before, once, for X years, since ….*

Nouns that go with *have* (Grammar pattern 6, to talk about actions and experiences) fall into these groups:

meals: *have lunch /a snack / something to eat*
food and drink: *have a sandwich / beer / a cup of coffee*
events: *have a meeting / a party / a lesson / a chat*
enjoyable experiences: *have fun / a good time / a laugh*
unpleasant experiences: *have a bad day / an accident / an operation*
daily routines: *have a bath / a rest /a walk*
other common general expressions: *have a look/go/try* etc.

(→ a/an)

Set phrases

· ' **have a seat / have a drink / have some crisps** '
Come in and have a seat. ~ Thanks.
▲ to invite someone, informally, to do something

· ' **I/you have to admit …** ' = speaking honestly
I have to admit, I don't know the first thing about computers.
You have to admit she's talented.

Exercises

1 **Look at these concordance lines with *have*, and classify them according to the Grammar pattern (1–6):**

a   An unexpected error **has** occurred.
b   What I want is to **have** my boat mended and re-equipped, and then to sail her away.
c   Do you **have** a pencil and paper?
d   How rude of me, I should **have** offered you some tea or coffee.
e   I'll **have** to be getting back, the guests are coming at four.
f   Miss Mayhew had gone off to **have** her hair done after my lesson.
g   Do you think Nicola's work might **have** put her in danger?
h   Did your parents **have** to move because of their work?
i   Another two seconds and I would **have** been Olympic Champion.
j   We tend not to change things unless we **have** to.
k   The media **has** been having a busy day.
l   My 3-year-old mongrel **has** just been to the vet to have his teeth cleaned.
m   We **have** played five games against First Division sides this season.
n   She **has** a terrific sense of humour.
o   How long **has** this been going on?
p   Things **have** changed so much since I lived here.
q   Thank you very much, we'll both **have** an orange juice.

2 **Make sentences using the present perfect, for these situations, using the correct form of the verb in brackets:**

I started work here ten years ago, and I'm still here. (work)
→ *I have worked here for ten years.*

a   We met each other six weeks ago. (know)
b   I bought this sofa five years ago. (have)

c   They got married six months ago. (be married)
d   I moved to this flat 15 years ago and I am still here. (live)
e   I loved opera as a child, and I still love it. (love)
f   Her family got the castle 500 years ago, and they still own it. (own)

Now, write questions for the sentences a–f, using the present perfect:

How long have you worked here?

3 **Put the word in brackets in the correct place in the sentence:**

a   (you) Have seen the Rothko exhibition?
b   (long) How have you known Joanna?
c   (yet) The post hasn't arrived.
d   (never) Peter has been on a plane.
e   (ever) Have you had Irish coffee?
f   (before) Has Trish been to Spain?
g   (read) I have already this book.
h   (have) She must forgotten the meeting was today.
i   (it) The flat looks nice. Have you had painted?
j   (to) It's late and I have go home.

4 **Complete these sentences with words from the list:**

fun	breakfast	a bad day	a chat	a try
a look	an accident	a heart attack	a swim	a beer

a   The camera doesn't work. Can you have .... at it?
b   Sit down and have .... I think there's a cold one in the fridge.
c   I got up late so I didn't have .... , and now I'm hungry.
d   I didn't have much .... at the party.
e   If you don't drive more carefully, you'll have ....
f   These new headphones are fantastic. Do you want to have .... ?
g   I just phoned up to have .... – or are you busy?
h   I've had .... – I got up late, I missed the bus, the boss shouted at me …
i   When I saw the bill, I nearly had .... !
j   Let's have .... and cool off.

how

[adverb] in what way or manner: *How did you get in?* • *Can you show me how the scanner works?* • *It's amazing how quickly they grow!*

Grammar patterns

1 how | + clause

How do you make onion soup?
How will you travel? ~ We're taking the train.
How was she looking? ~ A bit tired, actually.

▲ to ask about the way something happens or the way it is done or the way it appears

How was your weekend?
How did you like the film?

▲ to ask for an opinion

2 how | + adjective | + clause

How tall is the Great Pyramid?
How old are you?

▲ to ask about the dimensions, age, etc., of things

3 how | + adverb/determiner | + clause

How fast can you type?
How well does she speak French?

▲ to ask about abilities

How much does a litre of petrol cost?
How many eggs are there in a dozen?

▲ to ask about prices and quantities

How long have you been studying Portuguese?

▲ to ask about a period of time

4 verb | + **how** | + to-infinitive

Do you know how to skin an eel?
Someone came up and asked me how to get to Oxford Circus.

▲ to ask or talk about the way of doing something

5 how | + adjective/adverb | + !

I bought you some flowers. ~ How lovely!
How well you look!

▲ to express surprise, shock, etc.

6 it | + is/was etc. | + adjective | + **how** | + clause

It was funny how we met: I was standing at the bus stop …
Isn't it depressing how it gets dark so early?

▲ to comment on the way something happens (→ it)

Collocations

The following adjectives and adverbs frequently follow *how*: *old, big, tall, fast, high, heavy, long, often, well, many, much, far, good,* and *ever*.

How high is Mount Everest?
How long will you be in Athens?
How far is it to the next town?
How ever did you manage to wash the dog?

Set phrases

• ‛**how are you?**’
  Hi, Michael. How are you? ~ Very well. And you?
  ▲ to greet someone you know

• ‛**how do you do?**’ → do
  ▲ to greet someone more formally

• ‛**how are things?**’
  Hi, Birget. How are things? ~ Not bad, thanks.
  ▲ to ask about news, health, etc.

• ‛**how's it going?**’
  How's it going with the new job? ~ Pretty good.
  ▲ to ask if someone is happy with what they are doing

• ‛**how about you?**’
  Are you well? ~ I'm fine thanks. How about you?
  I feel like a swim. How about you?
  ▲ to return a question or suggestion

• ‛**how about …**’
  How about a coffee? ~ I've just had one.

How about watching a video?
▲ to make a suggestion

• '**how come?**' = why?
The meeting's been cancelled. ~ How come?
How come no one told me?

• '**how do you mean?**'
They're complimentary tickets. ~ How do you mean?
~ They're free.
▲ to ask for an explanation or clarification

Exercises

❶ **Put these words in order to make sentences:**

a do/know/well/how/Pat/you?
b him/to/the/how/ask/start/photocopier
c away/you/how/be/long/will?
d kilograms/many/there/how/a/are/in/tonne?
e book/you/did/the/how/like?
f was/the/him/much/suit/I/how/asked
g strange/they/was/it/met/how/
h know/to/egg/do/how/an/you/boil?

❷ **Choose one of the following words to complete each of these questions. (Use each word once only):**

heavy	far	big	tall	fast
deep	often	long	high	old

a How .... is a cheetah? ~ It can reach speeds of 110 kph.
b How .... is a giraffe? ~ About five and half metres.
c How .... is an elephant seal? ~ It weighs nearly four tons.
d How .... does Halley's comet come round? ~ Once every 76 years.
e How .... is Mount Kilimanjaro? ~ 5895 metres.
f How .... is a blue whale? ~ Thirty metres (or a hundred feet).
g How .... was Mozart when he died? ~ Thirty-five.
h How .... is Loch Ness? ~ 230 metres at its deepest part.
i How .... is the Moon? ~ It's 382,000 kilometres from the Earth.
j How .... is a jackal? ~ About the same size as a dog.

❸ **What were the questions? Write questions with *how*. For example:**

He asked how to get on to the coast road.
→ *'How do you get on to the coast road?'*
She suggested we go shopping.
→ *'How about going shopping?'*
They asked the price of the tomatoes.
→ *'How much are the tomatoes?'*

a They want to know how you make mayonnaise.
b He asked the price of the shirt.
c She wanted to know how far it was to Tulsa.
d The officer asked me my age.
e We were all asked how long we would be staying.
f He suggested we rent a car.
g Someone wanted to know the height of the mountain.
h I'll ask her how well she can cook.
i Ask him how to fill the tank.
j They asked me how long I'd been living here.

❹ **Choose phrases from the list to complete this conversation.**

How do you mean?
How about you?
How about that?
How much?
How are you?
How awful!
How come?
How's it going?

A: Hi, Bob. (a) ....
B: Not too bad. (b) ....
A: Pretty good. (c) .... In the new apartment, I mean?
B: I didn't get it.
A: Oh no! (d) ....
B: I was gazumped.
A: Gazumped? (e) ....
B: Somebody offered more money.
A: (f) ....
B: Two grand. And they accepted. So I lost it.
A: (g) ....
B: I know. I'm devastated.
A: Hey, I'll buy you lunch. (h) ....

if

Grammar patterns

1 **if**-clause, | + clause
   clause | + **if**-clause

   If he had no money, he would sometimes sleep in the station.
   Don't eat it if you don't like it.

   ▲ to talk about a possible situation and its results

1a **if**-clause (present tense), | + clause (future tense)

   If you're not careful, you'll break it.
   The price of oil will go up if there's a war.

   ▲ to talk about a possible situation in the future, and its results (This pattern is often called the first conditional.)

1b **if**-clause (past tense), | + clause (would/could etc.)
   (→ would)

   If you were a parent, you'd understand how I feel.
   I would vote for the Greens if I was allowed to vote.

   ▲ to talk about an unlikely or impossible situation in the present or future, and its hypothetical results (This pattern is often called the second conditional. → was, were)

1c **if**-clause (past perfect tense), | + clause (would have/could have etc.)

   It would've been more fun if it hadn't rained.
   If you'd booked, we might've got a table.

   ▲ to talk about an imaginary past situation and its results (This pattern is often called the third conditional.)

2 **if** | + so/not

   Are you going into town? If so, can you give me a lift?
   Check that the batteries are working. If not, recharge them.

   ▲ to make a condition by referring back to what has already been said

3 verb | + **if**-clause

   I asked her if she would like a dance.
   Do you know if Jan is coming to work today?

   ▲ to report a yes/no question, or to ask one indirectly

Collocations

If frequently follows these adverbs: *(but) only, even.*

   Ahmed said he'll join us in the restaurant, but only if we let him pay.
   Even if he tried, he'd never pass his exams.

If is often followed by these adjectives: *possible, necessary.*

   If possible, we'd like a room with a view.
   The police have threatened to use force, if necessary, to remove the protestors.

In Grammar pattern 3, the verbs that most frequently precede *if* are: *know, wonder, see, ask, doubt,* and *remember,* as well as *don't care, don't mind, doesn't matter.*

   I wonder if dinner's ready.
   See if this one fits.
   I doubt if Dieter will agree.
   I don't care if she's your sister: nobody says that to me.
   Do you mind if I take this chair?
   It doesn't matter if it rains because we can eat under the awning.

Set phrases

· ❛**if I were you …**❜
   If I were you, I would forget all about him.
   ▲ to give advice

· **if only …**
   If only dad could have been here. He would have loved it.
   If only it wasn't raining.
   ▲ to express a regret

· ❛**what if …?**❜
   What if we ask your mother to babysit?
   ▲ to make a suggestion

'**if you don't mind / if it's all right with you**'
I'll close the window, if you don't mind.
If it's all right with you, I'd prefer the window seat.
▲ to make a request

Exercises

❶ Look at these concordance lines with *if*, and classify them according to whether they belong to Grammar patterns 1a, 1b, 1c, or none of these:

a   She could have killed me **if** she'd wanted to.
b   **If** it fitted in with a family holiday, then I might go.
c   **If** I could just use the phone, I'll get a taxi.
d   Wouldn't Mummy have been horrified **if** she'd known?
e   **If** I've cooked it you'll eat it.
f   **If** customers think products are too expensive, they will go elsewhere.
g   The risk is even higher **if** you smoke and drink heavily.
h   **If** you go back to sleep you won't have time to have breakfast.
i   I am sure none of my clients would take me seriously **if** I didn't turn up in a sharp suit.
j   **If** I am going to buy a plane, how much will it cost me?
k   I think I could have done better **if** I had a different attitude.
l   **If** it hadn't rained the night before, there could have been a major forest fire.
m   You have to correct it **if** it is wrong.
n   I reckon I could sleep **if** I was warm enough.
o   They'll think I'm anti-social **if** I don't go.

❷ Put the word in brackets in the correct place in the sentence:

a   (will) What you do if they increase the rent?
b   (would) If I had the time, I do a computing course.
c   (if) The train may be late: so, I'll phone you.
d   (were) I'd see a doctor, if I you.
e   (if) Do you know Brian phoned?
f   (have) If I had known you were ill, I would phoned.
g   ('d) Would she have got the job, if she applied?
h   (if) It doesn't matter you are late: we'll wait.
i   (only) If I hadn't invited Martha!
j   (only) You can play inside but if you are quiet.

❸ Match the two parts of each sentence:

a   If you'd had my number …
b   If I had the money …
c   If you lend me the money …
d   If I'd had your number …
e   If I give you my number …
f   If I hadn't missed the train …
g   If I miss the train …
h   If I knew the way …

1   I wouldn't have been late.
2   I'll buy you a drink.
3   I'll be late.
4   will you call me?
5   I'd walk.
6   I'd rent a car.
7   I would've called you.
8   would you have called me?

❹ Complete these sentences by choosing the correct form of the verb in brackets:

a   If you (be) more thoughtful, you'd understand how I felt.
b   If you (be) in the supermarket, can you get me some fizzy water?
c   If you (be) more careful with it, it wouldn't have broken.
d   If you eat another cake, you (be) sick.
e   If she took more care of her appearance, she (be) really attractive.
f   If the traffic hadn't been so bad, I (be) here earlier.

in

[preposition and adverb] (1) indicates position or movement to a location: *The car is in the garage.* • *Come in!* • *When does the train get in?*
(2) indicates time: *It happened in January.* • *I'll be home in an hour.*

Grammar patterns

1 verb | (+ NP) | + **in** | + NP

Get in the back and sit next to Jordi.
They enjoy hiking in the mountains.

   ▲ to indicate position in a place, often enclosed or contained

I'll see you in two weeks, in June.

   ▲ to say when something happens, often with reference to a defined period of time, such as a month or a year

2 verb | + **in**

Come in! Sit down and have a drink.
I don't feel like going out this evening. ~ OK. Let's stay in.
They were practising a dance and I asked if I could join in.

   ▲ to indicate movement to, or position at, a place that is enclosed, or a situation that is viewed as being interior.

3 verb | + **in** | + NP
  verb | + NP | + **in**

We checked in our bags and went through customs.
The computer won't start. ~ Have you plugged it in?
As punishment, the headmaster kept the children in.

   ▲ to indicate that something or someone is moving to a place that is enclosed, or that they are positioned there, or contained by it

4 verb | + **in** | + preposition

I think we are in for a storm: look at those clouds.
The police burst in on them while they were having breakfast.

   ▲ conveys a variety of meanings, many of them idiomatic

Collocations

Common verbs with *in* (preposition) are followed by an object – Grammar pattern 1:

arrive in, believe in, be born in, deal in, get in, occur in, result in, be used in, involve yourself in, train someone in, interest someone in.

The following phrasal verbs are formed with *in* (adverb particle) – Grammar pattern 2:

Verbs denoting some kind of movement: *break in, come in, jump in, creep in, crawl in, run in, rush in, step in*
Other verbs: *be in, give in, join in, settle in, tune in*:

   We went to see Wayne and Shirley, but they weren't in.
   Thieves broke in and stole Maggie's jewels.
   What's the capital of Mongolia? ~ I give in. Tell me.

Grammar pattern 3:
ask/invite someone in, let something in, phase something in, shut something in, take something in (= learn something).

Grammar pattern 4:
fall in with, go in for, keep in with, zero in on:

   It was typical of my French teacher to zero in on my mistakes.

Nouns in the following groups commonly come after *in*:
emotions: *in love/pain/tears; in a bad mood* etc.
difficulty: *in trouble/danger; in a mess* etc.
places: *in bed/hospital/prison/town* etc.
areas: *in the north/south (of …); in front (of …); in the distance* etc.
times: *in autumn/spring, etc.; in the morning/evening* etc.
dimensions: *in height/length/shape/size* etc.

The following adjectives are followed by *in*:
interested/engaged/active/involved in
lacking/rich/low in
fluent/skilled/experienced in
dressed/clothed in.

Set phrases

• **in fact …**
   He looks fifty but in fact he's only 35 or so.

   ▲ to say that something is true, although surprising

- **in case …** = in order to be prepared for a possible situation
  Take a sweater in case it's cold.

- **in spite of …**
  In spite of her age, she still runs up the stairs.
  ▲ to indicate that something may be surprising

- **the in-thing** = the most fashionable thing
  Remember when mirror sunglasses were the in-thing?

- **in any case** → any

Exercises

❶ Put *in* in the correct place in these sentences:

a Do you take sugar your coffee?
b The train gets at 6.55 and leaves again at 7.00.
c Do you want to stay or go out?
d Janet is at the door. ~ Why don't you ask her?
e Eating foods high fat can result obesity.
f The government should step and do something about it.
g It's lovely here spring when the flowers are out.
h Will you be this evening? ~ No, we're going out.
i He's pain but he doesn't believe going to see a doctor.
j She's a good mood, spite of the fact she's hospital.

❷ *In*, *on*, or *at* (time).

Very generally, you use *in* with periods of time, such as months, years, centuries, periods in the day, and seasons:

in May, in 1492, in the 21ˢᵗ century, in the morning (but *at night), in summer*

You also use *in* to talk about the period of time before something happens in the future:

in ten minutes, in a few weeks, in fifty years

You use *on* for short periods of time, such as the days of the week, parts of a particular day, dates, and special days:

on Friday, on Wednesday morning, on January 14ᵗʰ, on my birthday

You use *at* for specific times, such as clock times, certain stages of the day, and meals:

at nine o'clock, at midnight, at sunrise, at breakfast

Choose the best way of completing these sentences:

a The baby was born at (*2001/midnight/May 1ˢᵗ*).
b The wedding will be in (*11 o'clock/Saturday/March*).
c Her first book was published on (*1997/January/her birthday*).
d I do all my best thinking at (*the morning/night/ Sunday evening*).
e The train leaves in (*five minutes/5.00/Monday evening*).
f I have a dentist's appointment on (*ten o'clock/Wednesday morning/the afternoon*).
g Oxford University Press was founded in (*the l6ᵗʰ century/ May 1ˢᵗ 1585/Christmas Day*).
h I'll phone you in (*night/Monday morning/a day or two*).

❸ Complete these sentences by choosing words from the list:

join   phase   invite   settle   break   let   take   jump

a Someone managed to .... in and steal a Picasso.
b His explanation was rather complicated and I didn't .... it all in.
c The cat's outside. Can you .... it in?
d Andrew's team lost, so he didn't .... in the celebrations.
e Why don't we .... the neighbours in for a drink?
f The new girl in my class is taking a while to .... in.
g Can you give me a lift into town? ~ Sure: .... in.
h They are going to .... in the new parking regulations slowly.

❹ Use expressions from the list to complete this dialogue:

in hospital   in fact   in luck   in trouble   in prison
in tears   in love   in case   in particular

A: What's the matter with Louise. She was (a) .... when I saw her a minute ago.
B: Yes, she's a little emotional at the moment. (b) .... , she's (c) ....
A: Oh really! Anyone (d) .... ?
B: Yes, someone she met when she was (e) .... He's a nurse.
A: Oh well, that's useful, (f) .... she gets ill again.
B: Yes, but the problem is, he's been (g) .... with the police and now he's (h) ....
A: Oh, dear. Poor Louise. She's never (i) .... , is she?

it

[pronoun] (1) refers to a thing, situation or place that has been mentioned or is understood: *What's that? ~ It's my new palm top.* • *I like São Paulo, even though it's enormous.*
(2) impersonal subject or object, to talk about the weather, the date, etc.: *It's a nice day.* • *It was Friday the 13th.* • *I don't like it here.*
(3) 'dummy' subject or object, to be expanded or detailed later in the sentence: *It's strange you should say that.* • *I hate it when people phone during dinner.*

NOTE: *it is* is contracted to *it's*.

Grammar patterns

1 **it** | + verb | (+ …)

It rains a lot on the west coast.
It was the first week of January. It was cold and wet.
It's another five miles to the lake.

▲ to talk about weather, times, dates, and distances

2 **it** | + verb | + clause

It looks as if the neighbours are back.
It appears that Mrs Hoskins is retiring.

▲ to talk about what you understand from the evidence
(→ seem, → look)

3 **it** | + is/was | + NP/ adjective | + clause

It's a shame you weren't at the party. (= that-clause)
It's funny how Jon and Ann argue all the time.
(= how + clause)
It was surprising to see his brother at the wedding.
(= to-infinitive clause)
It's nice having breakfast in bed. (= -ing clause)

▲ to express an opinion or an emotion

4 **it** | + verb | + clause

It helps to talk about it.
It doesn't matter if you don't finish.

▲ to say what is important or useful

5 **it** | + verb | + NP | + clause

It worries me that she won't eat anything.
It upset Claire to see all the animals in their cages.
It makes me laugh, hearing you say that.

▲ to say how someone reacts to a situation

6 **it** | + is/was etc. | + past participle | + clause

It was reported that there are a number of survivors.
It is not known if the virus is harmful.

▲ to report what people are saying or thinking about a situation

7 **it** | + is/was etc. | + NP | + wh/that-clause

It's cheese and butter that make you fat, not olive oil.
It was my brother you saw, not me.

▲ to emphasize the subject or object of the sentence

Collocations

Noun phrases that often go with Grammar pattern 3 (and their usual patterns) are:

+ that-clause: *a miracle, a disaster, a myth, no surprise, no wonder, a safe bet, my guess, your fault*
+ to-infinitive: *a joy, a relief, a shock, a mistake, a surprise, our aim, my hope, my decision*
+ that-clause/+ to-infinitive: *a pity, a shame, a good idea.*

It's no wonder you are exhausted.
It was a joy to hear her voice again.
It's a safe bet that your team will lose.
It was a shame not to have waited.

Adjectives that often go with Grammar pattern 3 (and their usual patterns) are:

+ that-clause: *(un)likely, (not) true, obvious, (un)lucky*
+ to-infinitive /+ -ing: *(not) easy, difficult, hard*
+ that-clause /+ to-infinitive: *(not) important, (im)possible*
+ that-clause /+ -ing /+ to-infinitive / how-clause:
nice, good, sad, amazing, funny, strange.

It's unlikely that they could have gone far.
It wasn't easy persuading Jacob to give blood.

It's amazing how fast the children grow.
It was impossible to find a taxi.

Set phrases

- ' **it's me / it's […] here** '
  Hello? ~ Hi, it's Kevin. Is Belinda there? ~ Just a second …
  ▲ to say that it is you who is at the door, or on the phone

- ' **we made it** ' = we succeeded
  There's the summit. We've nearly made it!

- ' **I can't help it** ' = I'm not able to control my feelings
  I'm sorry I laughed at you. I couldn't help it.

Exercises

1 There are sixteen examples of *it* in this story that have been removed. Can you put them back?

Was getting dark and the road was wet. Seemed to go on forever. 'Is another fifty miles,' said Tom. 'Will we make before nightfall?' Debbie asked. 'I hate when you keep asking that,' Tom said. 'I'm sorry,' she said. 'I can't help. Worries me to think of the children, alone in the house. Is not fair.' Was then that her phone rang. She picked up and switched on. 'Who is?' she asked. 'Is me, Jimmy,' said a little voice. 'Is late. Where are you?' 'We're nearly home,' said Debbie. 'Won't be long now. Are you OK?' 'Yes, but is a bit scary. Is lucky that Mr McOnion is here.' 'Mr who?' Debbie whispered, turning pale.

2 Change these sentences into sentences beginning with *it*:

To miss the start would be a shame.
→ *It would be a shame to miss the start.*

a To blame the students is unfair.
b What you think doesn't matter.
c The way she talks to herself irritates me.
d Not to be appreciated must be awful.
e That you have no job worries me.
f How much I've spent is unbelievable.
g That he has no friends doesn't surprise me.
h Being read to is nice.
i That Alex didn't bring Victor to the party is a pity.
j Not having to cook is a joy.

3 Choose words from the list to complete the sentences below:

funny	aim	guess	hard	obvious
fault	unlucky	wonder	shame	relief

a It's no .... you are hungry: you haven't eaten all day.
b It is .... to believe that my brother is a thief.
c It's not my .... we got lost: you are the one with the map.
d It is a .... that you will miss your son's graduation.
e It was a .... to hear that my wallet had been found.
f It is our .... to increase production by 50%.
g It is .... that she had cheated: her answers were the same as Kylie's.
h It is .... how the neighbours never answer the phone.
i It was .... that she failed the exam by just one mark.
j It is my .... that Gary will have forgotten the meeting.

4 Transform the following sentences according to Grammar pattern 7. For example:

I didn't break the window. Rob did.
→ *It was Rob who broke the window, not me.*
The dog doesn't like fish. The cat does.
→ *It's the cat that likes fish, not the dog.*

a Brenda didn't go to Rome. Elsie did.
b Their son didn't get married. Their daughter did.
c I'm not a vegetarian. My brother is.
d Sydney's not the capital of Australia. Canberra is.
e People aren't dangerous. Guns are.
f The coffee didn't keep me awake. The noise did.
g The protestors weren't to blame. The police were.
h Your genes don't make you fat. What you eat does.

just

[adverb] (1) very recently: *The plane has just arrived.*
(2) right now or soon: *We're just leaving.*
(3) exactly: *It's just what I thought.*
(4) equally: *This restaurant is just as expensive as the other one.*
(5) only: *By the end of the lecture there were just three people in the room.*
(6) almost not, barely: *I've only just got enough money.*
(7) to add emphasis (= so): *The sunset was just amazing.*
(8) to reduce emphasis (= simply): *I just wondered if you were free tonight.*

Grammar patterns

1 have/had | + **just** | + past participle

I've just seen Tony.
We had just got home when the alarm went off.

▲ to talk about something that happened very recently (using the present perfect)

2 am/is/was etc. | + **just** | + going to/about to

Have you packed? ~ I'm just going to.
We arrived at the station when the train was just about to leave.

▲ to talk about something happening in the immediate future

3 **just** | + as | + adjective/adverb | + as

She is just as nice as her sister.
The train is just as fast as the bus.

▲ to say that two things are equally the same

Collocations

Just frequently combines with the following words:
about, after/before, as, because, enough, like, then, and *yet.*

The report is just about ready: I need another day or two.
The phone rang just as she was leaving.
She got married just before her thirtieth birthday.
Just because I'm 16, it doesn't mean I'm a baby.
There's just enough bread for lunch.
It's just like Carlos not to leave a tip.
It was just then that the rain started.
I'm not finished just yet.

Set phrases

• **just in time** = with no time to spare
I arrived just in time for the start of the lesson.

• ‘**just a minute / just a second / just a moment**’
Is Ted there? ~ Just a minute, I'll get him.
▲ to tell somebody to wait for a short time

• ‘**just like that**’
She went out and got a job, just like that!
▲ to emphasize that something happens very easily

• ‘**I'm just looking**’
Can I help you? ~ It's OK. I'm just looking.
▲ to say that you don't need any assistance in a shop

Exercises

❶ Put *just* in the correct place in these sentences:

a I'm so tired.
b The bus has left.
c We're about to go out.
d Brian is as tall as Martin.
e There was one check-in desk for 250 passengers.
f I was getting in the shower when the phone rang.
g These shoes only fit me. Can I try a bigger size?
h That's the thing that Carol would say, wouldn't she?

❷ There are eight examples of *just* in this dialogue. Can you match each one with its meaning?

1 very recently
2 right now or soon
3 exactly
4 equally
5 only
6 almost not, barely
7 so (for emphasis)
8 simply (reducing emphasis)

A: I'm (a) just going to have lunch. Would you like to join me?
B: No, thanks, I've (b) just eaten.
A: Oh, go on. Have a spring roll.
B: All right, but (c) just one. Hmm.
A: Do you like it?
B: Yes. It's (d) just delicious. In fact it's (e) just as good as the ones you can order from the Chinese takeaway.
A: That's (f) just what I did: I ordered them!
B: Oh, I (g) just thought you made them yourself.
A: Me! Make spring rolls? I can only (h) just boil an egg!

❸ In British English, *just* is often used in present perfect structures (Grammar pattern 1). In American English, the past simple is preferred:

I've just had brunch. = BrE
I just had brunch. = AmE

'Translate' the following AmE sentences into BrE:

a Sheila just phoned.
b I just saw a great film.
c We just came back from a vacation in Europe.
d Maurice just wrote to me
e I just drove a hundred miles.
f The film just began.
g I just ate, thanks.
h Jo and Kim just went.

❹ Set phrases with *just*.
Can you match the two parts of each dialogue?

a Can I speak to Jean-Marc?	1 ~ Just like that?
b Have a coffee.	2 ~ Just my luck.
c Here comes the bus.	3 ~ Just a second.
d Have you heard? Gary's left Eileen.	4 ~ Only just.
e Did you catch the plane?	5 ~ I'm just looking, thanks
f I'm sorry, we are sold out.	6 ~ I've just had one.
g How many tickets do you need?	7 ~ Just in time.
h Can I help you?	8 ~ Just one.

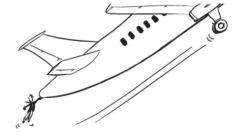

"DID HE CATCH THE PLANE?"

"ONLY JUST!"

keep

[irregular verb: *keep, kept, kept*] (1) to remain, continue: *Keep calm and don't panic.* • *Keep to the left.* • *The computer kept crashing, so I turned it off.*
(2) retain: *Can I keep this photo?*

Grammar patterns

1 **keep** | + NP

Can I keep this catalogue?
Do you want this folder back? ~ No, you can keep it.

▲ to talk about not losing things, or retaining things

2 **keep** | + adjective/adverbial

Keep out!
Keep left, until you come to the intersection.
I can't cut your hair if you don't keep still.

▲ to talk about things remaining in a particular state, or people remaining where or how they are

3 **keep** | + NP | + adjective/adverbial/-ing/
past participle

I'm so tired I can't keep my eyes open.
Where do you keep your rubbish bags? ~ Under the sink.
I'm sorry to keep you waiting.
Keep your arms covered or you'll burn.

▲ to talk about making things remain in a particular state, or place, or people remaining where or how they are

4 **keep** | (+ on) | + -ing

Keep going. We're nearly there.
They kept on driving all night.
Don't keep doing that: it's irritating.

▲ to talk about continuing to do an activity

Collocations

Keep combines with particles to form phrasal verbs:

If you *keep away/back,* or *keep* something or someone *away/back,* you put distance between yourself and something or someone. (*The police tried to keep the crowd back.*)
If you *keep* something *down,* you prevent it from increasing. If you *keep* someone *down,* you prevent them from achieving things.
If you *keep on,* you continue in the same direction, or you continue doing the same thing. (*Keep on until you get to the traffic lights, then turn left.*)
If you *keep off* something, you don't go on it, or you avoid it. (*Keep off politics and religion if you don't want an argument with my father.*)
If you *keep to* something like a plan, you don't deviate from it.
If you *keep* something *up,* you maintain it.
If you try and *keep up with* someone, or something, you try to stay at the same speed or level with them. (*They're always trying to keep up with the Joneses.*)

The most frequent verbs that follow *keep* are: *come, get, go, say, tell,* and *try.*

He keeps saying he's going to quit, but he never does.
I keep telling Jenny to take it easy, but she won't listen to me.
If the engine doesn't start immediately, keep trying.

Set phrases

· ❛**how are you keeping?**❜
How's your father keeping these days?
~ He's a lot better, thanks.
▲ to ask about someone's health

· **keep track (of) something** = have up-to-date information about something
I've got so many cousins I can't keep track of them all.

· ❛**it'll keep**❜
I'm dying to tell you about Sheila, but it'll keep.
▲ to say that something can wait for later

Exercises

1 Rewrite each of these sentences using the pattern 'keep + -ing':

a Joan of Arc heard voices all the time. *Joan of Arc kept hearing voices.*

b The musicians on the *Titanic* didn't stop playing.

c Even when he was deaf, Beethoven continued composing.

d Columbus never stopped looking for a western route to India.

e Borges went blind but continued to write.

f John Huston continued to make movies in his old age.

g Ann Frank didn't stop writing her diary, until the day she was captured.

2 There are eight examples of *keep* or *keeps* that have been taken out of this text. Can you put them back?

Dear Mabs,

I am 14. My older sister, who is 16, is driving me crazy. She's always picking on me. She telling me I am fat and useless, and she calling me names. If I lend her things, she them, and doesn't give them back. I try to myself to myself, but she won't leave me alone. My mother made her promise to be nice to me, but she didn't her promise. Also, she can't secrets: she tells everybody everything. I hoping things will change, as we get older, but they don't. What can I do, to from going crazy?

Desperate.

3 Phrasal verbs with *keep*. Complete these sentences by choosing particles from the list:

to   up   away   on   off   up with   in   down

a Piet keeps .... his Turkish by reading Turkish novels and listening to Turkish music.

b You should keep .... fatty foods if you want to lose weight.

c You probably find it hard to keep .... the rapidly changing world of technology.

d I expect you to keep .... the terms of the agreement.

e The government was unable to keep the cost of living ....

f Keep .... from the edge, or you might fall off.

g The guide book says we should keep .... until we reach the river.

h Doctor, my hair is falling out. I need something to keep it .... ~ Here, try this box.

4 Use phrases from the list to complete these idiomatic expressions:

... your fingers crossed
... you posted
... your wits about you
... it under your hat
... your eyes peeled
... an eye on things
... an open mind
... a straight face

a When I know what my travel arrangements are, I'll keep .... , so you know what's going on.

b I'm quitting this job, but keep .... : I don't want anyone else to know just yet.

c Keep .... for the airport sign: the turn-off is somewhere along this road.

d Our team is in the finals, so keep .... : we might just win.

e Can you stay here and keep .... while I go to lunch? I don't expect it will be very busy.

f As for blood sports, I try to keep .... : there are arguments for and against.

g The teacher's chair collapsed beneath him, and no one could keep .... It was so funny.

h Driving in Paris, you have to keep .... : it's quite terrifying.

know

[irregular verb: *know, knew, known*] to have learned something, or to be acquainted with a place or person; be certain about something: *I don't know what this word means.* • *How well do you know Gina?* • *I know that tune.* • *I knew you would say that.*

Grammar patterns

1 **know** | + NP | (+ adverb)

How long have you known Peter?
I know Bristol well.
His whereabouts are not known.

▲ to talk about your familiarity with a person, place or thing

2 **know** | (+ NP) | + about | + NP

He doesn't know about the accident.
Not a lot is known about the surface of Venus.

▲ to talk about knowledge of a topic or subject

3 **know** | + of | + NP

Do you know of anyone who wants a room?
I don't actually know her, but I know of her.

▲ to talk about a general but not detailed knowledge of something or someone

4 **know** | + that-clause

Did you know that Helen was a Mormon?
If only I'd known you were in town.

▲ to talk about your awareness of facts

5 **know** | + wh-clause

Excuse me, do you know where the nearest bus stop is?
I don't know why she married him.

▲ to talk about your familiarity with the circumstances

6 **know** | + wh | + to-infinitive

Do you know how to swim?
I don't know what to say.

▲ to talk about skills, or knowledge of what to do

Collocations

Adverbials that commonly occur with *know* are:
exactly, for certain, full well, perfectly well, and *very well.*

I know exactly what you mean.
I don't know for certain, but I think it's a llama.
She knows full well that she's on duty tonight.

Other verbs that collocate with *know* are: *let* and *get.*

If there's anything you need, let me know.
Once you get to know him, he's actually quite nice.

Set phrases

· **'I know'** = I agree
That programme is awful. ~ I know.

· **'I don't know'** = I disagree
Exercise makes you fat. ~ I don't know about that. I think it's the opposite.

· **'you know'** (1)
You should really be more careful, you know.
▲ to emphasize what you are saying

· **'you know …'** (2)
Mrs Thomas, you know, the substitute teacher, she was telling me …
▲ to give extra information about something or someone

· **'you know'** (3)
What is it with the au pair, you know, I mean, she … erm …
▲ to fill a pause

· **'you know what I mean'**
Danny is a bit unusual. You know what I mean?
▲ to indicate that your listener knows what you are talking about

· **'you never know'**
The law may change. ~ I doubt it, but you never know.
▲ to suggest that, although the future is uncertain, things may turn out for the better

· **'not that I know of'** = I'm not sure but I think not
Is Ciaran back from holidays yet? ~ Not that I know of.

Exercises

① **Classify these concordance lines with** *know*, **according to which Grammar pattern (1–6) they belong to:**

a Charlie would **know** what to do.
b No one **knows** how long the situation will continue.
c How much do you **know** about your own department?
d The public must not **know** that anything out of the ordinary has happened.
e The only trouble is, I don't **know** when to stop.
f I like him (or at least what I **know** of him) and I think he likes me.
g Did you **know** that Graham has been epileptic from birth?
h I **know** the style of his writing.
i I honestly don't **know** where all the money's gone.
j Do these people **know** each other?
k 'Tell me,' he said, very softly, 'what do you **know** of your mother's past?'
l In my view, the less people **know** about such things, the better.

② **Ten instances of the word** *know* **have been removed from this dialogue. Can you put them back?**

A: I'd like to enrol in the French class.
B: OK. Are you a beginner?
A: I don't exactly. I a lot of vocabulary, but my grammar is terrible. You what I mean.
B: Well, try Level 2. How does that sound?
A: You best. Where is it?
B: It's in Room 13. Do you where that is?
A: Yes. Who's the teacher?
B: Corinne.
A: Ah, Corinne.
B: Do you her?

A: No, not personally, but I of her. Is she Canadian?
B: Not that I of. But, you, I'm new here.
A: Oh really? I didn't.

③ Note the change of word order in indirect questions:

Where's the nearest bus stop?
→ *Do you know where the nearest bus stop is?*

What time does the train leave?
→ *Do you know what time the train leaves?*

Change these questions from direct to indirect (using *Do you know …?*), **and pay attention to the word order:**

a What's the time?
b Where's the bathroom?
c Who's the person in charge?
d When's the next bus?
e Where does the bus leave from?
f How much does a ticket cost?
g When did the plane arrive?
h Where is the check-in desk?

④ **Choose words from the list to complete these sentences:**

let get full well never about certain how

a I don't know for .... , but I think it's the next street on the left.
b Libby knows a lot .... computers: ask her.
c You know .... well that I'm not here on Tuesday.
d The restaurant's probably full. But you .... know: I'll phone and see.
e Now that we're going out together, I'd like to .... to know your family.
f Do you know .... to change the ink in the printer?
g I'm really busy next week, but if I have a moment, I'll .... you know.
h The dog knows perfectly .... she mustn't bark at the postman.

let

[irregular verb: *let, let, let*] to allow or permit something to happen: *Please let me through.* • *They wouldn't let us take photos.*

Grammar patterns

1 **let** | + NP | + verb

Let my people go!
Don't let the children play on the road.
My parents never let me stay up late.

▲ to ask for, or to give or refuse, permission

Let your arms hang loosely by your side.
Let us know what you decide.

▲ to give instructions or make requests

2 **let** | + NP | + adverbial

Don't let the dog in the garden.
Let us out!
The police are not letting the traffic through.

▲ to ask for, or to give or refuse, permission to go places

3 **let** | + myself/herself/themselves etc. | + verb/adverbial

I let myself in with the key.
Don't let yourself be talked into something you don't want to do.

▲ to talk about what you can allow yourself to do

4 **let** | + 's (= us) | + verb

Let's invite the neighbours to dinner.
Don't let's wash up now. Let's watch TV instead.
Let's not mention this to Alan.
Let's stop and have a coffee, shall we?
How about a game of chess? ~ Yes, let's!

▲ to make suggestions (that include the speaker)

Collocations

Let combines with particles to form phrasal verbs:

If you *let* someone *down,* you disappoint them. (*People are*

disappointed because they feel that the government has let them down.*)
If you *let* someone *in* or *out* or *back,* you allow them to enter or leave or return. If you *let* someone *in on* something, you tell them a secret.
If you *let* someone *off,* you release them, or you decide not to punish them. (*The judge let the defendant off lightly because it was her first offence.*)
If you *let on* (about something), you reveal something that you are not supposed to.
If something, like the rain, *lets up,* it slows down or stops. (*If the rain doesn't let up soon, the river will overflow.*)

Let combines with *go* to mean *release your hold on something*:

Let go! You're hurting!
Don't let go of the rope!

Set phrases

- **let alone …**
  There isn't enough food for us, let alone six guests.
  He can hardly walk, let alone drive.
  ▲ to follow a negative statement with something even more unlikely

- **' let me see / let's see / let me think … '**
  Let me think, where did I park the car?
  Let's see, where was I? Ah, yes. Another advantage of …
  ▲ to give yourself time to think, before saying something

- **' let's face it '** = you have to admit
  Let's face it, Dad, times have changed since you were a teenager.

- **' let's hope … '**
  Let's hope they remembered to turn the oven off.
  The key should be under the doormat. ~ Let's hope so.
  ▲ to express a hope

- **' let's suppose/say … '**
  Let's suppose Labour loses the election …
  Let's say – for argument's sake – that two and two make five.
  ▲ to suggest hypothetical situations

- **To let**
  ▲ to say that a house, flat etc., is available for rent

Exercises

1 Rewrite these sentences using *let*:

a Could you give me permission to see the ruins?
b They won't allow you to use your mobile phone on the plane.
c I asked to borrow the car but my father said no.
d May I have your autograph?
e Permit me to ask you a personal question.
f The landlady wouldn't allow me to have guests.
g I suggest we hire a car for the weekend.
h I don't think it's a good idea to invite the neighbours.
i Release the dog!
j Stop holding on to the dog!

2 In these sentences the verb particles (*up, out, down,* etc.) are mixed up. Can you put each one in the sentence where it belongs?

a The pain in my tooth didn't let off, even after I took two painkillers.
b Don't let down that I arrived late again – the boss will be furious if he finds out.
c Someone please unlock the bathroom door and let me on!
d Because it's a national holiday, we were let in work early, and we all went home.
e After you promised to take them to the park, you can't let the kids up now. They'll be so disappointed.
f I'm going to let you out on a secret: I'm going to have a baby!

3 Many idioms begin with *let*. Can you complete these sentences, using expressions from the list below?

the cat out of the bag	the side down	sleeping dogs lie
your hair down	it get you down	off steam
off the hook	yourself go	

a Everyone will be wearing a suit, so I'd better wear one too. I don't want to let ....
b It was my turn to cook dinner, but fortunately I was let .... because Tess offered to do it instead.
c I know that failing your driving test was a disappointment, but you mustn't let .... It's not the end of the world!
d She was trying to keep her engagement a secret, but her mother let .... and told all the neighbours.
e If you feel so angry about the situation, write a letter to the newspaper. At least, it will help you let ....
f You look terrible! Just because your girlfriend left you, you shouldn't let ....
g If I were you, I wouldn't mention the boss's personal problems to your co-workers. Better to let ....
h It's a good idea – once in a while – to go out with friends, stay out till five in the morning, and really let ....

4 Here are some song titles beginning with *let*. Can you complete them, using phrases from the list?

fall in love	drums	twist	go
night together	play	roll	be

a 'Let it............ .' (The Beatles)
b 'Let yourself ....' (Elvis Presley)
c 'Let's do it, let's ....' (Cole Porter)
d 'Let's spend the ....' (Rolling Stones)
e 'Let there be ....' (Sandy Nelson)
f 'Let the music ....' (Barry White)
g 'Let's .... again.' (Chubby Checker)
h 'Let the good times ....' (B.B. King)

LET
ME
OUT!

like

[regular verb: *like, liked, liked*] enjoy, find pleasant: *Steve likes cooking.* • *Which place did you like best?* • *I don't like parties.*
[plural noun] things you like: *What are your likes and dislikes?*
[preposition] similar to: *You look like your sister.* • *What was Moscow like?*

Grammar patterns

1 **like** | + NP | (+ adverbial)

Seamus likes fish but Joanne doesn't like it much.
How do you like our town?

▲ to talk about things, people, or places that please you

2 **like** | + -ing

I like reading in bed.
What do you like doing in your free time?

▲ to talk about activities that you enjoy, including your hobbies and interests

3 **like** | + to-infinitive

Sylvia likes to get up early and go for a run before breakfast.
We like to interview all applicants personally.

▲ to talk about what you prefer as part of your normal activity or routine

4 **like** | + NP | + to-infinitive

My father liked us to call him 'Sir'.
I'd like someone to help me with the accounts.

▲ to say what you prefer people to do

5 verb | + **like** (preposition) | + NP

Their dog is exactly like ours.
Who do you look like: your mother or your father?

▲ to talk about similarities between people, things, or actions

Collocations

Like (verb) frequently occurs after these adverbs: *really, quite,* and before these adverbs: *best, very much, at all.*

I really like Anthony Hopkins.
She says she doesn't like figs very much.
I don't like exercising at all.

Like (preposition) is often preceded by words like *feel, taste, sound, look,* and *smell*:

Why don't you want to come dancing? ~ I don't feel like it.
Ivan says he can't make up his mind. ~ That sounds like him.

Like (preposition) is often modified by words like *quite, rather, very, just, a lot,* and *exactly*:

She's a lot like her sister, isn't she?
Paragliding is rather like hang gliding.

You can also use *something* and *nothing*:

A quince is something like a big pear.
Your brother is nothing like what I expected.

Set phrases

- '**would you like …?**'
  Would you like a cup of tea? ~ I'd love one.
  What would you like to do this afternoon?
  ▲ to invite or offer someone something

- '**how do/did you like …?**'
  How did you like Luke's talk?
  How do you like your eggs?
  ▲ to ask people their opinions or preferences

- '**if you like**'
  We could have a break now, if you like.
  ▲ for making offers or suggestions

- '**what I (don't) like about …**'
  What I like about Madrid is the nightlife.
  What I like about Robin is her sense of humour.
  ▲ for stating opinions

• ' I (don't) like it when … / I (don't) like the way … '
I like it when the teacher lets us talk.
I don't like the way they fight all the time.
  ▲ to talk about things people do, or things that happen, that you enjoy

• ' what's […] like? '
What's Tony like? ~ He's all right, I suppose.
What was your hotel like? ~ Fabulous.
  ▲ to ask for an opinion or description of someone or something

• ' like I said '
It's sad, but, like I said, it's his own fault.
  ▲ to refer back to something you have already said

• ' like this / like so '
Tie the two ends together, like so.
  ▲ to show someone how to do something

Exercises

❶ Look at these concordance lines with *like*, and group them according to the patterns 1–5.

a Claudia doesn't **like** people to be late.
b I felt a little bit **like** Rambo.
c There are actors who **like** making movies, but I've never enjoyed it.
d When I was young, I thought I'd **like** a job helping people.
e My hands and feet were **like** ice.
f I'd **like** him to fall in love and get married.
g She's a good, clever girl. Try to be **like** her, Anne.
h She doesn't **like** dogs.
i I like to go on holiday but I always **like** to come back.
j I didn't actually **like** him very much.
k I **like** having long hair, it's so versatile.
l How could anyone work on a day **like** this?
m She **likes** to exercise to music.
n So, how do you **like** your steak, then?

❷ Put these words in order to make sentences:

a coffee/your/you/do/like/how?
b to/what/tomorrow/you/would/like/do?
c don't/horror/movies/very/I/like/much
d like/sandwich/I/a/feel
e way/she/I/the/laughs/like

f interrupt/it/him/he/doesn't/you/like/when
g mother/Hilary/like/her/looks
h to/classical/Jean/really/music/likes/listening
i a lot/her/likes/he
j breakfast/him/to/likes/her/she/make
k me/to/you/like/like/would/it/this/do?
l was/LA/like/what?

❸ *Like doing, like to do.*

> *Like doing* and *like to do* both mean 'to enjoy' but *like to do* can also mean that you think something is a good idea, even if you don't enjoy it:
>
> *I like to cook. I like cooking.* (= enjoy)
> *I like to have my teeth checked regularly.* (= it's a good idea)
>
> You always use a 'to-infinitive' after would:
> *'Would you like to come to the office?'*

Which is the best way of completing each of these sentences: -ing or to-infinitive? Or are both possible?

a I like (*to do/doing*) the dinner dishes before watching TV.
b What would you like (*to do/doing*) at the weekend?
c I don't like (*to go out/going out*) on week nights.
d She likes (*to do/doing*) her homework before dinner.
e Barry likes (*to play/playing*) computer games.
f I'd like (*to watch/watching*) the football this evening.
g I like my kids (*to be/being*) home before midnight.
h Do you like (*to dance/dancing*)?
i Would you like (*to dance/dancing*)?
j Would you like me (*to dance/dancing*)?

❹ Match these questions and answers:

a What does Max look like?
b What was the weather like?
c What's Robin's girlfriend like?
d What do you like doing?
e What does the cat like?
f What do you feel like doing?

1 ~ Swimming, windsurfing, things like that.
2 ~ Quite nice, but it wasn't very hot.
3 ~ She's got a great sense of humour.
4 ~ How about going to the cinema?
5 ~ Food out of a can, and a bowl of milk.
6 ~ He's tall, fair-haired, and he wears glasses.

little

[determiner and pronoun] not much: *There's little hope of finding survivors.* • *Do you take milk? ~ Just a little.*
[adverb] not much: *I'm afraid I'm a little late.* • *The town has changed very little.*
[adjective] not large: *They have a little house in the country.*

Grammar patterns

1   **little** | + uncountable noun
    little | + of | + the/this/your etc. | + uncountable noun

   They have very little food or water with them.
   There is little real evidence to support the theory.
   Little of the food reached the people who needed it.

   ▲ to say that there is hardly any of something (a negative sense)

2   a **little** | + uncountable noun
    a **little** | + of + the/this/your etc. | + uncountable noun

   I have a little cash, so let me pay.
   Can I put a little of this cheese on my pasta?

   ▲ to say that there is a small amount of something (a positive sense)

3   determiner | + **little** | + countable noun

   Look at the sweet little monkey!
   It was sad film about a little boy who ran away ...

   ▲ to talk about something that is small, often in contexts where you feel sympathetic

4   a **little** | + adjective

   It's a little cold in here: shall I put on the heating?
   Would you like to go out? ~ Actually, I'm a little tired.

   ▲ to reduce the importance of what you are saying (= a bit)

5   a **little** | + comparative | (+ than)

   How is your father? ~ He's a little better, thanks.
   I shop here. It's a little cheaper than the supermarket.
   Can I have a little more, please?

   ▲ to talk about small differences

6   verb | + NP | + a **little**

   Can you turn the volume down a little?
   Fry the vegetables a little and then add soy sauce.

   ▲ to talk about doing something to a small extent

NOTE: in spoken English *a bit* (*of*) is more commonly used than *a little* in Grammar patterns 2, 4, 5, and 6: *a bit of this cheese; it's a bit cold; he's a bit better; fry the vegetables a bit.*

7   verb | + very | + **little**

   On the way home they spoke very little.
   The situation has improved very little.

   ▲ to say that things rarely happen, or happen to a very small extent

Collocations

Abstract nouns that often follow 'little (+ real)' (Grammar pattern 1) include: *hope, chance, change, reason, effect, use, point, importance, news, evidence,* and *value.*

   There has been little change in the situation.
   The new law has had little real effect on immigration patterns.

A little combines with words like *while, way,* and *bit*:

   A little while later, the guests started arriving.
   It's a little bit warmer today, isn't it?

The adjective *little* (Grammar pattern 3) often combines with other adjectives: *tiny little, little tiny; nice/pretty/sweet/lovely/adorable* etc. *little; poor little.*

   They have a tiny little flat in Bayswater.
   What an adorable little kitten!

Set phrases

• **' just a little '**
   Would you like some more wine? ~ Just a little, thanks.
   ▲ to respond to an offer of a quantity of something

• **as little as possible** = the absolute minimum
   Does he help with the housework? ~ As little as possible.

- **little by little** = gradually
  Her Japanese is improving little by little.

- **little or no […] / little or nothing** = hardly any(thing)
  There is little or no money left for advertising.

Exercises

❶ Put *little* into the correct place in these sentences:

a There is a soup left. Shall I heat it up?
b There is point in saving money if inflation keeps going up.
c It's hot in here. ~ I'll open the window a.
d There is or no hope of finding survivors.
e What is your new apartment like? ~ It's a bit bigger than yours.
f The village has changed very since we were last here.

❷ *A little* or *a few*?

Note that *(a) little* is followed by uncountable nouns, and *(a) few* is followed by countable nouns:

Can I have a little more apple juice?
Can I have a few more chips?

Choose the word that best completes each sentence:

a She knows a few (*Italian/Italian words*).
b We're going away for a little (*while/days*).
c Malcolm has had a few (*trouble/problems*) with his teachers.
d The cake needed a little more (*eggs/butter*).
e What about leaving a tip? ~ OK. I have a few (*cash/coins*).
f What shall we have with the soup? ~ How about a few (*bread/crackers*)?
g What's the flat like? ~ It's OK but it needs a little (*furniture/chairs*).
h She says she's vegetarian but I've known her to eat a little (*sausages/salami*).

❸ *Little* or *a little*? *Few* or *a few*?
Look at the difference between these two sentences:

I have little time (so I can't help you).
I have a little time (so I can help you).

She has few friends (so she's lonely).
She has a few friends (so she's not lonely).

Complete these sentences with *little, a little, few,* or *a few*:

a The concert was so long that .... people stayed until the end.
b I speak .... Chinese: enough to get by.
c They had .... water so they managed to survive for .... days.
d There are .... good restaurants in the town, so we always eat at home.
e I have .... time for watching TV: I am far too busy.
f She's made .... friends at school so she's much happier now.
g How is your mother? ~ She's .... better. ~ Oh, I'm sorry.
h How is your father? ~ He's .... better. ~ Oh, I'm so pleased.

❹ Other ways of talking about small things or quantities.

Little suggests you feel sympathy for something (*sweet little girl*), or you think it's unimportant (*it's just a little thing, nothing special*). You use *little* before a noun, but not after the verb *to be*: *a little dog* but not (usually) ~~the dog is little~~. You can combine *little* with other adjectives: *a tiny little mouse*, but not (normally) with *very* or *too*: ~~a very little mouse~~.

Small simply means 'not large'. You can use *small* before a noun and after the verb *to be*: *a small house, the house is small*. You don't usually combine *small* with other adjectives (~~a tiny small mouse~~) but you can use *very* and *too*: *a very small mouse*.

Choose the best word – *little* or *small* – to complete these sentences:

a What a sweet .... boy: is he your son?
b The car was very .... but we all managed to get in.
c Thank you for the gift. ~ Oh, it's just a .... something.
d I'll just give you a .... injection: nothing to worry about.
e The necklace was made of tiny .... pieces of glass.
f If that towel is too .... , I'll try and find another one.

long

[adjective, gradable: *long, longer, longest*] to describe length; the opposite of *short*: *It's a long way to Tipperary.* • *Today is the longest day of the year.*
[adverb] for a long period of time:
I can't stay long. • *How long have you been married?*

Grammar patterns

1 how **long** | + is/was, etc. | + NP | + ?

How long is a stick insect?

▲ to ask about the length of things, even if they are short. (Other common adjectives that take this pattern are: *big, high, old, wide, deep, hot, heavy, thick.*)

2 [amount] | + **long**

A tennis court is 24 metres long and 11 metres wide.

▲ to give the dimensions of something. (Other adjectives include: *old, tall, deep, high, thick, wide, square.*)

3 how **long** | + verb | + ?

How long have you been living here? ~ Five years.
How long will you stay in Rome? ~ Not long: just two nights.

▲ to ask about duration

4 how **long** | + does/did/will etc. | + it take | + […] | + to-infinitive | + ?

How long does it take to get to work?
How long did it take you to write this book?

▲ to ask about the length of journeys, achievements, etc.

5 positive verb | + (for) a **long** time
positive verb | + too **long**/**long** enough/so **long**

The Curies worked together for a long time.
We've known each other a long time.
You've been on the phone too long.
I've waited long enough. Now I'm leaving.
It's been so long since you last wrote.

▲ to talk about a period of time.

6 negative verb | + **long**
question | + **long**?

It won't take long.
Have you been waiting long?

▲ to express a short period of time, and to ask about a period of time

Collocations

The most common verbs that go with *long* are: *be, look, seem.*

Those trousers look a bit long.
The train journey is not as long as it seems.

Some common nouns that go with *long* are: *time, way, distance, day, hair,* and *life.*

It's a long time since we heard from Julie.
He's got a long way to go as a football coach.

Some common adverbs that go with *long* are: *really, a bit, fairly, rather, too.*

I liked the concert but it was rather long.
It'll take a week or two to repair the DVD. ~ That's too long.

Set phrases

• ❛**long time no see**❜
  ▲ a humorous way of greeting someone after a long time

• ❛**it's a long story …**❜
  How did you miss your flight? ~ It's a long story. I'd arranged to …
  ▲ to introduce a complicated narrative

• ❛**to cut a long story short …**❜
  … so, to cut a long story short, when I got to the airport …
  ▲ to get to the point of a narrative

• **long ago** = a long time in the past
  Long ago, when dinosaurs ruled the earth …

• **at long last**
  At long last the waiter brought the bill.
  ▲ to express relief after waiting a long time

- **before long** = soon
  The bus should arrive before long.

- **all day/week/year** etc. **long** = the whole day/week/year etc.
  We waited all night long, but she never phoned.

- **no longer … / not any longer**
  I'm sorry, but we no longer produce that model.
  I thought you lived in Leeds. ~ Not any longer. I moved to London last year.
  ▲ to talk about something that happened in the past but doesn't happen now

- **be long** = take a long time to get ready
  Will dinner be long?
  Sit down, I won't be long.

- **in the long run** = not now, but sometime in the future
  The delay will cost more in the long run.

- **as long as / so long as …** = on condition that
  Can I borrow the car? ~ As long as you are back by 12.
  I don't care what you do, so long as you are happy.

Exercises

1 *Long* can be confused with *tall*, *high*, and *far*.

> *long* is used when you are measuring something from one end to another, such as a *river*, or to 'measure' time.
>
> *high* is used for talking about things that are a long way from the ground, or whose tops are a long way from the ground, such as *mountains*.
>
> *tall* is used when you are measuring thin things, like *trees*, or *people*, from their bottom to their top.
>
> *far* is used to talk about distances.

Choose the best word to complete each sentence:

a How .... is Mount Kilimanjaro? ~ Nearly 6000 metres.
b How .... is Boston from New York?
c He's very .... for his age, isn't he?
d I see that .... hair is back in fashion.
e We walked as .... as the market place.
f I like apartments with .... ceilings.
g I couldn't see much, because there was a .... woman in front of me.
h Where is the post office? ~ First on the right. It isn't ....

i How .... is the River Nile? ~ 6690 kilometres.
j How .... is the flight? ~ Two hours.

2 Look at this diagram and complete the sentences.

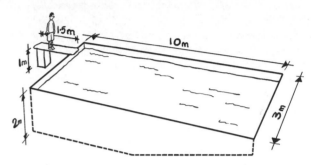

a The pool is 3m ....
b The board is 1.5m ....
c The pool is 2m ....
d The board is 1m ....
e The pool is 10m ....
f The boy is six years ....

3 Put *long* in the correct place in each of these sentences:

a Crocodiles can grow up to four metres.
b Have you been working here?
c How did it take you to paint the kitchen?
d The new bridge is finished, at last.
e This plant has flowers all year.
f Will the operation take?
g You can use the phone so as you don't make international calls.
h You've had the windsurfer enough. Now it's my turn.

4 Match the request with the condition:

a Can I use your mobile phone?	1 So long as you do the cooking.
b Will you lend me your suit?	2 As long as you are back in five minutes.
c Let's have a dinner party.	3 As long as you don't get it dirty.
d Can we have a break?	4 So long as you keep quiet.
e Can I have a ride on your motorbike?	5 As long as you don't speak for too long.
f Can I listen to you play?	6 As long as you wear a helmet.

look

[regular verb: *look, looked, looked*] (1) direct your eyes at something: *Who are you looking at?* • *I looked everywhere for the car keys.*
(2) seem, appear: *She looks like Rita Hayworth.* • *You look tired.*
[noun] (1) act of looking: *Have a look at this e-mail.*
(2) appearance: *I don't like the look of him.*

Grammar patterns

1 **look** | (+ adverbial)

Don't look! I'm getting dressed.
If you look carefully, you can see the island.

▲ to talk about focusing your attention

2 **look** | + at/for | + NP

Look at the moon!
I'm looking for my glasses. Have you seen them?

▲ to talk about focusing your attention in a certain direction, or in order to find something

3 **look** | + adjective

You look nice and cool in that frock.
This restaurant looks too expensive.

▲ to say how things appear

4 **look** | + like | + NP

He looks like a lawyer or a doctor or something.
You look like a clown in those trousers.

▲ to say what things resemble (→ like)

5 **look** | + as if/as though | + clause

You look as if you had seen a ghost!
They look as though they are enjoying themselves.
It looked as if the furniture had been moved.

▲ to talk about how things or people appear, and the cause

Collocations

Adverbs that often go with *look* (meaning 'direct your eyes') include: *carefully, closely, intently, longingly.*

He looked at the manuscript carefully.
The cat looked longingly at the fridge.

Verbs that frequently occur with *look* are: *turn* and *let.*

She turned to look in my direction.
Let me look at your wedding photos.

Adjectives and past participles that frequently occur with *look* include: *certain, likely, unlikely;* and *set, hurt,* and *lost.*

These trends look set to continue.
You look lost: can I help you?
Will we win? ~ It looks unlikely.

Look combines with a number of particles to form phrasal verbs:

If you *look after* somebody, you take care of them.
If you *look around* a place, you walk and look at what there is in the place.
If you *look forward to* (doing) something, you are excited about something in the future.
If you *look into* something, you investigate it.
If you *look out for* something, you pay attention, either to avoid something bad happening, or in order to notice something
If a situation *looks up* it improves.
If you *look up* something, or *look* something *up,* you search for particular information about it.
If you *look* someone *up,* you visit them when you are in the place where they live.
If you *look up to* someone, you respect them.

Set phrases

• ❝**look …**❞
Look, let's talk about this again in the morning.
▲ to draw attention to what you are going to say

• ❝**I'm just looking**❞ → just

- '**look out!** ' = Be careful!
  Look out! There's a bus coming …

- '**what does/do […] look like?** '
  I've lost my wallet. ~ What does it look like?
  ▲ to ask about the appearance of someone or something

Exercises

❶ Use the word in brackets to complete the sentence:

a (at) What are you looking?
b (for) I spend an hour a day looking my glasses.
c (as) You look though you got caught in the rain.
d (like) It looks it's going to be a nice day.
e (to) I look forward going home for my holidays.
f (me) She wouldn't let look at the letter.
g (set) The rain looks to continue for another week.
h (looks) It unlikely that they will sign the contract.
i (after) Can you look my things while I go for a swim?
j (out) I'll look for you at the conference.
k (like) I don't know your brother. What does he look?

❷ Choose the best particle(s), from the list , to complete these sentences with *look*:

after   around   out for   forward to   into   up (x2)   up to

a Do you mind if we look .... the apartment?
b The police are looking .... the causes of the accident.
c If you don't know what the word means, look it ....
d My dad is looking .... meeting you.
e Look .... pickpockets when you take the train.
f A man comes round to look .... the garden while we are away.
g Nerina really looks .... you, since you published that article.
h After a low period for investors, things are starting to look .... again.

❸ Other verbs like *look*. Study these definitions:

look (at): turn your eyes in a particular direction, investigate
see: become aware of somebody/something by using your eyes (→ see)
watch: look at somebody/something for a time, paying attention to what happens

[extracts from the *Oxford Advanced Learner's Dictionary*]

Choose the best of these three verbs (*look (at), see, watch*) to complete each of these sentences:

a Can you .... the baby while I go and get some milk?
b I asked the doctor to .... my eye, but he said it was OK.
c Goodness! .... the time. We'd better hurry.
d I can't .... the subtitles without my glasses.
e What shall we .... on TV tonight?
f Did you .... anything nice when you were shopping?
g Can you .... my homework and check I haven't made any mistakes?
h From the balcony you can .... Goat Island.

❹ Here are some more set phrases with *look*. Can you match them with what follows?

a Don't look now but …
b Look where you're going …
c Look after yourself …
d He's not much to look at but …
e Look what you've done …
f Look who's here …

1 take lots of vitamin C.
2 you've burnt a hole in the carpet.
3 he's got loads of money.
4 it's Diana and Phil. Come on in!
5 that man over there is my psychiatrist.
6 you nearly trod on my foot.

make

[irregular verb: *make, made, made*] produce or perform something: *She makes her own furniture.* • *The handles are made of plastic.* • *I'm making coffee.* • *Have you made any mistakes?*

Grammar patterns

1 **make** | + NP

I'll make breakfast if you make lunch.
Don't make any arrangements without asking me first.

▲ to talk about producing or performing something

2 NP | + is/was, etc. | + **made** | + of/from/out of …

Glass is made from sand.
Their headdresses are made out of feathers.

▲ to talk about how things are manufactured

3 **make** | + NP | + NP

My sister made me this T-shirt.
Can you make us all a cup of tea, Anthony?

▲ to talk about producing or performing something for someone

4 **make** | + NP | + adjective/NP

Pollution makes people ill.
It makes me sad to think of the money we wasted.
The Harry Potter *books made J.K. Rowling a millionaire.*

▲ to talk about causing things to be or to happen

5 **make** | + NP | + bare infinitive

Take this: it will make you feel better.
They made the passengers wait for an hour.
It's the wind that makes the windmill turn.

▲ to talk about causing or forcing someone or something to do something

6 is/was etc. | + **made** | + to-infinitive

We were made to empty our bags.

▲ to talk about being forced to do something

Collocations

Make combines with many nouns with the general meaning of 'perform an action'. For example:

make an appointment/an arrangement/a date
make a choice/a promise/ a plan
make an enquiry/an excuse
make a decision/a suggestion/a point
make a journey/trips/a visit
make a noise/a sound/a speech/a comment

Make combines with a number of particles to form phrasal verbs:

If you *make for* somewhere, you go in that direction.
If you *make* something *out,* you can only just see or hear it.
If you *make out* a cheque, you write the necessary information on it.
If you *make* something *up,* like a story or an excuse, you invent it.
If two people *make up,* they settle an argument.
If you *make up for* something, you do something that corrects a bad situation.

Set phrases

- **make it** = arrive on time, or succeed
  Do you think we will make it? ~ Yes, we've got plenty of time.

- **make do** = manage with something
  There's only a few vegetables in the fridge. ~ Well, we'll have to make do with those.

- **make your way** = move towards something, often with difficulty
  They made their way home in the wind and the rain.

- **make a start** = begin doing something
  OK, now that everyone is here, let's make a start.

Exercises

1 Put these words in order to make sentences:

a breakfast/makes/Gary/always
b make/coffee/shall/you/I/some?
c made/this/who/table?
d of/made/is/what/it?
e exercise/me/makes/better/sleep
f makes/sad/children/see/me/homeless/to/it
g tourists/bus/to/get off/made/were/the/the
h Hemingway/Paris/home/made/his

2 Use particles from the list to complete the sentences:

for   out (x2)   up (x 2)   up for

a Did you believe his excuse? I think he just made it ....
b I bought them some flowers to make .... being late.
c They were whispering, so I couldn't make .... what they were talking about.
d The weather turned bad so we made .... the harbour.
e I owe you $100. Who shall I make the cheque .... to?
f I'm sorry, Hilda. Let's kiss and make ....

3 Set phrases. Match the two parts of each exchange:

a Why didn't you come to class?
b Do you want tea or coffee?
c We don't often eat out.
d I don't understand her e-mail.
e I'm sorry to barge in like this.
f You only live once.

1 ~ That's OK. Make yourself at home.
2 ~ I don't know. I can't make up my mind.
3 ~ You're right. Make the most of it.
4 ~ Neither do we. But it makes a change.
5 ~ Neither do I. It doesn't make sense.
6 ~ I was busy. I couldn't make it.

4 Complete the crossword, using words from the collocation section to complete these sentences.

Across:
2 There are times in life when you have to make a .... For example, leave home or stay at home?
4 They gave us three days to make a .... , and in the end we said no.
7 To move all the furniture we had to make several ....s.
8 Don't make any .... : the baby has just gone to sleep.
10 I'd like to make an .... : do you sell rubber goods?
11 Let's make a .... to meet for lunch next week.

Down:
1 The Minister will make a quick .... to the hospital next month.
3 Sue makes the .... to Mongolia twice a year.
5 On accepting the prize he made a short .... in Spanish.
6 OK, you've made your .... Now, sit down and give the others a turn.
9 The thieves stripped the house without making a ....

may

[modal verb]: expressing possibility or permission: *I may be late this evening.* • *The brakes may have failed.* • *You may sit down if you like.* • *May I use your phone?*

Grammar patterns

1 **may** | + bare infinitive

The train may be late.
I may vote 'yes'. On the other hand I may not.
It may be snowing when you get there.

▲ to talk about present or future possibilities

May I use your bathroom? ~ Of course, you may.

▲ to ask for, and give, permission (more formally than → can → could)

2 **may** | + not | + bare infinitive

I may not be able to come to class on Friday.
Don't give them raw fish: they may not like it.

▲ to talk about present or future doubts and uncertainties

You may not take photos during the service.
Passengers are reminded that they may not smoke inside the terminal building.

▲ to refuse permission (formally)

3 **may** | (+ not) | + have | + past participle

Fiona's not here. She may have gone to lunch.
George may not have known about the party: that's maybe why he didn't come.

▲ to talk about past possibilities

4 it | + **may** | + be | + that-clause

I'm hopeless at languages. ~ It may be that you've never tried.
The TV won't work. ~ It may be that it's not plugged in.

▲ to talk about possible reasons for things

Collocations

The following adverbs commonly occur with *may*: *(very) well, (very) possibly, conceivably, (very) easily.*

Liverpool may well win. (= there's a strong possibility)
They may very easily have been delayed.
She may very possibly have left the country.
Interest rates may conceivably fall even lower. (= there's a weak possibility)

Set phrases

• **'may as well ...'**
We may as well go home: there's nothing happening here.
You may as well eat something, now that you're here.
▲ to suggest doing something, because there is no better alternative

• **'may I suggest / may I just say ...'**
May I suggest we take a break at this point?
▲ to introduce a remark or a suggestion, politely

• **may ..., but**
She may be the boss, but that doesn't mean she can do what she wants.
He may be 70, but he's still fit!
▲ to say that, although something is true, something else is also true

"THEY MAY NOT LIKE IT!"

Exercises

1

Six examples of *may* have been taken out of this text. Can you put them back in?

Instructions:

The examination takes three hours. You not begin until instructed. You use calculators but you not use any other electronic aid, such as portable computers. You not smoke or talk during the examination. You leave when you have finished. All papers must be handed in prior to leaving the room. Anyone found breaking these rules be asked to leave.

2 *May, may not, must, can't.*

You use *may* and *may not* to talk about possibilities. To say that something is certain, use *must*. To say that something is impossible, use *can't*.

Question: Is this David's bag?

Answers:
It *may not* be David's bag. It *may* be Derek's.
It *must* be David's bag. It's got his books in it.
It *can't* be David's bag. His bag is black, not brown.

Complete these sentences with *may, may not, must,* or *can't*:

a It .... be Friday, because yesterday was Thursday.
b Sharon may be at home. On the other hand, she ....
c This book .... be yours: it's got my name in it.
d The bus .... be late. Or we .... be early.
e Why hasn't Sarah phoned? ~ She .... have our number. Or she could be busy.
f Helen .... be married, because she calls herself Mrs Hayes. ~Yes, but she .... well be divorced.
g Who's that at the door? ~ It .... be Luis, because he's at work.
h What's that thing up in the sky? ~ It .... be a bird. Or a kite. Or a piece of paper.

3 *May have done.* In this dialogue, change Watson's statements of certainty into statements of possibility:

Watson: The thieves came in through a window
Holmes: Well, we don't know for sure. They may have come in through the window.
Watson: They were looking for diamonds.
Holmes: Well, they (a) .... for diamonds.
Watson: They didn't find anything.
Holmes: They (b) .... anything.
Watson: Lord Arnott surprised them.
Holmes: He (c) ....
Watson: He was shot by one of the intruders.
Holmes: He (d) .... by one of the intruders.
Watson: They threw the gun into the lake.
Holmes: They (e) .... into the lake.
Watson: They drove off in Lord Arnott's Rolls.
Holmes: They (f) .... in Lord Arnott's Rolls.
Watson: Or, the butler did it.
Holmes: He (g) ....

4 Other ways of expressing possibility and probability.

Possibility.
Rewrite these sentences, substituting *may* for the underlined expressions, and making any necessary changes:

a Maybe the meeting has been cancelled.
b Perhaps it will be a nice day tomorrow.
c It is possible she has lost the address.
d There's a chance Mary will phone.

Probability.
Rewrite these sentences, substituting *may well* for the underlined expressions, and making any necessary changes:

e Chances are the film won't have started yet.
f It's likely that Terry was lying.
g They will probably be having lunch now.
h It looks as if their plane has been delayed.

mean

[irregular verb: *mean, meant, meant*] (1) signify, represent: *What does this word mean?* • *Green means go.*
(2) intend: *I didn't mean to interrupt.* • *I've been meaning to call you.* • *You weren't meant to find out.*

Grammar patterns

1 **mean** | + NP

What does 'haere mai' mean in English? ~ It means 'welcome'.
You mean the world to me.

▲ to say what something signifies

2 **mean** | + that-clause

This red light means that the line is busy.
I'm tied up at the office. ~ Does that mean you will be late?

▲ to talk about the significance or implications of something

3 **mean** | + -ing

I'll finish this book even if it means staying up all night.
Love means never having to say you're sorry.

▲ to say that something involves doing or being something

4 **mean** | + to-infinitive

I didn't mean to upset you.
They meant to book a room, but they forgot.

▲ to talk about intentions

5 is/are etc. | (+ not) | + **meant** | + for/to-infinitive

These towels are meant for the guests.
I was meant to be here at nine, but I was held up.
You are not meant to eat the skin.

▲ to say what is expected, intended, or allowed

Collocations

Adverbs that frequently qualify *mean* and *meant* are: *really, simply*, and *always*.

> *To most people Hong Kong simply means cheap shopping.*
> *I didn't really mean to frighten you.*
> *I always meant to write and tell her.*

Other words the commonly occur with *mean/meant* are: *something* and *(absolutely) nothing*.

> *His phone call really meant something to her.*
> *The name means absolutely nothing to me.*

Set phrases

- **' I mean … '**
  It's not fair, I mean, you never let me drive.
  He's the president, I mean the prime minister, of France.
  ▲ to add a comment, explain, correct yourself, or fill a pause

- **' I mean it '** = I'm serious, I'm not joking
  You are the best cook in the world. I mean it.

- **' you mean …? '**
  Why don't you get up? ~ It's Saturday. ~ You mean, you don't have to go to work?
  ▲ to check if you have understood or interpreted correctly

- **' (do you) know what I mean? '**
  Beth is a little immature. Do you know what I mean?
  ▲ to check that your listener has understood

- **' what do you mean …? '**
  What do you mean, you're quitting your job?
  ▲ to express surprise

- **' I see what you mean '**
  I see what you mean: this knife is useless.
  ▲ to say that you now understand

- **' I didn't mean to '**
  I'm sorry: I broke the door of the washing machine. I didn't mean to.
  ▲ to make an excuse for something you did

Exercises

① Classify these concordance lines with *mean* according the Grammar patterns 1–5:

a What did they **mean** to do with him?
b Life was never **meant** to be easy.
c That would **mean** the end of the airline.
d Proofreading **means** reading each word of your work carefully.
e Their severe spinal injuries **meant** they couldn't even sit up.
f This **means** burning less, not more, fossil fuel.
g A 'snack' does not have to **mean** crisps, biscuits or chocolate.
h I'm very sorry. I never **meant** to fall asleep.
i It could **mean** that it is in the wrong position.
j Jane knew that the words were **meant** for her.
k It would be easier if people would say what they **meant**.
l Corrections **mean** retyping a whole line.
m This doesn't **mean** that you have to spend a fortune on tools.
n I don't know quite what I'm **meant** to do.
o And I didn't **mean** to say all this now.

② Choose symbols from the first box, and words from the second box, and make sentences. For example:

Number 1 means 'copyright'.

1 ©	2
3	4
5 ☺	6
7	8

just joking
danger: radioactivity
wheelchair access
no cycling
copyright
don't wash
peace
this way

③ Rewrite these sentences using forms of the verb *mean*:

a Did you intend to let the bird out?
b I'm sorry, I planned to phone you, but I was so busy.
c You were not supposed to read the letter.
d You are not allowed to sit in those seats.
e She was supposed to be here by now.
f I've been intending to e-mail you.

④ Complete this dialogue, using the expressions below:

I mean
you mean
do you know what I mean?
what do you mean?

A: You can't smoke here.
B: (a) ....
A: It's not allowed.
B: It's a restaurant, isn't it? (b) .... , it's a public place.
A: Yes, but it's an enclosed place, (c) .... , space.
B: (d) .... because we're inside I can't smoke?
A: Yes. Exactly.
B: That's ridiculous. If people don't like it, they can stay home.
   (e) .... no one's forcing them to go to a restaurant.
   (f) ....
A: (g) .... you think you have a right to smoke?
B: It's not a question of rights. It's a question of freedom.
   (h) .... , I'm free to smoke, and they're free to stay home.
   (i) ....
A: You really are impossible, (j) .... , really ...

more

[determiner and pronoun] comparative of *much, many*: *There are more rooms upstairs.* • *Can I have two more?*
[adverb] used with adjectives and adverbs to form comparatives: *The fish here is more expensive.* • *You should practise more often.*

NOTE: in adjectives of one syllable, or of two syllables ending in *-y*, *more* is usually replaced by the suffix *–er*: *cleaner, happier* (rather than *more clean, more happy*). Other two-syllable adjectives are variable: *more simple* or *simpler*; *more clever* or *cleverer*, etc. In one-syllable adverbs *–er* is also used: *faster, harder*. Irregular comparative forms include *better* (= ~~more good, more well~~), *worse* (= ~~more bad~~), and *farther* or *further* (= ~~more far~~).

→ most
→ much
→ than
→ as

Grammar patterns

1 **more** | + plural or uncountable noun

Can you make me some more copies?
They are predicting more rain.

▲ to talk about a greater or additional quantity

2 **more** | (+ of + NP)

This is delicious. ~ Would you like some more?
Do you have any more of these plastic folders?

▲ to talk about a greater or additional quantity

3 **more** | + than | + number/amount

There were more than a million people at the march.
The tank is more than half full.

▲ to say that the real number or amount is bigger

4 **more** | (+ and more) | + adjective | (+ than …)
adjective + -er | (+ and **adjective + -er**) | (+ than …)

Cities have become more crowded.
I was growing more and more impatient.

The days are getting longer. (= ~~more long~~).
Asthma is more common than it used to be.

▲ to describe processes of change.

This flat is nice but the other one was nicer.
Laptop computers are still more expensive than desktops.

▲ to make comparisons

5 verb | + **more** | (+ and **more**) | + adverb | (+ than)
verb | + **adverb + -er** | (+ than)

Since the accident, he drives more carefully.
She ran faster and faster.
Fred danced better than he sang.

▲ to talk about changes in the way things are done, and to compare how things are done

6 verb | + **more**

The front row seats are the best but they cost more.
You need to watch TV less and read more.

▲ to talk about an increase in a state or activity

7 the **more** | + adjective/adverb/NP, | + the **more** | + adjective/adverb

The more often you practise, the more confident you will get.
The more students, the better.
When do you want these copies done? ~ The sooner, the better.

▲ to say how one thing changes in relation to another

Collocations

More (as determiner and pronoun) is often preceded by words that express quantity, such as: *some, any, no; many, much, a few, several; a bit, a lot, lots,* and numbers: *one, two,* etc.

I'd like a few more of these please.
Do you have any more wrapping paper?
There are lots more chairs in the other room.

More as adverb is often preceded by *much, a bit, a lot*:

This restaurant is much more expensive than it used to be.
Jenny is a lot more friendly these days.

Set phrases

• **more and more …** = increasing numbers or an increasing amount of
There were more and more people arriving all the time.

• **more or less …** = almost
Are you ready to go? ~More or less.
The painting is more or less finished.

• **more than likely** = very likely
Do you think it will rain? ~More than likely.

• **(and) what's more …** = moreover
The 'Handy' is inexpensive and, what's more, it's economical on fuel.

Exercises

❶ Put *more* into the correct place in these sentences:

a The soup needs salt.
b I'd like three cups of coffee, please.
c How many of those chocolates are you going to eat?
d The plants need less water not.
e Do we need any ice or do we have enough?
f We are nearly out of lemons. Can you buy three?
g Mexico City is bigger and crowded than Guadalajara.
h Emma is older than James, but James is a bit independent.
i Housing is getting harder to find and much expensive.
j Excuse me, but can you repeat that slowly?
k I'd like a job where I could travel.
l The dangerous the sport, the she likes it.

❷ Change the word in brackets into a comparative form:

a The African elephant is (tall) and (heavy) than the Indian elephant and it has (large) ears.
b The killer whale is (small) but (aggressive) than the blue whale.
c The polar bear is a (good) swimmer than the grizzly bear; the grizzly bear is (dangerous).
d The octopus is (intelligent) than the squid. Squids are generally (active) and travel (far).

❸ *Less* is the opposite of *more*:

The bus is less expensive than the train.
= The train is more expensive than the bus.

To express the same idea, you can also use *not as … as*:

The bus is not as expensive as the train.
= The train is more expensive than the bus.
→ as

Rewrite these sentences using *more* or *-er*:

a The bus is not as comfortable as the train.
b The bus station is less convenient than the train station.
c The bus doesn't leave as often as the train.
d The bus stops less frequently than the train.
e The bus is not as safe as the train.
f The train doesn't go as fast as the bus.
g The bus takes less time than the train.
h The train is not as cheap as the bus.

❹ Look at these facts and then decide if the following sentences are true or false. Can you correct the sentences that are not true?

	Country A	Country B
Population density	12 people per sq km	250 people per sq km
Life expectancy	72 years	69 years
Spending on education (% of gross national product)	9.5	10.0
Pupils per teacher	28	35
People per doctor	250	275
Average income per person, per year	$22,000	$2,000

a Country B is much more densely populated.
b People live a lot longer in Country A.
c Country B spends a little more on education.
d In Country B there are a few more pupils per teacher.
e In Country B there are many more people per doctor.
f People earn a bit more in Country A.

most

[determiner and pronoun] superlative of *much, many,* nearly all:
Most birds can fly. • *Most of my friends are older than me.*
[adverb] used with adjectives and adverbs to form superlatives:
What is the most interesting place you have been to? • *Of all her books, I liked this one the most.*

NOTE: in adjectives of one syllable, or of two syllables ending in
-y, *most* is usually replaced by the suffix *-est: fastest, busiest*
(rather than *most fast, most busy).* Other two-syllable adjectives
are variable: *most cruel* or *cruellest; most common* or
commonest, etc. In one-syllable adverbs *–est* is also used:
hardest. Irregular superlative forms include *best* (= ~~most good,~~
~~most well~~), *worst* (= ~~most bad~~), and *farthest* or *furthest*
(= ~~most far~~).

→ more
→ much

Grammar patterns

1 **most** | + plural or uncountable noun

Most verbs are regular.
Most uranium comes from Australia.
I like most fish, but I don't like sardines.

▲ to talk about nearly all of a group in general

2 **most** | + of | + determiner | + NP

Most of the cotton grown in Egypt is exported.
My father-in-law painted most of these paintings.
Most of my relatives live in Australia.

▲ to talk about nearly all of a particular group

3 the | + **most** | (+ NP)

Everyone ate a lot, but Carol ate the most.
France produces the most wine.

▲ to talk about a larger amount than anything or
   anyone else

4 the/possessive | + **most** | + adjective | (+ NP) |
   (+ that/in/of …)
   the/possessive | + **adjective + -est** | (+ NP) |
   (+ that/in/of …)

He is India's most popular film actor.
This computer is the most powerful.
This is the most unusual present I've ever been given.
The biggest cathedral in Spain is in Seville.
Emma is the brightest of them all.

▲ to talk about people or things that have more of a quality
   than all others of that type

5 verb | + (the) | + **most**

What we need most is a decent map.
Which painting do you like the most?

▲ to say that something happens or is true to the greatest
   degree possible

Collocations

Common 'most + adjective' combinations include:
*most important, most likely, most beautiful, most popular,
most famous, most successful, most common, most effective,
most significant, most suitable, most useful.*

The most common adjectives formed with *–est* are:
best, biggest, highest, largest, latest, and *greatest.*

Adverbs that often precede *most* + adjective (or adjective +
-est) are: *by far, easily, much,* and *quite.*

This is easily the most affordable car on the market.
He was by far the most handsome man in the room.

Words or phrases that often follow 'most + adjective' (or
'adjective + -est') are: *ever, so far, yet, possible,* and *available.*

Our steaks are the best you've ever eaten.
This is the coldest day so far this winter.
He always orders the most expensive wine possible.

Set phrases

- **at (the) most** = the maximum
  It will take a week to write the report, or ten days at most.

- **most of all**
  Of the three apartments, this is the one I like most of all.

  ▲ to emphasize *most*

- **most of the time** = nearly all the time
  Most of the time she sits at home and watches TV.

- **make the most of …** = get the maximum out of
  It's only a short holiday, so make the most of it.

Exercises

❶ Put the word in brackets into the correct place in the sentence:

a (most) I like vegetables but I don't like courgettes.
b (of) Most the people at the party were Mike's friends.
c (most) Like people, I spend more money than I earn.
d (the) Saudi Arabia produces most oil.
e (the) Which is most expensive city in Europe?
f (the) They are all hardworking students but Andreas is most hardworking.
g (by) That was far the most delicious meal I've ever had.
h (most) Which of these shirts do you like?
i (ever) It was the most expensive movie.
j (of) You are only young once, so make the most it.
k (ever) What's the worst movie you've seen?

❷ Write the questions for these answers, using adjectives from list A and nouns from list B. For example:

Mount Everest. → *What is the highest mountain in the world?*

| A: ancient long small high deadly bright large heavy |

| B: lake animal star snake waterfall city bird river |

a The River Nile
b the blue whale
c The Caspian Sea
d Angel Falls
e Sirius
f Damascus
g the hummingbird
h the taipan

❸ Make sentences using this pattern:

it/beautiful place/see
→ *It's the most beautiful place I've ever seen.*

a it/boring film/see
b it/amazing book/read
c this/expensive hotel/stay in
d she/interesting person/meet
e it/boring conference/be to
f they/peculiar couple/know
g that was/delicious meal/have
h it was/exciting game/watch

❹ *More* vs *most*.
Choose the best word to complete these sentences:

a Which is .... expensive: a Volvo or an Audi?
b If you practised .... , you would be a good guitarist.
c The subject at school I enjoyed .... was history.
d .... people we know speak at least two languages.
e What was the .... difficult decision you ever made?
f The .... you study, the easier it gets.
g .... of the building was destroyed in the fire.
h I like the bus, but the train is .... comfortable.
i Which of the two girls has grown .... ?
j Which of the three girls has grown .... ?

much

[determiner] a lot: *The trip wasn't much fun.* • *Was there much discussion?*
[pronoun] a lot: *She didn't say very much.* • *Much of the book is unreadable.*
[adverb] a lot: *I don't like this colour much.*

Grammar patterns

1 how | + **much** | (+ uncountable noun) | + ?

   How much milk do you take in your tea?
   The meal cost a fortune. ~ How much?

   ▲ to ask about an amount of something

2 so/too/as | + **much** | (+ uncountable noun)

   I have so much work to do.
   They spend too much on their clothes.
   You can have as much as you like.

   ▲ to talk about the amount or degree of something

3 not | (+ very) | + **much** | (+ uncountable noun)

   There isn't much coffee left: shall I get some more?
   You haven't eaten very much.
   How much does he earn? ~ Not much.

   ▲ to talk about small quantities

4 **much** | + more/less | + adjective | (+ than)

   London is much more expensive than it used to be.
   Karen is looking much older, isn't she?
   How are you feeling? ~ Much better, thanks.

   ▲ to emphasize a comparison

5 **much** | + too | + adverb/adjective

   You are driving much too fast.
   This sofa is much too expensive.
   It's much too cold to go swimming.

   ▲ to emphasize that something is excessive.

6 verb | + very/so/too | + **much**

   I liked the concert very much.

Thank you so much for the flowers.
You worry too much.

   ▲ to say that you feel something, or that something affects you, a lot

7 not | + verb | (+ very) | + **much**
   verb | + **much** | + ?

   They didn't enjoy the party very much.
   Do you go back home much?

   ▲ to talk, or ask, about degrees and frequencies

Collocation

The following nouns commonly occur with *much* in Grammar patterns 3 and 4: *chance, difference, difficulty, fun, hope, money, space, time, work.*

   There isn't much chance of you winning the lottery.
   I'm afraid we don't have much time, so we'd better hurry.
   I like Australia because there is so much space.

Set phrases

• ‘ **how much does it cost? / How much is it?** ’
   This one is very nice. ~ How much is it?
   ▲ to ask about the price of something

• **much the same (as) ...** = almost the same (as) ...
   How are you feeling? ~ Much the same.
   The village is much the same as it was 50 years ago.

• **much too much** = an excessive amount of
   There is much too much unhappiness in the world.

• ‘ **not much / nothing much** ’
   Did you like the movie? ~ Not much.
   What did you do in the weekend? ~ Nothing much.
   ▲ to show that something is not very interesting or important

• ‘ **thanks so/very much.** ’
   Thanks so much for the ride. ~ You're welcome.
   ▲ to emphasize your gratitude

• ‘ **so much for ...** ’
   So much for imports. Now, what about exports?
   ▲ to show you have finished talking about a topic

Exercises

1 **Put the word in brackets into the correct place in the sentence:**

a (much) I don't know how it costs.
b (so) They have much money they don't know what to do with it.
c (as) You can have much salad as you like.
d (much) There isn't very time left.
e (much) Do you spend on clothes?
f (too) You shouldn't eat much sugar and fat.
g (more) This chair is much comfortable than the other one.
h (much) Slow down, or we'll arrive too early.
i (too) The meal was much expensive.
j (olives) I don't like very much.
k (much) Nowadays she doesn't go out.
l (much) Brighton and Eastbourne are the same.

2 **You use *much* with uncountable nouns, such as *food, fun,* and *work*. You use *many* with plural countable nouns, such as *children, chairs,* and *animals*. Choose *much* or *many* to complete these definitions:**

a 'Bald' means you don't have .... hair.
b 'Lonely' means you don't have .... friends.
c 'Poor' means you don't have .... money.
d A place is 'thinly populated' if there aren't .... people.
e You get 'drunk' if you drink too .... alcohol.
f You may get 'obese' if you eat too .... hamburgers.
g A 'lazy' person doesn't do .... work.
h You may go 'deaf' if there is too .... noise.
i Too .... cars can cause a 'traffic jam'.
j Too .... coffee can cause 'insomnia'.

3 You can use *much* in negative sentences and questions. You usually only use *much* in affirmative sentences after *so, too,* and *as,* or before comparatives. In other affirmative sentences, you use *a lot (of)*:

We haven't got much petrol. (OR: *We haven't got a lot of petrol.*)
Have we got much petrol? (OR: *Have we got a lot of petrol?*)
We've got so much petrol.
We've got much more petrol than before. (OR: *We've got a lot more petrol …*)
We've got a lot of petrol. (NOT: ~~We've got much petrol~~)

I don't like Brahms much. (OR: *I don't like Brahms a lot.*)
Do you like Brahms much? (OR: *Do you like Brahms a lot?*)
I like Brahms so much.
I like Brahms much more than Beethoven. (OR: *I like Brahms a lot more …*)
I like Brahms a lot.
(You can also say: *I like Brahms very much.* But NOT: ~~I like Brahms much.~~)

In which of these sentences can you replace *a lot (of)* with *much*?

a Has she got a lot of money?
b Nigeria is a lot bigger than Ghana.
c We enjoyed the concert a lot.
d I don't have a lot of time.
e The holiday was a lot of fun.
f There isn't a lot of difference between white and black rhinos.
g Does Bilbao get a lot of rain?
h Robin and Chris argue a lot.

Now, in which of these sentences can you replace *much* with *a lot (of)*?

i Will there be much traffic?
j Does it snow much in winter?
k You don't get much exercise, do you?
l I ate so much!
m Tell me how much I owe you.
n I don't like flying very much.

my

[possessive determiner] belonging to, or related to, me: *That's my glass.* • *Have you met my parents?*

The other possessive determiners are:

	singular	plural
1st person	my	our
2nd person	your	
3rd person	his	
	her	their
	its	

Nicola has lost her glasses.
That's my brother and those are his children.
Can I borrow your dictionary?
The neighbours haven't fed their dog.

Grammar patterns

1 **my** | + NP

> *Meet my mum and dad.*
> *I'm going on holiday with my boyfriend.*
> *My flatmate is from Buenos Aires.*

▲ to talk about your family members, partners, colleagues, the people you live with

> *I hurt my leg.*
> *I've got a pain in my chest.*
> *My hair needs cutting.*

▲ to refer to parts of your body

> *Have you seen my gym shoes?*
> *Is that my towel?*
> *Someone's been in my things.*

▲ to talk about your clothes and other belongings

> *Come round to my place.*
> *I've repainted my room.*
> *When I went back to my home town, I visited my old school.*

▲ to talk about your home, school, etc.

> *They asked for my date of birth, my address, and my passport number.*
> *My surname is Thornbury. My first name is Scott.*

▲ to talk about your personal information

> *In my opinion, they should get counselling.*
> *My passion is birdwatching.*
> *My theory is that children are over-protected.*

▲ to talk about your beliefs and desires

2 (all/both (of)) | + **my** | (+ number) | (+ adjective) | + NP

> *Both of my older brothers are married.*
> *All my new shirts are in the wash.*
> *My three former business partners have been arrested.*

▲ to talk more specifically about what belongs to or is related to you

Collocations

The most frequent nouns that follow *my* are family relationship terms (*father, mother, brother, wife, son, mum, dad,* etc.) and parts of the body (*hand, heart, eyes, hair, feet, face, ears,* and *arms*).

Adjectives that frequently go between *my* and its noun are: *own, old, favourite, best.*

> *It was one of my favourite churches.*
> *I've also still got my old Gibson Melody Maker.*

(→ own)

Set phrases

· **… of my/her** etc. **own**
I'd really like a room of my own: I'm tired of sharing.
▲ to emphasize the fact that something is personal, belonging to that person alone

· '**my goodness! / my God! / my!** '
My God! Look at the time!
My, how you've grown!
▲ for expressing surprise

Exercises

① Complete the sentences below using words from the list:

| elbow | flat | aunt | flatmate | bedroom | scarf |
| nephew | ankle | chin | slippers | village | belt |

a   My .... says he's coming to stay.
b   I went back to my .... last year: it's changed a lot.
c   Have you seen my .... – the black leather one?
d   I cut my .... while I was shaving.
e   Come up and see my .... : I've had the living room redecorated.
f   My .... died: she'd been ill for ages.
g   I twisted my .... when I was running to catch the bus.
h   Have you seen my .... – the brown leather ones?
i   After playing tennis yesterday day, my .... really hurts.
j   My new .... is called Andrew and he's 22.
k   I won't show you my .... because it's a mess.
l   I left my .... at the restaurant, but it was still there the next day.

② Complete these sentences by choosing the correct possessive determiner: *my, your, his, her, its, our, their*:

a   My grandfather fell and broke .... arm.
b   Open .... mouth wide, please.
c   My sister and .... husband live in Wales.
d   The goldfish jumped out of .... tank.
e   The children can't find .... toys.
f   My brother and I still live with .... parents.
g   Have you cleaned .... teeth?
h   The Queen had an operation on .... knee.
i   The school is proud of .... reputation.
j   It's time the guinea pigs had .... dinner.

③ In each sentence there is one unnecessary word. Can you delete it?

a   All the my three children are at college.
b   A my room-mate is from my home town.
c   Come round to the my place for a meal.
d   Both of my brothers married his school friends.
e   I fell over and cut the my knee.
f   My sister and his brother are both dead.
g   In the my opinion, you should see my dentist.
h   My ex-girlfriend stole all the my belongings.

④ *My* vs *mine*.

Is that *my* towel? ~ No, it's *mine*.

> *My* is a determiner – that is, it is always followed by a noun. *Mine*, on the other hand, is a pronoun, and stands alone. The possessive pronouns are:

	singular	*plural*
1st *person*	mine	ours
2nd *person*	yours	
3rd *person*	his	
	hers	theirs
	its	

Complete these sentences, choosing the correct determiner or pronoun:

a   Jon ordered chicken, so the chicken must be ....
b   I ordered steak, so the steak's ....
c   Who ordered an omelette? Jackie, is this .... omelette?
d   Anna ordered the fish, so the fish must be ....
e   Jackie and I are going to share a salad, so this salad must be ....
f   Whose is this soup? Nobody ordered soup. It must belong to that table over there. Ask them if it's ....
g   Now, the drinks. Jackie is the only one drinking juice, so this orange juice must be ....
h   This is .... glass, so this wine must be mine.
i   This is Jon's glass, so this is .... wine.
j   This is Anna's glass, so this must be .... wine.

need

[regular verb] to require something, or to be obliged to do something: *I need a break* • *The radio needs new batteries.* • *You don't need to come if you don't want to.*
[modal (questions and negatives only)] have to: *Need they wait?* • *I needn't have bothered.*
[noun] necessity: *There's no need to shout!*

NOTE: 'need + not' is contracted to *needn't*
→ have/has

Grammar patterns

1 **need** (verb) | + NP

Do you need anything from the shops?
Cathy needed an electrician so she phoned Jeff.

▲ to talk about things you require

2 **need** (verb) | + to-infinitive

We need to do something about the design.
Wendy won't need to retake her exam after all.

▲ to say what is required or not

3 **need** (verb) | + NP | + to-infinitive

She needs somebody to look after the baby for an hour or two.
I need a cloth to clean up this mess.

▲ to say who or what is necessary to help you with something

4 **need** (verb) | + -ing

The grass needs cutting.
Does this salad need washing?

▲ to emphasize that something should be done

5 **need** (modal) | + -n't/not | + bare infinitive

You needn't dry the dishes: just leave them to drain.
I needn't have got up so early: I could've stayed in bed.
You needn't start the course next year: you can wait until the year after.

▲ to say what isn't (or wasn't, or won't be) necessary

6 there | + is/was etc. | + determiner | + **need** (noun) | + to-infinitive

There was no need to phone the police, but they did.
There's an urgent need to protect the ozone layer.

▲ to talk about actions that are (not) necessary

Collocations

The most frequent infinitives following 'need + to' are: *be, know, do, have, make,* and *get.*

You need to be careful.
What we need to know is the exact cost.
Did you need to do that?

An adverb that frequently goes with *need* is *badly* (= very much):

He badly needs a haircut.
Money is badly needed to help restore the temple.

Set phrases

· **need a hand** = require help
  Do you need a hand with the packing?

· **be in need of** = require
  This house is in need of a coat of paint.

· **if need be** = if necessary
  We can always order a pizza, if need be.

Exercises

1 Look at these concordance lines with *need,* and classify them according to Grammar patterns 1–6:

a   If you **need** to apply for a passport, do so at least 12 weeks before departure.
b   They may **need** reminding of what to do.
c   There's no **need** to give up favourite foods.
d   That was what I **needed** – strong hot coffee.
e   She just **needed** someone to talk to.
f   Her father thought that her glasses must **need** adjusting.
g   Is there anything else you **need**?
h   There is seldom any **need** to apply the formula.
i   We really **need** an engineer to design us something better.
j   The teaching session **needn't** last more than 20 minutes.
k   The police **need** not have informed her.
l   If you **need** to see me again, you know where to find me.

2 There are three different ways of saying something isn't necessary, using *need*:

We don't need to hurry.
We needn't hurry.
There's no need for us to hurry.

Rewrite each of these sentences in at least two different ways, using *need:*

a   You needn't worry.
b   There's no need for you to shout!
c   Is there any need for us to book a table?
d   Need I stay?
e   She needn't have bought a ticket.
f   There was no need for you to tell your mother.

3 *Needn't/don't need to* and *mustn't.*

You needn't and *you don't need to* mean 'it is not necessary for you'. *You mustn't* means 'you are not allowed' or 'you shouldn't'.

Choose either *needn't* (or *don't need to*) or *mustn't* to complete these sentences:

a   You .... read that book: it's too shocking.
b   You .... read that book: it's the same as the other one your read.
c   You .... tell Mary about this: she will be very upset.
d   You .... tell Mary about this: I've told her already.
e   You .... walk until your leg is better.
f   You .... walk: I'll give you a lift in my car.
g   You .... photocopy these exercises: it's forbidden.
h   You .... photocopy these exercises, since you already have the book.

4 In this text, there are ten examples of *need* that have been taken out. Can you put them back in?

Nicky,
Thanks so much for offering to keep an eye on things while we are away. Just a few things you to remember: the plants watering every two or three days, especially if it's hot. There's no to water the cactus, though. The cat and the dog feeding every day: there are some tins of pet food in the kitchen. If you more, they sell it in the supermarket. You will to take the dog for a walk at least once a day. You don't to feed the snake, because it is asleep! If you something to read, there are lots of books in the study.

In case you to contact us, the phone number in Milan is 39 025094736. (You to dial 00 to get an international line.)

never

[adverb] at no time, in no situation: *She's never been on a plane.* • *I'd never go back there again.* • *It never rains in August.*

Grammar patterns

1 **never** | + imperative

Never let children play with matches.
Go away and never come back.

▲ for giving strong advice or commands

2 NP | + **never** | + present tense verb
NP | + is/are etc. | + **never**

She never helps with the cooking.
Mario is never late.

▲ for talking about present habits and routines. Other adverbs that fit this pattern are: *always, often, normally, usually, sometimes, occasionally, rarely, seldom.*

3 NP | + auxiliary/modal | + **never** | + verb
NP | + **never** | + past tense verb

Our team has never lost a game.
Before coming to Japan, I had never eaten sushi.
I'll never finish this assignment in time.
I'd never go on one of those TV game shows.
They can never have children
It never used to rain in August.
They never answered my letter.

▲ for emphasizing the fact that something didn't happen, won't happen, hasn't happened, etc.

4 **never** | + auxiliary | + subject | + verb

Never had it rained so much.
Never in my life have I seen such scenes of jubilation.

▲ a more emphatic way of expressing patterns 2 and 3

Collocations

Adverbs that often go with *never* are:
before, again, really, even, once.

I've never had pickled eggs before.
I'll never go back there again.
I've never really liked Hitchcock.
Has he got a job? He's never even applied for one!

Other words that occur frequently with *never* are:
any, anything like.

Jack never eats any vegetables.
Rain! I've never known anything like it.

Set phrases

· **'never mind'**
There's the phone! ~ I'm busy. ~ Never mind. I'll answer it.
The restaurant is closed. Never mind, we'll find another one.
▲ to tell someone not to worry about something

· **'never again!'**
I went to the opera once. Never again!
▲ to emphasize how upset or disappointed you are about something

· **never ever …**
She's suffered so much but she never ever complains.
You never ever do the shopping.
▲ an emphatic way of saying *never*

· **never once …**
Never once did she say 'Thank you'.
▲ to emphasize that something didn't happen at any time

· **'you never know'**
They'll probably reject our offer, but you never know.
You never know with Colin: sometimes he's in a good mood, and other times he's not.
▲ to say that anything is possible

Exercises

① Put the word in brackets into the correct place in the sentence:

a (never) The baby cries at night.
b (never) The neighbours are at home.
c (never) My parents have been overseas.
d (always) It rains in October.
e (often) Brenda is late for work.
f (usually) I have cereal and a cup of coffee for breakfast.
g (never) Take your things and come back here again!
h (have) Never I been so happy.
i (ever) They never say thank you.
j (never) I really enjoyed summer camp.
k (he) Never once did do the washing up.

② *Never* is often used with words like *any, anything, any more, much*, etc., that is, words that are used in negative contexts. (→ not)

Contradict these statements, using *any* etc. For example:

There's always something in the fridge.
~ *No, there's never anything in the fridge!*

a There's always some coffee left.
b There's always somebody at reception.
c We always go somewhere nice.
d We still have fun.
e There's always a lot of mail.
f I always bring you something.

③ *Never* is frequently used with the present perfect to talk about first time experiences:

I've never had tofu (before/until now).
= This is the first time I've (ever) had tofu.

Rewrite these sentences, using *never*:

a This is the first time she's failed an exam.
b This is the first time we've been to the opera.
c This is the first time you've ever called me 'Darling'.
d This is the first time I've flown first class.
e This is the first time Neil's been late.
f This is the first time it's ever snowed here.

④ Here are some expressions or catchphrases with *never*. Can you match them with their explanation?

a Better late than never.
b Never a dull moment.
c It never rains but it pours.
d You'll never walk alone.
e Never on Sunday.
f Never say die.
g Never the twain shall meet.
h It's now or never.

1 Song written by Oscar Hammerstein.
2 You say this when, as soon as one bad thing happens, lots of other bad things happen as well.
3 You say this when two things or people are so different they can never be together.
4 A film set in Greece, and the song that is sung in it.
5 You say this when something interesting or funny is happening, or when you are very busy.
6 Song made popular by Elvis Presley.
7 You say this when something good happens after a long wait, or when someone arrives late.
8 You say this to encourage yourself or someone in a difficult situation.

"MARRIED TO YOU THERE IS NEVER A DULL MOMENT."

no

[adverb] negative response: *Can you drive? ~ No, I can't.*
• *Coffee? ~ No, thanks.*
[determiner] not any, not a …: *No pets are allowed.* • *Is there no hope, doctor?* • *No news is good news.*

Grammar patterns

1 utterance, | ~ **no**

You told Sally. ~ No, I didn't. That's simply not true.
Can we sit on the grass? ~ No, I'm afraid you can't. It's not allowed.

▲ to deny something, or to refuse a request, offer, etc.

You don't smoke, do you? ~ No, I don't.
I don't like lychees much. ~ No, neither do I.

▲ to acknowledge a negative statement

The concert's been cancelled. ~ Oh no!

▲ to express shock or disappointment

2 **no** | + NP | + verb phrase

No dogs are allowed on the premises.
No players were sent off.

▲ to make a completely negative statement, such as making a prohibition

3 verb phrase | + **no** | + NP

There were no cucumbers in the market.
They made no effort to help.

▲ to emphasize that something does not exist or is not available

Contrary to popular belief, Cleopatra was no great beauty.
He is no fool.

▲ to express a judgement about someone

4 **no** | + comparative

I'm afraid my knee is no better, Doctor.
There were no more than ten people in the room.
You must register no later than the end of the month.

▲ to emphasize the opposite of what is expected, or to emphasise the limit that is set

Collocations

Some of the most common 'no + noun phrase' combinations are: *no doubt, no need, no way, no reason, no matter, no means, no idea, no time, no evidence.*

We had no doubt she was in Scotland.
He saw no reason to change it.
They had no means of telling.
There is no evidence to prove it.

Set phrases

· **no good … / no use … / no point …**
   It's no good complaining: they won't give you your money back.
   There's no point shouting at the dog: it doesn't understand.
   ▲ to say that something is a waste of time or effort

· **no end** = a lot
   The new regulations caused no end of confusion.
   Since taking lessons, her singing has improved no end.

· ‘**yes and no**’
   Was it difficult, telling your mum and dad? ~ Well, yes and no.
   ▲ to answer two ways to the same question

· **in no time** = very quickly
   Once in Turkey, Hugo learnt Turkish in no time.

· ‘**no wonder …**’
   No wonder you feel sick after all the chocolates you ate.
   ▲ to say that something is not surprising

Exercises

1 **Change these sentences with *not* into sentences with *no*:**

We haven't any bananas → *We have no bananas.*

a   There isn't any coffee left.
b   There weren't any parents at the meeting.
c   Isn't there any sugar?
d   They haven't won any games this season.
e   I haven't got any cousins.
f   Don't you have any money at all?
g   They didn't give us any information.
h   I haven't heard any news from Paul.

2 ***No, not, none.***

> Remember: *no* is used before nouns to mean *not any*. *No* is also used before comparative adjectives and adverbs (*no better, no later*).
>
> *Not* is used to make any word, phrase or clause negative. (→ not)
>
> *None* is a pronoun – the opposite of *all*.

Complete these sentences with *no, not,* or *none*:

a   I've got .... time to talk to you right now.
b   How many eggs are there? ~ ....
c   Ahmed is Egyptian, ... Lebanese.
d   There are .... many women in the class.
e   It's .... surprise that Allan failed his exams.
f   There is .... mail delivery on Sundays.
g   I invited my classmates, but .... of them came.
h   We go to the theatre, but .... often.
i   I have .... small change: can you lend me 20p?
j   I usually have some, but today I have ....

3 There are many other ways of saying *no*, for example:

I'm afraid not	I'd love to but …	Yes, but …
Not at all	Of course not	Not really
I don't think so	Certainly not	

Choose from the expressions in the box to complete these short dialogues. (Sometimes more than one choice may be possible.)

a   A: Do you feel like going out to eat?
     B: .... I'd rather stay at home this evening.

b   A: Is it going to rain, do you think?
     B: .... although the forecast said it would.

c   A: Television poisons the brain.
     B: .... it's a great way to relax, you must admit.

d   A: Excuse me, do you have a light?
     B: .... I don't smoke.

e   A: You won't tell Dad, will you?
     B: .... your secret is safe with me.

f   A: Are you free to come to dinner on Saturday?
     B: .... I've arranged to babysit for my flatmate.

g   A: Can I borrow the car tonight?
     B: .... you don't even have a driver's licence!

h   A: Did that hurt?
     B: .... I didn't feel a thing.

4 **Here are some more set phrases with *no*. Choose phrases from the list to complete the sentences:**

no way	no wonder	no longer
no sooner	no problem	no knowing

a   Isn't it amazing about Tina and Fred being a couple!
     ~ I know. There's .... , is there?
b   Thanks for putting up the shelf in the bathroom. ~ ....
c   .... had Sheila left than they started talking about her.
d   Jill and Pat have separated. ~ .... They were not very suited to each other.
e   Can you give me a hand with the weeding? ~ .... It's not good for my back.
f   Can I speak to Shirin, please? ~ I'm afraid she .... works here. She left about a year ago.

not

[adverb] used to make sentences, or parts of sentences, negative: *Sydney is not the capital of Australia.* • *Nick doesn't like oysters.* • *The meeting's on Friday, not Thursday.*

NOTE: in spoken language (when unstressed), *not* is usually contracted to *-n't* after the verb *to be* and auxiliary and modal verbs: *It isn't fair.* • *Haven't you finished yet?* • *Jenny can't swim.* The contraction of 'will + not' is *won't*. The uncontracted form of 'can + not' is always *cannot*.

Grammar patterns

1 am/is/are etc. | + not/n't

It's not my fault.
There weren't any cucumbers in the market.

1a auxiliary/modal | + not/n't | + verb

The lift isn't working.
Passengers must not stand in the aisle.
I'm sorry, I don't understand.

1b (first) auxiliary/modal | + not/n't | + (second) auxiliary | + verb

You shouldn't have gone to so much trouble.
Bridget hasn't been feeling well.

▲ to form negative statements

2 (wh) | + is/are | + n't | + NP | + ?
   (wh) | + (first) auxiliary | + n't | + NP | + verb | + ?

Why isn't Anna here?
Aren't you going to the wedding?
Why didn't you write?

▲ to form negative questions, informally.
   (More formally: *Are you not going to the wedding*?)

3 don't | + bare infinitive

Don't be inconsiderate; don't smoke in here!

▲ to prohibit someone from doing something or acting in some way

4 not | + -ing

She was silent, not knowing what to say.

▲ to negate an –ing word

5 not | + to-infinitive

Try not to think about it.

▲ to negate an infinitive

6 I think/suppose/hope etc. | + not

Is it going to rain? ~ I hope not.

▲ to answer questions about opinions, beliefs, hopes, etc.

7 not | + all/many/much | + NP [= subject]

Not all sharks are dangerous.

▲ to make statements about small quantities

8 clause/utterance, | + (but) not

You can swim in the big pool, but not in the diving pool.
I think of singing as a hobby, not a job.
I like Eskimo art. ~ Inuit, not Eskimo.

▲ to contrast one idea with another, or to make a correction

Collocations

Here are some frequent combinations of 'adverb + not/n't': *certainly not, maybe not, probably not, perhaps not, of course not, still not.*

Here are some frequent combinations of 'not/n't + adverb': *not necessarily, not even, not really, not yet, not exactly, not fully, not merely, not possibly, not quite.*

Verbs which frequently follow *n't* are: *bother, worry, realize, afford, know, want, seem, deserve, blame, forget, belong, remember, think.*

Don't bother with the dishes. I'll do them later.
You shouldn't blame the schools for every social problem.

Set phrases

- **not at all [adjective]**
  I'm not at all sure that this is my umbrella.
  ▲ to emphasize a negative statement

- **'not at all'**
  Thanks for helping to tidy up. ~ Not at all.
  ▲ to reply politely when someone thanks you for something

- **or not**
  I don't know if he's gay or not.
  ▲ to show a negative possibility

- **If not, …**
  Do we have any tomatoes? If not, I'll buy some.
  ▲ to make a conditional statement by referring to what has just been said

- **not only … (but) also/too**
  The flat is not only gorgeous, but it has a stunning view.
  Not only does he sing, he can dance too.
  ▲ to say that something else is also true

Exercises

❶ Correct these facts by using *not* (uncontracted):

a The earth is flat. The earth is not flat.
b The sun goes round the earth.
c Penguins can fly.
d Astronauts have been to Mars.
e Fish have lungs.
f Shakespeare wrote novels.
g The Pyramids could have been built by aliens.
h The continents are moving closer together.

❷ Question tags are little questions that come at the end of statements, in order to check if something is true, or to ask for agreement. If the statement is positive, the tag is usually negative, and vice versa:

You're not English, are you?
Jane works with you, doesn't she?

Add tags to these statements:

a It's a nice day, ... ?
b You're from Canada, ... ?
c Your brother is getting married, ... ?
d Amy and Michael live together, ... ?
e Trish has been skiing, ... ?
f Your bicycle was stolen, ... ?
g Bruno won a prize, ... ?
h I should sign the cheque, ... ?
i You used to smoke, ... ?
j The beach will be crowded, ... ?

❸ Correct these mistakes, using *not*:

Yesterday I go to the park. → Not 'go'–'went'.

a I have 22 years old.
b I no understand.
c I live with your wife and children.
d Harry is retired so now he don't work.
e I like pop music too much.
f How long do you live here now?
g It's the best film I have never seen.
h I didn't went to work yesterday.

❹ Rewrite these sentences so that they begin with *not much, not all, not many, not a lot,* or *not enough*:

A few snakes are not poisonous.
→ *Not all snakes are poisonous.*

a Only a few people came to the meeting.
b Only a little money was spent on publicity.
c Too little money is spent on education.
d A few birds can't fly.
e Too little help is given to the elderly.
f There are some Swedes who don't have fair hair and blue eyes.

now

[adverb] at this time or very soon, these days: *The doctor can see you now.* • *The bus should be here any minute now.*
• *They left New York and now they live in California.*
[conjunction] because: *Now you have a job, you should pay some rent.*
[discourse marker] *Now, what's this I hear about you and Bronwyn?*

Grammar patterns

1 **now** | + NP | + verb | (+ …)
   NP | + verb | (+ …) | + **now**
   NP | + **now** | + verb | (+ …)
   NP | + is/was, etc. | + **now** | (+ …)
   NP | + (first) auxiliary/modal | + **now** | (+ …)

   Now I feel much better, thanks.
   Jim and Chris are living in Sheffield now.
   She now works in advertising.
   It is now six-thirty.
   You can now go home.

   ▲ (with present tense verbs) to talk about a present situation that is different from a past situation

   We've known each other for six months now.
   How long have you been studying Hebrew now?
   I've now worked here for exactly a year.

   ▲ (with present perfect) to talk about an on-going situation from a present point-of-view

2 it | + is/has been | + (time) | + **now** | + since …

   It has been two years now, since we last had a pay rise.
   It's ages now since I saw a good film.

   ▲ to emphasize the period since something happened

3 **now** | + that-clause

   Now that it's stopped raining, we can go home.
   Now you're here we can open the wine.

   ▲ to say how a new situation means something can happen

4 (well +) **now** / **now** (+ then), | + utterance

   Now, let me think …
   Now then, let's move on to the next item on the agenda …
   Well now, what's this about the football? Someone was telling me …
   Now, where was I? Ah, yes, I was talking about …

   ▲ to mark a pause or a new stage in the development of the talk or conversation, or a return to a previous stage

Collocations

Now frequently combines with these adverbs: *right, just, not.*

   I can't come right now/just now (= at this moment), I'm busy.
   I saw your neighbour just now (= a moment ago).
   Can you have a look at the printer? ~ Not now. Ask me later.

Now also combines with these prepositions: *before, up to, until, by, for.*

   Until now, I'd never eaten lobster.
   Up to now the weather's been great.
   Phone Diane: she should be home by now.
   By now you will have heard the news about Brian …
   That's enough techno for now. Let's have some rock 'n' roll!

Set phrases

· **any minute/day/time now** = very soon
  Are you ready? The bus should be here any minute now.
  When's dinner? ~ Any time now.

· **now and then / now and again** = occasionally
  Do you hear from Ian much? ~ Now and again.

· **from now on …**
  From now on, smoking is not allowed inside the building.
  ▲ to announce a change starting from now

· **'now what?'**
  Andy? ~ Now what? ~ The printer still won't print …
  ▲ to express frustration at some new development
  (The word 'now' is pronounced with emphasis.)

Exercises

1 **Choose the best position (1 or 2) for *now* in these sentences:**

a I left my old job and (1) I work (2) for myself.
b What (1) are you doing (2)?
c (1) what's (2) the matter?
d She's been going out with him (1) for three months (2).
e It's been a year (1) since his wife (2) died.
f They (1) have (2) put traffic lights on that corner.
g (1) the baby is asleep, (2) we can have dinner.
h (1) she doesn't need a babysitter, (2) that she's older.

2 **Match the two parts of these exchanges:**

a	Can you give me a hand?	1	~ Any day now.
b	When is the baby due?	2	~ Now you tell me!
c	Erm, Gavin …?	3	~ Just now.
d	When did she phone?	4	~ Right now.
e	The lift doesn't work.	5	~ Not now. I'm busy.
f	When do you want the taxi?	6	~ Now what?

3 **Here are some synonyms, or near-synonyms, for *now*. Can you use them to complete these sentences?**

already: by or before now
yet: until now, in questions and negatives.
currently: at the present time, and for more time in the future
at the moment: at the present time, but for a short time
presently: soon
nowadays: now, compared to the past, especially when talking about changes
today: now, not the past
to date: up to now (formal)

a I graduated two years ago and I am .... doing research for my doctorate.
b Young people .... do everything in groups.
c We have received over a hundred enquiries ....
d It is only nine o'clock and he is .... in bed.
e The colours of the cave paintings are as fresh .... as they were 40,000 years ago.
f She is busy .... Can you call back later?

g Is Alan there? ~ No, he's not arrived ....
h He'll be arriving .... : can you wait one or two minutes?

4 **Here are some well-known song titles with *now*. Can you use words from the list to complete them?**

go   know   over   hour   altogether   friends   never

a 'Now is the ....' (traditional Maori song, recorded by Bing Crosby)
b 'It's now or ....' (Elvis Presley)
c '............ , now!' (The Beatles)
d 'It's all .... now.' (Rolling Stones)
e '............ now!' (The Moody Blues)
f 'If all my .... could see me now.' (Sammy Davis Jnr)
g 'Now you ....' (Little Willie John)

"IT'S NOW OR NEVER."

of

[preposition] connects nouns (see patterns below): *A cup of coffee, please.* • *There is a risk of fire.*

Grammar patterns

1 determiner | + **of** | + determiner | + NP

Some of my friends are vegetarians.
A lot of this furniture is antique.

▲ to specify the amount or number of things you are talking about

2 NP | + **of** | + NP

Everything was covered in a thick carpet of snow.
Can I have a packet of aspirins, please?
Do you want to see the video of our wedding?

▲ to say what something is made of, consists of, contains, or is concerned with

Do you like the cover of my book?

▲ to talk about parts of things

Have you seen the size of his feet!

▲ to say who or what has a particular feature

Who are the members of the committee?
I once saw the King and Queen of Spain.

▲ to say who something belongs to, or who it is connected with

The departure of the plane has been delayed.
The capture of the monkeys was big news.

▲ to say that someone or something performs or is affected by an action

It is a building of enormous architectural interest.

▲ to say what qualities a person or thing has

3 NP | + **of** | + NP | + 's
  NP | + **of** | + possessive pronoun

I met a friend of my father's at the launderette.

Have you seen that notebook of mine?

▲ to talk about one or more of a number of things that belong to someone

4 NP | + **of** | + -ing

Is there any way of getting tickets?

▲ to talk about how easy, difficult, likely, etc. a situation is

5 adjective | + **of** | + NP

Your mother and father must be very proud of you.
My little boy is afraid of dogs.

▲ to say who or what is the object or cause of a feeling

I quit my job. ~ That was brave of you!

▲ to say who has a particular quality

6 verb | (+ NP) | + **of** | + NP/-ing

They phoned to remind me of my doctor's appointment.
As a youth David dreamed of becoming a rock star.

▲ to say what a statement or thought is about

Collocations

In Grammar pattern 1, determiners that go before *of* include: *any, all, both, each, enough, every one, few, less, least, little, many, more, most, much, none, some,* and numbers (*one, two,* etc.).

any of these brown envelopes
twenty of my best friends

Many nouns are typically followed by *of*. Here are some of the most common: *sort, type; lack, shortage; advantage, disadvantage; front, back, top,* etc.; *a lot, lots, a bit,* etc.; *crowd, queue; bag, glass,* etc.; *rise, end, return.*

These nouns are often followed by 'of + ing' (Grammar pattern 4): *way, chance, idea, cost, intention, hope, means, task, danger, possibility, effect, problem, risk, point.*

These adjectives are commonly followed by *of* (Grammar pattern 5): *fond, proud, afraid, sick, tired, bored, certain, sure, aware, brave, clever, kind, stupid, rude, sweet, thoughtful, guilty, innocent.*

These verbs follow Grammar pattern 6:
'verb + of + NP/-ing':
talk, warn, dream, think, hear, know, learn, smell, taste, approve, complain.
'verb + NP + of + NP/-ing':
advise, inform, warn, remind, accuse.

Set phrases

· **'of course (not)'**
Can I use your phone? ~ Of course.
Are you angry with me about something? ~ Of course not.
▲ to say 'yes' or 'no' strongly, and to give, or refuse, permission

Exercises

❶ The word *of* has been taken out of this text. Can you put it back? (There are 8 examples.)

Most the world's water – 97 per cent it – is found in the oceans. The oceans also receive most the rain that falls. The rest falls on the land, where some it evaporates back into the atmosphere. Some water is returned to the atmosphere from plants. As the water in the atmosphere cools, it condenses to form clouds water vapour. Some this water falls to the Earth again as rain. If this process evaporation stopped, there would only be enough rain in the atmosphere to last for a couple weeks.

❷ Choose a word from list A and a word from list B to make *of*-phrases to complete the sentences that follow:

A: shortage	gang	pair	loads
beginning	slice	sort	middle

+ *of* +

B: food	books	the square	youths
shoes	bread	the movie	water

a I'm looking for a .... ~ What size do you take?
b Would you like a .... to have with your soup?
c Because of the drought there was a ....
d There is a fountain in the ....
e I was attacked by a .... and they stole my phone.
f We were late so we missed the ....
g There was .... left over after the party.
h What .... do like reading?

❸ *Of* vs. possessive *'s*.

To talk about 'belonging', you can use the possessive *'s*, especially when the first noun is a person, organisation, country, or animal: *Fred's trousers; the society's members; China's population; the cat's breakfast.* Otherwise, use *of*: *the roof of the house; the sound of a violin,* etc. You can also use possessive *'s* with time words and periods of time: *yesterday's paper; three weeks' holiday.*

Which of these sentences is correct? Correct the ones that are incorrect:

a Alexander Fleming is famous for penicillin's discovery.
b The government's proposal has been hotly debated.
c I'm studying art's history.
d Tomorrow's meeting has been postponed.
e Have you seen the neighbour's new car?
f I'll meet you at the tower's bottom.
g Your travel card is on the fridge's top.
h Daniel went into the lion's den.
i I really like your hair's colour.
j I read a book about Australia's wildlife.

❹ How many names of films can you find by connecting words in the two lists with *of*?

Lord		being Earnest
Planet		the Jedi
Return		the Third Kind
Raiders		the Living Dead
Night		the Rings
Lawrence	+ *of* +	Notre Dame
The Importance		Arabia
The Hunchback		the Bride
The Silence		the Lost Ark
Father		the Apes
Invasion		the Lambs
Close Encounters		the Body Snatchers

on

[preposition] (1) in contact with a surface or line: *There's something on your chin.* • *We live on 10th Avenue.*
(2) with time expressions: *I'll see you on Monday.* • *Phone me on my birthday.*
[adverb] connected, or continuing, or going forward: *Who left the lights on?* • *Keep on until you come to a roundabout.*

→ at
→ in

Grammar patterns

1 **on** (preposition) | + NP

Put the flowers on the shelf next to the TV.
Rosario is a large town on the river.
Most films are released on Fridays.

▲ to indicate position or specify a time

2 verb | + **on** (preposition) | + NP

I'm depending on you to help with the driving.
What does the generator run on? ~ Diesel oil.

▲ to talk about dependence and survival (Other verbs include: *bank, rely, count, survive, manage*)

At least we agree on one thing – the cost.

▲ to say what is talked about (Other verbs include: *advise, comment, remark, talk, lecture, disagree, vote.*)

3 verb | + NP | + **on** (preposition) | + NP

Why waste money on a taxi when we can walk?
How much did you spend on the groceries?

▲ to say what receives money, time, sympathy, blame, etc.

4 verb | + **on** (adverb)

Is Keith there? ~ Can you hold on a minute, and I'll get him.
The meeting dragged on and on, but no one could agree on a settlement.

▲ to emphasize that something is connected, continuing or going forward

5 verb | + **on** (adverb) | + -ing

Some people ignored the fire alarm and carried on working.
You can't go on pretending you love her.

▲ to talk about activities continuing or going forward

6 verb | + **on** (adverb) | + NP
verb | + NP | + **on** (adverb)

Can I try on these jeans?
What does this say? ~ Just a minute, while I put my glasses on.
We cheered our team on.

▲ to emphasize that something is connected, continuing or going forward

Collocations

These verbs follow Grammar pattern 4: *catch on, carry on, go on, move on, keep on, press on, push on, stay on, sign on.*

These verbs follow Grammar pattern 6: *hand (something) on, put (something) on, pass (something) on, switch or turn (something) on, take (something) on, try (something) on.*

Many nouns follow *on*. Here are some of the most common:

on board, on foot
on disk, on line, on the phone
on TV, on the radio
on business, on duty, on call, on holiday, on strike
on time, on track, on the way
on purpose
on sale, on loan
on fire, on ice, on tap
on a diet

These adjectives are usually followed by *on*: *keen, tough, dependent, based.*

Set phrases

• **on and on (and on)** = continuing for a long time
The lecture went on and on, and I nearly fell asleep.

• **❛what's going on?❜**
What's going on? Why aren't you ready yet?
▲ to ask about what is happening

'what's on (at …)?'
What's on at the Tivoli? ~ High Terminal Rise II.
▲ to ask about films, plays, etc.

- **have a lot on / have nothing on** = be very busy/have nothing planned
I've got a lot on at the moment so can we put the meeting off?
What's he doing this evening? ~ Nothing, he hasn't got anything on.

- **straight on** = continuing in the same direction
Drive straight on until you come to a gas station.

Exercises

1 **Look at these film titles. Which Grammar pattern is each one an example of?**

a *Strangers on a Train.* (Alfred Hitchcock, 1951)
b *Carry on Camping.* (Gerald Thomas, 1969)
c *And the Ship Sails On.* (Federico Fellini, 1983)
d *Blame it on Rio.* (Stanley Donen, 1984)
e *A Nightmare on Elm Street.* (Wes Craven, 1984)
f *Born on the Fourth of July.* (Oliver Stone, 1989)
g *Get on the Bus.* (Spike Lee, 1996)

2 **There are fourteen examples of *on* that have been taken out of this text. Can you put them back?**

I've had a lot lately, so I've been depending Ron to keep an eye the children while I'm away business. Monday evening I came home to find Ron asleep the couch, the television, and the baby crawling around the floor with nothing. 'What's going?!' I shouted. 'Come, Ron,' I said. 'This is not. I'm relying you.' From then things have improved … a bit.

3 **Complete these sentences with words from the list:**

| carry | catch | get | congratulate |
| survive | have | take | blame |

a I must .... you on your excellent keynote address.
b I don't think underwater mobile phones will .... on. They're too expensive, for a start.

c How many clothes do you .... on? Aren't you hot?
d They .... the rise in inflation on the price of oil.
e The firm did so well they had to .... on more workers.
f I'd like to .... on working after I retire.
g How do they .... on so little food?
h You pay when you .... on.

4 **Do the crossword by completing the *on* collocations:**

	¹P	U	R	P	O	²S	E			
						I				³D
		⁴B	O	A	R	D		⁵F	I
		U			E		⁶I	C	E	T
		⁷S	A	⁸L	E		L		T
		I		I		⁹T	I	M	E
		N		N		R			
		¹⁰E	V	E		¹¹A	L	E	R	¹²T
		S				C			A
		¹³S	T	R	I	K	E		P

Across:
1 Did he do it accidentally or on .... ?
4 How many people were on .... when the ship sank?
6 For lack of money, they've put the plan on ....
7 The latest *Harry Potter* book is now on ....
9 Is the Bedford train on .... ?
10 We usually watch the fireworks on New Year's ....
11 Because of the heat wave, the fire brigade was on ....
13 There are no buses today: the drivers are on ....

Down:
2 I have a full-time job but I do other things on the ....
3 No cream for me. I'm on a ....
4 Are you going away on .... or for pleasure?
5 A tourist caught the elephant stampede on ....
8 To send an e-mail you have to go on ....
9 Everything is going well and our plans are on ....
12 In this pub they have ice cold beer on ....

one

[number and determiner] *It's half past one.* • *We have one boy and two girls.* • *It happened one night.*
[pronoun] *He's selling the car and buying a bigger one.* • *Would you like one of my cards?*

Grammar patterns

1 **one** | + NP

We've only got one bedroom, but there's a sofa.
There's one person I'd like to thank in particular.
You can have one more chance.

▲ to emphasize that you are talking about a single person or thing

2 **one** | + of | + plural NP

Debbie is one of my oldest friends.
The cat broke one of Lynn's Mexican bowls.

▲ to talk about one member of a group of people or things

3 **one**
a/an | + adjective | + **one**
the/that/those, my etc. | (+ adjective) | + **one/ones**
the **one/ones**| + that-clause/adverbial

Would you like a coffee? ~ I'd love one.
I'll have a pizza: a small one.
Which sunglasses did you lose? ~ My Italian ones.
You take this suitcase and I'll take the other one.
Which is your house? ~ The one on the corner.

▲ to refer to something (countable) when that type of thing has already been mentioned

Collocations

The pronoun *one* most often follows these words: *this, that, the other,* and *which.*

Do you like this one or that one?
~ I prefer the other one, actually.

Set phrases

· **one by one / one after another** = first one, then another one, and so on
One by one, the passengers boarded the bus.

· **one another** = each other
We three have known one another since school.

· **one day / one morning / one evening** etc. = a particular day in the past or any day in the future:
One morning, Gregor woke up and found a cockroach in his bed …
We must get together one evening and have a drink.

· **all in one**
It's a scanner, photocopier, and printer all in one.
▲ to refer to something that has several functions

· **one or two …**
I just have one or two things to do before I go.
▲ to refer to a small number of people or things

"IT'S A CAR, BIKE, AND PLANE ALL IN ONE."

Exercises

1 Ten examples of *one* or *ones* have been taken out of this dialogue. Can you put them back in?

A: Can I help you?
B: Yes, I'm looking for a sweater.
A: These here are quite nice. They're reduced.
B: Do you have in grey?
A: What size?
B: Small. It's not for me: it's for of my grandchildren.
A: There are no grey left. I've got in charcoal.
B: I quite like this blue.
A: That is medium.
B: OK, I'll take the charcoal.
A: OK. Would you like of our catalogues?
B: I've got, thanks all the same.

2 *A* or *one*:

> We use *one* when the exact number is important:
>
> *He broke a leg playing football.*
> *Long John Silver had only one leg.*

Complete these sentences with *a/an* or *one*:

a   I've got .... idea: let's write a book together.
b   There's .... chocolate left: would you like it?
c   Can I have .... banana?
d   Do you take .... lump of sugar or two?
e   There's .... nice market near the station.
f   .... funny thing happened on the way to work.
g   The bus was completely full apart from .... empty seat.
h   .... TV is not enough for a family of six.
i   To make the perfect cup, use .... tea bag per person.
j   He was wearing a patch over .... eye.

3 *One* and *it*:

> *One* means 'one of a type of the thing mentioned': it does not refer to the exact same thing that was mentioned. If you are referring to the exact thing, use *it* or *them*.
>
> *Did you make these cakes? Can I taste one?* (any one of a group)
> *Did you make this cake? Can I taste it?* (the same cake already mentioned)

Replace the underlined words with *one, ones, it,* or *them*:

a   Is that <u>your newspaper</u>? Can I borrow .... ?
b   <u>This shirt</u> is too small. Can I try a bigger .... ?
c   I like <u>olives</u> but not the green ....
d   These are my <u>holiday photos</u>. Have you seen .... ?
e   We liked the <u>house</u> so much we bought ....
f   That's <u>my car</u> – the red .... I always park .... there.
g   I like <u>oranges</u>, especially Spanish .... , but I don't like peeling ....
h   Are these your <u>DVDs</u>? ~ Yes, do you want to watch .... ?
i   <u>My computer</u> was so old I gave .... away and bought a new ....
j   How do you cook <u>artichokes</u>? ~ Boil ....
k   If you'd like <u>a drink</u>, help yourself to ....

4 Here are some other ways of expressing the idea of 'one':

> first   single   only   solitary
> sole   once   unique   individual

Choose the best word from the list to complete each sentence. (You can use each word only once.)

a   This vase is the only one of its kind: it's ....
b   She has no brothers or sisters: she's an .... child.
c   Being a .... parent need not be a problem.
d   She's only been in a plane .... before.
e   The .... survivor of the accident is still in hospital.
f   She was always .... in her class.
g   Each student has their own .... style.
h   There was nothing for miles except a .... tree.

or

[conjunction] connects two or more possibilities: *Would you like tea or coffee?* • *Either we stay the night or we leave now.* • *I can't decide whether to buy it or not.*

Grammar patterns

1 word/phrase/clause/sentence | + **or** | + word/phrase/clause/sentence

I'd like some wine, please. ~ Red or white?
Is it a boy or a girl?
We can fix a time now or, if you like, I'll phone you tomorrow.
Cover your ferns in cold weather. Or bring them inside.

▲ to talk about alternatives

2 either | + word/phrase/clause | + **or** | + word/phrase/clause

The sentences are either true or false.
You can take either the bus or the train.
Either she finishes her degree or she gets a job.

▲ to say that there are two alternatives and no other alternatives are possible

3 not […] | + **or**

They can't read or write.
There isn't any soap or toothpaste or shampoo.
I'm not free on Tuesday, Thursday, or Friday.

▲ to include two or more things in a negative statement

4 verb | + whether […] | + **or** | + […]

I can't remember whether it's on the second floor or the third floor.
Do you know whether the plane has arrived or not?

▲ to report, or ask indirectly, questions about alternatives

5 clause | + **or** | + clause
don't | + verb | + **or** | + clause

We'd better hurry or we'll be late.
Don't tickle me or I'll scream.

▲ to warn or advise or threaten somebody that something bad or undesirable could happen

Collocations

Verbs that most frequently precede *whether* in Grammar pattern 4 are: *know, decide, see, wonder, (don't) mind, (don't) care, say,* and *remember.*

She doesn't know whether to go or to stay.
I'll see whether or not I'm available.
I wonder whether we should take the bus or phone for a taxi.
I don't care whether you like it or not.

Set phrases

• **or so** = approximately
It takes an hour or so by train.

• **a […] or two / one or two / two or three** etc.
I'll be a minute or two. Can you wait?
How many bags of chips did you have? ~ Two or three.
▲ to express an approximate quantity

• **or something / or anything**
His name was Fred, or Frank, or something
Would you like a sandwich or anything?
▲ to say vaguely that you mean another thing of the same type

• **or not?**
Is Jackie coming with us or not?
Have you phoned the estate agent or not?
▲ to make a yes/no question more emphatic

• **or else …** = otherwise …
They can't be home yet, or else they'd answer the phone.

• **or rather …**
We spent a few days in Bombay, or rather, Mumbai.
▲ to correct or explain what you have said

• **and/or** → and

Exercises

1 Put *or* (once only) into the correct place in each of these sentences:

a Do we go left here right?
b There isn't any bread, butter, milk, cheese.
c Either the dog goes I go.
d Do you want to serve yourself shall I serve it for you?
e Do you know whether she eats meat not?
f I can't decide whether not to pack my swimsuit.
g Shakespeare wrote forty so plays as well as a number of poems.
h Take your umbrella you'll get soaked.
i She doesn't know anything else she's lying.
j Are you feeling better now? ~ More less.

2 Match the two parts of these sentences:

a We could stay in …
b Don't make so much noise …
c She hasn't drunk anything …
d Stay away from the edge …
e I haven't seen the movie …
f Either be quiet …
g Ask him whether the train has left …
h It cost them a thousand pounds …

1 or eaten anything.
2 or so.
3 or you might fall in.
4 or you'll wake the baby.
5 or not.
6 or read the book.
7 or we could go out.
8 or go to bed.

3 Rewrite these sentences using *or*:

He doesn't drink and he doesn't smoke.
→ *He doesn't drink or smoke.*

a I haven't got the time and I haven't got the money.
b She hasn't been to Rome and she hasn't been to Florence.
c It isn't your business and it isn't anyone's business, how I live my life.
d They don't have clean water, they don't have shelter, and they don't have medicine.

Now, rewrite these sentences using *or*:

If you don't leave now, I'll call the police.
→ *Leave now or I'll call the police.*

e If you don't stop shouting, you'll wake the neighbours.
f If you drink any more, you won't be able to drive.
g If you are not careful, you'll hurt yourself.
h If your are naughty, I'll tell your mother.

4 *And* or *or*? Complete this text (part of the traditional marriage service) by choosing *and* or *or*:

We are gathered here this day to unite this man (a)............ .... this woman in the bonds of holy matrimony […] Into this, these two now come to be joined. If anyone present can show just (b) .... legal cause why they may not be joined, let them speak now (c) .... forever hold their peace. (Say after me:) I, Simon Simple, take Jane Lazy, as my wedded wife, to have (d) .... to hold from this day forward, for better (e) .... for worse, for richer (f) .... for poorer, in sickness (g) .... in health, to love (h) .... to cherish, till death do us part.

other

[determiner] (1) a second one, or more of the same: *I can't find my other sock.* • *They're expecting another baby.*
(2) a different one, or different ones: *You should see another doctor.* • *There are other ways of cooking potatoes.*
[pronoun] *Alistair is here but where are the others?* • *Can I have another?*

NOTE: When *other* follows *a/an* it is written as one word: *another*: *Would you like another cup of tea?*

Grammar patterns

1 **another** | + singular noun

Have another chocolate.
Let's discuss this another day.

▲ to talk about one more thing of the same type, or a different thing of the same type

2 determiner | + **other** | + singular noun

My other brother is a nurse.
Can I try on the other jacket?

▲ to talk about the second of two things of the same type

3 (determiner) | + **other** | + plural noun

You deal with the children; I've got other things to worry about.
There are many other problems, apart from the traffic.
Are there any other questions?

▲ to talk about the rest of the things, or different things

4 **another** | (+ one)
the | + **other** | (+ one)
(the) | + **others**

These kiwis are nice. ~ Would you like another one?
She was carrying a can in one hand and a cup in the other.
You take Andy in your car and I'll take the others in mine.
Some sharks are dangerous. Others are harmless.

▲ to talk about an additional thing, the second of two things, or the rest, when these have been mentioned before, or when they are obvious from the context

5 **another** | + number | + plural noun

It will take another three or four weeks.
Can I order another two tickets?

▲ to talk about a specific number of additional things

Collocations

The following words frequently occur before *other*:
each, any, some, no, many.

They are very fond of each other.
There is no other solution.

These words frequently occur after *other*:
one/ones, people, things, side, and *such.*

If other people don't like it, that's their problem.
… cheese, yoghurt, and other such products.
There are some more questions on the other side.

These two words frequently occur before *another*:
yet, and *just.*

This is yet another example of his skill.
You feel like just another member of the family.

These words frequently occur after *another*:
way, time, man/woman, thing, day, year, reason, person.

Is there another way to get there?
Another reason why the Internet is sometimes slow is … .

Set phrases

· **other than** = apart from, except for
Did you see anything else other than the Pyramids?

· ‘**the other day/afternoon** etc.’
I ran into Yasmeen the other day.
▲ to talk vaguely about some time in the past

· **every other day/week** etc. = every second day/week etc.
I get the kids every other weekend.

· ‘**someone or other / something or other** etc.’
Where did you get that bowl? ~ I can't remember. Somewhere or other.
▲ to talk vaguely about a person, thing, place, etc.

- **on the other hand**
  Reptiles are cold-blooded. Birds, on the other hand, are warm-blooded.
  ▲ to give a contrasting point of view

- **in other words**
  I'm afraid we won't be renewing your contract. ~ I'm fired, in other words.
  ▲ to say something in another way, usually more simply

Exercises

1 **Put the word in brackets into the correct place in the sentence.**

a (another) This pen doesn't work. Have you got one?
b (other) All the students are better than me.
c (others) Some dogs are easy to train but are impossible.
d (another) Can you make hundred copies of this letter, please?
e (the) One of my brothers is retired and other is out of work.
f (another) You have this sandwich while I order.
g (other) The children seem to like each a lot.
h (the) If we order ice creams, others will want one, too.

2 *Another, more, other, others.*

You use *another* to mean 'one more' with singular countable nouns. If you want to talk about more things or stuff, use *more*, or *some more*:

Would you like another cup of coffee?
Would you like more milk in your coffee?
Would you like some more sugar?

You can use *other* or *more* with plural nouns when you mean 'more of the same':

Are there any other questions?
Are there any more questions?

But, when you mean 'different', you use *other*, not *more*:

I don't like beans. Are there any other vegetables?

When *other* is used as a pronoun, it has *–s* in the plural:

I don't like these vegetables. Are there any others?

Complete these sentences, with *another, more, other,* or *others*. (Sometimes two answers are possible.)

a This apple juice is delicious. Is there any .... ?
b I don't like apple or pear juice. Is there any .... ?
c I'm looking for .... apartment because the one I've got is too small.
d I've seen one apartment and tomorrow I'm going to see two ....
e I want to stay at home but my partner has .... plans.
f I like some modern artists but not ....
g Would you like .... slice of cake?
h Are there any .... blankets? I'm freezing.
i We have arguments, just like .... couples.
j And .... thing: you didn't clean the bath.

3 **Complete these sentences by choosing from this list of set phrases with *other*:**

one after the other
this, that, and the other
one another
in other words
someone or other
on the other hand
the other way round
one way or another
among other things

a Don't worry, we'll find you a ticket, ...
b What did you do at the weekend? ~ Not much: ....
c There was a series of disasters, ...
d Who phoned? ~ I'm not sure: ....
e You can tell they love ....
f Tobacco is bad for the lungs, ...
g A pizza would be nice; .... , we had pizzas yesterday.
h Poverty causes crime, not ....
i I got a D grade. I failed, ...

own

[determiner, pronoun] belonging to someone, done by someone: *Everyone in our office has their own computer.*
• *I'd prefer a room of my own.* • *Is that your own work?*
[verb] possess: *We don't own our house: we just rent it.*

Grammar patterns

1 possessive | + **own** | + NP

The boys each have their own room.
You have to trust your own judgement.

▲ to say that something belongs to, or is used by, someone

Can you make your own arrangements to get there?
We grow our own vegetables.
It's your own fault you are cold. You should've brought a sweater.

▲ to say that something is personal, without help from other people

2 a | + NP | + of | + possessive | + **own**

Gordon left his job to start a business of his own.
Can I borrow your grammar book? ~ Don't you have one of your own?

▲ to say that something belongs to someone and to no one else

3 (all) | + on | + possessive | + **own**

She sat all on her own, eating her lunch and reading a book.
This is a game that children can play on their own.
Susan is old enough to go to school on her own now.

▲ to say that someone is alone, or does something without help

Collocations

You can emphasize *own* with *very*:

At last, we have a car of our very own.
The village now has its very own web site.

The verb *own* is often used in the passive with these adverbs: *jointly, partly, wholly, privately, publicly.*

The company is jointly owned and operated.
All the apartments in this block are privately owned.

There is one phrasal verb formed with *own*:
If you *own up* to something, you confess that you did it:

OK, own up! Who ate the last plum?

Set phrases

• **through no fault of my/his** etc. **own**
Through no fault of their own, they missed the plane.
▲ to say that someone is not responsible for a mistake, accident, etc.

• **as if he/they** etc. **own/owns/owned the place**
The new assistant is carrying on as if she owned the place.
▲ to say that someone behaves over-confidently

• **for your/her** etc. **own good** = for personal benefit
You should be nicer to the boss. It's for your own good.
She's too clever for her own good.

All my own work

Exercises

1 Put *own* in the correct place in these sentences:

a   The furniture is all their design.
b   We grow the wheat ourselves and make our bread.
c   I don't want to share. I'd rather have my room.
d   This is a test, so work on your and don't talk to each other.
e   Each room has a TV, minibar, and its bathroom.
f   Each guest was given their very box of chocolates.
g   She is not well enough to leave the house on her yet.
h   How much of this land does the prince?

2 *Own* must always follow a possessive form, such as a possessive determiner (→ my) or a noun + *'s: Jacob's, the landlord's,* etc. Complete these sentences with the correct form of possessive determiner:

a   She's sixteen but she still doesn't have .... own room.
b   I got called away suddenly and had to leave the children on .... own.
c   Don't you have a dictionary of .... own?
d   Their dog is so spoilt: it even has .... own chair.
e   I don't have .... own computer but I do have a desk of .... own.
f   My wife and I make .... own yoghurt.
g   Jimmie, are you sure that this is .... own work?
h   The flat has .... own entrance.

3 Other ways of saying *own:*

She found the way on her own.
(= She found the way by herself.)
The neighbours own the garden.
(= The garden belongs to the neighbours.)

Rewrite these sentences, using the word in brackets.

a   These paintings belonged to my father. (own)
b   Who does this car belong to? (own)
c   The company is owned by the workers. (belong)
d   Do you own this apartment? (belong)
e   I don't like living on my own. (myself)
f   Can you get home on your own? (yourself)
g   We don't like leaving the children by themselves. (own)
h   Delia prefers to work by herself. (own)

4 Spot the mistake. In this text one of the examples of *own* is incorrect. Can you identify it?

My family is totally self-sufficient. We own our own home and the house has its own garden, so we grow all our own vegetables and even make our own bread. We own three goats so we make our own cheese and yoghurt. (I have to own up, though: we don't make an own coffee.) We are educating our children on our own, too. We even write our own schoolbooks!

place

[countable noun] a particular position or building, town, etc.:
Rio is a fantastic place. • *Come back to my place and have
something to eat.* • *This is the place where I lost the ring.*
[verb] put: *Place the chicken in a large pot.*

Grammar patterns

1 its/my/her etc. | + **place**

   Put the books back in their place.
   Julia's having a party at her place on Saturday.

   ▲ to talk about where something goes, or about where
   someone lives

2 a/an | (+ adjective) | + **place** | + to-infinitive

   We're looking for a place to eat.
   Where's the best place to buy shoes?

   ▲ to talk about where you do things

3 the | + **place** | (+ where/in which) | + clause

   This is the place where I usually park the car.
   You can visit the place in which Wordsworth wrote 'The Prelude'.
   What's that place you went to last summer?

   ▲ to identify a place

Collocations

Place combines with a number of verbs:

If something *takes place*, it happens. (*The World Cup takes place
every four years.*)
If you *take your place*, for example at a table, you go to the
place chosen for you. If someone *takes the place of* someone,
they replace them.
If you *get a place* on a team, or at a university, you become a
member, student, etc.
If you *lose your place,* for example in a book, you don't know
where you finished.
If someone *saves* or *keeps a place* for you, they guard it until
you arrive. You can also *go back to your place,* and *change places*
with someone.

The following adjectives and nouns frequently occur before
place: *good, best, safe, right, wrong, nice, busy, quiet, strange,
public, meeting, hiding,* and *market*.

The verb *place* is often followed by these nouns:
an order, an advertisement, a bet.

   We placed an ad in the local paper.

The participle *placed* is often used after these adverbs:
well, ideally, uniquely, conveniently.

   *If you speak several languages you are well placed for a range
   of interesting jobs.*

Set phrases

· **in place** = ready, or in the correct place
   Plans are in place for the development of the area.

· **in the first place**
   *I don't understand why you chose to study archaeology in the
   first place.*
   ▲ to talk about the beginning of a situation, especially to
   criticize it

· **all over the place** = in many different places, or in
   a state of disorder
   She travels all over the place as part of her job.

· **in his/her** etc. **place / in place of ...** = instead of
   For the sauce, you can use hazelnuts in place of almonds.

· **(if I was/were) in your place ...**
   In your place, I'd get a lawyer.
   ▲ to give someone advice

· **it's not my place to ...**
   *It's not my place to criticize Aisha, but I think she's made the
   wrong choice.*
   ▲ to say that something is not appropriate for you

· **out of place** = inappropriate or uncomfortable
   Doug's comments about John were out of place, I thought.
   *He felt out of place at the party; all the other guests knew
   each other.*

- **no place for/to …** = not an appropriate place
  The inner city is no place to bring up children.

- **'how are you placed?'**
  How are you placed on Thursday? ~ I'm free in the afternoon.
  ▲ to ask if someone is available for a meeting, for example

Exercises

❶ Common meanings of the word *place* include:

place (noun)
1 a particular position, point, or area: *Is this the place where it happened?*
2 a particular city, town, building, etc.: *I used to live in York and I'm still fond of the place.*
3 (especially in compounds or phrases) a building or an area of land used for a particular purpose: *a meeting place* • *The town has many excellent eating places.*
4 a point in a book, speech, piece of music, etc., especially one that somebody has reached at a particular time: *She had marked her place with a bookmark.*
5 a position, seat, etc., especially one that is available for or is being used by a person or vehicle: *Come and sit here: I've saved you a place.* • *Don't lose your place in the line.*
6 a house or flat/apartment; a person's home: *What about dinner at my place?*
7 a position among the winning competitors in a race or competition: *He finished in third place.*

place (verb)
8 to put something in a particular place, especially when you do it carefully or deliberately: *He placed his hand on her shoulder.*

[adapted from the *Oxford Advanced Learner's Dictionary*]

Match these concordance lines containing *place* with the definitions above:

a I'd never been to her **place** before.
b Phone in advance to reserve your **place.**
c I must have lost my **place** in the script.
d A handy and popular eating **place** for travellers!
e He carried a leather bag which he **placed** on the floor.
f He had a reserved parking **place** behind the building.
g This is my favourite **place** in the universe.
h Allan qualified in third **place**.
i The orchestra were coming back to their **places**.

j **Place** in a bowl with the milk and gently heat.
k I remembered this **place** when it was called Back Hill.

❷ There are ten examples of the word *place* (or *places*) missing from this dialogue. Can you put them back in?

A: This is my. Come in. Sorry about the mess. Things are all over the.
B It's nice. It must be nice to have a of your own. How did you find it?
A: It wasn't easy. I looked at a lot of. I was looking for a to work and to live at the same time.
B: I know what you mean. You've seen my, haven't you? It's a wonderful to live, but it's not big enough. There's simply no to work.
A: Yes, I was happy in the where I was living before. But now I wouldn't change for the world.

❸ Collocations.
Choose words from the list to fill the spaces in these sentences:

public   safe   wrong   quiet   best   strange

a What's the .... place around here to eat sushi?
b Here's the money: now, go and put it in a .... place.
c Why are you late? ~ I went to the .... place. I thought you meant in front of the park, not opposite it.
d This place is too noisy. Can't we find a .... place where we can talk?
e The meat factory? That's a .... place to take the children.
f Smoking is now forbidden in most .... places.

Now, choose the right verb for these sentences:

take (x2)   get   lose   save   change

g Do you mind if we .... places? I'd like to sit next to Ed.
h I'd like to .... a place at Bristol, in the drama school.
i Can you .... my place for me? I'm just going to the toilet.
j The annual general meeting will .... place next Friday, after the conference.
k I always fold the page over so I don't .... my place.
l The treasurer has resigned and there's no one to .... her place.

put

[irregular verb: *put, put, put*] to move or place something or someone in a position: *Put the milk in the fridge.* • *Put your hands up.* • *That puts me in a difficult situation.*

Grammar patterns

1 **put** | + NP | + preposition | + NP

I put the key under the mat.
Don't put your feet on the seat!

▲ to talk about moving or placing things or people

She put a lot of effort into learning Chinese.
You should put your theory into practice.
The government is putting pressure on the unions.
The accident put an end to our holiday.

▲ to talk about applying non-physical things, such as effort, pressure, ideas, etc.

2 **put** | + NP | + adverb particle
put | + adverb particle | + NP

Put your clothes away.
The neighbours put up a wall next to our garden.
Put your coat on. It's freezing outside.
I can't put this book down, it's so interesting.

▲ to talk about moving or placing physical objects somewhere

We'll have to put the meeting off. Jack is away on Thursday.
They put the fire out before it could do any damage.
We put our name down for one of the new apartments.

▲ to express a variety of idiomatic meanings to do with changing the state of things, or moving them in time or space, or writing things, etc.

Collocations

Nouns that frequently follow *put* are:
money, way, hand.

They put their money into real estate.
To put it another way, you're fired!
She put her hand on my shoulder.

Other combinations with *put*:

put pressure/strain/stress on someone (*The recession put a lot of strain on small businesses.*)
put somebody in a difficult/awkward/embarrassing situation
put a case (for something)/a point of view/suggestions
put an argument/an idea etc. clearly/well/in writing
put something into practice/action/operation/effect
put somebody out of work/a job/business
put somebody into a good/bad/lousy mood
put something right/straight; put somebody right/straight
(*Let me put you straight: I didn't touch your computer.*)

Put combines with particles to form many phrasal verbs:

If you *put* something *back,* you return it to where it was, or you postpone it.
If you *put forward* an idea, you suggest it.
If you *put* something *off,* you postpone it; if you *put* someone *off* something, you do something to discourage them.
If you *put out* a fire, you extinguish it. If you *put* your back/shoulder etc. *out,* you injure it.
If you *put* someone *through,* by phone, you connect them.
If you *put* something *together,* you (re)assemble it.
If you *put* something *up,* or *down,* or *in,* or *out,* you place it in those directions. If you *put up* the price of something, you increase it. If you *put* someone *up,* you accommodate them.
If you *put up with* something, you tolerate it.

Set phrases

• ' **put yourself in my place/position** '
  Put yourself in my place: how would you feel if you lost your job?
  ▲ to appeal for sympathy, understanding

• **to put it bluntly**
  Well, to put it bluntly, you don't study very hard.
  ▲ to warn someone you are going to speak honestly

• **to put it another way**
  Let me put it another way. Imagine that this is the house and this is …
  ▲ to make something easier to understand

'**how can I put it? ...**'
The children are (how can I put it?) little monsters.
▲ to prepare a listener for something that may sound unpleasant

put simply
Put simply, I'm sick to death of my job.
▲ to say that you are going to give just the basic facts about something

... put together = all included
Brazil is bigger than all its neighbours put together.

put yourself out = inconvenience yourself
Please don't put yourself out: I can sleep on the sofa.

Exercises

❶ Put the word(s) in brackets in the correct place in the sentence:

a (put) Where did you the key?
b (it) I put on the shelf beside the door.
c (it) Smoking's not allowed so please put out.
d (in) Have you got a jug I can put the water?
e (in) Have you got some ice I can put the water?
f (out) She really put herself to make sure we enjoyed ourselves.
g (it) I don't know how to put: you've failed.
h (it) Can you please put in writing?
I (it) Put back before someone finds out.
j (up) You see what I have to put with!

❷ Phrasal verbs with *put*.
Replace the words in italics with a phrasal verb with *put*. Choose from these adverb particles: *through, back, together, off, out* (x2), *up* (x2).

a Hold the line and I'll *connect* you.
b We can *accommodate* you for the night.
c The landlord is going to *increase* the rent.
d Please *extinguish* your cigarettes.
e Can you help me *assemble* this bookcase?
f Please be quiet. You are *distracting* the players.
g *Replace* all the books on the shelves.
h I *injured* my knee playing tennis.

❸ Idioms with *put*.
Match the two parts of these idiomatic expressions:

a	Don't put all ...	1	my finger on it.
b	I can't put ...	2	my foot down.
c	I'm going to put ...	3	money on it.
d	I put ...	4	foot in it.
e	I really put my ...	5	your eggs in one basket.
f	I wouldn't put ...	6	two and two together.

Now, use expressions from the above list to complete these short conversations:

a How do you know they are living together?
~ I just worked it out. ....
b The noise upstairs is driving me crazy.
~ I've had enough too. ....
c You were so indiscreet, asking Jimmy about his exam results, when you know he failed everything.
~ I know. ....
d Do you think the Social Democrats will win the next election?
~ Unlikely. ....
e I'm going to invest my savings on the stock market.
~ Be careful. ....
f Denise has changed, but I can't work out how.
~ Neither can I. ....

❹ Ten examples of the word *put* have been removed from this text. Can you put them back?

HEALTH TIPS FOR OUR PASSENGERS:

Here are few tips for your safety and comfort.

To sleep more comfortably: take off your shoes and on the sleeping socks we have provided. The footrest down and your feet on it. The seat back. The eye mask on; and the ear plugs in. Don't forget to out the overhead light. If you don't want to be disturbed during the flight, the 'Don't disturb' sticker on your head rest.

We recommend regular exercise. For example, your feet flat on the floor and press down firmly ten times. Your arms above your head and stretch.

Now, sit back and enjoy the flight!

say

[irregular verb: *say, said, said*] (1) to express in words: *She says she is tired.* • *'Let's go,' he said.*
(2) to think, have an opinion: *How about a dance? What do you say?*
(3) to mean: *Are you saying you don't care anymore?*

→ tell

Grammar patterns

1 **say** | + NP

Can I just say a few words?
She didn't say very much.
What did you say?

▲ to talk about speaking, without saying exactly what is said

2 **say** | + that-clause

The agency said that the tickets should arrive tomorrow.
They say you should get up and stretch every half hour.
The recipe says you need two eggs.

▲ to report statements or opinions (written or spoken)

3 **say** | + wh-clause

Did Martin say when he was leaving?
The advert doesn't say how much it costs.

▲ to ask about what is said, or to specify what isn't said

4 **say** | (+ to + NP) | + quote
'quote' | + **say** | (+ to + NP)

The label says, '100% authentic'.
'You're late', I said to the driver.

▲ to report, directly, what is spoken or written

5 **say** | + so

Is it going to rain? ~ They say so.
If you don't like the proposal, you should've said so.

▲ to refer back to what someone has expressed (→ so)

6 it | + is/was etc. | + **said** | + that-clause

It is often said that practice makes perfect.

It is said that the Queen was furious.

▲ to report what was said, without saying who said it

7 NP | + is/was etc. | + **said** | + to-infinitive

At least two people are said to be in a critical state.
The President is said to have amassed a huge fortune.

▲ to say what is reported or believed

Collocations

Adverbials that frequently occur with *say* and *said* are: *aloud, out loud; at last, finally; again, repeatedly,* plus many adverbs that express mood or manner of expression, such as *angrily, cheerfully,* and *vaguely.*

'Oh no!' she said out loud, 'my handbag!'
As I've said repeatedly, you're too young to go out on your own.

Verb phrases that occur with *say* include: *be about to, be going to, want to, hate to, be fair to.*

I forgot what I was going to say.
I hate to say it, but it's time we went.
It's fair to say that this wasn't her best performance.

Prepositions that commonly go with *say* are: *about* and *to*:

What did Jane say about the meeting?
Barry said hello to Margaret.

Set phrases

- **'let's say …'** = for example
  We'll have a break for, let's say, ten minutes.

- **'having said that … / that said …'** = despite that
  They are not paid enough. Having said that, it's not merely a question of money.

- **'that's not to say …'**
  It seldom rains in August. That's not to say it won't.
  ▲ to add something that corrects or qualifies what you have just said

- **'don't say …'**
  Don't say you hadn't heard!
  ▲ to show surprise

Exercises

1 **Put the word in brackets into the correct place in each sentence:**

a (to) 'Go home', I said her.
b (she) 'It's getting late,' said.
c (what) Debbie wouldn't say she had been doing.
d (is) The menu doesn't say what the soup.
e (so) I didn't agree and I said.
f (is) It sometimes said that English has no grammar.
g (to) He is said have fallen into a crevass.
h (about) I've forgotten what I was to say.
i (cheerfully) 'Good morning, all,' said Arthur.
j (about) What did you say me to Jacky?

2 **These sentences are in direct speech (Grammar pattern 4). Change them to indirect speech (Grammar pattern 2). Pay attention to tense and pronoun changes:**

'It's going to rain,' she said. → *She said it was going to rain.*
'I've lost my scarf,' said Andrew. → *Andrew said he had lost his scarf.*

a 'I'm hungry,' she said.
b 'I'll be late,' said Susan.
c 'I've been robbed,' said the sailor.
d 'The bus didn't stop,' he said.
e Donald said, 'It may rain'.
f 'I can hear voices,' said Lydia.
g 'I'm going to complain,' said Mrs Adams.
h 'We have to work,' they said.

3 **Tenses and *say*.**

Study these different forms of *say*:
1 In literature: *'A river runs near our village,' said Ishvar. 'You can see it shining, and hear it sing.'*
2 Introducing a topic in conversation: *Tom was saying, the other day, that he's thinking of moving to the States …*
3 Telling a story in conversation: *… so Mary says, 'I have to go into hospital,' and I say, 'Oh no, what's the matter?' and she says …*
4 Quoting from a written text: *The instructions say you have to shut down the computer first.*

Choose an appropriate form of *say* to complete these extracts:

a The rules ………… you have to deal out all the cards.
b Adam glanced at the letter. 'It's for you,' he ………… .
c I ran into Peter and he ………… that Derek and Sue have split up.
d The label ………… it has no artificial preservatives.
e … then this man ………… 'What are you doing in here?' and Dick ………… : 'What business is it of yours?' and I'm going, 'Oh no!' …
f The door opened slowly. 'Come in, my dear,' ………… the Count.

4 **Use expressions in this list to complete these exchanges:**

Easier said than done
You can say that again
Whatever you say
I wouldn't say no
I'd rather not say
That goes without saying
Who says?

a You're not allowed to smoke in here.
~ ………… .
There's a sign. Look.

b This bus needs a good clean.
~ ………… . It's filthy.

c Can I count on you if I need you?
~ ………… .
You're a true friend, Amos.

d Try and persuade the boss to give you a raise.
~ ………… .
Come on. She's not that difficult, is she?

e Do you fancy some juice?
~ ………… .
Apple or orange?

f Who told you about Robin and Jan?
~ ………… . /
Come on. We have no secrets.

g Let's not have any starters.
~ ………… . You're the one who's paying.

see

[irregular verb: *see, saw, seen*] (1) sense something by means of the eyes: *Bats can see in the dark.* • *I saw someone climbing in the window.*
(2) understand, realize: *I see what you mean.*
(3) meet, visit: *You ought to see a doctor.*
(4) find out: *Can you see who is at the door?*

→ look

Grammar patterns

1 **see** | (+ adverbial)

Turn on the lights: I can't see.
From the top you can see for miles.

▲ to talk about visibility in general

2 **see** | + NP

Did you see the monkeys?
I saw a good film last weekend.

▲ to talk about what you watch or look at

3 **see** | + NP | + -ing

I can see something moving.
Did you see the dolphins performing?

▲ to talk about seeing things in progress

4 **see** | + NP | + bare infinitive

We saw the rocket lift off.
The police didn't see anyone arrive or leave.

▲ to talk about seeing entire actions

5 **see** | + that-clause

I see that the price of petrol has gone up.
I don't see that it matters.

▲ to talk about things that you have learned or realized

6 **see** | + wh-clause
see | + if-clause

I'll see what I can do.
Do you see what I'm getting at?

Can you go and see if there's any mail?

▲ to talk about discovering and finding out things.

Collocations

See (in the sense of using your eyes) very commonly occurs after modal verbs: *can, could, be able.*

I can't see a thing.
You'd be able to see much better if you cleaned your glasses.

See often follows these verb phrases: *be surprised, be amazed, be glad, be pleased, be relieved.*

I was surprised to see Christine at the launch.
I'm relieved to see that there was no damage.

These adverbs often occur with *see: just, hardly, clearly, dimly.*

We could just see the ship on the horizon.
From where we are, you can dimly see the lights of Vic.

There are a few phrasal verbs formed from *see:*

If you *see* someone *off,* you accompany them to their point of departure. (*I'll come to the airport and see you off.*)
If you *see through* something, you are not deceived by it. (*They saw through my little scheme.*)
If you *see* something *through,* you continue doing it until it is finished. (*Now that we have started, we have to see it through.*)
If you *see to* something, you deal with it. (*I'll see to dinner: you deal with the baby.*)
If you *have something seen to,* you get someone to deal with it. (*You should have that tooth seen to.*)

Set phrases

· '**I see**' = I understand
It's a fungal infection. Nothing serious. ~ I see.

· '**you see**'
I didn't go to work. Jamie's not very well, you see.
▲ to say that you are explaining something

· '**see you (later) / (I'll) be seeing you**'
Bye, Jim. ~ See you later.
▲ to say goodbye, informally

- ' **as I see it** ' = in my opinion
  As I see it, the project is not going to work.

- ' **let me see / let's see** '
  Shakespeare was born in, let me see, 1564, I think.
  ▲ to show you are thinking about, or trying to remember, something

- ' **we'll see** '
  Can we go to the zoo? ~ We'll see.
  ▲ to say that you will decide later

- ' **you'll see** '
  Don't worry. The exam will be easy. You'll see.
  ▲ to tell someone that they will find out that you are right

Exercises

① Classify these concordance lines with *see* according to the Grammar patterns 1–6.

a   I could **see** his lips moving.
b   Cats can **see**, hear and smell with more sensitivity than we can.
c   I might stay in. I'll **see** how I feel.
d   Warren was the only witness to **see** him fall.
e   I didn't believe her for a minute but I didn't **see** what I could do.
f   They couldn't **see** properly through their masks.
g   Michael wouldn't like to **see** her cry.
h   All I could **see** of her was the top of her nose.
i   Aha! I **see** that you are not afraid to speak the truth.
j   How nice to **see** a friendly face.
k   Let's **see** if we can find the Colombi Hotel.
l   If you **see** someone acting suspiciously by the house, just call the police.
m   It is encouraging to **see** that the Society is also moving with the times.

② Eight instances of *see, saw,* or *seen* have been taken out of this text. Can you put them back in?

I think I may have a UFO[1]. Last night, the dog was barking so I went out to what was disturbing it. It was a clear night. You could the stars. Suddenly, I an object above me travelling at high speed. At first I thought it was a plane. But I was amazed to it change direction sharply, before it disappeared. That was all I. It was like nothing I have ever before. I don't believe in aliens, but how else can I explain what I?

[1] Unidentified Flying Object

③ Convert these pairs of sentences into one sentence. For example:

The man fell over. I saw him. → *I saw the man fall over.*
The train was arriving. I saw it. → *I saw the train arriving.*

a   The sun set. I saw it.
b   The lights were coming on, one by one. I saw them.
c   People were coming and going. I saw them.
d   A car stopped suddenly. I saw it.
e   A man got out. I saw him.
f   He was pointing a gun at someone. I saw him.
g   He was shouting something. I saw him.
h   He pulled the trigger. I saw him.

④ Put the following expressions into the best place in the dialogue:

let me see   you'll see   I see   see you   you see   we'll see

A: Hi Jane. Can I ask you a favour?
B: What?
A: Well, (a) .... , my brother's coming next weekend and we don't have room in the flat.
B: (b) ....
A: So, I was wondering if he could stay with you.
B: For how long?
A: Erm, (c) .... , about two or three days, I think. Please.
B: Well, (d) .... I'll have to talk to the others.
A: He'll be no trouble. He's very nice: (e) ....
B: I'll get back to you, OK.
A: OK, (f) ....
B: Bye now.

seem

[regular verb: *seem, seemed, seemed*] (a linking verb) appear:
Everyone seems very busy. • *The house seemed to be empty.*
• *It seems to me that we've been overcharged.*

Grammar patterns

1 NP | + **seem** | + adjective/past participle

You seem confused.
The government seems unable to decide.
The woman seemed lost.

▲ to say how someone or something appears to be

2 NP | + **seem** | + like | + NP
(→ like)

Erica seems like a nice person.
Berlin seems like an interesting place to visit.

▲ to say what your impression is, of someone or something

3 NP | + **seem** | + to-infinitive

The bus seems to be late.
Your dog doesn't seem to like me very much.
I seem to have lost my glasses.

▲ to say what appears to be the case, or to say what is the case

4 it | + **seem** | + as if/as though | + clause
it | + **seem** | + like | + clause (= informal usage)

It seems as if everyone is invited to their wedding.
It seemed as though a bomb had hit the town.
It doesn't seem like your boss appreciates you.

▲ to say what you think is true from the evidence you have

5 it | + **seem** | (+ to + NP) | + that-clause

It seemed to me that she had been crying.
It seems you don't have a lot of experience in this field.

▲ to say what you think is true from the evidence you have

6 it | + **seem** | + NP/adjective | + that-clause
it | + **seem** | + NP/adjective | + to-infinitive

It seems a pity that Gabriel can't get the day off.
It seemed unfair to keep the children inside.
It seems highly likely that share prices will fall.

▲ to state an opinion or a prediction

Collocations

In Grammar pattern 1, frequent adjectives occurring with *seem* are: *odd, strange; pleased, surprised; possible, impossible; certain, likely, unlikely; clear, reasonable.*

It seems odd to think that he was once a millionaire.
She seemed surprised to see me.
It now seems unlikely that London will host the Games.

In Grammar pattern 3, the most frequent infinitives following *seem* are: *to be, to know, to do, to have, to make,* and *to get.*

You two seem to know each other.
I don't seem to have my credit card.

Set phrases

· **it seems ages since …**
   It seems ages since I read a good novel.
   ▲ to emphasize the time since something happened

· **' so it seems '** = it appears to be the case / people say so
   I hear Adrian is quitting. ~ So it seems.

· **' I can't seem to … '**
   I can't seem to open this jar.
   I couldn't seem to find your phone number.
   ▲ to say that you can't manage to do something

Exercises

1 **Identify the Grammar pattern (1–6) in these concordance lines with *seem*:**

a   They did not **seem** pleased to see me.
b   It **seemed** a shame that it couldn't be in time for my mother's birthday.
c   Children were playing with what **seemed** like wonderful toys.
d   It **seems** likely that Mozart made use of the interlude.
e   It **seemed** like it was the hardest decision I ever had to make.
f   This program would **seem** to be very limited in its usefulness.
g   It may **seem** obvious to you.
h   It **seemed** to him that he at last had a friend.
i   Now it **seems** that the disease builds over a period of years.
j   The journey would have **seemed** like an eternity.
k   It **seemed** pointless to continue.
l   He can't **seem** to make up his mind who he is.
m   It **seems** as though you may run into opposition.

2 **Transform these sentences, so as to include the word(s) in brackets, and without altering the meaning:**

a   He seems to be a nice guy. (like)
b   It seemed as though the crowd was going to riot. (if)
c   It seems impossible that Ben could fail. (possible)
d   It seemed that they had been arguing. (to have)
e   It seemed like a good idea at the time. (to)
f   The doctor seems to have called. (that)
g   His heart seemed to have stopped. (as if)
h   It doesn't seem likely that Catherine will marry. (seems)
i   You seem to be enjoying yourselves. (It)
j   It seems to me that Bronwyn is lying. (be)

3 We often use *seem* in order to reduce the force of statements, so as to be more polite, for example:

This bill is wrong. → *This bill seems to be wrong.*
The total isn't correct. → *The total doesn't seem to be correct.*
You've made a mistake. → *You seem to have made a mistake.*

Make these statements less forceful, by using *seem*:

a   The television is broken.
b   The phone doesn't work.
c   The towels are dirty.
d   I've broken the toilet seat.
e   There's no hot water in our room.
f   I've lost my key.
g   There's nothing in the mini-bar.
h   The room hasn't been cleaned.

4 Other verbs that take Grammar pattern 1 and Grammar pattern 2, with a similar meaning to *seem*, are: *smell, taste, feel, look,* and *sound.*

That smells nice.
The soup tastes burnt.
The piano sounds like it needs tuning.

In this text, the underlined verbs are in the wrong place. Can you put them where they belong?

My friend Max has opened a restaurant, so I went to eat there. At first sight, the restaurant <u>felt</u> promising: well decorated and nicely lit. But when Max greeted us, he <u>smelled</u> worried and his hand <u>tasted</u> damp when I shook it. I soon realized why. From the kitchen I could hear the cook: he <u>looked</u> drunk. Sure enough, when the first course arrived, it <u>seemed</u> disgusting: undercooked and oversalted. And when the cook came out to say hello, his breath <u>sounded</u> strongly of cheap wine. Not a good beginning …

should

[modal verb] (1) expresses desirability: *You should take it easy.*
• *I shouldn't have eaten all those chips.*
(2) expresses probability: *It should be a nice day tomorrow.*
• *She should have had the baby by now.*

NOTE: 'should + not' is contracted to *shouldn't;*
'should + have' = *should've;*
'should + not + have' = *shouldn't have*

Grammar patterns

1 should | (+ not/n't) | + bare infinitive

We should phone your mother.
Are you coming to the gym? ~ Maybe I should.
You shouldn't work so hard.

▲ to say what is (not) a good thing to do; to give advice

You should answer all the questions.
Heavy items should not be placed in the overhead lockers.

▲ to say what is necessary or forbidden (often in written contexts, to state rules and regulations)

Phone Oliver: he should be home by now.
They say the weather should clear up tomorrow.
I've phoned for a taxi: it shouldn't be long.

▲ to say that you expect or hope something to be the case (or not)

2 should | + have | + past participle

The bus should've been here half an hour ago.
We should've finished by the end of the week.

▲ to say that you expect something to have happened already, or by the time specified

You should've told me that you were ill.
The government should've acted immediately.

▲ to say that something was expected or desirable, although it didn't happen; to criticize

3 should | + not/n't | + have | + past participle

They shouldn't have pulled that building down: it was unique.
I shouldn't have said that: I'm sorry.

▲ to say something was not a good thing to do, although it happened; to criticize

Collocations

The following are common combinations of adjectives/participles with *should*:

should be able	should be encouraged
should be possible	should be considered
should be grateful	should be avoided
should be clear	should be treated

It should be possible to sustain life on Mars.
War should be avoided at all costs.
It should be clear that we stand united on this issue.

Set phrases

• ⟨ **I should think/hope so** ⟩
Evan says he'll tidy up the mess. ~ I should hope so.
▲ to strongly agree with something

• ⟨ **you shouldn't have!** ⟩
Here's a going-away present. ~ Oh, you shouldn't have!
▲ to show surprise when someone has given you a present

• ⟨ **you should have seen …** ⟩
You should've seen the look on Barry's face when I proposed!
▲ to emphasize how surprising or funny something was

Exercises

1 *Should* is a modal verb, and therefore:

- has no special third person form: *He should go …*
- makes questions and negatives without *do/does*: *Should we wait?* • *They shouldn't laugh.*
- has no future form: *Tomorrow you should make an appointment.*
- has no past form, so uses 'have + past participle' in the past: *We should have phoned yesterday.*

Change these sentences into the form indicated in brackets. (Use contractions where appropriate.)

a We should be there by now. (she)
b They should drink. (not)
c The boys should wear jackets. (question)
d I should go. (tomorrow)
e I should go. (yesterday)
f I should go. (not; yesterday)
g I should go. (he; not; yesterday)
h We should do something. (he; not; question)
i We should do something. (he; yesterday)
j We should do something. (he; not; question; yesterday)

2 *Should* and *must*.

'Should + bare infinitive' and 'must + bare infinitive' are similar in meaning. *Must* is a bit stronger than *should*:

You should go and see this film.
(= It's a good idea to see this film.)
You must go and see this film.
(= It's a very good idea to see this film.)

But in the past, they are very different in meaning:

She should have phoned. (= It would have been a good idea to have phoned, but she didn't.)
She must have phoned. (= It's very probable she phoned.)

Rewrite these sentences with either *must* or *should*, or, if possible, both:

a I really need to get a hair-cut.
b I recommend you read this book.
c It's very probable Dennis was delayed.
d It would have been a good idea if you'd apologized.
e It's very probable I left my wallet in the supermarket.
f It's a good idea to eat more fresh fruit.
g It would've been a good idea if you'd eaten more fresh fruit.
h It wasn't a good idea, losing your temper.

3 Read the conversation and say what they *should have done* or *shouldn't have done*:

A: How was your trip to the national park, Emma?
B: It was a disaster, literally.
A: Oh, no. Why? What happened?
B: Well, we went on a hike, just Wayne and me, and it started out quite nice, but then the weather turned bad, and we didn't have any raincoats or anything. So we decided to turn back, and Wayne had this idea that we could take a short-cut through the forest, but we got lost. So we decided to light a fire, but it started to spread, it was so windy, and we were trying to put it out, and I burned myself. And we didn't have anything to put on the burn. Meanwhile it was getting later and later, and we didn't have anything to eat or drink. Nobody knew where we were. And then Wayne decided to go on ahead without me. Oh it was terrible …

Write sentences:

They didn't take protective clothing.
→ *They should've taken protective clothing.*

a They didn't take a map.
b They took a short-cut.
c They didn't follow the signs.
d They lit a fire.
e They didn't take a first-aid kit.
f They didn't take food or water.
g They hadn't told anyone where they were going.
h They didn't stay together.

so

Grammar patterns

1 **so** | + adjective/adverb

You're so clever.
He drives so fast.
I thought I would faint, it was so hot.

▲ for emphasizing qualities and feelings

2 not | + **so** | + adjective/adverb

Julia passed her exams. Jim wasn't so lucky.

▲ for making comparisons

3 **so** | + adjective/adverb | + that-clause

The water was so clear that you could see the bottom.
I'm so hungry I could eat a horse!

▲ to emphasize the quality of something by talking about its effects

4 **so** | + much/many/few/little | + NP | (+ that-clause)

There were so many people you couldn't move.
It's not surprising he has so little money.

▲ to emphasize the amount of something (and its effect)

5 **so** | + clause

It was starting to get dark so they headed for home.
The sofa looked dirty so we had it re-covered.

▲ to say what the consequence of a situation is

6 **so** that | + clause

Take a map so that you don't get lost.

▲ to state the purpose of an action

7 I think/suppose/hope etc. | + **so**
I don't think | + **so**

Is that our bus? ~ I hope so.
Is it going to rain? ~ I don't think so.

▲ to answer questions about opinions, beliefs, hopes, etc.

8 **so** | + auxiliary | + NP

I quite like this track. ~ So do I.
Luke is off work and so is Mrs Britton.
We never take taxis. ~ Neither do we.
I didn't enjoy the party and nor did Ruben.

▲ to say that something is also true for someone else. (Note that if the first verb is negative, you use *neither* or *nor*.)

9 do/did | + **so**

If you haven't voted yet, you should do so as soon as possible.

▲ to refer back to an action that has just been mentioned

10 **so** | + utterance

So, how's your dad?
… so, anyway, when the police finally arrived …

▲ to introduce something new into the conversation, or to return to a topic

Collocations

These adjectives frequently follow *so*:
long, angry, bad, pleased, easy, beautiful, worried, glad.

I'm so angry with Robert. Do you know what he's done now?
How are you feeling? ~ Not so bad, thanks.

These adverbs frequently follow *so*:
far, much, badly, quickly, long, frequently.

I haven't seen him for so long.
I need a haircut so badly.

Set phrases

- **even so, ...** = despite that
  It's not late, I know. Even so, I think we should be going.

- **if so ...**
  Are you hungry? If so, we can stop and eat.
  ▲ to make a conditional statement by referring to what has just been said

- **' ... or so '**
  Cook the sauce for twenty minutes or so.
  ▲ to be vague about an amount or quantity

- **' ... and so on, and so forth '** = et cetera
  We'll need a tent, sleeping bags, back pack and so on.

- **' ... like so '**
  Fold the paper in two, like so.
  ▲ to demonstrate something, with a gesture or action

Exercises

1 Match the two parts of these sentences:

a	It was so hot ...	1	I fell asleep.
b	I'm so hungry ...	2	I laughed and laughed.
c	It was so boring ...	3	my ears have gone numb.
d	I'm so thirsty ...	4	I screamed.
e	I'm so tired ...	5	I had a cold shower.
f	It was so funny ...	6	I can't keep my eyes open.
g	I'm so cold ...	7	I could eat ten burgers.
h	I was so frightened ...	8	I could drink a gallon of water.

2 *So* or *such*?

Note that so goes before adjectives and adverbs, while *such* goes before noun phrases:

It was so hot we went to the beach.
It was such a hot day we went to the beach.

Choose *so* or *such* to complete these sentences:

a You'd be .... nice to come home to.
b It's .... a wonderful life!
c The baby's .... cute, and she's got .... a sweet smile.
d It's .... a pity that you can't come to the wedding.
e It's a nice house, but it's .... a long way to the station.
f You're .... right. I am .... an idiot.

3 Put *so* in the correct place in these sentences:

a Jenny likes opera and do I.
b It was pretty that I took a photo.
c Take an umbrella that you don't get wet.
d It was Roger's birthday we phoned him.
e Our neighbours are friendly. They have nice kids, too.
f Terry has confidence in the stock market, but I'm not sure.
g They say it will snow tomorrow, but I don't think.
h She nearly dropped the salad bowl, it was heavy.
i I'm glad you could come to the opening.
j I took the rubbish out. As I was doing, I heard a strange noise.

4 Respond to these statements, showing that they are true for you, too, using *so* or *neither/nor*:

I come from Leeds. → *So do I!*

a I really liked Lisbon. ~
b I'm learning Arabic. ~
c I don't know anyone here. ~
d My brother has seen a panda. ~
e I've never read a *Harry Potter* book. ~
f I can stand on my head. ~
g A friend of mine has a pet rat. ~
h I won't be long. ~

5 In this dialogue there are a number of set phrases with *so*. Can you find expressions that mean the following:

a	goodbye	e	you're right
b	neither good nor bad	f	very very
c	really?	g	you should've listened to me
d	according to the experts	h	that's the way things are

A: How was the concert?
B: So-so. I'd rather have gone to the movies with you.
A: I told you so. You missed a great film.
B: Is that so?
A: It's going to win several Oscars, so they say. You really should have come. It was ever so good.
B: Well, so be it. Another time, perhaps. Wow, look at the time: it's nearly five.
A: So it is.
B: I must dash. See you later.
A: So long.

some

[determiner and pronoun] indicates an indefinite quantity of something; not all: *I'd like some bread, please.* • *Let me give you some advice.* • *The peaches looked nice so I bought some.*

→ any
→ a/an

Grammar patterns

1 **some** | + plural or uncountable noun

There are some more cups on the top shelf.
I bought some paint for the kitchen.
Some languages don't have tenses.

▲ to refer to a certain amount of some thing or things

2 would you like/do you want etc. | + **some** | + plural or uncountable noun | + ?

Would you like some more pasta?
Shall I order some firewood?

▲ to make polite offers, suggestions, where you want to encourage a 'yes' answer

3 **some** | + of | + NP

Some of the seats were empty.
I can take some of you in my car.
She ate some of her dinner.

▲ to refer to a certain amount of a group of things, or part of something (→ of)

4 **some** | + countable noun

Some man phoned.
I read it in some newspaper.

▲ to refer to a thing or person without saying which or who exactly

Collocations

Some common abstract uncountable nouns that follow *some* (OR → any) are: *information, advice, accommodation, evidence, experience, help, knowledge, news, progress, research, success, work.*

I need some information about buses, please.
She's done some research into hormone replacement therapy.
There's some evidence that flax seeds are good for you.

Some common concrete uncountable nouns that follow *some* (OR → any) are: *money, furniture, software, traffic,* as well as lots of foods and drinks, e.g.: *meat, chicken, cheese, rice, bread, water, wine, coffee, sugar,* and *milk.*

We bought some new furniture for the front room.
There's always some traffic at this time of day.

Set phrases

• **' some kind of … / some […] or other '**
She works in some kind of office.
Briony married some actor or other.
▲ to talk about something vaguely, because you don't know, or you think it doesn't matter

• **some more** = an extra amount of something
The fruit salad is delicious. ~ Would you like some more?

• **some time** = a fairly long period of time
He lived in China for some time.

Exercises

1 Put *some* in the correct place in these sentences:

a I haven't got any apple juice but I've got orange.
b You didn't ask for any cheese but I bought anyway.
c There are more eggs in the fridge, if you need any.
d Katie ate of her vegetables but she didn't eat the meat.
e There's plenty of rice left if you'd like more.
f I think there must be mistake: this is not my bill.
g Harry spent time in Africa, studying the chimpanzees.
h We need bread and a cup of hot milk, please.

2 *Some* and *a/an*.

> Many nouns are countable (if we think of them as units) or uncountable (if we think of them as masses):
>
> *I'm sorry, I broke a glass.* = countable
> *Be careful, there's some glass on the floor.* = uncountable.

Complete these sentences using *a/an* or *some,* depending on the meaning:

a Would you like .... lemon in your tea?
b You've got .... egg on your shirt.
c Can you buy .... paper: *The Times,* for example?
d I bought Jessica .... ice cream, but she dropped it.
e Cut .... lemon in half.
f There's .... writing paper in the desk.
g Break .... egg and beat it with a fork.
h Would you like .... ice cream with your fruit salad?
i We bought .... live chicken from the farmer.
j Add .... cold chicken to the salad.

3 *Some* vs 'zero':

> You use *some* when the quantity is limited, but no determiner ('zero') when the quantity is not limited:
>
> *Would you like some water?*
> *Plants need water, or they will die.*

Complete these sentences, using *some* or leaving them as they are ('zero'):

a All birds lay .... eggs.

b Do you mind if I use .... eggs to make an omelette?
c The house is full of .... furniture.
d She found .... nice furniture on the street.
e Pasta is made from .... flour.
f The bath is too full. Let .... water out.
g My bike got a puncture when I ran over .... glass.
h The green bin is for .... glass.

4 *Something.*
Here are some set phrases with *something.* Can you use them to complete the sentences below?

quite something
something to do with
something of
something wrong with
something about
something like

a They say that .... ten thousand people are homeless.
b Jeff is .... an expert on computers: why don't you ask him?
c I wish you'd do .... that tap: it's still dripping.
d I don't know what he does, but it's .... banking.
e There's .... the cat and I think we should take it to the vet.
f She made her first film when she was 25, which is ....

5 Complete these song titles using words or phrases from the list:

somebody
someone (x 2)
something (x 2)
some day
somewhere
some

a '............ my prince will come'. (Morey and Churchill)
b '............ enchanted evening'. (Rogers and Hammerstein)
c 'You do .... to me'. (Cole Porter)
d '............ to watch over me'. (Gershwin)
e 'I finally found ....'. (Barbra Streisand)
f '............ happened on the way to heaven'. (Phil Collins)
g '............ 's crying'. (Chris Isaak)
h '............ , my love'. (from *Dr Zhivago*)

sort

[noun] type, kind: *What sort of bird is that?* • *For problems of this sort, you should see a doctor.* • *You'll meet all sorts of people there.*
[adverb] a little; more or less: *She's sort of strange.* • *It's sort of square-shaped.*
[verb] arrange things: *Can you sort these words into two groups?*

Grammar patterns

1 **sort** | (+ of + NP)

I don't like jasmine tea. Do you have another sort?
What sort of books do you read?
This is my sort of place.

▲ to talk about a class of people or things

2 all/many/most | + **sorts** | (+ of + NP)

What sort of pizzas do they do? ~ All sorts.
They sell all sorts of different spices here.
I like most sorts of music.

▲ to talk about multiple categories of things

3 **sort** of | + […]

What's Janine like? ~ She's sort of tall and pretty.
The car is a sort of blueish colour.
What's the weather like? ~ It's sort of raining.
Are you ready yet? ~ Sort of.

▲ to describe people or things or events inexactly

So, I was standing there, and there was a sort of, a sort of, this sort of, noise …

▲ to fill a pause when speaking

Collocations

Adjectives that frequently occur with *sort* include: *best, worst, right, wrong, funny, odd,* and *strange.*

What's the best sort of engine oil?
She was nice, in an odd sort of way.

The verb *sort* combines with two adverb particles to form phrasal verbs:

If you *sort* something *out,* you organize it;
If a problem *sorts* itself *out,* it stops being a problem without anyone having to take action.
If you *sort through* something, you go through things, to organize them or to find something:

I'm trying to sort out my travel arrangements but the agency never answers.
~ Don't worry. It'll sort itself out.
She sorted through the family photos, looking for one of her grandfather.

Set phrases

- **of sorts** = not a typical or good example of a thing
  The hotel does a breakfast of sorts.

- ❛ **… (and) that sort of thing** ❜ = and more things of that general type
  You get bread, jam, honey, rolls, that sort of thing.

- **out of sorts**
  What's the matter with Alison? ~ I'm not sure. She's just out of sorts.
  ▲ an informal way of saying you are ill, or upset

- ❛ **it takes all sorts …** ❜
  Did you see the way he ate his spaghetti!
  ~ It takes all sorts.
  ▲ to say that someone is behaving unusually, but that this is because people are different

Exercises

1 Look at these concordance lines with *sort*. Classify them according to whether:

a it means 'type' (Grammar patterns 1 and 2)
b it means 'not exactly' or it is a pause-filler (Grammar pattern 3)
c it is a verb.

a It can also **sort** of recognize your handwriting and convert it into text.
b I've always wanted to be the **sort** of woman who drove men wild.
c I had a few **sort** of pains, but I didn't think anything of them.
d Then she flopped on the sofa to **sort** through the letters.
e It just seems to me that we can get better results if we treat the, if we treat the **sort** of, well, for want of a better word, the local inhabitants with a certain amount of, of, of respect.
f How did they **sort** out the mess?
g You must have some **sort** of career.
h He started to **sort** his papers into a neat pile.
i 'Well, had you and Cindy had any – uh – **sort** of, you know, marital difficulties?'
j It's the **sort** of book that requires two hands to lift.
k People buy things for all **sorts** of reasons.

2 Use *sort of* to make the answers to these questions even less exact:

Did you like the film? ~ I liked it. → *I sort of liked it.*

a What colour are your boyfriend's eyes? ~ Blueish-green, I think.
b Do you know London well? ~ I know it, but not very well.
c Did Mark apologize? ~ Well, he apologized.
d Who do you look like? ~ Like my father, when he was young.
e How is your Russian? ~ I can speak it, but I can't write it at all.
f Can you play the piano? ~ Yes.

3 Other words for classifying things.

Look at these dictionary definitions:

sort: a group or type of things that are similar in a particular way
kind: a group of people or things that are the same in some way
type: a class or group of people or things that share particular features and are part of a larger group
make: the name or type of a machine, piece of equipment, etc. that is made by a particular company
brand: a type of product made by a particular company
model: a particular design or type of product
breed: a particular type of animal that has been developed by people in a controlled way

[from the *Oxford Advanced Learner's Dictionary*]

Choose words from the above list to complete these sentences. (Sometimes more than one word may be possible.)

a The latest .... s will be on display at the boat show.
b What .... of car does he drive? ~ A Peugeot.
c Do you know what your blood .... is?
d What .... of dog is that? ~ I think it's a Pekinese.
e They didn't have my usual .... of soap powder, so I had to buy this one.
f Do you know what .... of doctor she is? ~ She's a pediatrician.
g Why don't you fancy him? ~ He's not really my ....
h What is a quince? ~ It's a .... of fruit.

4 In this text one example of *sort/sorts* is used incorrectly. Can you find it?

My parents were moving house so they asked me to sort through my things. I'm the sort of person who tends to collect things, so you can imagine the sorts of things that had accumulated in my room over the years. I decided to sort everything into two piles: the things I didn't want, and the things I wanted to keep. Into the first pile went all sorts of toys and games. They were not worth keeping, since I don't have any sort of children of my own. It was more difficult when it came to the books, many of which had a sort of sentimental value for me. I am still attached to them, in an odd sort of way …

start

[regular verb: *start, started, started*] to begin, or to cause to begin: *It started to rain.* • *She started the engine.*
[noun] a beginning, e.g. of a period of time: *At the start of the school year …*

Grammar patterns

1   **start** | (+ adverbial)

The car won't start.
The concert started on time.
About the new job: when can I start?

▲ for talking about things getting into action

2   **start** | + NP

When do you start school?
We had just started dinner when the phone rang.
Shall I start the dishwasher?

▲ to talk about beginning a process, or causing it to begin

3   **start** | + -ing

It started snowing.
Has she started walking yet?
You can start writing now.

▲ to talk about an action or process beginning

4   **start** | + to-infinitive

I started to feel tired.
It was starting to get dark.
The baby started to cry.

▲ to talk about an action or process beginning.
   (Note that patterns 3 and 4 have the same meaning:
   It started snowing = It started to snow. However, you can't
   use –*ing* after *starting*: NOT ~~It was starting snowing.~~)

5   **start** | + NP | + -ing

That started me thinking.
Let's start the ball rolling (= let's make something begin
happening)

▲ to talk about causing a process to begin

6   a/the | (+ adjective) | + **start**

We'll need to make an early start.

▲ to indicate a positive or negative beginning to an action
   or process

Collocations

Some common nouns after *start* are: *a family, a/the fire, a list,
a (new) business, a new career, a new life, the day, the engine,
the process, the season, the week, things, work.*

Start combines with particles to form phrasal verbs:

If something *starts off,* it begins, or begins moving. (*The holiday
started off OK, but then …*)
If something *starts out,* it begins as one thing and changes into
something else. (*Frogs start out life as tadpoles.*)
If you *start out* on a journey, you begin it.
If you *start* something *up,* like an engine, you cause it to work.
If you *start up* a business, you bring it into existence. (*They're
planning to start up a travel agency.*)

Adjectives that frequently qualify *start* (noun) are:
good, great, bad, early, fresh, false, and *shaky.*

The meeting got off to a shaky start.
This plan won't work. I think it's time we made a fresh start.

Set phrases

·   **for a start / to start with …**
    *Why don't you like this restaurant? ~ Well, for a start, it's
    overpriced …*
    How can I help? ~ To start with, you could wash the glasses …
    ▲ for introducing a list of reasons or instructions

·   **from start to finish** = from the beginning to the end
    Their marriage was a disaster from start to finish.

·   **(right) from the start** = from the very beginning
    They never liked each other right from the start.

·   **get started** = start now what was planned
    It's getting late so I think we should get started.

- **give somebody/have a head start**
  My knowledge of Spanish gave me a head start when I went to Mexico.
  ▲ to talk about giving somebody an advantage or having an advantage

Exercises

❶ Look at these concordance lines for *start*. Identify the Grammar pattern (1–6) in each case. (There are two examples of each pattern.)

a People might also **start** to make a freer kind of music.
b I'm going to **start** working there part-time.
c He walked to his school, ready to **start** a new day.
d We are going to **start** to combat the transport congestion.
e Newsome had a bad **start** but ended up doing OK, I thought.
f Something outside **started** the dogs barking.
g Get a good night's sleep and **start** fresh in the morning.
h When pupils **start** playing, go round the class helping.
i New courses **start** every 2 weeks throughout the year.
j And after a nervous **start** he brought off some important saves.
k Someone always has to **start** the clapping.
l We'll get over to Number 10 and **start** the wheels turning.

❷ *Start* vs *begin*.

> You can often replace *start* with *begin*:
> It started to rain → *It began to rain.*
> However, this is not possible when *start* has the meaning of 'start a journey', 'cause something to happen', or 'start a machine working'.

In which of these sentences can you not replace *start* with *begin*?

a Your favourite programme starts in ten minutes.
b When does the lesson start?
c Kate's always trying to start an argument with me.
d The bus starts for Stonehenge in half an hour.
e The car won't start.
f It started snowing heavily.
g I usually start work at eight.
h Who started the fire?

❸ Complete these sentences with words from the list:

early	fresh	flying	on	a rumour
school	life	an argument	up	a fire

a Charlie Chaplin started .... as a music-hall artiste.
b If we are going to get there before dark, we need to start ....
c Someone started .... that she was not married.
d After his business collapsed he decided to make a .... start.
e I heard the noise of a car starting ....
f The appeal got off to a .... start when someone donated $1000.
g Kevin started .... about politics with his father.
h I started .... when I was five, but I didn't like it much.
i Sparks from the chimney started .... which quickly spread.
j I think you should make a start .... your project, if you are going to finish it by Friday.

❹ Read these instructions for a clothes dryer. The word *start(s)* is missing eight times. Can you replace it?

To the dryer, press the green button (A). If the dryer does not immediately, check that the door is closed properly, then it again. If it still won't, check that it is not overloaded. Remove some items if necessary.

Occasionally the dryer may to vibrate. If this happens, stop it, reload it, and it again.

Warning: do not the dryer if the red light (B) is flashing; this means the machine has overheated. If the red light flashing during a cycle, stop the dryer, and wait until the light stops flashing before re-starting it.

still

[adverb] (1) continuously, not finishing: *The electricity is still off.*
• *Are you still working for ABC?*
(2) however, despite this: *Even with a bad knee, he still managed to win.* • *Five euros is not much. Still, it's better than nothing.*
[adjective] not moving: *Keep still while I do your hair.*

Grammar patterns

1 NP | + **still** | + verb (+ …)
   NP | + is/was etc. | + **still** | (+ …)
   NP | + auxiliary/modal | + **still** | + verb

   He's 80, but he still swims every day.
   It was hot yesterday and it's still hot.
   I'm still waiting for a refund.

   ▲ to say that a situation continues to exist at or up to a
     particular time

2 NP | + **still** | + […] | + not

   The potatoes still aren't ready!
   The post still hasn't arrived.
   The lift still isn't working.

   ▲ to say that there's no change in a situation in which a
     change is expected

3 **still** | + comparative adjective or adverb
   comparative adjective or adverb | + **still**

   The bus got still more crowded at each stop.
   It was cold yesterday, but today is colder still.

   ▲ to emphasize a difference

4 utterance. | + **Still** | + utterance

   I'm not earning much. Still, it's better than nothing.
   He's totally unreliable. Still, he is my brother.

   ▲ to say that what you have just said is not really a problem

Collocations

Still is the adverb most frequently used with continuous verb
structures:

   It was still raining.
   Are you still living in Ealing?

'Still + not' is common with the present and past perfect:

   I still haven't paid the electricity bill.
   It was midnight and the band still hadn't arrived.

Still often occurs in contexts with *even if* or *even though*:

   Even though you are a tourist, you still need a visa.
   The coast is still beautiful, even if it is a bit touristy.

Set phrases

• **still […] to go** = remaining
   There are still ten days to go before the wedding.

• **it's still early days**
   She doesn't like her new job but it's still early days.
   ▲ to say it's too early to know what will happen

"ARE YOU STILL HERE?"

Exercises

❶ Position of *still* in the sentence.

In Grammar patterns 1 and 2, *still* usually comes:

- before the main verb (*my tooth still hurts; they are still eating.*)
- after the verb to be (*the baby is still asleep.*)
- after positive modal verbs (*I can still smell it.*)
- before any negative words or contractions (*It still hasn't rained.*)
- less usually, it can go at the end of the sentence (*I can hear it still.*)

Put *still* in the correct place <u>inside</u> these sentences (i.e. not at the end):

a   I am learning Chinese.
b   They won't answer the phone.
c   At 5 a.m. it is dark.
d   I can remember the song you taught me.
e   Is it raining?
f   Even twenty years later, I dream of Milford Sound.
g   It was not summer.
h   I can't drive.
i   Do you live in Maple Terrace?
j   The water should be hot.

❷ Complete these sentences like this:

It was raining yesterday and *it is still raining.*

a   He was lazy as a child and ....
b   I have been waiting for an hour and ....
c   My tooth hurt yesterday and ....
d   He was watching TV three hours ago and ....
e   They were learning English when they were eight and ....
f   I felt ill this morning and ....
g   She loved horse riding when she was young and ....
h   The tap was dripping last week and ....

❸ *Still* contrasts with the adverbs *yet* and *already*.

Already is used in positive sentences to talk about things happening earlier than expected:

I've already had breakfast. (OR: *I've had breakfast already*)
Have you had breakfast already? (OR: *Have you already had breakfast?*)

Yet is used in negative sentences and questions to talk about something that has not happened before a particular time, but is expected to happen later:

I haven't had breakfast yet.
Have you had breakfast yet?

Still means that a situation is continuing, or has continued longer than you expected:

I am still having breakfast.
I still haven't had breakfast.

Note that these two sentences are similar in meaning:

I haven't had breakfast yet.
I still haven't had breakfast.

But the second sentence is more emphatic, and may mean you are annoyed.

Put *still, yet,* or *already* into the underlined sentences:

a   I asked you to write an essay. <u>Have you done it</u>? ~ No. <u>I am doing it</u>.
b   <u>Have you had lunch</u>? That was quick!
c   I've tried and tried, but <u>I haven't passed my driving test</u>.
d   I've been in Egypt one day but <u>I haven't seen the Pyramids</u>.
e   I've been in Egypt five months and <u>I haven't seen the Pyramids</u>.
f   Do you want to read the newspaper? ~ No. <u>I've read it</u>.
g   <u>He's only 19</u> and <u>he's graduated</u>.
h   You go on without me. <u>I'm not ready</u>. <u>I'm getting dressed</u>.

stop

[regular verb: *stop, stopped, stopped*] to move no longer; to end, or prevent, something happening; opposite of *start*: *The bus didn't stop.* • *Stop doing that!* • *I stopped a policeman and asked him the way.*
[noun] action or place of stopping: *Is this our stop?*

→ start

Grammar patterns

1 **stop** | (+ adverbial)

The clock just stopped.
Let's stop now, and have something to eat.
We'll stop at one o'clock.

▲ to talk about an activity ending or pausing

2 **stop** | + NP

Stop that taxi!
A woman stopped me and tried to sell me flowers.
He was stopped by the police, and searched.

▲ to talk about causing something or someone not to move

3 **stop** | + -ing

My knee got better when I stopped running.
Stop playing with your food!

▲ to talk about not doing something any more

4 **stop** | + NP | (+ from) | + -ing

How do you stop the engine overheating?
They managed to stop him from jumping.

▲ to talk about preventing someone or something from doing something

5 **stop** | + to-infinitive / for + NP

Half way up the tower we stopped to admire the view.
If you always stop to think about the grammar, you'll never be fluent.
Let's stop for lunch.

▲ to talk about pausing one activity in order to do something else

6 **stop** | + and | + verb

A number of people stopped and stared.

▲ to talk about pausing one activity in order to do something else

Collocations

Adverbials that often go with stop are: *abruptly, dead* (*in your tracks*), *immediately, short,* and *suddenly.*

The train stopped abruptly.
There was a noise in the other room, and we stopped dead in our tracks.
He heard his name and stopped short.

Stop combines with some adverb particles to form phrasal verbs:

If you *stop by,* you visit someone briefly.
If you *stop off* or *stop over* at a place when you are travelling somewhere, you break your journey there.

I'll stop by and see if you are feeling better.
On our way to Townsville we stopped off in Rockhampton.
I'd like to stop over in Singapore for a day, if that's possible.

The phrase *a stop* is used to talk about a complete halt:

If you *bring something to a stop,* you make something stop. (*He managed to bring the lorry to a stop.*)
If you *put a stop to something,* you prevent something from happening. (*The government wants to put a stop to under-age drinking.*)

Set phrases

· **' stop it! '**
Stop it! You're hurting me!
▲ to tell someone not to do something, usually unpleasant

· **stop at nothing**
He'll stop at nothing to get what he wants.
▲ to be prepared to do anything, even if it is wrong, to obtain something

Exercises

1 Classify these concordance lines with *stop*, according to their Grammar pattern (1–6). (There are two of each.)

a If you get lost just **stop** and ask.
b He would have liked to **stop** for a chat.
c When they **stop** working they need to readjust.
d The train was a slow one that **stopped** at every station.
e It was lack of money that **stopped** them going away.
f He **stopped** me last Friday in the High Street.
g It never **stopped** raining and our clothes were wet through.
h If a stranger **stops** and offers to help, don't get out of the car.
i Instead of **stopping** to help her, he carried on driving.
j There is nothing **stopping** you from using your machine.
k The family **stopped** to watch the band as they went by.
l The film had to be **stopped** for seven minutes.

2 *-ing* or *to-infinitive*.
Choose the best way of completing these sentences:

a When it got too dark, we stopped (*to play/playing*) and went inside.
b In Crewe we stopped (*to change/changing*) trains.
c For your health's sake, you should really stop (*to smoke/smoking*).
d He stopped (*to smoke/smoking*) a cigarette and consult the map.
e Your tennis serve will improve if you stop (*to think/thinking*) about it.
f I'm sorry we are late: we had to stop (*to change/changing*) a tyre.

3 *Stop* is an 'ergative verb' – that is to say it has two patterns, one without an object and one with an object:

The car stopped.
Jeff stopped the car.

The meaning is similar, but in the first we don't know what caused the car to stop. In the second we do know.

Other ergative verbs used in similar contexts to *stop* are:
start, begin, end, open, shut, close, and *continue.*

Look at this dialogue:

A: **Did you stop the dishwasher?**
B: *No, it just stopped.*

Write similar responses to these questions:

a Did you break the door handle? ~ ....
b Did you crack the mirror? ~ ....
c Did you shut the garage doors? ~ ....
d Did you burn the potatoes? ~ ....
e Did you start the pump? ~ ....
f Did you open the windows?~ ....

4 *Stop, end, finish.*

End and *finish* have the idea of completion. (→ end)
Stop has the idea of halting or pausing, often with a notion of incompletion.

Completion:
The teacher ended the lesson with a game.
The lesson ended and we went home.
Finish your homework/dinner/work!
Have you finished writing? ~ Yes, I've done all the exercises.

Incompletion:
The teacher stopped the tape and asked us some questions.
Why have you stopped writing? ~ I'm tired.

Choose the best verb (*end, finish, stop*) to complete these sentences. (In some cases there are two possible answers.)

a We'd like to .... the concert with a song we wrote ourselves.
b They had to .... the football match because of the rain.
c What time does the film .... ?
d I don't know how to .... the printer.
e You didn't .... your breakfast.
f Our lifestyles were so different, we had to .... our relationship.
g The trains .... running at midnight.
h When you .... doing the last exercise, you can have a break.

take

[irregular verb: *take, took, taken*] (1) move something to another place: *Take your umbrella with you.* • *I'll take Gran her tea.* (2) perform an action: *Stand there and I'll take a photo.* • *Let's take a walk.* (3) accept or receive: *Do you take travellers' cheques?*

Grammar patterns

1 **take** | + NP | (+ adverbial)

Take these trousers to the drycleaners.
I was taken to a very smart restaurant.

▲ to talk about moving something or someone from one place to another

2 **take** | + NP | + NP

Can you take Graham this book?
I was thinking of taking my mother some flowers.

▲ to talk about moving something to someone

3 **take** | (+ NP) | + time expression | (+ to-infinitive)

How long does the flight take?
It takes me twenty minutes to get to work.
This painting must have taken you ages.

▲ to talk about the duration of journeys or actions

Collocations

Take collocates with many nouns to form compound verb phrases. For example:

transport: *take the bus, take the train, take a taxi, take the metro.*
food and medicine: *take milk (in your coffee), take sugar, take drugs, take a pill.*
daily routine: *take a shower, take a nap, take a break, take a walk.*
exams: *take an exam, take a test.*
control: *take control, take the lead, take power, take responsibility, take office.*
others include: *take place, take part, take pity, take offence, take advice.*

Take combines with many particles to form phrasal verbs:

If you *take after* someone, you resemble them in some way.
If you *take* something *away*, you remove it to another place.
If you *take* an amount *away* from another amount, you subtract it.
If you *take back* something that you have bought, you return it to the shop where you bought it.
If you *take back* something that you have said, you admit you were wrong.
If you *take in* (or *up*) an item of clothing, you make it narrower (or shorter) so that it fits.
If you are *taken in* by something, you are tricked by it.
If you *take off* your clothes, you get undressed.
If a plane *takes off,* it leaves the ground.
If a business or an idea *takes off,* it becomes successful.
If you *take on* a job or an assignment, you agree to do it.
If you *take* someone *out,* you take them to be entertained.
If you *take* something *over,* you become responsible for it, or in control of it.
If you *take to* something or someone, you start to like it or enjoy it.
If you *take up* an activity or an offer, you start doing it or you accept it.
If something *takes up* your time, it consumes your time.

Set phrases

· **take […], for example …**
Not all teachers are good learners. Take me, for example …
▲ to give an example of what you have been talking about

· ‘**I take your point**’ = I see what you mean (although I may not agree with you).
I take your point, but don't you think …?

· ‘**take it from me / take my word for it**’
Aliens are watching us. Take it from me.
▲ to persuade someone that what you are saying is true

Exercises

1 Take and bring.

> You *take* something when you *go* to a place, and you *bring* something when you *come* to a place.

Choose the best word to complete these sentences:

a When you come, can you .... your camera with you?
b If you go to the mountains, ... lots of warm clothes.
c Can you .... this bowl back to Mrs Denham?
d We'd love to come to your party. What shall we .... ?
e We're going to Lucy's party. Shouldn't we .... something?
f Can I help? ~ Yes, can you .... this rubbish out?
g Can I help? ~ Yes, can you .... in some firewood. It's cold in here.
h What shall I do with your suitcase? ~ .... it here.

2 In these sentences the words beginning with *p* have been misplaced. Can you put them where they belong?

a I was invited to take pity in a television discussion.
b The council hopes citizens will take part in their city, and not throw rubbish everywhere.
c The army took pleasure by means of a military coup.
d The Olympic Games take power every four years.
e I took pride on the homeless cat and gave it some milk.
f She took place in simple things, like gardening and cooking.

3 Rewrite these sentences, using phrasal verbs with *take* in place of the underlined words or phrases:

a My new hairdryer doesn't work! ~ Well, <u>return</u> it!
b I was <u>fooled</u> by the letter, and sent them $100.
c My time is <u>filled</u> just looking after the children.
d Who do you <u>resemble</u>: your father or your mother?
e In his old age he <u>started doing</u> dangerous sports like hang-gliding.
f I've <u>agreed to do</u> the job of designing our new catalogue.
g <u>Remove</u> your shirt so the doctor can X-ray your chest.
h Would you like to <u>relieve me of</u> the driving: I'm feeling tired.
i I think the cat has <u>started to like</u> you.
j We opened a branch in Beijing and the business really <u>became successful</u>.

4 Idioms with *take*.
Match the two parts of these sentences:

a It was a really convincing speech. You have to take …
b I'm offering you a 5% increase. That's my last offer. Take …
c The case for better schools is inarguable. It is taken …
d The government will fight back. It's not going to take …
e When they suddenly announced their engagement everyone was taken …
f Ben, you're going to have to decide. It's time you took …
g You paid $1000 for this rubbish! I think you've been taken …
h I'm afraid you're going to have to believe me. You have to take …

1 the bull by the horns.
2 it or leave it.
3 this lying down.
4 for a ride.
5 as read.
6 your hat off to her.
7 my word for it.
8 by surprise.

"YOU'LL HAVE TO TAKE MY WORD FOR IT!"

tell

[irregular verb: *tell, told, told*] (1) give or reveal information: *You should tell the doctor about it.* • *Who broke this? ~ I'm not telling.* (2) order: *They told us to go away.* (3) recognize, judge: *Both cars look the same: I can't tell which is mine.*

Grammar patterns

1 tell | + NP | (+ about) | + NP

I told Jeremy the facts.
Did you tell your dad about the accident?

▲ to talk about giving information to someone, about something

2 tell | + NP | + that-clause

The receptionist told me that Mr Hobbs was in a meeting.
Did I tell you Marilyn's had a baby?

▲ to report what people say

3 tell | + NP | + wh-clause

You have to tell the immigration officer how long you are staying and how much money you are bringing with you.

▲ to report answers to questions

4 tell | + NP | + wh | + to-infinitive

Could you tell me when to get off, please?
Stop telling me what to do.

▲ to report orders or advice

5 'quote' | + **tell** | + NP

'I love you, Diana,' Gregory told her, adoringly.
'You can do it,' I told myself.

▲ to report speech or thoughts directly

6 tell | + NP | (+ not) | + to-infinitive

Tell the children to be quiet.
I told her not to worry.

▲ to give orders or advice

7 tell | + that-clause/wh-clause

His mum could tell he was lying.
I can't tell which is which.

▲ to talk about forming a correct judgement about something

Collocations

The following nouns often follow *tell* in the pattern 'tell + NP': *the truth, a lie, a story, tales, a joke, the time, the difference.*

I cannot tell a lie: it was me who did it.
He started his talk by telling a joke.
Has she learned to tell the time yet?

The modal verbs *can't/couldn't/not be able* are often used with *tell,* in the sense of recognizing or judging things:

I can't tell who it is from here.
What piece were they playing? ~ I couldn't tell.

Two phrasal verbs are formed from *tell*:

If you can *tell* people or things *apart,* you can recognize the differences between them. (*I can't tell the twins apart.*)
If you *tell* someone *off,* you criticize them for something they have done. (*She told the children off for throwing stones.*)

Set phrases

- **'I tell you / I'm telling you'**
  I'm telling you, it was an accident.
  ▲ to emphasize that what you are saying is the truth

- **'to tell (you) the truth'**
  You look tired. ~ I'm not feeling very well, to tell you the truth.
  ▲ to indicate what you really think or feel

- **'don't tell me …'**
  Don't tell me you forgot the onions!
  ▲ to show surprise

- **'you're telling me!'**
  That was a really dull class! ~ You're telling me!
  ▲ to say that you strongly agree

- ' **I'll tell you what … / I tell you what …** '
  I tell you what, why don't we move the table against the wall?
  ▲ to introduce a suggestion

- **time will tell**
  Do you think their marriage will work? ~ Time will tell.
  ▲ to say that the outcome will be clear later

Exercises

❶ Study these concordance lines with *tell* and classify them according to the Grammar patterns 1 to 7. (There are two examples for each pattern.)

a Give my regards to your father and **tell** him not to worry.
b The state should **tell** firms how to attract and keep good staff.
c His father **told** him the names of the stars.
d 'Oh, no,' Annabelle **told** them, 'I think you've got the wrong idea.'
e You'd better not **tell** Clare why I'm leaving.
f I can't see the park any more, so it's hard to **tell** where I am.
g He didn't **tell** anyone about her visits.
h Mrs Dean **told** him she had some news.
i Should she **tell** Hassan what she knew?
j The young man said he would **tell** her when to get off.
k 'Don't be stupid ,' Marie **told** herself, sternly.
l Thieves can **tell** who is at home and who is out at work.
m You can **tell** her that I'll be calling on her tomorrow.
n I meant to **tell** Mrs Hennessey not to disturb you.

❷ Put the word in brackets in the correct place in each sentence:

a (you) Would you like me to tell a story?
b (it) I know a good joke. ~ Tell to us.
c (that) She told her boyfriend she didn't want to see him any more.
d (myself) I told to be brave and not to worry.
e (to) The teacher told him go home.
f (one) How do you tell from another?
g (told) 'The car won't start,' Matthew me.
h (how) Can you tell me to use the scanner?
i (to) Tell me when we get the turn-off.
j (what) I tell you: let's go to the beach.

❸ *Tell* and *say*.

Note that, when you are reporting speech, *tell* always has a person as its object, but *say* can never have a person as its object. If you want to mention the person, you have to use *to* after *say*:

I told him he was late. 'You are late,' I told him.
I said he was late. 'You are late,' I said (to him).

Choose the correct verb to complete these sentences:

a Can you (*tell/say*) us the way, please?
b 'It's getting late,' I (*told/said*).
c (*Tell/Say*) the waiter to bring some more wine.
d Terry (*said/told*) she was going to have a bath.
e Andy McKay (*was telling/was saying*) me about his son's operation.
f Can you (*tell/say*) me the time, please?
g The guidebook (*tells/says*) that the cathedral is Romanesque.
h 'The museum is closed,' the woman (*told/said*) me.
i Can you (*tell/say*) me where the nearest bank is?
j Why didn't you (*tell/say*) you were hungry?

❹ Complete the text, by choosing the correct form of either *say* or *tell* to fill each space:

Derek (a) ………… me this rather pathetic joke the other day. There is this woman on a train, carrying a baby, a really ugly baby, and this drunk man sits down opposite her, and he (b) ………… to the woman, 'That's a really ugly baby.' And she (c) ………… , 'I beg your pardon?' and he (d) ………… , 'That's the ugliest baby I've ever seen'. And he carries on (e) ………… her how ugly the baby is, until eventually she pulls the emergency cord, and the guard comes. The guard (f) ………… , 'What's the matter?' And the woman (g) ………… him that the drunk man has been insulting her. So the guard (h) ………… the drunk to go away, and he (i) ………… to the woman, 'I'm very sorry about that. Look, as an apology, we will give you a free meal in the dining car'. And he (j) ………… , 'What's more, I'll see if I can find a banana for your monkey'.

than

[conjunction and preposition] joins two parts of a comparison:
She earns more than I do. • *It is warmer today than yesterday.*
• *I would rather read a good book than watch TV.*

→ more
→ as

Grammar patterns

1 comparative adjective/adverb | (+ NP) | + **than** |
   + clause

   The city was much less chaotic than I expected.
   Madonna can sing better than she can act.
   My dad has more hair than I do.

   ▲ to make comparisons

1a comparative adjective/adverb | (+ NP) | + **than** |
   + NP/-ing

   William is a bit older than me.
   Is this a more powerful computer than your old one?
   E-mailing is so much easier than writing letters.

   ▲ to make comparisons

1b comparative adjective/adverb | (+ NP) | + **than** |
   + adjective/adverb/preposition

   Jennifer seemed less talkative than usual.
   In those days people were more friendly than now.
   Air travel is much more of a hassle than in the old days.

   ▲ to make comparisons

2 would rather | + bare infinitive | + **than**

   I'd rather go to the movies than go bowling.

   ▲ to state preferences

Collocations

More than and *less than* are often followed by amounts:

> *There were more than a million people on the march.*
> *The amount of plastic that is recycled is less than 1%.*

Adjectives and participles that follow *than* in Grammar pattern
1b include: *normal, usual, average, expected,* and *predicted.*

> *The rainfall was higher than average.*
> *The results of the tests were better than predicted.*

Adverbs that follow *than* in Grammar pattern 1b include:
before, ever, then, and *now.*

> *The beach was more crowded than ever.*

The adjective *different* is often followed by *than*, especially in
American English (where British English prefers *from*):

> *The response to the survey was different than expected.*

Other and *rather* can be followed by *than*:

> *We didn't have time to see much, other than the
> main monuments.*
> *I think it was a case of stupidity rather than bravery.*

Set phrases

· **more often than not** = usually
  More often than not he'll be wearing odd socks.

· **better late than never**
  I'm sorry I'm late. ~ Better late than never!
  ▲ to excuse the lateness of something or somebody

Exercises

1 **Put the words in brackets into the correct place in each sentence:**

a (do) You seem to have more work than I.
b (than) The rock concert was attended by more two thousand fans.
c (much) He can write more correctly than he can speak.
d (than) You'll find the place less peaceful before.
e (to) I go home less often than I used.
f (rather) I'd eat in than go out.
g (other) She doesn't see anyone than her immediate family.
h (not) More often than the train is late.

2 **Match the two parts of these sentences:**

a The pace of life was slower then …
b I'd rather walk …
c Bob found Chinese more difficult …
d Your mobile phone is heavier …
e Ellen can speak better Chinese …
f The bus is less expensive …
g Carmen is a much better cook …
h This month has been colder …

1 than mine.
2 than take a taxi.
3 than normal.
4 than I can.
5 than it is now.
6 than a taxi.
7 than he expected.
8 than me.

3 **Rewrite these sentences so that they include *than*:**

Jules is not as tall as Simon. → *Simon is taller than Jules.*

a White-o is not as expensive as Blanc-o.
b My brother isn't as old as me.
c I'm not as intelligent as him.
d It doesn't rain as much here as it does on the coast.
e Madonna can't dance as well as she can sing.
f It isn't as cold today as it was yesterday.
g Spanish isn't as easy as I expected.
h The milkman doesn't pass by now as often as he used to.

4 **Idioms and sayings with *than*.**
Match the two parts of these exchanges:

a Let's try and persuade the boss we need a pay rise.
b Rather than appoint me, he appointed his brother.
c At last! Here comes Henry with the photocopies.
d I couldn't have done the report without your help.
e The topic I chose for my assignment is turning into a real headache.
f I don't think we know enough about this new pay deal yet.

1 ~ Better late than never.
2 ~ It seems that you've bitten off more than you can chew.
3 ~ Yes, there's more to it than meets the eye.
4 ~ As they say, blood is thicker than water.
5 ~ Easier said than done.
6 ~ Two heads are better than one.

that

Grammar patterns

1 **that** | (+ NP/one)

That is your bed there.
This is my racket so whose is that one?
I'm not well. ~ Why's that?

  ▴ to refer to things or people not near you, or to refer to what has just been said or done (→ this)

2 verb | + **that**-clause

Sandy said that you phoned.
We all agreed that it was a difficult exam.

  ▴ to report what people say, with verbs like *say, agree, deny, suggest,* etc. (→ say)

The police don't think that it was an accident.
I hope that Khaled can come.
Did you notice that she was crying?

  ▴ to talk about what people believe, hope, or remember, or what they see, hear, etc. (→ think)

3 verb | + NP | + **that**-clause

Someone told me that she had resigned.
I reminded Nat that he owed me a meal.

  ▴ to report what people say, using verbs like *tell.* (→ tell)

4 it | + is/was etc. | + past participle | + **that**-clause

It is reported that three people are still missing.
It has been suggested that Mr MacFee was lying.

  ▴ to say that something is said or believed without saying by whom

5 is/was etc. | + adjective | + **that**-clause

I was sure that it was Friday.
We are glad that our team won.

  ▴ to express beliefs and feelings about situations

6 NP | + **that**-clause

Rescue efforts continue in the hope that more survivors are found.
It's always been a great regret that I never met Freire.

  ▴ to express beliefs and feelings about situations

7 NP | + **that** [= subject] | + verb
  NP | (+ **that** [= object]) | + NP [= subject] | + verb

Have you seen the new guy that works here?
The woman (that) you spoke to is called Maria.

  ▴ to identify the exact person or thing you are referring to. (This is called a defining relative clause. → who)

Collocations

Common verbs in Grammar pattern 2 are: *believe, feel, find, guess* (AmE), *know, say, see, show,* and *think.*

Common verbs in Grammar pattern 3 are: *advise, inform, persuade, promise, remind, show, teach, tell, bet, advise, inform, persuade, promise,* and *warn.*

Common adjectives in Grammar pattern 5 are:
(to express beliefs) *sure, certain, confident, positive, right*
(to express feelings) *afraid, amazed, disappointed, glad, pleased, proud, sorry, surprised, worried.*

Common nouns in Grammar pattern 6 are: *fact, idea, hope, possibility, doubt, impression, suggestion, belief, sign, conclusion.*

Set phrases

• **'that's right.'**
  You're a new student here, aren't you? ~ That's right, yes.
  ▴ to say that you agree or understand

• **'that's all right / that's OK'** = it doesn't matter
  I'm sorry about the mess. I'll clean it up. ~That's all right. Don't worry about it.

- **that is / that is to say**
  The book is autobiographical: that is to say, it's based on his childhood memories.
  I like cooking, that is, if I have the time.
  ▲ to explain something more clearly, or to correct yourself

- **'that's that'**
  It's settled: we're going to Benidorm, and that's that.
  ▲ to say that you have finally finished or decided something

Exercises

❶ Where *that*-clauses follow verbs or adjectives (Grammar patterns 2, 3, and 5), the word *that* can usually be omitted, especially in informal language and after *think* and *say*:

She said that she was not feeling very well.
(= She said she was not feeling very well.)
It's likely that the match will be postponed.
(= It's likely the match will be postponed.)

In Grammar pattern 7, *that* can be omitted only if it stands for the object of the relative clause:
Is this the book (that) you wanted?
But NOT: ~~Is this the book has the answers?~~

Look at these concordance lines, and decide if *that* can be omitted or not:

a Sales in April from stores **that** were open a year ago rose 2%.
b Deep down my wife thinks **that** I'm a pessimist.
c My father tried making me a wooden train but **that** didn't satisfy me.
d Is there a cure **that** they do not know about?
e They write good solid songs **that** are tuneful.
f Before you begin, make sure **that** you are comfortable.
g Never tell anyone **that** you are alone in the house.
h He always got **that** train, he was entirely reliable.

❷ Classify these concordance examples of *that*, according to the Grammar patterns 1–7. (There are two of each pattern.)

a Tell her **that** she can stay if she likes.
b It was said **that** a massacre had followed.
c What was **that** animal? Would it have killed us?
d The wildlife **that** we destroy has as much right to be on the planet as us.
e She told me **that** she did not quite know where to begin.
f Before you begin, make sure **that** you are comfortable.
g They write good solid songs **that** are tuneful.
h They say **that** cleanliness is a virtue.
i Freud introduced the idea **that** a part of the ego is unconscious too.
j I know you will all be happy **that** we have chosen your magazine.
k Would you say **that** you have many people you could talk to?
l I'll come down and talk to you about **that**.
m It is believed **that** more can be done to reduce risk.
n Be conscious of the fact **that** this is a tranquil and a peaceful place.

❸ Six obligatory and two optional examples of *that* have been removed from this text. Can you put them back?

The stethoscope is an instrument is used to listen to a patient's breathing and heart beat. It was an invention changed medical practice. It enabled doctors to diagnose diseases were concealed until then, such as tuberculosis.
   But it should not be assumed all doctors and patients were enthusiastic about the invention. When they saw the doctor with his stethoscope some patients thought they were going to be operated on, because, at time, it was only surgeons used medical instruments. The idea people were afraid of stethoscopes now seems ridiculous.

❹ Use words from the list to complete these sentences:

news   agreement   evidence   suggested   fact
doubt   realize   impression believe   seems

a We are both in .... that Tomas is the best student.
b I was under the .... that you were available.
c People used to .... that the world was flat.
d Andrew .... that we should buy Fiona a book.
e It .... that Petra is having problems at work.
f It is a well-known .... that smoking is bad for you.
g There was no .... that things were cheaper then.
h I was surprised by the .... that he'd resigned.
i When did you .... that Jan and I are married?
j There is .... that someone has been cheating.

the

[definite article] (1) used before all types of nouns when your listener or reader knows which person or thing you are referring to, because:
(a) it is the only one present: *It's in the oven*; or
(b) it is the only one in your shared world: *I'll meet you at the station;* or in the whole world: *The moon was full that night;* or
(c) because it has been referred to before: *Put a pin close to a magnet and the pin will cling to the magnet;* or
(d) because you are specifying which one, by adding more information: *The woman sitting next to me teaches yoga.*

(2) used before singular countable nouns and some adjectives when you are talking about all things of that type: *The Blue Whale grows to 30m long.* • *I am teaching myself to play the guitar.* • *The aged outnumber the young.*

→ a/an

Grammar patterns

1 **the** | + NP

Can I borrow the lawnmower?
The neighbours are arguing again.

▲ to refer to things when both the speaker and the listener know what is being referred to

The computer has changed our lives.
She has written a book about the chimpanzee.

▲ to make general statements, using one thing as an example of its class

2 **the** | + adjective/NP | + NP

You put bottles in the green bin, and paper in the blue one.
I'll meet you at the train station, not the bus station.

▲ to say which thing you are talking about

3 **the** | + first, last etc. | (+ NP)

I was the last to arrive and the only man there.
What would you like to drink? ~ The usual.

▲ to specify things that are unique, using adjectives like *first, last, next, same, main, only, usual, wrong,* etc.

4 **the** | + superlative | (+ NP)

Everest is the highest mountain in the world.
Who is the tallest in your class?

▲ to talk about the one person or thing that has more of a quality than others of that type

5 **the** | + NP | + preposition | + NP
the | + NP | + relative clause or participle

The letters on your desk arrived this morning.
Who is the President of Peru?
The place we liked best was Queenstown.
Go and talk to the woman sitting by the door.

▲ to specify exactly which thing or things you are talking about

6 **the** | + adjective

The rich are getting richer, and the poor are getting poorer.

▲ to talk about all the people who have the same characteristic

7 **the** + comparative, | … **the** + comparative

The more you practise, the better you will become.

▲ to say how one thing changes in relation to another

Collocations

The following noun groups are usually preceded by *the*:

nationalities: *the Irish, the Swiss, the Japanese,* etc.
geographical regions: *the north, the coast, the mainland,* etc.
times and events: *the holidays, the nineties, the summer, the war,* etc.
shops, etc.: *the chemist's, the doctor's, the supermarket,* etc.
transport: *the bus, the metro, the train,* etc.
musical instruments: *the piano, the violin, the drums,* etc.
jobs around the home: *the ironing, the shopping,* etc.
many proper names: *the UN, The Times, the South Pole,* etc.

Set phrases

- **the sooner the better** = as soon as possible
  You'll have to tell him, and the sooner the better.

- **the more the merrier**
  I like big classes: the more the merrier, I say.
  ▲ to say that it doesn't matter how many people participate

Exercises

❶ There are ten examples of *the* in this text. How do you know which thing or person the writer is referring to, in each case?

a because it is the only one in the immediate situation.
b because it is the only one anywhere.
c because it has been referred to before, in the text.
d because the writer is specifying which one, by adding extra information:

Neil Armstrong was <u>the</u> first person to set foot on <u>the</u> surface of <u>the</u> moon. In <u>the</u> picture you can see him stepping out of <u>the</u> spacecraft *Eagle*. <u>The</u> words that he then said are famous: 'That's one small step for a man, one giant leap for mankind'. He and his co-pilot Buzz Aldrin then planted a flag and collected rocks. <u>The</u> flag is probably still there. <u>The</u> rocks have helped scientists understand <u>the</u> history of <u>the</u> solar system.

❷ Put *the* where it belongs in these contexts (one example per context):

a She speaks French and is learning violin.
b What is best restaurant in town?
c My favourite room at home is kitchen.
d A couple walked in and man was carrying a big bunch of flowers.
e Generally I like fish but I don't like ones with bones.
f In our town there are two banks. One is next to Town Hall.
g You can borrow any coat except red one: it's mine.
h Valencia is famous for oranges and beauty of its women.
i I saw Michael Douglas last night. ~ Not Michael Douglas?
j A taxi stopped and two men got out. Taxi drove off.

❸ To make general statements about a class of things, you can use *the* with countable nouns:

The brown bear hibernates in winter.

To make general statements about uncountable or plural things, use no article ('zero article'):

Bears hibernate in winter. (NOT ~~The bears …~~)
Bears like honey. (NOT ~~the honey~~)

To talk about specific and definite things, use *the* with all nouns (countable and uncountable; singular and plural):

The bears in the zoo never hibernate.
I like the honey they make in my village.

To talk about specific but indefinite things, use *a/an* with singular countable nouns, and zero article with plural and uncountable nouns:

He was chased by a bear.
I saw bears in the zoo, eating honey.
(→ a/an)

Complete this text by adding *the*, but only where necessary:

DODO: .... dodo is an extinct bird, belonging to .... pigeon family. .... dodos lived on .... islands and couldn't fly. In .... seventeenth century, ... sailors started visiting .... islands, looking for .... food and .... water. .... sailors hunted .... dodos and ate them. .... last dodo died in 1790.

then

[adverb] (1) at that time: *We moved to Bristol in 1986. ~ How old were you then?* • *I'll be home at eight. Can you phone me then?* (2) after that: *Type your user name and then your password.* • *Fry the onions and then add chopped ham.* (3) in that case: *If you are going to the conference then I will go too.* • *Are we all agreed then?*

Grammar patterns

1   clause | + **then**
    then | + clause

We met in 1998. We were both students then.
I'm seeing Jeff tonight so I'll ask him then.

▲ to refer to a previously mentioned time in the past or in the future

My shoes are wet. ~ Then put them in front of the fire.
The phone's ringing and I'm in the bath. ~ I'll get it then.

▲ to show that what you are saying is a consequence of what has just been said

2   first/to start with etc. … | (+ and) **then** …

First you chop some tomatoes. Then you fry them …
First of all, close all programs you're working on. Then shut down the computer …

▲ to give instructions in sequence

To start with, I do a rough sketch. Then I ink in the outline. Then I scan it …
First, we took the ferry across and then we caught the local bus.

▲ to recount events in sequence

3   when/if | + clause, | + **then** | + clause

If she finds out, then I am in trouble.
If you like spicy food, then you will like this.

▲ to talk about the logical result of a situation

Collocations

Then, as a time adverb, is often preceded by prepositions or adverbs, such as *back, by, from […] (on), since, just,* and *until*:

I first went to Cairns in the sixties. Back then, it was a real frontier town.
We got there at twelve but by then the restaurant had closed.
She started acupuncture six months ago, and since then her back has improved a lot.
Just then, I heard a shout.

In conversation, *then* is often preceded by other discourse markers, to show a change of topic, to get attention, or to sum up what has been said:

Now then, what's this about you going to Brussels?
OK then, who's going to serve?
Right then, are we ready to go?
Well then, that explains everything.

Set phrases

· **then and there / there and then** = immediately
  If you are lucky they will give you the visa there and then.

· **but then / but then again**
  The train is late. But then, it is always late.
  ▲ to show that what you said is not surprising

· **now and then** = occasionally
  Do you see Deborah much? ~ Now and then.

· **from then on**
  From then on, everything went well.
  ▲ to say that something started at a point in time and continued

Exercises

1 **Linking events in a sequence. Choose linking words from the list to complete this text:**

then (x 2)   finally   next   first   before that   eventually

How do you climb Mount Hopeless?

(a) .... you walk up the valley, following the river.
(b) .... you start climbing. Oh, I forgot, (c) .... you have to cross the river. You go through a forest and (d) .... you come to a lake. (e) .... it's a long climb, but (f) .... you come out onto a plateau, and, (g) .... , after a short climb, you reach the summit.

2 **Match the two parts of each exchange:**

a   I'm cold.
b   Arnie is being awful.
c   The baby is crying.
d   Mother is coming to stay.
e   I'm starving.
f   It's getting late.
g   This shirt doesn't fit.
h   Let's have an omelette for supper.

1   ~ Then feed her.
2   ~ I'll make lunch then.
3   ~ Then try another size.
4   ~ Put a sweater on then.
5   ~ Let's call a taxi then.
6   ~ Then I'm leaving.
7   ~ I'll get some eggs then.
8   ~ Then leave him.

3 **Choose words from the list to complete these sentences:**

since   from   just   back   until   by

a   I started writing in 1970. .... then I was using a typewriter.
b   She stopped smoking ten years ago. .... then she's never had a single cigarette.
c   He left Australia in 1992. .... then on he travelled a lot before settling in Japan.
d   I lit the barbecue. .... then the rain started.
e   I'll pick you up at eight thirty. Will you be ready .... then?
f   When I was 12 my mother took me to see *The Magic Flute*. .... then I had never been to the opera.

4 **Ten examples of *then* have been taken out of this text. Can you put them back? (Sometimes there is a choice of position.)**

The waiter refilled their glasses. It was that Albert produced the ring. She stared at it for a minute or so and she put it on. 'You do love me?' she breathed. 'Passionately.' 'I've always loved you, too, Al,' she murmured. 'Will you marry me?' he asked. 'Yes, but I'll have to ask daddy. Only can I give you a firm answer.' 'When will you see him?' 'Next summer. Not before.' 'But I can't wait until,' Albert sobbed. 'By it will be too late.' 'Take the ring back,' she sighed. 'If you cannot wait, you do not truly love me.'

"NOW THEN, WHERE'S THIS RHINO?"

there

[pronoun] introduces the fact that something or some person or some event exists: *There's a market on Saturdays.* • *There was someone at the door.* • *Will there be music?*
[adverb] in or to or at that place: *Leave the books on that desk there.* • *I know Cairo well: I used to live there.*
→ here

Grammar patterns

1 **there** | + is/was etc. | + not any/no/a few etc. | + NP

There was water all over the floor.
Is there meat in this sauce?
How many students are there in your class?
There's been an accident.
There aren't any tickets left.
Have there been any phone calls?

▲ to say that (or to ask if) something exists or happens or that something is in a particular place

1a **there** | + is/was | + NP | + -ing

There was a young woman sitting next to me.
There were people running around and shouting.

▲ to introduce new things or people into a description, and say what they are doing

1b **there** | + modal verb | + be | + NP
there | + seems | + to be | + NP
there | + used | + to be | + NP

There must be a light switch somewhere.
Will there be anything to eat?
There seems to be a hole in it.
There used to be a forest here, but they cut it down.

▲ for talking about the likelihood, desirability, etc. of things existing

2 **there** | + pronoun | + verb

Can you see Mike anywhere? ~ Yes. There he is!
Have we missed the bus? ~ Yes, there it goes.

▲ to indicate people or things at some place away from you

Collocations

There are is often followed by numbers, amounts, quantities, e.g. *lots, a few, hundreds, some, two, many,* etc.:

There were hundreds of people at the airport.
Are there many mosquitoes?

There is/are is often followed by impersonal pronouns: *no one, nothing, someone, anyone, anything.*

We called by, but there was nobody home.
There's nothing to do.
There's someone here to see you.
Is there anything we need from the supermarket?

Prepositions that often go before *there* include: *in, up, over, down, under, back.*

The bank is over there.
Put the suitcase up there, on the rack.
We should have taken the by-pass back there.

Set phrases

- '**hi there … / hello there …**'
  Hi there, Annabelle, how are things? ~ Hi, Chuck.
  ▲ for informal greetings

- '**is […] there?**'
  Yes? ~ Hello. Is Darko there? ~ Yes, just a minute …
  ▲ to ask for someone, when telephoning

- '**there you are …**'
  That'll be £2.50. ~ There you are. ~ Thanks.
  ▲ for giving something to someone, such as money or goods in a shop

Exercises

1 Look at these concordance lines, and identify the meaning of *there* in each case. Is it a pronoun (showing that something exists) or is it an adverb (saying where something is)?

a **There**'s a bar and a lecture room for guests' use.
b **There**'d been another quake at 4am, a 6.5 shock.
c It was only in my third year that I really felt happy **there**.
d You say **there**'s a certain amount of risk. How much?
e I was **there** for her birth and it was the most exciting thing.
f But **there**'ll be no alcohol on sale.
g He was standing **there** with Mrs Kasmin as she tried to give him tea.
h He had been **there** since he left the Pit a year earlier.
i He was confident **there**'d be no problem. So was I.

2 In this dialogue all the examples of *there* have been taken out. Can you put them back in? (There are ten.)

A: Excuse me. Is a cashpoint near here?
B: Well, used to be one over. But it seems to have gone. Let me think: I think is another one in the Ellis Arcade.
A: Where is that?
B: Do you see that tall building over?
A: Yes.
B. Turn right and keep going for two blocks. Is a cinema and next to that is a shopping centre. It's called Ellis Arcade. Is a cashpoint in.
A: Thanks very much.

3 *There* vs *it*.

Generally, you use *there* to introduce new information (in the form of nouns). You use *it* (or *they* in the plural) to refer to information that has already been mentioned:

There's a big square in Marrakesh. It's called Djemaa el Fna. (→ it)

Complete this text with *it, they*, or *there*:

(a) (*There/It*) is nowhere in the world like Djemaa el Fna. By day (b) (*there/it*) is basically a market. In the evening (c) (*there/it*) is more like a carnival or a circus. (d) (*There/They*) are musicians, clowns, acrobats and snake charmers. (e) (*There/they*) are also dentists, herb doctors and barbers. And of course (f) (*they/there*) are lots of tourists. (g) (*There/They*) are sometimes as unusual as the local people. All in all, (h) (*it/there*) is a fascinating place. And if you are hungry (i) (*there/they*) are hundreds of food stalls. But don't go around the middle of the day: (j) (*there/it*) can be very hot.

4 Here are some more set phrases with *there*. Can you use them to complete the sentences?

there and back
then and there
there you are, you see
there you go
there, there
here and there
so there!
so there I was

a I liked the coat so much I bought it ....
b I'm not going to the party and you can't make me, ...
c That's £12.50. ~ .... ~ Thanks. There's your change.
d … And .... , in the middle of the night, with no money and my cell phone not working …
e How long will it take to get .... ?
f .... I told you the museum would be closed.
g So, where did you go in Brussels? ~ Oh, ... – nowhere special.
h I'm so nervous. ~ .... , don't worry: it'll be OK.

thing

[countable noun] (1) an object, idea, event, remark, that is not precisely identified: *Have you got a thing for opening bottles?*
• *A funny thing happened on the way to work.*
(2) (plural) objects in general, clothing, equipment: *I'll just put my sewing things away.*
(3) the general situation: *I'll have to think things over.*

Grammar patterns

1 it | + is/was etc. | + a/an | + adjective | + **thing** | + to-infinitive

It was a stupid thing to say.
It's not a nice thing to do.

▲ for stating an opinion about an action, behaviour, etc.

1a it | + is/was etc. | + a | + adjective | + **thing** | + that-clause

It's a good thing that we booked.
It was a lucky thing you checked the ticket.

▲ to comment on, or evaluate, an action or behaviour

2 the | + adjective | + **thing** | + is/was etc. | + to-infinitive

The important thing is to be careful.
The best thing is to drink lots of water.

▲ for giving advice or recommendations

2a the | + adjective | + **thing** | + is/was etc. | + -ing

The dumb thing was forgetting the tickets.
The hardest thing will be finding a taxi.

▲ to talk about one part or aspect of an event

2b the | + adjective | + **thing** | + is/was etc. | + that-clause

The good thing about Venice is that there are no cars.
The funny thing is, the door was locked.

▲ to introduce a point of view or an opinion

Collocations

These adjectives often go with *thing*:
good/best, bad/worst, nice, horrible, funny, strange, weird, stupid, main, important, hard, and *last.*

> *The worst thing about flying is the hanging around beforehand.*
> *It's a weird thing, but I feel that we've met before.*
> *The main thing is that you're safe.*
> *The last thing I expected was a glass dolphin.*

Verbs that frequently precede *things* (with the meaning of a general situation) include: *think over, discuss, sort out, speed up.*

> *You'll have to sort things out with Jeremy.*
> *We'll need to speed things up, if we are to meet that deadline.*

Verbs that frequently follow *thing(s)* include: *go on, happen,* and *occur.*

> *There were strange things going on next door.*

Set phrases

• **(not) a thing** = (not) anything
From where we were sitting we couldn't see a thing.
I haven't eaten a thing all day.

• ❛**the thing is …**❜
Aren't you hungry? ~ Well, the thing is, I had a late lunch.
▲ for introducing an explanation

• **for one thing …**
Why didn't you like the film? ~ Well, for one thing, it was too long.
▲ to introduce one of several possible reasons

• ❛**… and things**❜
She collects old maps and things.
▲ for talking vaguely about a category

• ❛**… and that sort of thing**❜ = etc.
They repair TVs and computers and that sort of thing.
▲ for expanding a category

• **just the thing**
Lemon and honey: it's just the thing for a sore throat.
▲ for recommending

Exercises

1 Read these concordance lines with *thing*. Which of the 5 Grammar patterns is each one an example of? (There are two examples of each pattern.)

a The sensible **thing** is to try to stop worrying.
b For me the important **thing** was winning the match, the money is very much the second thing.
c It was a very sensible **thing** to do.
d The great **thing** about tea drinking is that so many varieties are available.
e It was a good **thing** he knew the way so well.
f 'What an odd **thing** to do,' remarked Endill.
g The most important **thing** is to achieve the right balance.
h It's a good **thing** we got here in time, he thought.
i The hardest **thing** is knowing where to go to get help.
j The main **thing** is that you're not injured.

2 Match the two parts of these sentences:

a The nice thing about Paris is …   1 they are clean.
b The worst thing about Barcelona is …   2 you can use it everywhere.
c The strange thing about Gary is …   3 the verbs.
d The hardest thing about Turkish is …   4 there was nothing to eat.
e The best thing about the euro is …   5 the traffic noise.
f The good thing about cats is …   6 the street cafés.
g The odd thing about the party was …   7 it takes so long.
h The only thing about the bus is …   8 he can't cook.

3 Choose words from the list to complete these sentences. (Use each word only once.)

odd   main   first   whole
worst   best   strange   important

a He said he wasn't hungry, but he ate the ………… thing.
b The most ………… thing to pack is your passport.
c The ………… thing to remember is not to panic.
d That's the ………… thing about university – the exams.
e An ………… thing happened to me when I was in the supermarket this morning.
f When you arrive, the ………… thing you should do is turn on the electricty.
g The ………… thing about Athens? The Parthenon, of course.
h An electric iron – that's a ………… thing to give a child.

4 Here are some more fixed phrases using *thing* or *things*. Can you put them into their contexts?

of all things   just one of those things
all things considered   a thing of the past
the latest thing   the thing with him
no bad thing   no such thing

a That's ………… : he says one thing but he does another.
b He came to work wearing his slippers, ………… !
c The flight took 12 hours but it wasn't too bad, ………… .
d It's ………… that she lost that job, because she was miserable working there.
e You have to try these new snacks: they're ………… .
f It's not your fault we missed the bus – it was ………… .
g There's ………… as a free lunch.
h Look, forget what I said. It's over. It's ………… .

"THIS IS JUST THE THING FOR THE BIRDS TO NEST IN."

think

[irregular verb: *think, thought, thought*] (1) have an opinion, idea, or belief: *I think that this is their street.* • *What do you think of my haircut?* • *It's thought to be over a hundred years old.* (2) consider: *I'm thinking of changing jobs.*

Grammar patterns

1 **think** | (+ about + NP)

Shh! I'm trying to think.
What are you thinking about?

▲ to talk about reflecting, using your mind

2 **think** | + of | + NP

No one could think of a good excuse.
I couldn't think of his name.

▲ to talk about imagining or remembering things

3 **think** | + that-clause

I thought that you knew about me and Jerry.
Do you think it will rain?

▲ to talk about opinions, beliefs

4 **think** | + of/about | + -ing

Have you ever thought of going freelance?
I'm thinking about opening a flower shop.

▲ to talk about making plans

5 **think** | + wh-clause
   think | + wh | + to-infinitive

Try to think where you left the keys.
I can't think what to do.

▲ to talk about making a mental effort

6 NP | + is/was etc. | + **thought** | + to-infinitive
   it + was/were etc. | + **thought** | + that-clause

The area is thought to be frequented by polar bears.
It is thought that the fire was started deliberately.

▲ to say what is believed, but not known for certain

Collocations

Adverbials that commonly go with *think* include: *carefully, honestly, long and hard, personally,* and *really.*

Diane thought long and hard before she accepted the offer.
Personally I think she's made the right choice.

Verb phrases that precede *think* include: *dread to* and *hate to.*

I dread to think what she was wearing.

Think combines with particles to form phrasal verbs:

If you *think back* to something, you think about something that happened in the past. (*Try and think back to the last time you saw her.*)
If you *think* something *over,* you consider it carefully. (*Have you had time to think over my offer?*)
If you *think* something *through,* you think about it in a thorough way. (*I don't think she's thought the whole thing through.*)
If you *think* something *up,* you invent it. (*I'm sure he thought the whole story up.*)

Set phrases

• **'... I think'**
The party's on Saturday, I think.
▲ to express uncertainty or to make what you say less forceful

• **'I think so / I don't think so'**
Are we ready to go? ~ I think so.
Is Joan married? ~ I don't think so.
▲ to answer yes, or no, but less forcefully

• **I should think / I would think.**
It will take about six to eight weeks, I should think.
▲ to say that you think something may be true

• **who would have thought ...?**
Who would have thought Emma was so tough!
▲ to express surprise

• **'just think ...'**
Just think: this time next week we'll be in Mexico.
▲ to emphasize your excitement or surprise

· ' I was thinking … '

I was thinking: would you like to have the afternoon off?

▲ to indicate an idea, or suggestion

· ' I wasn't thinking '

I'm sorry I said that. I wasn't thinking.

▲ to apologize

· **think twice**

I'd think twice before getting a snake, if I were you.

▲ to think carefully before doing something

Exercises

❶ Study these concordance lines with *think* and classify them according to the Grammar patterns 1–6. (There are two examples of each pattern.)

a The gossip is that she is **thinking** of resigning.
b I married you **thinking** you were like me.
c Mr Kelsey, who is **thought** to be in his forties, was taken to hospital.
d Then she **thought** of Charles and the laugh died away.
e He is **thinking** about what is in the back of the plane.
f It is **thought** that development at the chosen site could endanger wildlife.
g Now she had to **think** how to survive.
h Deep down my wife **thinks** that I'm a pessimist.
i He is so quiet; I never know what he is **thinking**.
j She **thought** of what her colleagues and students might be doing.
k **Think** about cycling more or travelling on public transport.
l I can't **think** where I've seen her before.

❷ Put the word in brackets in the correct place in the sentence:

a (don't) I think it will rain.
b (about) What are you thinking?
c (of) We can't think a good name for the baby.
d (so) Janet says the hotel is expensive but I don't think.
e (he) Do you think will get first prize?
f (honestly) Do you think it's well written?
g (to) The Library of Alexandria is thought have been destroyed by fire.
h (and) I would think long hard before you say yes.

i (it) Before you decide you should think over.
j (have) Who would thought that Joshua would win!

❸ Note that *think* in the sense of talking about beliefs, opinions, and ideas is not used in the continuous. But *think* in the sense of considering something is often used in the continuous:

I think she did the right thing. (NOT: ~~I am thinking she~~ …)
I am thinking of working part-time. (NOT: ~~I think of~~ …)

Choose the best form of the verb to complete these sentences:

a What (*are you thinking/do you think*) of the new carpet?
b Terry and Kim (*are thinking/think*) of adopting a baby.
c What (*are you thinking/do you think*) of cooking for the party?
d I (*'m not thinking/don't think*) much of this new series on TV.
e How long (*have you been thinking/have you thought*) about moving to Italy?
f You look sad. What (*are you thinking/do you think*) about?

❹ Choose expressions from the list to complete this conversation:

I think
You'd think
Do you think you could
Just think
Do you think so?
Come to think of it
Who would have thought?
I was thinking

A: (a)............ , our own home! At last!
B: I know (b) .... !
A: (c) .... , why don't we have a house-warming party?
B: (d) .... It's a lot of trouble and expense.
A: I know. But (e) .... our friends are expecting it. (f)............ , Jack asked me just the other day if we were going to have a party.
B: (g) .... they would wait until we'd moved in.
A: I'm going to make a guest list. (h) .... hand me that pen?

this

[determiner and pronoun, plural *these*] the one here, or near me: *Have you tried this dip?* • *Is this your towel?*

→ that

Grammar patterns

1 **this** | (+ NP/one)

This is nice, this music.
Which colour do you prefer? ~ I quite like this one.
Do these glasses suit me?

▲ to refer to things near you

This is where I met Danny.
Is this your first visit?

▲ to refer to the place or situation you are in now

Margaret, this is my partner, Hugo. ~ Hi, Hugo, nice to meet you.
Is this your mother in the photo?

▲ to refer to people when you are identifying or introducing the person or asking who they are

The level of the sea is rising. This is due to global warming …
In 1987 he wrote Bird Song. In the introduction to this book he said …

▲ to refer back to something that has been mentioned

This is how it happened: I was on my way to …
Listen to this: 'A man has been arrested for …'

▲ to refer forward to something you are going to mention

I was in this pub, and this man comes up to me …
There were these three little pigs, and the first pig was called Gregory …

▲ to refer informally to someone or something for the first time, when you are telling a story

2 **this** | + adjective/adverb

I need a piece of wood, about this long.
Now add some flour: about this much.

▲ to indicate the size of something with your hands

Collocations

This frequently goes with time expressions, to mean 'the one that's coming':

What are you doing this evening?
I'm busy this Friday. How about next Friday?
They say this summer is going to be very hot.

In writing, *this* frequently goes with words that refer back, in a general way, to the topic: e.g. *problem, question, idea, situation, topic, state of affairs, issue.*

People complain most about the traffic. This problem is made worse by …
Chimpanzees can be taught to speak. This idea has been around for years now …

This also goes with words that refer back, in a general way, to what has been said, e.g.: *comment, remark, proposal, argument, explanation, point, story,* etc.

'The team is useless,' said the club president. This remark caused anger among the players …
'Some people like arts programmes,' said the minister. She made this point when she was …

Set phrases

• **'this minute'** = immediately
  You'd better hurry because the bus is leaving this minute.

• **these days** = at the present time
  How are things in Auckland these days?

• **'this and that'**
  What've you been doing lately? ~ Oh, this and that. Nothing special.
  ▲ to talk vaguely about a variety of things

Exercises

1 *This* or *that*?
Complete the sentences with *this/that/these/those*:

a Does .... dress look OK? ~ Yes, it looks good on you.
b Did you like .... book I gave you for your birthday?
c Can you bring me .... folders, please?
d .... film is terrible. Let's go.
e Who is .... woman standing by the bar?
f Do you remember .... party we went to last New Year?
g Emma, I'd like you to meet my brother, Ewan. Ewan, ... is Emma.
h What are you looking at? ~ .... are the photos of Marta's birthday.
i Hello? .... is Graham Sharpe. Is .... Angela McKay?
j .... large room we're now standing in used to be the ballroom.
k I'm going to study ichthyology. ~ What's .... ?
l I'd like to change .... shoes: they're the wrong size.
m What's .... good news you were about to tell me?
n I hear you were on holiday. ~ Oh, ... was ages ago.
o I must tell you .... joke: .... woman is on a train with her baby …

2 *This*, *that*, or *it*?

In writing you can refer back to previous topics by using *this, that,* and *it*.

You use *it* to continue what you have been talking about. You use *this* to draw attention to new or important topics. You use *that* to put distance between yourself and the topic.

Decide which is the best alternative to fill each gap:

The <u>grasshopper</u> is an insect that lives in fields. (a) .... makes a chirping noise by rubbing its legs against its wings. (b) .... does (c) .... to attract its mate.

<u>Japan</u> used to be mainly agricultural. (d) .... was a long time ago. Now (e) .... is mainly industrial. (f)............ means that most people live in big cities.

<u>Italy</u> is a food-loving country. (g) .... is famous for pasta. (h) .... comes in a wide variety of shapes. (i)............ is also famous for pizza. But (j) .... is another story.

3 **Read this text and identify what *this* refers to, in each case. For example:**

The streets were empty. ◀ *This* seemed strange.

This is a picture of my family. As you can see, we were a big family. This meant that, as a child, I always had company and never felt alone. I sometimes miss this, now that I am living on my own. But I don't miss the noise. This is because I am a quiet person by nature. If you don't believe me, how about this: when I left college I spent three months alone living in a lighthouse! I think that this was probably the happiest period of my life.

time

[uncountable and countable noun] (1) what you measure in minutes, hours, etc.: *Excuse me, have you got the right time?* (2) when something happens; an event, occasion or period: *Did you have a good time?* • *She lived in Lille for a time.*

Grammar patterns

1   all (of)/some of/most of etc. | + determiner | + **time**

Most of the time they stayed in and watched TV.
Why do you keep singing all the time?

▲ to talk about a period spent doing something

2   in | + a day's/three weeks'/five years' etc. | + **time**

I'll phone you back in a couple of hours' time.
The bridge will be completed in a year's time.

▲ to say when something will happen

3   determiner | + **time** | + when-clause/that-clause

Do you remember that time when Stig's car broke down?
There was a time when he never drank or smoked.
You say that every time you walk in the door.

▲ to define a period or point of time

4   **time** | + to-infinitive

Is it time to light the barbecue?
The best time to plant tomatoes is in late spring.

▲ to say when something should happen

I didn't have time to wash my hair.
The students needed more time to practise.

▲ to talk about the amount of time available to do something

5   it's | + **time** | + that-clause (past tense)

It's time that the government did something about it.
I think it's time you kids went to bed.

▲ to say that something should happen now

6   have | + a/an | + adjective | + **time**

Did you have a nice time?
What an awful time they had!

▲ to talk about good or bad experiences

Collocations

Common verb phrases with *time* include: *have time, make time, find time, pass the time, spend time (doing), take time, save time, waste time.*

If you don't have enough time to do it, then you will have to make time.
It will save time if you take the shortcut.
Don't waste time watching TV: do something useful.

Adjectives that frequently fit into the pattern 'have + *time*' (Grammar pattern 6) are: *enjoyable, fun, good, grand, great, marvellous, pleasant, splendid, wonderful;* and *awful, dreadful, miserable, sad, terrible.*

Did you have a fun time at the beach?

Set phrases

· ' **about time** '
  Here's the bus. ~ About time!
  ▲ to show you are annoyed because someone or something is late

· **at the same time**
  He writes beautifully. At the same time, his books can be quite heavy-going.
  ▲ to say that two things are true, even if they seem different

· **it's high time …**
  It's high time you got your hair cut.
  ▲ to say that something should happen now

· **in no time** = very quickly, or very soon
  They changed the tyre in no time, and we were on our way again.
  Hurry up. The taxi will be here in no time!

· **from time to time** = occasionally
  Dad likes a nice cigar from time to time.

- **time and (time) again / time after time** = repeatedly
  I've told you time and again: the bottles go in the green bin.

- **once upon a time …**
  Once upon a time there was a selfish giant …
  ▲ to begin a fairy story

Exercises

❶ There are fourteen examples of the word *time* (or *times*) that have been taken out of this dialogue. Can you replace them?

A: Did you have a good in Mexico?
B: We had a great, apart from Jack, who was sick the whole. It's the first I've been there. So we spent most of the in Mexico City, which is nice at this of year: not too hot, and clear blue skies. We didn't have to go to Yucatan and we didn't want to waste on buses and things, so we mainly stayed around the capital. There's so much to see, although at you get a bit overwhelmed by the size of the place. But, at the same, it's actually quite easy to get around: we took the metro all the. You can get around in no. And most of the it's not too crowded. Yes, it was fantastic. I'd like to go back some.

❷ Choose verbs from the list to complete these sentences with *time*:

spend   save   waste   find   take (x2)   have   pass

a They ………… their free time doing charity work.
b If you ………… time, you should visit the art museum.
c Why ………… time learning Latin if no one speaks it?
d I'm very busy but I'm sure I can ………… time to meet your new boss.
e One way to ………… the time in an airport is to play cards.
f Learning a language does ………… time: you're not going to do it overnight.
g Take the tunnel: it's much quicker. You will ………… a lot of time.
h Is the exercise too difficult? Well, ………… your time. I'll come back in ten minutes.

❸ Choose the best preposition to complete these sentences:

a Was the train (*in/at/on*) time? ~ Yes, it arrived at 5.49, as scheduled.
b (*By/On/At*) the time we arrived, the film had already started.
c He's 19 but he behaves like a ten-year-old (*in/on/at*) times.
d (*From/For/At*) a time, we were happy together. Then the trouble started.
e Did you arrive (*in/on/by*) time for the speeches? ~ No, we were too late.
f The building work is due to start (*on/at/in*) two or three weeks' time.
g I hadn't seen Derek (*since/for/from*) some time.
h (*In/On/At*) what time would you like me to call you?

❹ Compounds with *time*. In these sentences, the word compounds with *time* (e.g. *part-time, time bomb*) are in the wrong place. Can you put them were they belong?

a Van Gogh never achieved recognition in his own part-time.
b In her lunchtime she likes making things out of stuff she finds on the beach.
c Listen, I'm busy all morning. Let's meet at lifetime.
d San Francisco is not in the same timetable as New York.
e Someone phoned up and said they had put a time limit on the plane.
f Could I have a time bomb for the bus, please?
g She works free time in a day care nursery.
h The tutor set a time zone for the history assignment.

❺ Expressions and idioms with *time*.
Match the two parts of these exchanges:

a I never thought I'd jump out of a plane!
b There's going to be a nasty accident on this corner one day.
c Did you catch the train OK?
d I keep putting off the decision to sell the house.
e Did you enjoy Las Vegas?
f Do you really think I should get a DVD player?

1 ~ Well, there's no time like the present.
2 ~ Yes, it's only a matter of time.
3 ~ Yes, you have to move with the times.
4 ~ Yes. We arrived just in the nick of time.
5 ~ Well, there's a first time for everything.
6 ~ Yes, we had a whale of a time.

to¹

[infinitive marker] (1) goes before the base form of the verb
(e.g. *do, be, get, have,* etc.) and is used after certain verbs,
adjectives, nouns, and *wh*-words: *I'd like to pay.* • *She was afraid
to ask.* • *They have the ability to win.* • *I don't know what to
wear tonight.*
(2) substitutes for the infinitive : *Don't go if you don't want to.*
(3) in order to: *I'm writing to ask about the job.*
[preposition] → to²

Grammar patterns

1 verb | + **to** | + infinitive

Jeff has agreed to give us a quote.
Lola and Jürg have decided to move.

- ▲ to express your willingness or commitment to a future
  action, using verbs such as *promise, hope, want, decide,
  offer, refuse, intend,* etc.

Try to get some rest.
The government failed to act.

- ▲ to talk about attempting, succeeding, or failing to achieve
  something, using verbs like *try, manage, remember,* etc.

The lock seems to be broken.
Students tend to arrive late.

- ▲ to express lack of certainty about a situation, using verbs
  like *appear, seem, tend, happen*

2 verb | + NP | + **to** | + infinitive

They ordered the youth to empty his pockets.
Marilyn advised me not to apply for the job.

- ▲ to talk about getting people to do things, using verbs like
  want, ask, advise, get, help, force, etc.

3 verb | + wh-word | + **to** | + infinitive

I don't know where to go this summer.
Did you remember what to say?

- ▲ to talk about knowing and learning things, using verbs
  like *explain, understand, discover, find out, forget,* etc.

4 verb | + NP | + wh-word | + **to** | + infinitive

Can you tell me when to get off, please?
Who taught the children how to swear?

- ▲ to talk about telling or showing someone something, with
  verbs like *teach, show, tell, advise,* etc.

5 clause | + **to** | + infinitive

We went on to the roof to watch the fireworks.
The bus stopped to let some passengers off.

- ▲ to say what the purpose of an action is (This is called the
  infinitive of purpose.)

6 NP | + **to** | + infinitive

Do you have permission to make copies?
People have a duty to vote.

- ▲ used with abstract nouns that express willingness, ability,
  obligation, etc.

7 adjective | + **to** | + infinitive

I'm sorry to hear you're leaving.
The children are afraid to go in the water.

- ▲ to describe how you feel about a situation, using
  adjectives like *(un)likely, (un)able, difficult, easy, free, glad,
  hard, ready,* and *willing*

It's sure to rain.

- ▲ to talk about how certain something is

Collocations

Verbs that occur with Grammar pattern 1 are: *like, begin,
attempt, fail, continue,* and *agree.*

A veterinary surgeon attempted to revive the elephant.
Prices have continued to rise.

The most frequent nouns in Grammar pattern 6 are: *time, thing,
way, place, stuff, a lot.*

What a horrible thing to say!
She needs a nice place to live.
I've got a lot to do this afternoon.

Set phrases

- **in order to / so as (not) to**
  Salmon travel upstream in order to breed.
  She wrote in the kitchen so as not to disturb the children.
  ▲ for expressing purpose

- **'to be honest / to tell you the truth** etc.**'**
  I think they should get a new manager, to be honest.
  Well, to sum up, it was a fairly disastrous trip.
  ▲ to comment on what you are saying

- **[…] enough to [+ infinitive] …**
  She's old enough to drive but not old enough to vote.
  ▲ to say that something is sufficient in order to do something

- **too […] to [+ infinitive] …**
  It was too dark to see clearly.
  I was too tired to concentrate.
  ▲ to say that a limit has been exceeded, so it's impossible to do something

Exercises

❶ Many reporting verbs take Grammar patterns 1 or 2:

'If I were you, I'd see a dentist,' Angel said to me.
= Angel advised me to see a dentist.

Rewrite the direct speech as reported speech, using verbs from this list:

promise (GP 1)	remind (GP 2)	threaten (GP 1)
agree (GP 1)	advise (GP 2)	warn (GP 2)
permit (GP 2)	invite (GP2)	

a 'I'll call the police!' she said.
b 'You can leave now,' the teacher said to the class.
c 'I'll be home before midnight, believe me,' Julia said.
d 'Don't go near the dog,' Brad said to the boy.
e 'Would you like to come to dinner?' Anna said to me.
f 'Don't forget to turn out the lights,' said Ian to the others.
g 'OK, I'll sign the contract,' Tom said.
h 'You should take some painkillers,' I said to Ellie.

❷ Many verbs can take both 'to + infinitive' or the -ing form of the verb. With some verbs there is no change of meaning; with other verbs, the meaning is completely different.

Decide if these pairs of sentences mean the same, or are different:

a 1 They continued to argue all through the meal.
   2 They continued arguing all through the meal.
b 1 You must remember to post the letter.
   2 You must remember posting the letter.
c 1 Let's stop to watch the news.
   2 Let's stop watching the news.
d 1 It began to rain so we ran for cover.
   2 It began raining so we ran for cover.
e 1 After college he went on to teach French.
   2 After college he went on teaching French.
f 1 Don't you think it's time you started to pack?
   2 Don't you think it's time you started packing?

❸ Giving advice. Use words and phrases from lists A, B, and C to write sentences with *to*:

To change money, you should go to a bank.

A:	B:	C:
book	~~money~~	the post office
borrow	a magazine	a gym
buy	a parcel	a travel agency
~~change~~	fit	a library
send	a key made	a book shop
keep	a book	~~a bank~~
have	a holiday	a hardware store

❹ In this text all the examples of *to* have been taken out. Can you put them back? (There are twelve.)

Dear Babs,
I am 16 and I have a problem. I have decided be a singer and I want leave school so I can follow this dream. But my parents won't allow me leave. They have ordered me stay at school and told me keep studying until I am 18. I have begged them let me leave, but it's no use. What should I do? It's impossible stay at school when I have this burning desire be a singer. Is there no way convince them give me my freedom? Please advise me what do. I hope hear from you soon.

to²

[preposition] in the direction of a place or time: *She ran to the bus stop.* • *It's ten to two.*
[infinitive marker] → to¹

Grammar patterns

1 **to** | + NP (place)

I went to the bank and then took a bus to the office.
Is this the way to the beach?
It used to take several days to fly from Cape Town to London.

▲ to talk about a place that you move or travel towards

He was sitting to the left of the President.
Alicante is to the south of Valencia.

▲ to talk about the position of something, in relation to another thing

2 from | + NP | + **to** | + NP (time)

The office is open from Monday to Friday.
The plant flowers from May to July.

▲ to talk about a time period from beginning to end

3 verb | + NP | + **to** | + NP

I sent a text message to Diane.
What shall I do with these? ~ Give them to Misha.
Who did you sell your old laptop to? ~ To Chris.

▲ to talk about an action where someone receives something, using verbs like *give, offer, pass, pay, send, write,* and *show*

4 verb | + **to** | + NP | + that-clause

Evelyn explained to the policeman that she was a tourist.
I mentioned to José that you are looking for a flatmate.
Colin admitted to me that he had been seeing someone.

▲ to report a communication, using verbs such as *explain, complain, confess, report,* and *suggest*

Collocations

To follows these adjectives: *similar, different, identical, equal; close, next; married, engaged;* plus those adjectives that describe ways of treating people, such as *kind, polite, rude, cruel, nice, friendly, faithful, mean, horrible*:

Your backpack is similar to mine.
It was due to Gavin that you got this job.
He's so rude to the customers …

To commonly combines with these verbs: *listen, see, belong, object, refer, appeal, lead, take, get.*

What's that you're listening to?
The motorbike belongs to the next door neighbour.
Can you see to (= attend to) the potatoes while I chop the onions?
I didn't take to (= like) Belinda: she seemed a bit snooty.

To forms the third element of a number of three-word phrasal verbs, such as: *face up to, get down to, get round to, lead up to, look forward to, look up to,* as well as the expression *get/be used to.* (→ used)

You're an adult now: it's time to face up to your responsibilities.
OK, that's enough chatting. Let's get down to work.
I look forward to hearing from you.
I'm not used to climbing all these stairs.

Set phrases

· **face to face / back to back / cheek to cheek**
Shall we do the interview over the phone, or face to face?
▲ to describe how two people are positioned in relation to each other

· **ten to one / a hundred to one** etc.
There's a million to one chance you'll win the lottery.
▲ to say what the chances are of something happening

· **to and fro** = from one place to another and back again
I've been going to and fro all morning.

Exercises

1 **This text has twelve examples of *to* that have been removed. Can you put them back in the correct place?**

Dear Mrs Brennan,

Here is my report on your ex-husband's activities yesterday.

He left the house at 8.04 and walked the station, where he took a train the city centre. On the train he read a newspaper and listened music on his portable stereo. He didn't talk anyone, apart from giving directions a passing tourist. He then walked work, arriving there at 8.37. He came out at 12.31 and went a café opposite his office, where he had lunch, alone, until 13.29. He then went back the office, and was there from 13.30 18.00. I followed him home. He got there at 18.43, and he did not come out again that evening.

As I explained you in my last report, I do not believe that Mr Brennan is concealing anything. I will send you an invoice at the end of the month, as usual. I will also enclose the photo that belongs you. Looking forward hearing from you,

Monty Dagg
(Private Detective)

2 **Transform the following sentences from 'verb + noun phrase + to + noun phrase' → 'verb + noun phrase + noun phrase':**

I sent a message to Diane → *I sent Diane a message.*

a Send an e-mail to the boss.
b The teacher taught the alphabet to the children.
c A friend of mine sold a painting to me.
d Show your arm to the doctor.
e I told the bad news to the neighbours.
f Can you take this letter to Mrs Lowe?
g We gave a skateboard to Tom and a football to Josh.
h Read the article to me.

3 ***To* can be used to indicate the end point in a process, or the result of an action:**

He smashed the bowl to bits.

Match the two parts of these sentences:

a	The film was so sad it reduced her …	1	to pieces.
b	The sailor was stabbed …	2	to nothing.
c	She cried herself …	3	to green.
d	I tore the letter …	4	to death.
e	The lights changed from red …	5	to sleep.
f	New treasures have been brought …	6	to tears.
g	A chorus brought the opera …	7	to light.
h	All my wonderful plans came …	8	to an end.

4 ***To* is also an infinitive marker (→ to[1]). Look at these concordance lines and separate them into two groups, according to whether *to* is (a) the infinitive marker, or (b) a preposition. If it is a preposition, does it follow a noun, verb, adverb, or adjective?**

a She felt it was her duty **to** ask certain questions.
b Catastrophes are familiar **to** all of us.
c He stopped by the hospital on his way **to** a tennis match.
d We need **to** ask you some questions.
e 'I'd like **to** be a policeman,' he said.
f I made my second journey **to** Cosford in 1980.
g The younger boys go **to** bed at nine o'clock.
h He had been particularly close **to** his mother.
i I'm pleased **to** announce the winner of the competition.
j They had moved **to** a smaller, less fashionable apartment.
k I have a suggestion **to** make on this point.
l We'll see if we can find something good **to** eat.
m There's no need **to** feel sorry for him, Jen.
n We look forward **to** meeting you there.
o They don't want **to** get their hands dirty.

too

[adverb] (1) more than enough: *The coffee was too hot to drink.*
• *Can I try another size? These ones are too big.*
(2) in addition, as well: *I took Jane to the movies and her mother came too.* • *Snakes and lizards are reptiles. Turtles, too.*

→ and

Grammar patterns

1   **too** | + adjective | (+ for | + NP)

Is the doctor in? ~ I'm afraid you're too late. She's just left.
He's too old for her, in my opinion.
The food was too rich for my tastes.

▲ to talk about things being excessive

1a   **too** | + adjective/adverb | + to-infinitive

Ten blocks! That's too far to walk.
She sang too softly to be heard at the back of the hall.

▲ to talk about things being excessive for a certain purpose

1b   **too** | + much/many/little/few | (+ NP)

Have some more ice cream. ~ Stop! that's too much!
There were too many people and too few seats to enjoy the concert properly.

▲ to talk about quantities that are more or less than desirable or necessary

2   NP | + **too**
clause/utterance | + **too**

You, too, could have soft, lustrous hair.
It really works, and it's safe, too.
I'm staying at the Nile Hilton. ~ I'm staying there, too.
I'd love a coffee. ~ Me, too.

▲ to add something to what has already been said

Collocations

Adjectives and adverbs that frequently follow *too* are: *early, easy, hard, late, little, long, low,* and *small*.

> *It's too early to predict when a vaccine will be available.*
> *Are we too late to get a table?*
> *We had to wait too long, so we left.*
> *The government has done too little, and too late.*

Adverbs that go before *too* include: *a bit, much, far, a lot,* and *rather*:

> *Friendly? He was a bit too friendly!*
> *There are far too many cars on the road.*
> *The film was enjoyable but rather too long for my liking.*

Set phrases

• '**too bad**'
Judy didn't get that job. ~ Too bad.
▲ to say that you are sorry about a situation

• '**me, too**'
I'm freezing. ~ Me, too. Let's go inside.
▲ to include yourself in what has just been said

• **(all/only) too true**
That many athletes take drugs is all too true.
▲ to say that something is true when you wish it was not

• **too good to be true**
He's handsome, intelligent, and rich.
~ It's too good to be true. I bet he's married.
▲ to show your doubts about a surprisingly good situation

• **too clever by half**
The film was too clever by half: all those flashbacks and endless close-ups.
▲ to show you don't like the way someone or something is trying to appear intelligent

Exercises

1 Put *too* in the correct place in these sentences:

a It's far expensive for me. Have you got anything cheaper?
b Is it late to phone for a pizza? ~ Yes, it's after midnight.
c The concert was very good but I thought the music was rather loud.
d I'm much busy to see him now.
e Ten miles! That's far far to walk.
f The soup was very salty but the fish was salty.
g Rich? He's got much much money.
h You're making much noise and it's very late.
i I'll have some milk. I'll have some sugar.
j We're going to the beach. ~ Can I come?

2 *Too* is similar in meaning to *not* […] *enough*:

It's too big to send by post. → *It's not small enough to send by post.*
There was too little information. → *There wasn't enough information.*

Change these sentences from *too* to *not* […] *enough*:

a The ceilings are too low.
b The kitchen is too small.
c The rooms are too dark.
d The apartment is too expensive.
e There are too few balconies.
f There is too little ventilation.

Now, change these sentences from *not* […] *enough* to *too*:

g The train station is not close enough.
h The apartment is not clean enough.
i There are not enough bedrooms.
j There is not enough light.
k It's not big enough for our family.
l It's not modern enough for our tastes.

3 *Too* and *very*.

Both *too* and *very* add emphasis, but *too* means that there is some problem:

The car was very expensive, but I bought it.
The car was too expensive, so I didn't buy it.

Complete these sentences with either *too* or *very*:

a I like Andrew .... much. He's really nice.
b The ceiling is .... high to paint without a ladder.
c The beach was .... crowded, but we found a nice spot to ourselves.
d The book is difficult, but not .... difficult. I managed to finish it.
e He drove .... fast and was stopped by the police.
f If we drive .... fast we will get there before dark.
g We are .... grateful for everything you have done.
h He's .... old and .... rich, and she married him.

4 Can you complete these film and song titles, using words from the list?

Big   Far   Easily   Much   Heaven   Far   Hot (x2)   Busy

a *A Bridge Too* .... (war film made in 1977)
b *The Man Who Knew Too* .... (Hitchcock film, made in 1956)
c *All This And* .... *Too*. (film starring Bette Davis, 1940)
d *Too* .... *To Handle*. (film starring Clark Gable, 1938)
e 'Too .... Thinking About My Baby.' (Marvin Gaye song, 1969)
f 'Your Feet's Too ....' (Fats Waller song)
g 'Too Darn ....' (Cole Porter song)
h 'I Fall In Love Too ....' (Frank Sinatra song)

up

[preposition] to or in a higher place: *Climb up the rope.*
[adverb] towards a higher place: *Why don't you come up?*

Grammar patterns

1 verb | + **up** (preposition) | + NP

Jack and Jill climbed up the hill.

▲ to indicate direction and destination

2 verb | + **up** (adverb)

Stand up!
The price of petrol has gone up.
Can you speak up, please?

▲ to indicate movement to a higher position or increase in degree

This man came up and asked me the time.
Go up and ask the receptionist.

▲ to indicate movement towards a person or place

Drink up!
You did the cooking so let me wash up.

▲ to talk about doing something to completion

The ship started to break up.

▲ to talk about something becoming lots of pieces

3 verb | + **up** | + NP
  verb | + NP | + **up**

I picked up my knife and fork and started eating.
These trousers are too long. Can you take them up, please?

▲ as in pattern 2, to indicate increase in height and size, or movement towards a place, or completion, or destruction

4 verb | + **up** | + preposition | + NP

You go ahead and we'll catch up with you.
The children get up to no good if you leave them alone.

▲ conveys a variety of meanings, many of them idiomatic

Collocations

Up can combine with these verbs to make Grammar pattern 2:
come, get, go, let, meet, pay, pop, speak, stay.

Come up and I'll show you the view.
The rain didn't let up (= stop) for several days.
The kids want to stay up (= not go to bed) to watch TV.

Up can combine with many verbs to make Grammar pattern 3,
e.g.: *bring, call, cut, eat, fill, fix, hold, lift, put, send, take, tie, use.*

Cut the meat up into small cubes.
Dad helped me put some kitchen shelves up.
Turn the torch off: you'll use up the batteries.

Up can combine with some verbs to make both Grammar pattern 2 and Grammar pattern 3, but with a difference of meaning, e.g. *add, give, keep, look, turn:*

Slow down: I can't keep up.
They sang hymns to keep their spirits up.
We weren't expecting Uncle Ted to come but he just turned up.
Can you turn the TV up? I can't hear it.

Some common Grammar pattern 4 combinations are:
put up with (= tolerate), *come up with* (= devise), *keep up with* (= maintain the same pace or standard with), *run up against* (= encounter e.g. a problem).

Set phrases

· **'what's up?'**
   What's up? ~ Not a lot.
   You look worried. What's up?
   ▲ for asking about news, or to find out what's wrong

· **up and down** = into the air and back to the ground
   The kids were jumping up and down.

· **up and running** = working effectively
   Our new website is up and running at last.

· **'it's up to you'** = it's your decision or responsibility
   You're welcome to stay. It's up to you.

· **up to …**
   The tank will take up to 60 litres of fuel.
   I sometimes work up to 12 hours a day.
   ▲ for stating the limit

Exercises

1 **What is the meaning of each underlined example of *up* in this dialogue?**

a to a higher position   c to completion
b to a bigger size   d into pieces

A: What are you doing?
B: I'm getting the room ready for the party.
A: Can I help? Shall I cut <u>up</u> the cake?
B: No. But you can help me blow <u>up</u> the balloons.
A: OK.
B: And then you can put them <u>up.</u>
A: How?
B: Climb <u>up</u> on that ladder.
A: … OK, that's done.
B: Now, can you wrap <u>up</u> the presents?
A: OK. Shall I bring <u>up</u> some wood for the fire?
B: Yes, but chop it <u>up</u> first.
A: What now?
B: OK, now help me tidy <u>up</u> …

2 **Preposition or adverb?**

> a *She looked up the chimney.*
> b *She looked up the word (in the dictionary).*
>
> Note that in sentence (a) *up* is a preposition, but in sentence (b) it is an adverb. As an adverb, it can change position: we can say *She looked up the word* and *She looked the word up*, but NOT ~~She looked the chimney up.~~

Decide if the following examples of *up* are prepositions or adverbs. If they are adverbs, rewrite the sentence with *up* in a different position.

a The cat climbed up the tree.
b Please pick up your clothes off the floor.
c Can you bring up the mail when you come?
d The thieves blew up the safe and stole the diamonds.
e Be careful going up the ladder.
f Eat up your vegetables.
g Where shall I hang up my jacket?
h A fly crawled up my nose.

3 **Verbs with *up*.**
Replace each underlined verb with a phrasal verb from the list below, so that the meaning of the sentence stays the same (although possibly less formal).

give up   set up   put up   pick up   bring up
do up   look up   make up   take up   get up

a 'I shall <u>arise</u> and go now, and go to Innisfree ….' (W.B.Yeats)
b I had to <u>invent</u> an excuse for not having a bus ticket.
c We're not going on holiday this year. We're going to <u>renovate</u> our apartment instead.
d I'm too old to <u>get into the habit of</u> skiing. I prefer walking in the mountains.
e Next time you're in Leicester, you should <u>visit</u> my parents.
f He plans to <u>establish</u> his own web design business.
g If you lived in France you'd <u>acquire</u> French quite quickly.
h When their parents died, their aunt offered to <u>raise</u> the children herself.
i Last New Year I resolved to <u>quit</u> smoking.
j It's good to have an extra bedroom so you can <u>accommodate</u> guests.

4 **Idioms and expressions with *up*.**
Complete these sentences, choosing words or expressions from this list:

right way up   up to something   up to scratch
ups and downs   up-and-coming   what's up
up to you   time is up   up and about
up to my ears

a You have to finish writing your exam now. Your ………… .
b Hello, Harry, ………… ? You look terrible.
c I'm suspicious. Where are the boys: they must be ………… .
d You can come with us or you can stay at home: it's ………… .
e 'Don't worry,' the doctor said. 'It's not serious. You'll be ………… in no time.'
f She is one of the new, ………… , country and western stars: you'll be hearing a lot about her soon.
g I can't possibly do this assignment. I am ………… in work.
h Their marriage has been fairly successful although they've had their ………… .
i I'm sorry, your homework wasn't ………… . You'll have to do it again.
j The painting is upside down. Put it the ………… .

used

[past tense of verb *use*] *I used a knife to open the letter.* (pron. /juːzd/).
[adjective] something that has been used: *a used car* (pron. /juːzd/).
[modal verb: *used to*] to talk about past habits: *She used to work here but she left.* (pron: /juːst/)
[adjective + preposition: *used to*] accustomed, familiar with: *You'll soon get used to the lifestyle in Madrid.* (pron: /juːst/)

Grammar patterns

1 **used** to | + bare infinitive (action verbs)

When we were kids we used to cycle to school.
They never used to park in this street.
I don't smoke now, but I used to.

▲ for talking about things that happened (or didn't happen) regularly in the past

1a **used** to | + bare infinitive (state verbs)

It used to be much quieter here in the old days.
A loaf of bread used to cost 50p.
I never used to like fish, but now I prefer it to meat.

▲ for talking about how things were (or weren't) in the past

2 be/get | + **used** to | + NP

I'm used to kids: I've got three of my own.
It's hard work, but you'll soon get used to it.

▲ for talking about things you are familiar with, or becoming familiar with, and accept

2a be/get | + **used** to | (+ not) | + -ing

Living in LA, I'm used to driving everywhere.
Are you getting used to working at home?
It took me a long time to get used to not having the children around.

▲ for talking about things you are accustomed to doing, or situations you are becoming familiar with

3 is/was etc. | + **used** | + for | + -ing
is/was etc. | + **used** | + to-infinitive

The lever can be used for adjusting the height.
Solar panels are used to provide heating.

▲ for describing how and why things are used

Collocations

Time expressions that frequently go with Grammar patterns 1 and 1a are: *then, before, often, always, never, in the old days, in those days, when I/he/she etc. was young.*

In those days, we never used to stay out after midnight.
When I was young, we used to call the teacher 'Sir'.

Expressions that frequently go with Grammar patterns 2 and 2a are: *by now, finally, slowly, gradually.*

I think the children are used to me by now.
We're slowly getting used to all the stairs.

Set phrases

· **… than it/they** etc. **used to be**
It's a lot more expensive than it used to be.
He's much less touchy now than he used to be.
▲ for making comparisons with states of things in the past

· ❛**things ain't what they used to be.**❜
It's impossible to get a decent cup of tea nowadays. ~ I know, things just ain't what they used to be.
▲ to comment nostalgically and humorously on what's changed

Exercises

1 Study these concordance lines and classify the examples of *used* according to its grammar pattern:

GP 1: used to + action verb
GP 1a: used to + state verb
GP 2: be/get + used to + NP
GP 2a: be/get + used to + -ing

a   There **used** to be a sign on the tower.
b   I'm **used** to sharing rooms with friends.
c   We were still getting **used** to the idea.
d   Two of my brothers **used** to be car mechanics.
e   His eyes were getting **used** to the dim light.
f   My Mum **used** to take me when I was very little.
g   It is like trying to get **used** to driving a new car.
h   The boys at school **used** to make fun of me.
i   It's really hard to get **used** to something different.
j   His family **used** to come and stay for a week.

2 Note that there is no present form for 'used + to + bare infinitive'. You cannot say I use to study a lot these days. Instead, you can say *I study a lot these days* or *I study all the time these days* or *I'm always/forever studying*.

Complete these sentences about past and present habits using this model:

I never used to study, but now I study all the time.

a   She never used to read, but now ….
b   … but now they argue all the time.
c   You never used to worry, but now …
d   … but now I swim a lot.
e   Andy never used to smoke …
f   We never used to get junk mail, but now …

3 'Used to + bare infinitive' and 'would + bare infinitive' (→ would) can both be used to talk about past habits:

The bus used to stop here.
The bus would stop here.

But 'would + infinitive' is used for past actions, not past states. You can say *There used to be a pub here then*. But you can't say There would be a pub here then.

In the following text, delete any examples of *would* that are not acceptable:

When I was young we (a. *used to/would*) live near a river. We (b. *often used to/would often*) go and swim there. It (c. *used to/would*) be very clean in those days. There never (d. *used to/would*) be any factories or houses nearby. Now it's changed. It's no longer safe to swim there. But in those days we (e. *used to/would*) spend most of the summer there. Sometimes we (f. *used to/would*) take tents and spend the nights there. We (g. *used to/would*) light a fire and cook sausages and things. In those days we (h. *used to/would*) think that nothing would ever change …

4 Rewrite these sentences, using *be/get used to*:

I didn't like the food here at first, but now it's not so bad.
→ *I'm getting used to the food here.*
I didn't like the weather then and I still don't like it.
→ *I haven't got used to the weather.*

a   We found the noise intolerable at first, but now it's bearable.
b   The humidity was unbearable, initially, but now I don't notice it at all.
c   At first the pace of life was difficult for us. But now it's not so bad.
d   When he started this job, Derrin hated getting up early, and he still hates it.
e   Going to work on the underground was an awful shock, and I still dislike it.
f   Sharing a room was awkward at first, but it doesn't seem quite so awkward now.

very

[adverb] to emphasize adjectives and adverbs: *His books are very good.* • *You play the guitar very well.* • *We don't have very much time.*
[adjective] exact, extreme: *He arrived at that very moment.*
• *I stayed to the very end.*

Grammar patterns

1 **very** | + adjective/adverb

The hotel was very expensive, but it was worth it.
We'll be late, but not very late.
Do you eat out very often?

▲ to emphasize the quality of something

2 **very** | + much/many or little/few

I like your sister very much.
There are very few good film critics.
Did you like the book? ~ Yes, very much.

▲ to emphasize the quantity of something

3 **very** | + superlative

This is the very latest fashion.
I want you to do your very best.

▲ to add emphasis to a superlative

4 **very** | + NP

This is the very thing I was looking for.
They climbed to the very top.

▲ to emphasize the exactness or extremeness of something

Collocations

Adjectives that commonly occur with *very* are: *good, nice, difficult, important, different, hard,* and (*not*) *likely.*

This cake is very nice: did you make it yourself?
It is very difficult to predict earthquakes.
They may accept our offer, but it's not very likely.

Other words that commonly occur with *very* are: *much, well, little, few, often,* and the combination 'adjective + *indeed*'.

There was very little hope left that they would be rescued.
I don't go out very often.
Some parts of the city are very old indeed.

Set phrases

- '**very well, thanks**'
  How are you? ~ Very well, thanks. And you?
  ▲ to respond to the greeting 'How are you?'

- '**thank you very much**'
  Here's your receipt. ~ Thank you very much.
  ▲ to thank someone politely

- **not very**
  What's his German like? ~ Not very good.
  You're not very strong, are you?
  ▲ to say that something has the opposite quality, often to be polite, or less forceful

- **can't/couldn't very well …**
  We can't very well leave her there. We'll have to take her.
  I couldn't very well refuse.
  ▲ to say that it is not right or possible to do something

- '**very much so**'
  Does the smoke annoy you? ~ Very much so.
  ▲ to agree or say 'yes' emphatically

- […] **very own**
  At last she had her very own office.
  This is Derek's very own work.
  ▲ to emphasize that something belongs to somebody and to nobody else

- **the very same** = exactly the same
  We discovered we had been to the very same school.

Exercises

1 Change the underlined adjectives into a less forceful form, using *not very*:

He's <u>unfriendly</u>.
→ *He's not very friendly* (OR: *He isn't very friendly.*)
They seemed <u>unwelcoming</u>.
→ *They didn't seem very welcoming.*

a She was <u>unhelpful</u>. She didn't do a thing.
b Your suggestion is <u>unrealistic</u>. It won't work.
c The children seemed <u>uninterested</u>. Perhaps they were tired.
d The cabin attendants were <u>unattractive</u>, which is unusual.
e The results of his study are <u>insignificant</u>. But I didn't say so.
f I'm feeling <u>unwell</u>. I think I'll go home.
g Your writing is <u>illegible</u>. I can't read it.
h The waiters were <u>impolite</u>. I'm not eating there again.

2 You use *very* (and *extremely*) with gradable adjectives, such as *good, unusual, attractive*, that have degrees:

The film was very good.
This building is very unusual.
The women were extremely attractive.

You don't usually use *very* with ungradable adjectives, like *brilliant, unique,* or *stunning*. Ungradable adjectives are absolute and don't have degrees. Instead, you use adverbs like *absolutely, totally, completely*:

The film was absolutely brilliant.
This building is totally unique.
The women were completely stunning.

Choose the best adverb to complete these sentences:

a What was the weather like? ~ It was (*very/absolutely*) freezing.
b Take a pullover with you: it's (*very/absolutely*) cold.
c This salad is (*very/absolutely*) delicious: what's in it?
d Try this Mexican tomato dip: it's (*extremely/totally*) tasty.
e How was your holiday? ~ (*Very/Totally*) brilliant!
f Did you meet Sue at the party? ~ Yes, I thought she was (*very/totally*) nice.
g The problem was (*very/absolutely*) difficult to solve.
h I'm trying to do this exercise but it's (*extremely/completely*) impossible.

3 Note that you can use *really* for both gradable and ungradable adjectives:

The film was really good.
The film was really brilliant.

Rewrite sentences a–d in exercise 1, using *really*.

4 *Very* is used with adjectives, but not comparative forms:

It was much cooler inside.
OR: *It was very much cooler inside.*
OR: *It was far cooler inside.* (NOT ~~It was very cooler …~~)

You can use *very* with adjectives that end in *–ed,* especially those describing feelings:

I am very interested in how the brain works.
She was very frightened, but she didn't show it.

But if the *-ed* word is a past participle with a passive meaning, you can't use *very*. You have to use expressions like (*very*) *much* or *greatly*:

He was greatly admired by his people.
Your help has been (very) much appreciated.

Decide which of these sentences is correct. Correct the ones that are not:

a I'll be very disappointed if Ivan doesn't remember my birthday.
b The government's position has been very criticized.
c London was very warmer than I expected.
d They were very worried about the future.
e The speaker told a joke, but no one was very amused.
f This hotel is very more expensive than the other one.
g Your Spanish is very improved: what have you been doing?
h Bernhardt was very loved by her fans.
i I am feeling very confused. Can you explain it again?
j Her early poetry was very influenced by Yeats.

want

[regular verb: *want, wanted, wanted*] to desire or need something or someone: *Do you want a drink?* • *The dog wants to go for a walk.* • *They wanted me to pay a deposit.*
[countable noun] lack of something: *I'm suffering from want of sleep.*

Grammar patterns

1 **want** | + NP | (+ adverbial)

I want a long holiday.
What do you want for dinner?
They say they want breakfast in the garden.
I want it now!

▲ to express a wish or need for something
(*I'd like … would you like …* is less forceful.)

2 **want** | + to-infinitive

Do you want to go out for a drink? ~ No, I don't really want to: not in this rain.
I wanted to phone, but I didn't have my mobile.
I've been wanting to meet you.

▲ to express a wish or need to do something

3 **want** | + NP | + to-infinitive

They wanted me to go to the police station.
I don't want anyone to use my computer while I'm away.

▲ to talk about needs or wishes involving other people

Do you want me to post these letters?
I want you to check these proofs.

▲ to offer to do things, or to ask people to do things

4 **want** | + NP | + past participle/adjective

Sue wants this report photocopied and sent out to all our members.
I want the living room nice and tidy before the guests arrive.

▲ to say how you need or wish something to be done

Collocations

Adverbs that frequently occur with *want* are: *always, just, never,* and *really.*

I just wanted to have a good time.
This is what I have always wanted.
I really wanted this part badly.
Nigel never wanted to be captain.

The most common infinitives that follow *want to* are: *be, do, get, go, know, say, see,* and *talk.*

We don't want to get lost, do we?
I want to know what she said.
I just wanted to say thank you.

Set phrases

• **' do you want …?'**
Do you want some more coffee?
▲ to offer something to somebody

• **' did you want …?'**
Did you want to see me?
Did you want a cup of tea?
▲ to ask what someone wants, politely

• **' who wants …?'**
Who wants more turkey?
▲ to offer something to a group

• **' if you want'**
I'll clean up, if you want.
▲ to make an offer

• **' what I (really) want is …'**
What I really want is a nice cup of tea.
▲ to make explicit what you want

• **' I just wanted to say …'**
I just wanted to say that it's been really nice working with you.
▲ to introduce, politely, an announcement

• **for want of […]** = because of a lack of something
She took unskilled work, for want of a better job offer.

Exercises

1 Classify these concordance lines with want according to their Grammar pattern (1–4). There are three of each pattern.

a   Do you **want** to borrow my car?
b   He didn't **want** anyone else to suffer.
c   We **want** Annabelle and Steven to enjoy the things we never had.
d   All customers – international and external – **want** quality.
e   I want a job done and I **want** it done properly.
f   I **want** to apologise. I should have been here to meet you.
g   I'll take over here, if you **want** a break?
h   There are many things I **want** to do.
i   I'm sure you'll find what you **want** amongst this lot.
j   Patients **want** their treatment carried out by a competent trained doctor.
k   Do you **want** someone to come and fetch you?
l   Staff clearly **want** the issue resolved quickly.

2 Put the word in brackets in the correct place in the sentence:

a   (to) I want you marry me.
b   (you) Do want to come with us?
c   (never) I wanted to go to university.
d   (her) They wanted to sign a contract.
e   (put) I want the books back on the shelves.
f   (don't) What we want is a lot of noise.
g   (just) I want you to sit down and be quiet.
h   (always) Jamie wanted to be a cook.
i   (I) What really want is a glass of water.
j   (painted) We wanted the chairs not varnished.

3 Note that:

want does not usually take the continuous form.

want is not usually used in the passive (except in the sense: *He's wanted by the police; You're wanted on the phone.*)

want is never followed by a that-clause

to negate *want* you say, for example, *I don't want to do it,* NOT ~~I want not to do it.~~

Decide which of these sentences are correct, and then correct the incorrect ones:

a   I want that you return my money.
b   What are you wanting to eat?
c   I don't want that they wear their shoes in the house.
d   Tell Christie that she is wanted on the phone.
e   The police want you not to park here.
f   A sandwich is wanted by the boys.
g   I am wanting that you don't smoke in here.
h   What do you want that I do?

4 Here are some scrambled song titles with *want* or *wanna* (= *want to*). Can you unscramble them?

a   love/I/want (Elton John)
b   you/I/tell/to/want (The Beatles)
c   man/wanna/your/I/be (The Beatles)
d   hand/to/I/your/want/hold (The Beatles)
e   dance/you/do/want/to? (Bette Midler)
f   to/really/I/all/do/want (Cher)
g   to/fool/want/I'm/you/a (Frank Sinatra)
h   higher/you/take/want/I/to (Sly and the Family Stone)
i   you/want/I/be/only/with/to (Dusty Springfield)
j   secret/to/a/you/do/know/want? (The Beatles)
k   wanted/doesn't/be/want/somebody/to? (The Partridge Family)

was / were

[past tense of irregular verb *be*] (1) a lexical verb, linking two ideas: *Yesterday was Thursday.* • *Were Jane and Robin at the concert?*
(2) auxiliary verb: *It was raining when we arrived.* • *Their bags were opened and searched.*

The forms of the verb *be* in the past are:

	singular	*plural*
1st person	I was	we were
2nd person	you were	
3rd person	he was	
	she was	they were
	it was	

→ be
→ being
→ am/ is/are
→ been

Grammar patterns
(main verb)

1 NP | + **was/were** | + NP/adjective/adverbial

The woman you spoke to was our next-door neighbour.
What was the match like? ~ It was a bit disappointing.
Why weren't you at work last week? ~ I was off sick.

▲ to give more information about the subject, such as who, or what, or where, or when, or how

(auxiliary verb)

2 NP | + **was/were** | + -ing

It was getting dark and the streetlights were going on …
How did you break your arm? ~ I was skiing and I fell.

▲ to say that something was in progress at some time in the past, often to provide the background for an event
(This pattern is called the past continuous.)

3 NP | + **was/were** | + past participle

Paper was first used in China.
We were given a guided tour of the palace.

Where was your camera stolen?

▲ to talk about things that happened, without needing to say who or what caused them
(This is the simple past passive.)

4 if | + NP | + **was/were** etc. | + NP | + would/might etc.

If I was in such pain, I would see a doctor.
If it wasn't for you, I don't know what I'd do.
What would you do, if you were me?

▲ to talk about hypothetical present states
(This is called the second conditional. → if)

Collocations

Was/were are auxiliary verbs which help to form the past continuous tenses.
The most frequent verbs with the continuous (all tenses) are (in order of frequency): *go, do, get, come, try, look, make, work, talk, wait,* and *think*.

He was going too fast and the car went out of control.
Everyone was looking at me.
I was thinking, maybe we should get a dog.

The most frequent adverbs that combine with continuous forms (all tenses) are: *still, now, also, already, just, always, currently, only, really, actually, constantly,* and *simply.*

It was still raining when we woke up the next morning.
Several people were already queuing …
We were just talking about you.

Set phrases

- **was/were born**
  Where were you born? ~ I was born in New Zealand.
  ▲ for talking about a birthplace

- **' if I were you … '**
  If I were you, I would forget all about him.
  I'd put in central heating, if I were you.
  ▲ for giving advice

- **wish you were here!**
  Having a lovely time in Nice. Wish you were here. Love, G.
  ▲ a common expression when writing postcards on holiday

- **as it were**
  Fiona is my right-hand man, as it were.
  ▲ to make what you are saying sound less exact, less literal

- '**was telling / was saying …**'
  Mike was telling me they have this tradition in Ireland that …
  I was saying to Ron, they can be very nice, noodles …
  ▲ an informal way of reporting speech

Exercises

❶ Study these concordance lines with *was* and classify them according to the Grammar patterns 1–4:

a The girl who **was** driving smiled at Roger and pulled up.
b Thanks to proper medical care the infection **was** cured.
c The street below **was** in darkness.
d I **was** sent to what were known as elocution lessons.
e Corman **was** following me around with the camera.
f We rang Duncan to ask where he **was** going on holiday.
g If there **was** anything she could do to help she would.
h She **was** about forty and a little fat.
i She fainted and **was** taken to hospital.
j If you knew which horse **was** going to win the Grand National you could make a fortune.
k Ryan's father **was** in the music business.
l If the airline **was** to succeed it needed to be sold to the public.

❷ Choose the most likely form of the verb in these sentences:

a We (*played/were playing*) tennis, when it (*started/was starting*) to rain, so we came inside.
b The doorbell (*rang/was ringing*) just as I (*got/was getting*) into bed. So I ignored it.
c We (*got/were getting*) to the station just as the train (*left/was leaving*), but we managed to catch it in time.
d I hurt my back: I (*rode/was riding*) a horse and I (*fell off/was falling off*).
e I'm sorry I haven't finished the assignment: I (*worked/was working*) on it, when my computer (*crashed/was crashing*).
f My mother and father (*met/were meeting*) because she (*worked/was working*) as a nurse when he had to have an operation.

g Bruno (*came down/was coming down*) in the lift, when the power (*went out/was going out*). He was stuck there for more than an hour.
h When I (*woke up/was waking up*), it (*snowed/was snowing*), so I (*went/was going*) skiing.

❸ Here are some famous achievements and discoveries. Make sentences about them, using the past passive with these verbs:

invent	discover	write	climb
make	compose	build	paint

1593 Thermometer
The thermometer was invented in 1593.

a 1506 *The Mona Lisa*
b 1603 Shakespeare's *Hamlet*
c 1800 the electric battery
d 1824 Beethoven's *Ninth Symphony*
e 1889 the Eiffel Tower
f 1930 Pluto
g 1939 *Gone With the Wind*
h 1953 Mount Everest

❹ Here are some film titles that include forms of the verb *be*: *am, is, are, was, were*. Can you complete them?

a *I .... Sam.* (starring Sean Penn, 2001)
b *I .... a Teenage Werewolf.* (directed by Gene Fowler, 1957)
c *The Devil .... a Woman.* (starring Marlene Dietrich, 1935)
d *How the West .... Won.* (with Gregory Peck and James Stewart, 1963)
e *Guess who .... coming to Dinner?* (directed by Stanley Kramer, with Sidney Poitier)
f *A Star .... Born.* (last remade in1976, with Barbara Streisand)
g *Everything you wanted to know about Sex but .... afraid to Ask.* (directed by Woody Allen,1972)
h *Those .... the Days.* (with William Holden, 1940)
i *........... Paris Burning?* (French war film with Jean-Paul Belmondo, 1966)
j *I .... a Male War Bride.* (directed by Howard Hawks, with Cary Grant, 1949)
k *The Russians .... Coming, the Russians .... Coming.* (Norman Jewison, 1966)

way

[countable noun] (1) method, style, behaviour: *I liked the way she did the presentation.* • *Do it your way, if it's easier.* • *You'll get used to our strange ways.*
(2) route, road, direction, distance: *Can you tell me the way to Harrods?* • *Which way did they go?* • *We're still a long way from the turn-off.*
[adverb] by a large amount: *I'm way behind in my work.*

Grammar patterns

1 determiner | (+ adjective) | + **way** | + of | + -ing

A good way of curing hiccups is to drink lots of water.
What's the most effective way of removing wine stains?

▲ to talk about how to achieve a particular result

2 determiner | (+ adjective) | + **way** | + to-infinitive

The best way to get to Harlem is to take the A-train.
One way to preserve lemons is by using salt.

▲ to talk about how to achieve a particular result (Patterns 1 and 2 are interchangeable.)

3 in | + a/an | (+ adjective) | + **way**

He did it in an underhand way.
Can you do my hair in a different way this time?

▲ to talk about the manner or style of doing something

4 the | + **way** | + that-clause
  the | + **way** | + in which | + clause

I'll show you the way that my grandmother used to poach eggs.
There are some problems regarding the way in which the data were collected.
I don't like the way Gary shouts at the kids.

▲ to identify the manner or style of doing things

5 verb | + your/his etc. | + **way** | + preposition | + NP

We made our way towards the lighthouse.
She elbowed her way to the front.
Harry munched his way through two huge bowls of chips.

▲ to talk about doing something progressively and purposefully

Collocations

The following adjectives often go with *way*, in the sense of method, style, behaviour: *easy, good, best, proper, hard, ideal, quick, right, wrong, possible, new, old, different, same, funny,* and *strange.*

What's the proper way to tie a bow tie?
You always do it the hard way.
That's a funny way of writing a seven.

These adjectives go with *way*, in the sense of route, road, direction, distance: *best, long, quickest, shortest, right, wrong, own,* and *separate*:

What's the quickest way to Rye from Hastings?
After we split up, we each went our separate ways.

Verbs that often go before 'determiner + way' are: *go, lose, find, make, ask, tell, know, show,* and *lead.*

We lost our way in the darkness.
We made our way towards the shore.
Can you show us the way to the bypass?
You lead the way: I'll follow.

Verbs that go with *way* (without *the*) are *give* and *make*:

Make way! There's a houseboat coming.
You have to give way to the traffic on your right.

Set phrases

• '**no way**'
Would you ever go on a quiz show? ~ No way!
▲ to say that something is impossible

• '**by the way**'
By the way, do you remember that couple we met in Benidorm? Well …
Are you doing the cooking tonight? I've done the shopping, by the way.
▲ to introduce a topic that is not directly related to what has been said, or to add something extra that you have just thought of

• **in a bad way** = ill or not well
The business is in a bad way. We may have to reduce our staff.

- **all the way / the whole way** = during the entire journey, or time
  The baby cried the whole way.

- **either way ...**
  You can take the old road or the new one: either way, it will take an hour or so.
  - ▲ to say that it doesn't matter which of two possibilities you choose

Exercises

① Look at these concordance lines with *way* and classify them according to the Grammar patterns 1–5. (There are three for each pattern.)

a The best **way** to get there is to hire a car and driver.
b The **way** in which we breathe affects our physical, mental and emotional well-being.
c I was making my **way** slowly up Granville Street.
d Evening classes are a good **way** of meeting people.
e Sam has a strange **way** of showing gratitude.
f He entered the room in an awkward blundering **way**.
g That's the **way** they do things in LA.
h It's a good **way** to get attention.
i This boy behaved in an underhand **way**.
j He pushed his **way** through the shoppers.
k What's the best **way** of relieving low back pain?
l There is no perfect **way** to bring up children.
m They're disgusted that anyone would abandon the puppies in such a cruel **way**.
n You don't like the **way** they dress.
o I spotted Dad edging his **way** through the throng.

② Ten examples of *way* have been removed from this text. Can you replace them?

Q: What's the best of cooking artichokes?
A: One is to cut off the leaves and boil the hearts (or 'chokes'), and toss them into a salad. That's the they eat them in Spain. That, you don't have to bother with the leaves. Another is to deep-fry the baby ones in oil, the same you fry chips. I had them done that in Rome and it's the I prefer. Either, artichokes are delicious, and very good for you. There's no you are going to get fat, eating artichokes!

③ Choose words from the two lists to complete these sentences:

adjectives: own   hard   funny   possible   wrong
verbs: ask   make   clear   lead   find

a You've put your pullover on the .... way again: it's back-to-front.
b When the band split up, each musician went his .... way.
c The government promises it will .... a way out of the present crisis.
d There's a policeman. Why don't you .... him the way?
e There are several .... ways of cooking an egg: frying, boiling, poaching, etc.
f The resignation of the government will .... the way for fresh elections.
g MacDuff: you .... the way and we'll follow.
h I learned to cook the .... way: through trial and error.
i If there is a fire you should .... your way quickly to the ground floor.
j That's a .... way to drink coffee: through a straw!

④ Many set phrases with *way* are formed from prepositions. For example:

in a way = to some extent
in the way = causing an obstruction
on the way / on your way = on your journey
out of the way = no longer causing an obstruction
out of your way = inconveniently far
by way of = as a form of

Complete these sentences by choosing an appropriate phrase:

a 'Hello,' he said, ... conversation.
b .... , I regret what I said, although she deserved it.
c I'll move this chair .... , so you can see the TV.
d I'm sorry, I didn't mean to make you go ....
e Can you pick up some milk .... home?
f Excuse me, your car is .... I can't get out.

well

[irregular adverb: comparative and superlative forms are *better, best*] in a good or skilful or thorough way: *The band played well.* • *How well can you speak Thai?* • *Mix the ingredients well.*
[irregular adjective: comparative and superlative forms are *better, best*] healthy, good: *You look well.* • *He's not a well man.*
[discourse marker] to signal a pause or change of direction in the conversation: *Well, let me think, I suppose, erm …;* • *Well, I'm not sure I agree …* • *Well, what about the football …?*

→ good

Grammar patterns

1   verb | (+ very/fairly/quite etc.) | + **well**
   well | + past participle

   I thought you handled the situation very well.
   She sings well.
   The boys are well behaved.

   ▲ to talk about things being done in a good way, or to say with approval how things are

   How well do you know Adrian?
   The salad should be well tossed.

   ▲ to talk about doing things in a complete way

2   could/might/may | + **well** | + bare infinitive

   Who's phoning at this time of night? ~That may well be the doctor.
   Jim could well have left town by now.

   ▲ to express strong possibility (→ may, could)

3   to be/feel/look etc. | + **well**

   Are you well?
   I'm feeling much better, thanks.
   You look well.

   ▲ to talk about a person's health

4   **well** | + adverbial

   We didn't get home until well after midnight.
   Arsenal are well on the way to victory.

Please let us know your plans well in advance.
There were well over a hundred people there.

▲ to add emphasis to adverbs and prepositions

Collocations

Well is often qualified by the following words: *very, quite, rather, fairly, pretty.*

   He played that quite well, didn't he?
   She writes pretty well for a beginner.

Well combines with many past participles to form compound adjectives: *well prepared, well paid, well built, well dressed, well known,* plus the expression *well off.*

   The job is not very well paid but I enjoy it.
   You can tell by their fur coats that they are well off.

Well commonly adds emphasis to these two adjectives: *aware* and *worth.*

   I am well aware that you are busy, but it's not an excuse.
   The pyramids are well worth visiting.

Set phrases

· **as well (as …)** = in addition to
   Can I have a three black marker pens, and a blue one as well?
   As well as my family, all my wife's family came too.

· **do well to …** = be advised to
   You'd do well to get a second opinion.

· **may/might (just) as well …**
   The bus is never going to come. We may as well walk.
   ▲ to talk about doing something which you don't really want to do, but there's not much choice

· **well and truly** = totally
   The rain came down and I got well and truly soaked.

· **just as well**
   It's just as well we had a spare key, or we might have been locked out.
   ▲ to say that something is convenient or helpful

Exercises

1 Order the words to make sentences with *well*:

a plays/Fiona/well/piano/the
b type/can/well/how/you?
c children/not/well/the/very/were/behaved
d is/read/can/but/he/well/his/terrible/writing
e taken/they/well/the/may/bus/have
f look/don't/very/you/well
g castle/visit/worth/is/the/a/well
h was/a/just/taxi/as/it/took/we/well

2 Like *well*, the following adverbs have identical adjective forms: *fast, hard, early, late*:
(adjective) *the fast car; hard work*, etc.
(adverb) *he ran fast; she worked hard*, etc.

Choose from the above words the best word to complete each of these sentences. Then say if the word is an adjective or an adverb.

a He drove too .... and was booked for speeding.
b Teaching children is .... work, but it's very rewarding.
c If you arrive .... , you'll miss the best bit.
d She sings .... but she can't act.
e I like to get up .... , even at the weekend.
f 'The .... bird catches the worm'. (expression)
g You will have to study .... if you want to pass the exam.
h Because of the .... start, the game didn't finish until 11pm.
i She wasn't feeling .... so she went home.
j The .... train takes an hour. The slow one takes 90 minutes.

3 Match the two parts of these short dialogues:

a How would you like your steak?
b How are you?
c It's OK, the train hasn't left yet.
d I want you to do this essay again.
e I passed my final exams.
f There's nothing on TV. Shall we go to the movies?

1 ~ Just as well.
2 ~ Well done!
3 ~ Well done, please.
4 ~ We might as well.
5 ~ Very well.
6 ~ Very well, thanks.

4 In conversation, *well* can be used for different discourse purposes, such as:

1 to fill a pause
2 to indicate a new topic, or return to an old topic
3 to introduce direct speech that is being reported
4 to indicate the end of the conversation
5 to express your doubt about what someone has said
6 to indicate that you are waiting for someone to speak

Identify the purpose of each instance of *well* in this dialogue:

A: (a) Well, as I was saying, I'm looking for someone to share my flat with. I phoned Gary and asked him and he said (b) 'Well, I'll let you know,' but that was six weeks ago, so then I thought of you, and how you're not happy where you are.
B: (c) Well, that's not entirely true, it's just that (d) well, erm, you know, the room is a bit small, that's all.
A: So you don't want to move?
B: Erm …
A: (e) Well?
B: Not really.
A: (f) Well, that's all I wanted to know. I'll speak to you later …

what

[question pronoun **and** determiner] to ask questions (see patterns below) about something or someone: *What's that on your nose?* • *What did Cheryl say?* • *What music do you like?*
[relative pronoun] to identify the thing you are talking about, or to add extra information about it: *This is what I wanted to give you for your birthday.* • *What I like about you is your smile.*

Grammar patterns

1 **what** | (+ NP) | + verb | + ?

What happened?
What kind of person would do a thing like that?

▲ to ask about the agent or cause of something (this is called a subject question)

1a **what** | (+ NP) | + is/was etc. | + NP | + ?

What's your job?
What colour are his eyes?

▲ to ask about the identity or characteristics of something or someone

1b **what** | (+ NP) | + auxiliary | + subject | + verb | + ?

What did Dan say?
What are the children doing?
What kinds of books do you read?

▲ to ask about the thing or activity etc. that is the object of the verb (This is called an object question.)

2 question | + **what** | (+ NP) | + clause | + ?
statement | + **what** | (+ NP) | + clause

Do you know what time it is?
Tell me what happened exactly.

▲ to make a question indirect, perhaps in order to be polite

2a question | + **what** | (+ NP) | + to-infinitive | + ?
statement | + **what** | (+ NP) | + to-infinitive

Did you understand what to do?
Now I remember what verb to use.

▲ to talk about the objects of your thoughts, memories, understanding, etc.

3 **what** | + clause | + is/was etc. | + NP

What tourists like about the place is the colour and movement.
What I really need is a new bank card.

▲ to draw extra attention to the idea in the second part of the sentence

4 **what** | (+ adjective) | + NP | + !

What a lovely day! What a change!
What ugly buildings!

▲ to show surprise, pleasure, or shock

Collocations

As a determiner, *what* is frequently followed by these words: *kind of, type of, sort of.*

What type of contact lenses do you wear?

like (→ like) is also frequently used with *what*:

What does she look like?

What is often followed by *do you think* to form indirect questions:

What do you think the time is?
What kind of bird do you think that is?

The verbs that most frequently precede *what* in Grammar patterns 2 and 2a are: *know, see, tell, wonder, ask, understand, show,* and *remember.*

I know what you must be thinking.
I wonder what's for dinner.
Show me what you wrote.
Can you remember what they said?

Set phrases

• **'guess what! ...'**
Guess what! I passed my driving test!
▲ to announce good news

• **'I know what ...'**
I know what. We could borrow dad's car.
▲ to introduce an idea or suggestion

- **what's more …** = moreover
Green tea tastes delicious. What's more, it's good for you.

- ' **what about …?** '
I'm busy on Thursday. ~ What about Friday?
  ▲ to make a suggestion

- **what if …?**
What if your boyfriend finds out?
  ▲ to ask about or present a hypothetical situation

- ' **so what?** '
You're blocking my view. ~ So what?
  ▲ to say, impolitely, that something doesn't concern you

Exercises

❶ **There are twelve examples of** *what* **that have been taken out of this text. Can you put them back?**

Dear Belinda,
I don't know to do about my parents. I am sixteen, and, 's more, I'm very grown up for my age. But my mum and dad won't let me do I want. They tell me to wear and to do, and even to think! Do you know I mean? And, really drives me mad is that they ask me I want to do but they never listen to I tell them. A disaster! Tell me you think I should do.

Desperate.

❷ **Choose words from the list to complete these questions:**

make   breed   size   nationality
model   colour   type   time

a What .... shoes do you take? ~ 42.
b What .... does the bus leave? ~ At 6.00.
c What .... of music do you like? ~ Reggae and jazz mainly.
d What .... would you prefer? ~ A light blue, a duck-egg blue.
e What .... is your watch? ~ It's a Rolex.
f What .... of dog is that? ~ I think it's an Irish setter.
g What .... are you? ~ I'm Canadian.
h What .... of Nokia are you interested in? ~ The latest one.

❸ **Add** *do you think* **to these questions, to make them less direct. Make any other necessary changes.**

What is the time? → *What do you think the time is?*
What does this mean? → *What do you think this means?*

a What is that black thing?
b What are you doing?
c What will the weather be like?
d What can we do to help?
e What do spiders eat?
f What does Jack do?
g What did the teacher say?
h What would the police have done?

❹ **Here are some song titles with** *what*. **Can you complete them by choosing words from the list?**

love   found   friends   want   morning
wonderful   deserve   thing   fool   world

a 'What is this .... called love?' (Cole Porter)
b 'Oh what a beautiful ....' (Rogers and Hammerstein)
c 'What kind of .... am I?' (Frank Sinatra)
d 'What a .... world.' (Louis Armstrong)
e 'I still haven't .... what I'm looking for.' (U2)
f 'What have I done to .... this?' (Dusty Springfield)
g 'That's what .... are for.' (Dionne Warwick)
h 'You can't always get what you ....' (Rolling Stones)
i 'What the .... needs now is love.' (Burt Bacharach)
j 'What now, my .... ?' (Sonny and Cher)

when

Grammar patterns

1 **when** | + is/was etc. | + NP
   when | + auxiliary | + subject | + verb

   When is lunch?
   When does he arrive?
   When will you be having dinner?

   ▲ to ask questions about the times of things

2 question/statement | + **when** | + clause

   Do you know when the film starts?
   I asked the receptionist when the next course would begin.

   ▲ to ask indirect questions or to report questions about time

3 question/statement | + **when** | + to-infinitive

   Do you remember when to pay?
   I don't know when to tell Derek.
   The brochure tells you when to register for the conference.

   ▲ to talk about the time for doing things, including scheduled events

4 clause | + **when** | + clause
   when | + clause | + clause

   We were halfway up when the lift stopped.
   When I was at university I shared a house with friends.

   ▲ to talk about events in relation to other time periods

5 will | + bare infinitive | + **when** |
   + (present tense) clause

   I'll phone you when I have more news.
   When the clock strikes twelve the fireworks will begin.

   ▲ to talk about future events in relation to other future events

6 **when** | + -ing

   Please switch out the lights when leaving.
   Make sure your back is straight when working at the computer.

   ▲ to talk about routine processes or procedures

Collocations

When often follows the following nouns relating to time: *time, day(s), occasion(s), moment(s), bit, season, case(s),* and *period(s).*

   Do you remember that day when the garage roof blew off?
   There are still some occasions when you have to wear a tie.
   I liked the bit when James Bond was escaping from the sharks.
   What happens in cases when the correct blood type is not available?

When can also follow these expressions: *love it, like it, hate it, enjoy it,* etc.

   I like it when you rub my back.
   I hate it when the train is crowded and you have to stand.

Set phrases

- '**since when?**' = how long?
   Since when have you had a dog? ~ *Over a month now.*

- '**when you like**' = at a time that is convenient
   Come round when you like: we'll be home.

- '**when in Rome … (do as the Romans do)**'
   I don't usually wear shorts – but 'when in Rome' …!
   ▲ to say you should follow the local customs

Exercises

1 Put the word in brackets into the correct place in each sentence:

a (are) When you leaving for New York?
b (are) Do you know when they arriving?
c (does) 'When the bank open?' she asked.
d (opened) She phoned and asked when the bank.
e (to) You should find out when check-in.
f (will) When you arrive you phone?
g (when) Turn the lights off you go to bed.
h (when) Do you remember the time I lost my keys?
i (when) Since did you take sugar in your coffee?
j (it) I don't like when you work late and don't phone.

2 Write the actual questions:

I asked the caretaker when the park closed.
→ 'When does the park close?'

a He asked someone when the shops opened.
b At the ticket office I asked when the last bus left.
c I asked the receptionist when the next course would start.
d She asked me when I was going on holiday.
e Someone asked me when the bridge had been destroyed.
f She asked when she could see the doctor.
g Hamish asked when he had to pay.
h I asked the nurse when I would know the results.

3 Match the two parts of these sentences:

a Say hello to Gran …
b I'll be staying with a friend …
c I had lunch with Gran …
d Will you see Gran …
e Did you see Gran …
f I always have a nice time …
g I was having lunch with a friend …

1 when you are in Stockport?
2 when I'm in Stockport next week.
3 when you see her.
4 when I see Gran.
5 when you were there?
6 when Gran walked in.
7 when I was in Stockport.

4 The action in the *when*-clause can happen before, during or after the action in the main clause, depending on the tense of the verb in the main clause:

When I arrived, she made coffee.
(= I arrived and then she made coffee.)
When I arrived, she was making coffee.
(= I arrived at the same time as she was making coffee.)
When I arrived, she had made coffee.
(= She made coffee and then I arrived.)

Choose the best form of the verb to complete these sentences:

a When we got there, the film (*started/had started/was starting*) so we missed the first five minutes.
b The band waited for the President to arrive. When he arrived, they (*played/had played/were playing*) the national anthem.
c When the power went off I (*worked/had worked/was working*) at my computer, and I lost everything.
d When we (*went/had gone/were going*) through the mountains, the bus broke down.
e When the bus broke down, we all (*got off/had got off/were getting off*).
f When I first met Nick, I (*didn't read/hadn't read/wasn't reading*) any of his books.
g I (*studied/was studying/had studied*) Korean when I went to Seoul, so I could speak to people from day one.
h The ship (*left/was leaving/had left*) when all the passengers were aboard.
i It (*rained/was raining/had rained*) when the match started, and the grass was still wet.
j When you phoned I (*had/was having/had had*) dinner: that's why I didn't answer.

who

Grammar patterns

1   **who** | + verb | (+ object)

Who phoned?
Who's going to the party?

▲ to ask which person does, did, or will do something (This is called a subject question.)

1a   **who** | + is/was etc. | + NP

Who was Maria Callas? ~ She was a famous singer.

▲ to ask about the identity of someone.

1b   **who** | + auxiliary | + subject | + verb | (+ preposition)

Who do you prefer: Domingo or Pavarotti?
Who were you talking to?

▲ to ask about the person who is the object of a verb, or the object of a preposition (This is called an object question.)

2   question/statement | + **who** | + verb

Do you know who won?
Can you tell me who is on duty?
I don't know who she married.

▲ to speculate about people, or to ask a question about someone indirectly, perhaps in order to be polite

3   NP | + **who** [= subject] | + verb
    NP | (+ **who** [= object]) | + NP[=subject] | + verb

I don't like that man who reads the news.
The person (who) you should see is not here today.

▲ to identify the exact person you are referring to (This is called a defining relative clause.)

4   NP, | + **who**

Evelyn, who you met here once, she's our new boss.
James Dean, who died in a car crash, was a Hollywood icon.

▲ to add extra information about the person you are talking about (This is called a non-defining relative clause.)

Collocations

Verbs that frequently come before *who* in Grammar pattern 2 are: *know, decide, mention, say, ask, wonder, care, decide, remember, tell,* and *see.*

I don't know who my teacher is.
I wonder who that could be?
Go and see who that is.

Nouns and pronouns that frequently come before *who* in Grammar pattern 3 are: *those, people, someone, anyone, man, woman, person.*

Those who had tickets were allowed in.
Do you know anyone who speaks Turkish?

Set phrases

• **who knows?**
Where's Elef? ~ Who knows? She could be anywhere.
▲ to show that you don't know, and that probably no one else knows

• **who cares?** = I don't care
You'll break the chair! ~ Who cares? It's old anyway.

• **who's there? / who's that?**
Knock knock. ~ Who's there?
Amos. ~ Amos who?
A mosquito!
▲ to ask who is at the door

• **who's calling?**
Could I speak to Trevor McEwan, please? ~ Certainly. Who's calling? ~ This is Madhur Patel.
▲ a formal way of asking who is phoning

• **who else?**
I've invited Benny and Dan. ~ Who else? ~ Jane and Tibor.
▲ to ask about other people who may be included

- **to whom it may concern**
  To Whom It May Concern:
  I have known Professor Grundy for …
  ▲ a formal way of beginning a written testimonial

Exercises

❶ Subject and object questions.

Look at this diagram and write questions for the answers provided.

Who phoned Dawn? Jenny did.
Who did Dawn phone? Andy.

a	.... ? Andy and Bill did.	d	.... ? Andy.
b	.... ? Jenny.	e	.... ? Dawn did.
c	.... ? Dawn.	f	.... ? Nobody did.

❷ Direct and indirect questions. Put the word in brackets in the correct place in the sentence.

a (is) Who my teacher?
b (is) Can you tell me who my teacher?
c (was) Who that woman I saw you with last night?
d (was) I wonder who that.
e (is) Guess who coming to dinner!
f (is) Do you know who Marion seeing?
g (are) I don't care who you!
h (is) … or who your father!

❸ *Who* and *that*.

You can use *that* instead of *who* in defining relative clauses. But in direct questions (Grammar pattern 1) and indirect questions (Grammar pattern 2), and in non-defining relative clauses (Grammar pattern 4), you have to use *who*.

In this text, decide which examples of *who* can be replaced by *that*:

Who was Selwyn Toogood? You don't remember who he was? Well, he's that chap who did the quiz show on the telly in the seventies. Toogood, who died last week, was a household name. I remember him particularly well, because I was one of the many thousands of people who took part in that show. You probably don't remember who I am, either. But I was the spotty teenager who, when asked: 'Who wrote Beethoven's *Ninth Symphony*?' answered: 'Was it Brahms?'

❹ *Who* in defining relative clauses.

Note that you can leave out *who* when it is the object of the relative clause, but not when it is the subject:

The person who I spoke to had dark hair.
OR: *The person I spoke to had dark hair*

The person who spoke to me had dark hair.
but NOT: ~~The person spoke to me had dark hair.~~

In non-defining clauses, you have to use *who* (or some other relative pronoun):

My uncle, who you never met, lives in Montreal.
My uncle, who never met you, lives in Montreal.

Put *who* in these sentences, only where necessary:

a Jane Arnold, lives in Seville, is a good friend of mine.
b What's the name of that actor was in *Gladiator*?
c That woman you met at the conference just phoned.
d The waiter served us was incredibly slow.
e The children I taught spoke excellent English.
f Have you got the address of the man did your kitchen?
g My herbalist, is Chinese, recommends green tea.
h That writer you like, wrote *Emma*, what's her name?

why

Grammar patterns

1 **why** | + is/was etc. | + NP
   why | + auxiliary | + subject | + verb

   Why is the oven on?
   Why did Andrew quit his job?
   Why haven't you been to see the doctor yet?

   ▲ to ask the reason for something

2 question/statement | + **why** | + clause

   Do you know why Ellen phoned?
   I don't understand why they still teach Latin.

   ▲ to ask indirectly, or talk about, reasons

3 (the reason +) **why** | + clause | + clause

   The reason why I phoned is to ask you to dinner.
   Why they need another car is beyond me.
   (= I don't understand why they need another car.)

   ▲ to emphasize the reason for something

4 **why** | + determiner | + NP
   why | (+ not) | + infinitive

   Why all this fuss about the football?
   Why so many knives and forks?
   Why go to Dublin? Why not stay at home?

   ▲ to ask informal questions, where the verb or auxiliary
     can be omitted because it's obvious

Collocations

Why frequently follows *reason*:

   What is the reason why so many children suffer from asthma?
   The reason why I'm writing is to ask your advice.

Why questions are typically answered with *because*:

   Why are you leaving? ~ *Because it's late.*
   The reason why you haven't been paid is because you didn't invoice us.

Set phrases

• **(yes) why not?**
  Would you like to come back to my place? ~ *Why not?*
  ▲ to agree with something someone has suggested

• **why not …?/ why don't …?**
  How shall we feed everyone? ~ *Why not phone for some take-away pizzas?*
  My hair is a mess. ~ *Why don't you have it cut?*
  ▲ to make a suggestion

• **why ever …?**
  Miranda doesn't want any curry. ~ *Why ever not?*
  ▲ to emphasize a question, e.g. to show surprise or annoyance

• **why on earth …?**
  Why on earth did she have to bring Simon with her?
  ▲ to emphasize a question, e.g. to show surprise or annoyance

• **why me?**
  Chris, you can do the washing-up. ~ *Why me?*
  ▲ to show surprise that you have been chosen, blamed, etc.

• **why is it that …?**
  Why is it that women are better language learners? One reason may be …
  ▲ to frame a rhetorical question

Exercises

❶ Put the words in order to make sentences:

a you/moved/why/the/have/sofa?
b why/work/know/TV/doesn't/you/the/do?
c you/why/crying/me/tell/are
d late/must/why/a/they/there/are/reason/be
e understand/needs/don't/why/an/she/I/operation
f that/popular/are/why/theme parks/is/so/it?
g we/why/invite/neighbours/don't/the?
h you/eyes/love/why/your/are/I

❷ Can you match the two parts of these (corny) jokes?

a Why did the tomato go red?
b Why can some teachers see well?
c Why was the cucumber arrested?
d Why did the child study in the plane?
e Why do birds fly south in winter?
f Why is that man standing in the sink?
g Why did the fly fly?
h Why did the boy throw the clock out the window?

1 Because it's too far to walk.
2 Because it was pickled.
3 Because he's a tap dancer.
4 Because he wanted a higher education.
5 Because the spider spied her.
6 Because they have good pupils.
7 Because it saw the salad dressing.
8 Because he wanted to make time fly.

❸ What were the actual questions?

He asked the reason why the buses were running late.
→ *'Why are the buses running late?'*

a James asked me why I was wearing a tie.
b Someone asked why the road was blocked.
c I'll ask the mechanic if he knows why the car won't start.
d The teacher asked the boy why he hadn't done his homework.
e The interviewer asked the singer why she wouldn't sing in English.
f Can you ask your friend the reason why he parked his car on the lawn?
g The neighbour asked me if I knew why the lights had gone out.
h A person is at the door asking why we don't vote Labour.

❹ Eight examples of *why* have been taken out of this conversation. Can you put them back?

Dad: Alan, don't you help your brother with his homework?
Alan: Me?
Dad: Because you are good at history.
Alan: Well, all right. But I don't know you can't help him.
Dad: Because I'm cooking dinner, that's.
Alan: So, what's the question?
Gerry: 'Were the pharaohs buried in tombs?' Explain in one hundred words.
Alan: They want to know the pharaohs were buried in tombs? That's easy. Because they were dead.
Gerry: That can't be right.
Alan: Not?
Gerry: Because it's not a hundred words.
Alan: Look, I don't know you asked me in the first place.

will

[modal verb] (1) be willing: *Will you answer the phone?* • *She won't eat anything.*
(2) for predictions: *They'll be here soon.* • *If you take an umbrella, you won't get wet.*
(3) expresses habitual, expected behaviour: *She'll spend hours on the Internet every evening.* • *Snakes won't bite unless attacked.*

NOTE: The contraction of 'will + not' is *won't*.

Grammar patterns

1 will/won't | + bare infinitive

Terry will give you a lift to the football, if you like.
Will you have some more soup?
I'll pick you up at the airport.

▲ to make offers and promises

Will you get a loaf of bread, please?
Turn the TV down, will you?
I'll have the mixed salad followed by the fish.

▲ to make requests or orders

They say it will rain all weekend.
Will it take long? ~ No, it won't take a minute.
You'll love Hong Kong.

▲ to make statements and predictions about future events

Babies will utter their first words around the age of one.
On a good day, I'll run 15 miles.

▲ to talk about predictable behaviour, such as habits

2 will | + have | + past participle

I will have worked 60 hours this week.
Come round at 9. We will have eaten by then.

▲ to predict something that will be finished at a certain time

3 will | + be | + -ing

I'll be working late this evening.
The board of directors will be meeting on Monday.

▲ to talk about something that is in progress in the future, especially when talking about future plans and arrangements

The plane will be landing in ten minutes.
Will you be using your webcam this weekend?

▲ to talk about something that will happen as a matter of course

4 if-clause, | + NP | + will/won't | + bare infinitive

If your there are no tickets left, we'll go again another day.
The plants will die if you don't water them.

▲ to say what will happen, given a certain condition

(This is called the first conditional. → if)

Collocations

Will frequently combines with the semi-modal verbs *have to, need to,* and *be able to*:

I will have to call you back.
Will we need to bring our passports?
Patrick won't be able to attend the meeting.

Will commonly occurs with the adjectives *likely* and *unlikely* in the pattern: *it is likely/unlikely that X will happen.*

It is likely that DVDs will replace videos within five years.

Will commonly occurs with verbs that express our hopes and expectations, such as: *hope, think, know, guess, doubt, reckon, believe, imagine,* and *expect.*

Do you think it will rain?
I doubt very much if Michael will want to go.

Set phrases

· ' **I'll see / we'll see** '
Can we go to the beach? ~ We'll see.
▲ to say that you will decide something later

· **that'll be the day**
Arsenal will beat Manchester United. ~ That'll be the day.
▲ to say that you don't believe something will happen

Exercises

① Put the word in brackets in the correct place in the sentence:

a (will) They say it rain tomorrow.
b (won't) A lion attack an elephant.
c (will) Who be at the meeting?
d (will) When you have finished your exams?
e (will) I have to talk to Jonathan about it.
f (won't) If you hurry now, you be late.
g (will) The doctors think you be able to go to work soon.
h (will) When you be having lunch?
i (will) You need to go on-line to access the Internet.
j (won't) We start eating until you get here.

② *Will* is the most common way of talking about the future. But there are other ways. For example, you can use present tenses to show that the future event is connected to the present in some way:

I'm going to make myself a sandwich. (= to talk about arrangements, plans, intentions → going)
It looks like there are going to be lots of people at the march. (= to make a prediction, based on present evidence → going)
Jenny and I are having lunch together tomorrow. (= to talk about a planned arrangement)
The train leaves at 6.00 tomorrow morning. (= to talk about scheduled or timetabled events)
It is likely/It is bound to be crowded. (= to make predictions based on present evidence)

Note that *will* is the only choice when making offers, requests, promises, etc., and the most frequent choice when making predictions:

I'll help you with your French homework, if you like. (NOT: ~~I'm going to~~ …)
I imagine it will be a difficult decision. (*I imagine it's going to be* … is possible, especially in spoken language.)

Choose the best option in these pairs of answers. (Sometimes both options are possible.)

a A: The phone's ringing.
B: 1 I'll answer it.
   2 I'm going to answer it.
b A: What's the weather forecast for the weekend?
B: 1 It'll be cold and wet.
   2 It's going to be cold and wet.
c A: Are you ready to order, sir?
B: 1 Yes, I'll have a Pizza Margherita, please.
   2 Yes, I'm going to have a Pizza Margherita, please.
d A: How old are you?
B: 1 I'll be 29 next June.
   2 I'm going to be 29 next June.
e A: What are your plans for the weekend?
B: 1 I'll paint the kitchen.
   2 I'm going to paint the kitchen.
f A: I need a lift to the station.
B: 1 I'll take you.
   2 I'm going to take you.
g A: Can you come to lunch on Friday?
B: 1 No, I'll meet Dr Hockly at the airport.
   2 No, I'm meeting Dr Hockly at the airport.
h A: Are we very late?
B: 1 No, the concert will start at 8.30.
   2 No, the concert starts at 8.30.

③ Complete this conversation by choosing expressions from the list. (There are more expressions than spaces.)

I guess I'll	we'll see	I'll say
it won't	will you?	you're sure you won't?
will it?	that'll do	what'll it be?

A: (a) ....
B: I'll have a pint of lager, thanks.
A: Cheers.
B: Cheers. Any plans for the weekend?
A: Nothing special. (b) .... just take it easy. (c) .... What about you?
B: We were going to the car racing but they say it'll rain.
A: (d) ....
B: So they say. Another one?
A: No, (e) .... I'd better go.
B: (f) ....
A: OK, just the one.

with

[preposition] accompanying, having, by means of: *His mother went with him to the doctor's.* • *I'd like one of those suitcases with little wheels.* • *She tied up the parcel with string.*

Grammar patterns

1 NP | **with** | + NP

Who's the girl with red hair?
They have a house with a view of the sea.

▲ to talk about the features that something or someone has

2 verb | (+ NP) | + **with** | + NP

I've been dancing. ~ Who with? ~ With Alfonso, of course.
What shall we bring with us? ~ Bring some fruit.

▲ to say who or what accompanies something, or goes together

I fixed the TV antenna. ~ What with? ~ With a piece of wire.
Fill the tank with diesel, not petrol.

▲ to talk about what you use to do something

I totally agree with you.
He works with disabled children.

▲ to talk about doing things together (Other verbs include: *collaborate, discuss, go along, play, share, socialize, speak.*)

He's always fighting with his older brother.
Don't argue with me.

▲ to talk about doing things competitively (Other verbs include: *compete, clash, disagree, struggle.*)

Can you help me with the washing up?
My dad gave us a hand with the decorating.

▲ to talk about giving assistance (Other verbs include: *assist, help out.*)

The meal ended with cheese and dessert.

▲ to talk about what happens at the beginning or end of something (Other verbs include: *start, conclude, open.*)

She was shaking with fear.

▲ to talk about how people behave because of what they feel (Other verbs include: *cry, groan, laugh, scream, sigh, tremble.*)

3 is/was, etc. | + adjective | + **with** | + NP

The crowd was wild with excitement.
My ears were numb with cold.

▲ to talk about emotional or physical states

Collocations

Other verbs usually followed by *with* include:
bargain, check, identify, interfere, keep up, and *collide.*

They're always trying to keep up with their neighbours.
The bus collided with a lorry.

Nouns that are often followed by *with* include:
sympathy, relationship, argument, disagreement, peace, appointment, meeting, contact, problem, and *trouble.*

Do you have much contact with Leon?

Noun combinations with *with* include: *with pleasure, with pride, with feeling, with style, with care, with practice, with time, with difficulty, with ease, with […]'s permission, with […]'s help, with a view to …, with reference to …, with regard to … .*

With your permission, I'd like to take some photographs.

Adjectives that are often followed by *with* include: *angry, bored, fed up, satisfied, pleased, impatient, honest, familiar,* and *popular.*

To be honest with you, I don't think it's authentic.

Some more combinations of 'adjective + *with* + noun' to talk about emotional and physical states (Grammar pattern 3): *sick with fear, breathless with excitement, blue with cold, weak with exhaustion, blind with rage, speechless with terror.*

Set phrases

· **to be with someone** = to be having a relationship with someone
Is Andy still with Monica?

· ❛**I'm (not) with you**❜ = I don't understand what you're saying
I beg your pardon? I'm not with you. Can you explain?

Exercises

① Put *with* in the correct place in each sentence:

a   Who did you go home?
b   It's a house two bedrooms and a garden.
c   Can you pull out those nails? ~ What?
d   The boy next door helps the garden.
e   I'm having problems the computer. It keeps crashing.
f   Slow down. I can't keep up you.
g   I'm not going to argue you about it.
h   She's fed up her job and is threatening to quit.

② Make sentences about these tools and appliances according to this pattern:

(can opener) *You use a can opener to open cans with.*
(foot warmer) *You use a foot warmer to warm your feet with.*

a   cheese grater
b   hairdryer
c   bottle-opener
d   potato peeler
e   nail clippers
f   fire extinguisher
g   rice cooker
h   coffee grinder

③ Choose words from the list to complete these sentences:

care   pleasure   ease   reference
help   view   feeling   practice

a   With .... to your advertisement in *The Post*, I would like to apply …
b   Can you take a photo of us? ~ With ....
c   Your English will improve with ....
d   We're calling a meeting with a .... to organizing a street party.
e   She spoke with .... about the plight of homeless children.
f   Handle these documents with .... as they're very old and valuable.
g   She beat her opponent with .... to win 6-1, 6-0.
h   With Evelyn's .... we finished the testing in an hour.

④ Complete these film titles by choosing a word from the following list:

The Man   Travels   Sleeping   From Russia   Interview
Gone   Dances   To Sir   A Room   The Trouble

a   .... *with the Vampire.* (with Brad Pitt and Tom Cruise)
b   .... *with the Enemy.* (with Julia Roberts)
c   .... *with Wolves.* (with Kevin Costner)
d   .... *with a View.* (a Merchant-Ivory production)
e   .... *with the Golden Gun.* (with Roger Moore)
f   .... *with my Aunt.* (with Maggie Smith)
g   .... *, with Love.* (with Sidney Poitier)
h   .... *with Love.* (with Sean Connery)
i   .... *with Harry.* (directed by Alfred Hitchcock)
j   .... *with the Wind.* (with Vivien Leigh and Clark Gable)

work

[regular verb: *work, worked, worked*] (1) do a job or make an effort: *Where do you work?* • *You'll have to work hard if you want to pass.*
(2) function: *How does the photocopier work?*
[uncountable noun] a job, or place of work, or effort: *I'm looking for work.* • *You've done a lot of work on the garden.*
[countable noun] something produced by an artist, or (plural) construction and repairs: *This is not one of Miró's best works.*
• *The by-pass is closed because of road works.*

Grammar patterns

1 **work** (= verb) | (+ adverbial)

Nigel works in a hairdressing salon.
How long have you been working here?

▲ to talk about the jobs people do

The lift's not working.
The phone works best if you stand on the balcony.

▲ to talk about things functioning properly or succeeding

2 **work** (= verb) | + NP

Do you know how to work the coffee machine?
Our boss works us hard.

▲ to talk about making things or people work

3 (determiner and/or adjective) | + **work** (= noun)

His work involves caring for disabled children.
I started work when I was fifteen.

▲ to talk about your job

She's going out with a guy she met at work.

▲ to talk about the place were you work

Going up the mountain was hard work but coming down was easy.

▲ to talk about what takes effort

Collocations

These adverbials often go with *work* (in the sense of doing a job): *hard, steadily, round the clock.*
These adverbials go with *work* (in the sense of function): *perfectly, properly, smoothly, well.*

They worked steadily all morning.
To finish my dissertation I had to work round the clock.
The electric drill doesn't seem to be working properly.

These prepositions often follow *work* (in the job sense): *as, at, for, on, with.*

She works as a cab driver.
Who do you work for?
I'm working on a new project at the moment.

These prepositions often precede *work* (the noun): *at, in, out of, off.*

There are over five million people out of work.
I'm thinking of taking a bit of time off work.

There are some phrasal verbs with *work*:

If you *work out* something, or *work out* how to do something, you solve it: (*I haven't worked out how to send attachments.*)
If a situation *works out,* it ends satisfactorily (*I'm sorry their marriage didn't work out.*)
If you *work out,* you do physical exercise (*Tony's working out down in the gym.*)
If you *work up* enthusiasm, or interest, or a thirst, or a hunger, etc. you make these things happen through effort (*I'm trying to work up enough courage to ask for a pay rise.*)

Set phrases

• **' nice work! / good work! '**
I came first in my class. ~ Nice work!
▲ to congratulate someone on an achievement

• **get (down) to work** = start doing work
OK, now that the formalities are over, let's get down to work.

• **work your way ...** = make slow progress
Hamish started as an office boy and then worked his way up.
The rescuers worked their way through the ruins.

- **work it / work things …** = arrange for something to happen
  I'll see if I can work it so that you get free seats.

- **work wonders** = produce good results
  Take these pills: they'll work wonders.

- **in working order** = functioning properly
  You'll find the facilities are all in working order.

Exercises

1 Ten examples of the word *work* (or *working* or *worked* or *works)* have been removed from this dialogue. Can you put them back in?

A: How was?
B: Up and down. I got to late, and found that the photocopier wouldn't. By the time we had out what was wrong with it and got it again, it was practically lunchtime. So I didn't get much done in the morning.
A: And in the afternoon?
B: Well, you know James (he's been on that Beech-Reeds contract), well, he's decided to quit and become a musician. So they've asked me to take over his. That might mean a pay increase.
A: Nice!

2 Collocations.
Here are some adjectives and verbs that frequently go with *work* (noun). Choose words from these lists to complete the sentences below:

Adjectives:
tedious   light   heavy   shoddy   your own   steady
Verbs:
going   take on   get done   get down to

a   How much work did you .... this morning?
b   Until you recover from the operation, you should only do .... work.
c   I'm looking for some .... work that will give me guaranteed income.
d   Let's turn the TV off and .... work.
e   Look at this .... work! ~ Well, if you pay so little, what do you expect?

f   How's work? ~ It's .... very well, thanks.
g   You shouldn't .... so much work: you simply don't have the time.
h   Is this .... work? ~ Well, my brother helped me with some of it.
i   It's such .... work I sometimes think I will die of boredom.
j   I did most of the renovations myself, but I employed a man to do the .... work.

3 Many compound nouns are formed 'noun + work', or 'work + noun'. For example, *woodwork* and *workbook*. Make compounds from the words in these two lists that match the definitions below. (Note there are more words than you will need.)

metal				day
group				force
course				load
spade				man
body	**+ work**	**work +**		mate
patch				place
wood				sheet
home				shop
ground				station

a   the outside part of a car
b   a piece of paper with exercises for students
c   the craft of making things out of iron, copper, brass, etc.
d   the work that students do over a term or year
e   the amount of work a person or machine is expected to do
f   the person you work with
g   uninteresting work that has to be done in preparation for something else
h   all the people who work for a business or in a factory

would

[modal auxiliary verb] expresses a range of meanings including possibility, hypothetical events, and past habit: *It would be nice to see you again soon.* • *What would Gandhi have done?* • *We would often meet at the local café.*

→ if
→ had

NOTE: *would* is commonly contracted to *'d*: *I'd see a dentist.* 'Would + not' is contracted to *wouldn't*; 'would + have' is contracted to *would've*.

Grammar patterns

1 if | + past tense, | + **would** | + bare infinitive

If Dad was still alive, he'd be proud of you.
I'd drive you myself if I had the car.
If you could, would you live abroad?

▲ to talk about hypothetical situations in the present or future (This is known as the second conditional.)

2 if | + past perfect, | + **would** | + have | + bare infinitive

If I'd known, I would've given you a lift.
We wouldn't have been late if we'd taken a taxi.

▲ to talk about hypothetical situations in the past (This is known as the third conditional.)

3 I | + **would** | + infinitive | + if I were you

I'd get a second opinion, if I were you.
If I were you, I'd ask for my money back.

▲ for giving advice (→ was/were)

Collocations

Would often occurs with adverbs like *never, probably*:

You would probably be more comfortable sleeping on the sofa.
I'd never do a thing like that!

Would often follows *I wish*:

I wish you wouldn't leave your shoes lying around.
I wish Jake would hurry up.

When talking about past habits, *would* occurs with time expressions like: *sometimes, often, always; in those days, when I was young*, etc.

In those days we would often play football in the street.

Would is often followed by *rather* or *sooner* to mean *would prefer to*:

I'd rather watch the football.
Would you rather sit inside?
I'd sooner die than wear a suit!

Would is frequently followed by verbs of liking and disliking: *like, prefer, love, hate.*

Wouldn't you love to live on a boat?
I would hate to be outside in this weather.

Set phrases

- ' **would you mind [+ -ing]?** '
  Would you mind sitting in the front?
  ▲ for polite requests

- ' **would you mind if [+ past tense clause]** '
  Would you mind if I closed the window?
  ▲ for asking permission

- ' **would you like [+ to-infinitive]** '
  Would you like to try one of these? ~ I'd love to /Yes, I would.
  ▲ for inviting and offering

- ' **I'd say … / I'd imagine … / I'd have thought …** '
  I'd say it was going to rain.
  I'd imagine they're on their way.
  I'd have thought she was too old.
  ▲ for stating a tentative opinion or deduction

- **would-be [+ noun]** = hoping/wanting to be
  The would-be occupants were disappointed when the flat was let to someone else.

Exercises

1 *Would* has a range of meanings and uses. The most common are:

1 in hypothetical situations: *Would you ever change your name?*
2 when making requests and offers: *Would you give me a hand?*
3 for past habits: *They would often visit us.*
4 as the past of *will* in reported speech: *They said it would probably rain.*
5 for the 'future-in-the-past': *This was the man she would one day marry.*

Match each of the concordance examples below with one of the above five uses of *would*. (There are three examples of each.)

a In the evenings we **would** walk round town and maybe go the cinema.
b I kept telling myself it **would** be all right.
c The consumer might get cheaper CDs, but he **would** also get less choice.
d I **would** appreciate a response on this matter by Monday.
e My mother **would** help me with my schoolwork and I would help her with the housework.
f A world without music **would** be a very dull place.
g Mr Goodman's solicitor said his client **would** appeal.
h When we went out to a restaurant together, he **would** always complain.
i He said it **wouldn't** stop raining.
j **Would** anyone like to volunteer to organize the party?
k When he was sixty years old he retired and, thinking he **would** be happy there, bought a cottage in Hampshire.
l I **would** be grateful for the papers back in due course.
m When **would** I be expected to start?
n In 1949 it was agreed that in future no person under the age of twenty-one **would** be allowed to enter.
o I could tell that the marriage **would** never last.

2 **Put the word in brackets into the correct place in each sentence:**

a (if) Would you leave home you could afford to?
b (had) If I my own car, he thought, I would leave.
c (would) If you wanted to, you be a good tennis player.
d (have) If I'd known you were coming, I would prepared your room.

e (be) He promised me he would home in time for dinner.
f (mind) Would you turning the TV down? I'm trying to study.
g (were) I'd wear a tie if I you.
h (often) When I was young we would go swimming in the canal near our house.
i (rather) Would you have tea or coffee?
j (to) Wouldn't you prefer have breakfast on the terrace?

3 **Write sentences for these situations, using *would* and an if-clause. For example:**

I don't have the money, so I can't buy an apartment, but …
if I had the money, I'd buy an apartment.

a It's not a nice day, so we won't go to the beach, but …
b It wasn't a nice day, so we didn't go to the beach, but …
c Elvis isn't alive, so he's not in his seventies now, but …
d Martha doesn't speak French, so she won't go to France, but …
e I'm not in your position, so I won't start looking for a job, but …
f We didn't change money at the airport, so we didn't have money for the taxi, but …
g Suzy didn't study hard for her exams, so she didn't pass, but ….
h My uncle didn't write his life story, so he wasn't famous, but …

4 **On the left are some common ways of starting sentences using *would*. Can you match them with the sentence endings in the right-hand column?**

a It'd be nice if …	1 it started to rain.
b If you'd just like to …	2 tea, actually.
c It wouldn't surprise me if …	3 piece of cake?
d She would say that, …	4 follow me.
e You'd think …	5 the sun comes out.
f Would you like some …	6 wouldn't she?
g I'd prefer …	7 she owned the place.
h Would you like a …	8 milk?

you

[pronoun, subject and object] (1) personal pronoun that refers to the person, or people, you are addressing: *You eat meat, don't you?* • *Can you all see the screen?* • *That colour suits you.* • *Can I sit next to you?*
(2) impersonal pronoun that refers to people in general: *On a clear day you can see Mount Fuji.* • *There's a bus that takes you down to the main shopping area.*

NOTE: contracted forms of *you* are: *you're* (you are), *you've* (you have), *you'll* (you will), *you'd* (you had *or* you would).

The other personal pronouns are:

	singular		plural	
	subject	object	subject	object
1st person	I	me	we	us
2nd person	you			
3rd person	he	him		
	she	her	they	them
	it	it		

Grammar patterns

1 **you** | + verb
   verb | + **you**

   You look tired.
   I can't hear you. Can you speak up?

   ▲ to refer to the person you are talking to, either as subject or object of the verb

   You sometimes see eagles here, if you are lucky.
   How do you say 'Hello' in Chinese?
   I hate it when people phone you and try and sell you things.

   ▲ to refer to people in general, either as subject or object of the verb

2 (don't) | + **you** | + verb
   imperative | + will | + **you**

   You go to bed now.
   Don't you touch the heater, do you hear?
   Come this way, will you?

   ▲ to tell people to do things, or not to do things

Collocations

When *you* is used to address more than one person, it is often followed by words like: *all, two, guys* (informal), *both, folks* (informal, American English), *children*, etc.

   You all know the rules: no running or diving.
   You two go in the back and I'll sit in the front.
   You both can have a chocolate.

You and me, or *you and I* (= we), are common combinations:

   We should stay in touch, you and me.
   You and I have the same sunglasses. (OR: more informally: *You and me have the same sunglasses.*)
   Between you and me, I think she may be pregnant.

Set phrases

• **you see →** see

• **you know →** know

• '**bless you**'
  Ah-choo! ~ Bless you. ~ Thanks.
  ▲ a phrase to say when someone sneezes

• '**same to you**'
  Happy New Year. ~ Same to you.
  ▲ to return a greeting

• '**you too**'
  Take care of yourself. ~ You too.
  ▲ to return someone's wishes or hopes

• '**right you are**'
  Can you move your bike, please? ~ Right you are.
  ▲ to say you accept a statement or request

Exercises

1 Use the table opposite to complete these sentences with personal pronouns:

a Can .... get .... something to drink? ~ I'd love a glass of water.

b Barry looks sad. What's the matter with .... ? ~ .... 's lost his job.

c Angie, can .... do .... a favour? Call the children in and give .... their dinner. .... are starving.

d I'll give .... my e-mail address. ~ Just a minute. I'll write .... in my address book. Now, where is .... ?

e How do .... make a vinaigrette? ~ .... mix oil and vinegar together.

f Where's mother? ~ I think .... 's in the garden. Why do you want .... ?

g How long have .... and Cherry know each other? ~ Well, ... met at a party. A friend of mine introduced .... and .... have been going out together ever since.

h Whose is this bag? ~ I think .... 's Barbara's. Give .... to ....

2 Look at these concordance lines with *you*. Decide, in each case, if *you* is:
• personal subject or object, singular or plural
• impersonal subject or object

For example: *You two have been married for ages, haven't you?* personal subject, plural

a How did **you** build up this vocabulary, Adrian?
b I've told all **you** boys a thousand times!
c It's times like that when **you** find who your friends are.
d If **you** speak a language well, accents are a minor problem.
e There is a help screen showing **you** how to use the help system.
f This is to invite **you** to join a new Special Interest Group.
g I offered **you** brandy because I thought it might steady your nerves.
h So **you** offered to marry her?
i Remind me to tell **you** sometime over a beer.
j The program allows **you** to draw lines and boxes as well.
k Are **you** children in bed yet!
l The first thing was to find a school for **you** three.
m Do **you** remember how we met?

3 Fourteen examples of *you* have been taken out of this dialogue. Can you put them back?

Dermot: Hi, Natasha.
Natasha: Dermot! How are?
Dermot: Fine, and?
Natasha: Very well, thanks.
Dermot: What are doing here?
Natasha: I'm looking for the Polish Consulate. Dermot, are from around here, aren't? Do know where the Polish Consulate is?
Dermot: It's best if take the next street on the right, and go down two blocks. Can't miss it. But why are looking for the Polish Consulate?
Natasha: I need a visa.
Dermot: But don't need a visa to go to Poland!
Natasha: Forget I'm from New Zealand. Not like. New Zealanders need visas.
Dermot: Oh, yes. Right are. Well, good luck.
Natasha: Thank.

4 Can you complete these Beatles song titles, adding *you*, plus words from the list :

girl	life	cry	love	man
without	money	away	secret	dance

a 'All .... need is ....'
b 'Baby, ... 're a rich ....'
c 'Do .... want to know a .... ?'
d 'Got to get .... into my ....'
e 'Within .... , ...'
f '............ never give me your ....'
g '............ 've got to hide your love ....'
h 'I'm gonna sit right down and .... over ....'
i 'I'm happy just to .... with ....'
j '............ 're going to lose that ....'

key

a/an

1 b *an amphibian* c *an insect* d *a reptile*
e *a bird* f *a mammal* g *a fish* h *a bird*

2 a *an architect* b *a mechanic* c *a teacher*
d *a taxi-driver* e *a doctor* f *a lawyer*
g *a soldier* h *a waiter/a cook*

3 b *a* d *a* g *a* h *a*

4 a *have a drink* b *drink* c *have a chat*
d *chat* e *look* f *have a swim* g *have a*
look h *swim*

5 a – 3 b – 1 c – 8 d – 6
e – 4 f – 5 g – 2 h – 7

all

1 a correct b *All tap water …* c d e correct
f *… all of them* g *All babies …*
h i correct j *… all of you!*

2 a *Every* b *whole* c *Both* d *whole* e *all*
f *Both* g *all* h *Every* i *whole* j *every* k *all*

3 a *all along* b *all being well* c *by all*
accounts d *all the better* e *in all* f *all*
too soon g *of all things* h *all right*

am/is/are

1 a What *is* your brother doing these days?
b The price of oil is *not* going up. c You're
not Canadian, *are* you? d Where are *you*
from? e Alessandro is *always* late for
class. f Our team is not *playing* on
Saturday. g Are you making lunch or
am I? h It's not snowing but it *is* raining.
i The conference is *to* start on Saturday.
j What *is* a scanner used for? k Some
chopsticks are *still* made of wood.
l Chinese *is* also spoken in Singapore.

2 a *'m writing* b *is making* c *are watching*
d *are playing* e *is reading* f *is having*
g *is staying* h *'s going* i *'s doing*
j *are you doing*

3 b *is rising* c *is increasing* d *is falling* e *is*
improving f *is getting* g *are disappearing*
h *is spreading* i *is expanding*

4 a – 6 b – 5 c – 7 d – 1
e – 8 f – 2 g – 3 h – 4

*Tea is produced in Sri Lanka.**
Farsi is spoken in Iran.
An axe is used for chopping wood.
Leningrad is now called St Petersburg.
Koala bears are found in Australia.
Spaghetti is made from flour.
*Toyota cars are manufactured in Japan.**
*Cricket is played in India and Australia.**
(*other country names possible)

and

1 a *… and* some carrots? b *… and* it has
a garage. c *… and* throwing things.
d *… and* turned on the TV. e *… and*
fifty copies. f *… and* have some
chocolate cake if you like. g *… are nice*
and comfortable. Try *and* remember …

2 a *back and forth* b *there and then*
c *First and foremost* d *off and on* e *in*
and out f *here and there*

3 a *ends* b *sound* c *early* d *tired* e *sweet*
f *dry* g *bounds* h *knees*

4 Some possible answers:
Klean-Kat is fast. What's more, it's safe./
It's also safe./ It's safe, too./Moreover, it's
safe./ It's safe, as well./In addition, it's safe.

any

1 a Ask *any* policeman … b … but they
didn't have *any*. c I can't wait *any* longer
… d There wasn't *any* bottled water …
e … at *any* branch of our bank.
f … because there isn't *any* coverage.
g It isn't *any* use learning Latin: no one
speaks it *any* more. h… In *any* case, the
news… i If you see *any* melons in the
market… j… without *any* food, …
k She refused to take *any* money …
l If Eva grows *any* taller…

2 a *There isn't any coffee left.* b *There*
weren't any parents at the meeting.
c *Isn't there any sugar?* d *They haven't*
won any games this season. e *I don't*
have/haven't (got) any cousins. f *Don't*
you have any money at all? g *They didn't*
give us any information. h *I haven't*
heard any news from Paul.

3 a *some, any* b *any, some* c *any, none*
d *no* e *any* f *some* g *any* h *none* i *no*
j *some, none*

4 a *somewhere* b *anyone/anybody*
c *something* d *anything* e *anywhere*
f *someone/somebody* g *anyone/*
anybody h *anything*

as

1 a *… as you are both Canadians.*
b *… just as I got up.* c *… wasn't as*
difficult *as I thought.* d *… is the same*
as yours. e *Tom looks as if …* f *… He*
works *as an air-traffic controller.*
g *…, as you probably know.* h *…twice*
as expensive as that one. i *Some sports,*
such as hang-gliding, are known as …
j *It's too early to say, as yet, …*

2 a *Iron is not as hard as steel.*
b *Alexandria is not as hot as Cairo.*
c *April was not as bad as March.* d *The*
bus doesn't leave as often as the train.
e *Edinburgh doesn't have as many people*
as Glasgow. f *Manchester is not as far*
away as Liverpool. g *Gary doesn't earn*
as much as Lilian. h *Hugo isn't as good-*
looking as Toni.

3 a *As it was Sunday, I got up late.* b *As I*
was getting out of my car, I heard the
explosion. c *The Indian elephant isn't as*
big as the African elephant. d *It isn't as*
windy today as it was yesterday. e *As you*
weren't home, I left a note. f *Woody Allen*
isn't as funny as Groucho Marx. g *As you*
are not busy, can you set the table? h *Your*
sunglasses are the same as mine. (OR: *My*
sunglasses are the same as yours).

4 a *old as the hills* **b** *white as a sheet*
c *warm as toast* **d** *good as gold* **e** *sick as
a dog* **f** *hard as nails* **g** *thin as a rake*
h *flat as a pancake*

ask

1 1: e, h 2: d, j 3: b, m
4: f, i 5: c, k 6: g, l 7: a, n

2 a I'd like to ask *you* your opinion …
b … asked Jason *to* move his car.
c I asked you *not* to … **d** We *were*
asked if we … **e** Chuck asked his boss
for a day off … **f** Why don't you ask a
policeman *if* he … ? **g** … where the
station *was*. **h** … if they *do* takeaways.
i … and ask what *to* do. **j** 'Where are
you going?' *I* asked her.

3 a opinion **b** favour **c** way **d** permission
e price **f** time **g** question **h** advice

4 a *Roger asked Matt if he was taking a
taxi.* **b** *The waiter asked us to follow him.*
c *I asked the man sitting next to me if this
was Reading.* **d** *Harry asked Rita to
marry him.* **e** *The customs officer asked
Mr Vázquez what his first name was.*
f *The teacher asked the children to be
quiet.* **g** *I asked the shop assistant if they
took credit cards.* **h** *Mrs Hill-Smith asked
the waiter to bring her a fork.*

at

1 a … can you stop *at* the chemist's?
b There's a train that arrives *at* Stansted
Airport … **c** … *at* the corner of Queen
and Market Streets. **d** Is Melanie here *at*
the moment? –No, I think she's *at* lunch.
e … started *at* eight o'clock and finished
at midnight. **f** What are you staring *at*?
~ Nothing. I was just looking *at* myself
…. **g** … she's clever *at* drawing.
h … while you're *at* it? ~ I'll do it *at* once.

2 a – 7 **b** – 4 **c** – 2 **d** – 8
e – 3 **f** – 6 **g** – 1 **h** – 5

3 a *the dentist's* **b** *the airport* **c** *the top*
d *breakfast* **e** *the wedding* **f** *home*
g *work* **h** *the bottom*

4 a *in* **b** *on* **c** *at* **d** *on* **e** *at* **f** *at* **g** *in* **h** *in*,
on **i** *at* **j** *at* **k** *at, in*

back

1 The journey *back* from the beach was a
nightmare. We had to take the *back*
roads because of the traffic on the main
roads. By the time we got *back*, it was
midnight and the kids were asleep on
the *back* seat. I *backed* the car into the
garage, and went to open the front
door. It was then that I realized I didn't
have the key. I must have left it *back* at
the hotel. I went round to the *back* of
the house and tried to force open the
back door. Then I felt a terrible pain in
my *back*. I haven't been able to go *back*
to work for a week.

2 a *background* **b** *setback* **c** *backup*
d *backlog* **e** *cutbacks* **f** *backpack*
g *backlash* **h** *backdrop* **i** *paperback*
j *fullback*

3 a *call* **b** *bring* **c** *turn* **d** *put* **e** *come*
f *pay* **g** *take* **h** *lie*

4 a – 4 **b** – 6 **c** – 1 **d** – 5
e – 2 **f** – 7 **g** – 8 **h** – 3

be

1 A home can *be* improved by removing a
wall between two small rooms, to create
one big room. Removing a wall needn't
be a big job. It can *be* done easily and
quickly. But before you go ahead, ask
yourself the following questions:
Will the loss of a room *be* inconvenient?
If you have a growing family, for
example, you may *be* needing extra
bedrooms in the future. And, will the
shape of the new room *be* suitable for
your needs? What family activities will
be carried out there? Will it *be* used both
for having meals and for watching TV?

Will children *be* doing their homework,
while others are listening to music? And,
be careful! If the wall is structural, it
could *be* dangerous to remove it. To *be*
sure, consult an architect first.

2 b *It must be a gorilla. It can't be a shark,
rhino/ostrich, etc.* **c** *It could/might/may
be an ostrich/an albatross.* **d** *It must be
an ostrich. It can't be an albatross/
penguin etc.* **e** *It could/might/may be an
elephant/a rhino/a giraffe. It can't be a
kangaroo, etc.* **f** *It must be a penguin. It
can't be an ostrich, etc.* **g** *It could/
might/may be a kangaroo/an ostrich. It
can't be a giraffe/a shark etc.* **h** *It could
be a shark/a gorilla/a whale/an
elephant/a rhino. It can't be a penguin,
etc.* **i** *It must be a shark. It can't be a
rhino, etc.* **j** *It must be a kangaroo. It
can't be a rhino/a whale etc.*

3 b *Hard hats must be worn.* **c** *Cars
may/will be towed away.* **d** *Seat belts
must be fastened.* **e** *Arms and legs
must/should be covered.* **f** *Goods must
be declared.* **g** *Young children must be
carried.* **h** *Smokers may/will be fined.*

been

1 a How long have *you* been waiting?
b My father-in-law has *not* been feeling
well lately. **c** I'm feeling sick. ~ It must
have been the fish you ate. **d** Have you
ever been *to* Brazil? ~ Yes, I've been
once. **e** I see that the classrooms have
been repainted at last. **f** Where have
you *been* lately? I haven't seen you
around. **g** Who phoned? ~ I don't know.
It *may* have been Martin. **h** The sheets
have *been* washed and ironed. **i** He *had*
been drinking and he had a headache.

2 How long … **a** *have you been staying
with him?* **b** *has she been living with her?*
c *have you been working on it?* **d** *have
they been studying it?* **e** *have you been
looking for one?* **f** *have you been waiting
for it?*

3 **a** *for* **b** *since* **c** *since* **d** *since* **e** *for*
f *since* **g** *for* **h** *for*

4 **a** *It's been repaired.* **b** *They've been
cleaned.* **c** *It's been fixed.* **d** *They've been
watered.* **e** *It's been cut.* **f** *It's been
looked after.* **g** *It's been tidied up.*
h *It's been washed.*

being

1 1: d, m 2: e, h, k 3: b, f, i, l 4: a, c 5: g, j

2 **b** *It's being ironed.* **c** *He's being
interviewed.* **d** *It's being painted.* **e** *They're
being questioned.* **f** *It's being repaired.*
g *It's being printed.* **h** *It's being defrosted.*
i *It's being restored.* **j** *They're being fed.*

3 **a** – 3 **b** – 4 **c** – 2 **d** – 1
e – 7 **f** – 8 **g** – 5 **h** – 6

4 **a** *been* **b** *be* **c** *been* **d** *be* **e** *been*
f *Be, be* **g** *being* **h** *be* **i** *been* **j** *be*
k *being* **l** *been* **m** *be*

but

1 **a** – 8 **b** – 4 **c** – 1 **d** – 7
e – 6 **f** – 2 **g** – 3 **h** – 5

2
A: How about a game of tennis tomorrow?
B: I'd love to, *but* I've got a lot to do.
A: *But* you promised!
B: I know, *but* I'm just so busy. I thought I'd
finish everything today *but* I haven't.
A: You do nothing *but* work. *But* for tennis
you'd get no exercise at all. Remember,
Tom, I'm not only your friend, *but* I'm also
your doctor. You need to take it easy.
B: Yes, *but* don't forget I actually enjoy
work, Ed. *But* you're right: let's play
tennis tomorrow.
A: Great.
B: *But* just one game.

3 **a** *because* **b** *so* **c** *and* **d** *but* **e** *so* **f** *but*
g *because* **h** *so* **i** *and* **j** *because*

4 **a** *Although wind power is a viable energy
source it is still underused./ Wind power is*
a viable energy source.
*However/Nevertheless/Even so/And
yet/Yet it is still underused.*
b *Although it is difficult to breed pandas
in captivity, it is not impossible./It is
difficult to breed pandas in captivity.
However/Neverherless/Even so/And
yet/Yet it is not impossible.*
c *Although the fight against malaria
continues, a cure is still a long way off./
The fight against malaria continues.
However/Nevertheless/Even so/And
yet/Yet, a cure is still a long way off.*

by

1 1: c, f, j 2: d, k 3: b, g 4: a, h 5: i, l 6: e, m

2 Please send it by *air/sea/road/rail.*
They sell them by *the dozen/ the kilo/
the box/the pound.*
She became an actor by
accident/luck/choice/necessity.
Can I pay by *credit card/cash/
bank draft/cheque?*

3 **a** *at* **b** *by* **c** *by* **d** *at* **e** *by, at* **f** *on* **g** *By*
h *at, by* **i** *in* **j** *on*

4 **a** *The electric guitar was invented by
Leo Fender in 1948.* **b** *'Happy Birthday'
was written by Mildred and Patty Hill in
1893.* **c** *Microsoft was started by Bill
Gates in 1975.* **d** *Palmyra was ruled by
Queen Zenobia in the third century.* **e**
*Penicillin was discovered by Alexander
Fleming in 1928.* **f** *Radium was
discovered by Marie and Pierre Curie in
1898.* **g** The Body Shop *was started by
Anita Roddick in 1976.*

can

1 ability: a, d, g possibility: b, f, h
permission: c, e, i

2 **a** false: *Cats can see in the dark.* **b** true
c false: *Most bats can fly.* **d e** true **f** false:
Kangaroos can jump long distances.
g false: *Penguins can't fly.* **h i j** true

3 *You can't …* **b** *take photos here* **c** *play
music here.* **d** *use a mobile phone here.*
e *walk on the grass here.* **f** *park here.*
g *cycle here.* **h** *bring your dog in here.*

4 **a** *Camels are equipped to travel long
distances without water.* **b** *Is Matthew
able to talk yet?* **c** *I think Robin is capable
of doing much better at school.* **d** *Do you
know how to write in Arabic script?*
e *We are looking for someone who has
the ability to inspire confidence.* **f** *Some
people are incapable of teaching.* **g** *We
regret that we are unable to accept your
offer.* **h** *Does anyone here know how to
change a tyre?*

come

1 **a** *come* **b** *going* **c** *coming* **d** *come*
e *goes* **f** *go* **g** *come* **h** *go*

2 1: a, i 2: b, c, f, g, l 3: e, h, j 4: d, k

3 **a** *came to* **b** *came down* **c** *came out*
d *come through* **e** *comes up* **f** *came into*
g *came off* **h** *come back*

4 **a** *to an end* **b** *here* **c** *first* **d** *along* (come
along = hurry) **e** *true* **f** *again* (come
again = can you repeat that?) **g** *into
view* **h** *right* (come right = get better)

could

1 **a** *It could be the postman.* **b** *He could've
got lost.* **c** *It couldn't have been Karl.*
d *It could be hot.* **e** *It could break.*
f *It could've been Sheila.* **g** *It couldn't
have been the children.* **h** *You could've
left them in the car.*

2 *Could we …* **b** *see the room (first)?*
c *have a room with a view?* **d** *have some
sandwiches and soft drinks in our room?
Could you …* **e** *recommend a good local
restaurant?* **f** *give us a wake-up call at
eight tomorrow morning?* **g** *Could we
have breakfast for two in our room?*
h *Could you tell the people in room 102 to
be quiet?*

3 **a** *managed to* **b** *could* **c** *couldn't*
d *could* **e** *couldn't* **f** *could* **g** *managed
to* **h** *were able to*

did

1 *did* as auxiliary verb: a, b, c, d, g, h, l
did as main verb: e, f, i, j, k, m

2 **a** *buy* **b** *eat* **c** *feel* **d** *meet* **e** *spend*
f *feed* **g** *see* **h** *win*

3 **a** *have you lived* **b** *Did you see* **c** *did you
do* **d** *did you buy* **e** *Did the doctor call* (=
this morning is not connected to now)
f *Has the doctor called* (= *this morning* is
still connected to now)
g *have you read* **h** *did you read*

4 **a** – 3 **b** – 5 **c** – 6 **d** – 2 **e** – 4 **f** – 1

do / does

1 **b** *Where do you work?* **c** *When/What time
do you get up?* **d** *How far do you run
before breakfast?* **e** *How long do you
spend in the gym?* **f** *How far do you swim?*
g *How far do you cycle?* **h** *What do you
eat and drink?* **i** *What do you hope to win?*

2 **a** *Is Ana single?* **b** *Does Gregor have a new
job?* **c** *Can Miriam sing well?* **d** *Will you
be busy?* **e** *Has Monica arrived?* **f** *Does
she like world music?* **g** *Does she have a
lot of CDs?* **h** *Does Jo do up old cars?*

3 **a** *do* **b** *does* **c** *do* **d** *does* **e** *do* **f** *does*
g *does* **h** *does*

4 **a** *sandwiches* **b** *kung-fu* **c** *shopping*
d *hair* **e** *economics* **f** *140 miles an hour*
g *homework* **h** *dishes*

for

1 Have you planned *for* your retirement
and old age? It is common *for* people to
postpone these important life decisions,
to put them off *for* another day. But you
should be preparing *for* your future now.
For a start, will you have enough money
for your needs? If you don't, who will

provide *for* you, and care *for* you if you
are ill? Even if you have been working *for*
a long time, your pension may not pay
for a comfortable life style, nor be
enough *for* emergencies. What are you
waiting *for*? Sign up *for* our Lifesaver
Guaranteed Capital Growth Fund now! If
not *for* you, do it *for* your loved ones.

2 **a** *for* **b** *since* **c** *during* **d** *since* **e** *during*
f *for* **g** *since* **h** *during* **i** *during* **j** *for*
k *since* **l** *for*

3 **a** *A hammer is used for banging nails in.*
b *A glass jar is useful for keeping herbs in.*
c *Ice is good for relieving burns.* **d** *Wine
bottles are useful for putting candles in.*
e *An axe is used for chopping wood.* **f** *Salt
is good for removing stains.* **g** *Sticky tape
is useful for repairing torn paper.* **h** *A cigar
box is good for keeping stamps in.*

4 **a** *It is usual for bats to sleep upside-down.*
b *It is normal for bears to sleep through
the winter.* **c** *It is easy for cats to see in the
dark.* **d** *It is difficult for seals to run fast.* **e**
It is common for owls to hunt at night. **f** *It
is not usual for chimpanzees to eat meat.*

get

1 1: g, p 2: a, b 4: d, n 5: i, m
6: k, r 7: f, l 8: c, e, q 9: h, s 10: j, o

2 **a** – 6 **b** – 4 **c** – 5 **d** – 1
e – 7 **f** – 8 **g** – 3 **h** – 2

3 **a** *get back* **b** *get away* **c** *get down to*
d *get up* **e** *get out of* **f** *get over* **g** *get on*
h *get in*

4 **a** *getting crowded* **b** *getting older*
c *getting late* **d** *getting warmer*
e *getting fat* **f** *getting tired*

5 I got up, dressed and *made* the children
their breakfast. I *bought* a paper and
caught the bus early, but it *was* held up
in the traffic, so I *arrived at* the meeting
late and I *was* shouted at by the boss.
Things *became* worse when I *received* a
call on my phone in the middle of the

meeting. Then I spilt my coffee and had
to *fetch* a rag to clean it up. After the
meeting I *received* an angry note from
the boss, saying my behaviour had
better improve, or I'd *be fired/lose my job.*

give

1 **a** *Natalia has given him her car.*
b *The children are giving them bread.*
c *I'm going to give her my books.*
d *The government gave us a pension.*
e *What did the teacher give them?*
f *Do you think the committee will give
you the prize?* **g** *Someone gave it milk.*
h *Who will give me my money back?*

2 *Bill gave Dawn a CD. Dawn was given a
CD. The CD was given to Dawn.
Dawn gave Bridget a bowl. Bridget was
given a bowl. The bowl was given to
Bridget.
Bridget gave Jenny a fern. Jenny was
given a fern. The fern was given to Jenny.*

3 **a** *a call* **b** *a big smile* **c** *a push* **d** *an
example* **e** *a talk* **f** *some advice* **g** *an
interview* **h** *a shout*

4 **a** – 3 **b** – 7 **c** – 8 **d** – 1
e – 4 **f** – 5 **g** – 6 **h** – 2

go

1 Every summer, when we *go* on holiday,
we *go* to a place in the mountains
called Blue Lakes. There are lakes,
mountains and forest, so it's perfect for
the kids. The boys like to *go* fishing
while me and the girls *go* hiking and
bird watching. Sometimes we all *go*
sailing together and you can also hire
kayaks and *go* kayaking on the lake.
There's a local store where we *go* and
buy basic stuff, and there's a village a
few miles away where we *go* once a
week to do the shopping or *go* to the
cinema if the weather is not good and
where you can *go* and have a meal in
the one or two restaurants.

2 a *gone* **b** *been* **c** *gone* **d** *gone*
e *been* **f** *been* **g** *gone* **h** *gone*

3 a *up* **b** *out* **c** *away* **d** *on* **e** *together*
f *back* **g** *ahead* **h** *off*

4 a – 5 **b** – 8 **c** – 1 (goes to show =
proves something) **d** – 6 (on the go =
busy doing things) **e** – 7 (from the
word go = from the beginning);
f – 2 **g** – 4 **h** – 3

going

1 a What *are* you going to do this
weekend? **b** I'm going *to* the
supermarket: can I get you anything?
c I *was* going to come to the party but I
got lost. **d** You're *never* going to get
into college if you don't study. **e** I'm
going to have *to* get a new computer.
f Jakob is *probably* going to hand in his
resignation. (OR: Jakob is going to hand
in his resignation, *probably.*) **g** It looks
like it's going to *be* wet again
tomorrow. **h** I think we should *keep*
going until it gets dark. **i** We are *not*
going to stay with your mother. **j** How
long are *you* going to be?

2 a *They are going to build a new bridge.*
b *We are going to discuss this at the next
meeting.* **c** *I won't be flying. I'm going to
take the train.* **d** *What are you going to
say to the lawyer?* **e** *We are going to sign
the agreement.* **f** *We are not going to
take any action.*

3 a *Do you intend to place a large order?*
b *I will be discussing this with Jean-Pierre.*
c *They have decided not to reconsider our
offer.* **d** *Our lawyers plan to keep you
informed.* **e** *It is not our intention to
pursue the matter.* **f** *I'm planning to
spend a week in Brazil.*

4 a *he's got a lot going for him* (= he has a
lot of good qualities in his favour)
b *which was good going* (= which was
good progress) **c** *he's going on 40* (=
he's nearing 40) **d** *the way things are*

going (= given the present situation)
e *it was tough going* (= the process was
difficult) **f** *while the going is good* (=
while the present good situation
continues) **g** *to be going on with* (= to
keep you occupied) **h** *if I'm coming or
going* (= what I feel about the situation
– it's so hectic)

good

1 a … but only if you are *good*. **b** That
soup smells *good*. … **c** It's a good *thing*
that … **d** … but I'm not very good *at* it.
e It's *no* good shouting at them …
f … You're so good *with* your hands.
g … A walk will do *you* good. **h** What
good is a degree … **I** Is this book *any*
good? … **j** They say they will make
good any damage ….

2

A: *Good* morning, Jeff.
B: Hi, Natalie. How are you?
A: *Good*, thanks. Did you have a *good*
weekend?
B: Not bad. We went to that exhibition.
A: Any *good*?
B: Not really. It's a *good* thing you didn't
go. What about you?
A: Yeah, I won a medal, playing chess.
B: *Good* for you! You must be *good* at it.
A: Well, I practise a *good* deal. But what
good is it, if you can't make any money
out of it?
B: Yeah, well. Hey, feel like a drink later on?
A: That's a *good* idea. How about six?
B: That's no *good*. I'm busy. Seven?
A: Fine. See you then.
B: *Good*bye.

3 a *better* **b** *best* **c** *well* **d** *better* **e** *good*
f *good* **g** *best* **h** *Better* **i** *best* **j** *good,
well*

4 a *far* **b** *true* **c** *new* **d** *thing* **e** *turn* (one
good turn deserves another = if
someone does something for you, you
should do something for them) **f** *books*
(to be in someone's good books = to be

in favour with them) **g** *news* **h** *time* (all
in good time = be patient)

got

1 1: past of *get*: b, f,
2: present perfect of *get*: c, d, j,
3: *have got* for possession: e, g, h, l
4: *have got to* for obligation: a, i, k,

2 a How many children *have you got*?
b Sam *has got* blue eyes and fair hair.
c Don't kiss me: I've *got* a terrible cold.
e *Has* your flat *got* central heating?
h I *haven't got* any change, I'm sorry.

3
A: Excuse me, can I ask you some
questions?
B: Well, I haven't *got* much time. But … OK.
A: Have you *got* a mobile phone?
B: Yes, I have. I've *got* two in fact.
A: Why have you *got* two?
B: One's for work and one's for family and
friends.
A: Have you *got* a big family?
B: No, I haven't. Look …
A: Have you seen the new Magifone?
B: No, I haven't.
A: Here, I've *got* one here. It's *got* lots of
exciting new features. It's *got* a hundred
different ring tones. And it's *got* an
integrated digital camera and colour
display. And …
B: Look, really, I've *got* to go. I've *got* an
important meeting.
A: OK. But take one of these brochures. It's
got all the details of our special offer.
B: Thanks

4 Possible answers:
You've got to … **a** *… provide a work
contract.* **b** *… have a valid passport.*
c *… provide photocopies of your work
contract and your passport.* **d** *…
have/provide three passport-sized
photographs.* **e** *… provide a valid
medical certificate.* **f** *… prove (that) you
have no criminal record.* **g** *… complete
Form WP100.* **h** *… pay $US 75.*

had

1 Tom sat down to dinner and reflected on his day. It *had* begun badly. He *had* been worrying about things the night before, so he *had had* a bad night, and he *had* overslept. Consequently he *had* arrived late for his class. What's more, he *had* forgotten there was an exam. If he *had* known, he would have stayed in bed. He *had* his dinner in silence. He *had* to do his homework, but he didn't feel like it. He *had* a cup of coffee and turned on the TV. He asked himself what he *had* done to deserve a life like this.

2 As he entered his room Otto knew that the game was up. He had taken a train *the night before*. He had arrived in the town early in the morning. He had found a hotel, and had checked in. He had taken a walk around the town and had eaten in a cheap restaurant. He had spoken to nobody. Nobody had spoken to him. He had written a couple of postcards. He had gone back to his hotel. He had opened the door and had entered his room …

3 a *She said (that) they'd had an accident.* **b** *He asked Derek if he had eaten yet.* **c** *He told me (that) he had spoken to the boss.* **d** *She admitted (that) she had broken the fax machine.* **e** *He complained (that) they hadn't rung him.* **f** *She asked me why I hadn't written.*

4 *She had …* •to take the kids to playschool •to take the dog to the vet •to take the car to the garage •to buy groceries •to go to the dentist •to pick up the car from the garage •to pick up the kids •to make dinner.

have / has

1 1: a, l, m, p 2: d, g, i 3: k, o 4: e, h, j 5: b, f, 6: c, n, q

2 a *We have known each other for six weeks.* **b** *I've had this sofa for five years.* **c** *They've been married for six months.* **d** *I've lived here/I've lived in this flat for 15 years.* **e** *I've loved opera since I was a child.* **f** *Her family has/have owned the castle for 500 years.*

Questions:
How long … a have you known each other? b have you had this sofa? c have they been married? d have you lived here/in this flat? e have you loved opera? f has/have her family owned the castle?

3 a Have *you* seen the Rothko exhibition? **b** How *long* have you known Joanna? **c** The post hasn't arrived *yet*. **d** Peter has *never* been on a plane. **e** Have you *ever* had Irish coffee? **f** Has Trish been to Spain *before*? **g** I have already *read* this book. **h** She must *have* forgotten the meeting was today. **i** The flat looks nice. Have you had *it* painted? **j** It's late and I have *to* go home.

4 a *a look* **b** *a beer* **c** *breakfast* **d** *fun* **e** *an accident* **f** *a try* **g** *a chat* **h** *a bad day* **i** *a heart attack* **j** *a swim*

how

1 a *How well do you know Pat?* **b** *Ask him how to start the photocopier.* **c** *How long will you be away?* **d** *How many kilograms are there in a tonne?* **e** *How did you like the book?* **f** *I asked him how much the suit was.* **g** *How strange it was they met.* **h** *Do you know how to boil an egg?*

2 a *fast* **b** *tall* **c** *heavy* **d** *often* **e** *high* **f** *long* **g** *old* **h** *deep* **i** *far* **j** *big*

3 a *'How do you make mayonnaise?'* **b** *'How much is the shirt?'* **c** *'How far is it to Tulsa?'* **d** *'How old are you?'* **e** *'How long will you be staying?'* **f** *'How about renting a car?'* **g** *'How high is the mountain?'* **h** *'How well can you cook?'* **i** *'How do you fill the tank?'* **j** *'How long have you been living here?'*

4 a *How are you?* **b** *How about you?* **c** *How's it going?* **d** *How come?* **e** *How do you mean?* **f** *How much?* **g** *How awful!* **h** *How about that?*

if

1 1a (1st conditional): f, h, o 1b (2nd conditional): b, i, n 1c (3rd conditional): a, d, l None of these: c, e, g, j, k, m

2 a What *will* you do if they increase the rent? **b** If I had the time, I *would* do a computing course. **c** The train may be late: *if* so, I'll phone you. **d** I'd see a doctor, if I *were* you. **e** Do you know *if* Brian phoned? **f** If I had known you were ill, I would *have* phoned. **g** Would she have got the job, if she'd applied? **h** It doesn't matter *if* you are late: we'll wait. **i** If *only* I hadn't invited Martha! **j** You can play inside but *only* if you are quiet.

3 a – 8 **b** – 6 **c** – 2 **d** – 7 **e** – 4 **f** – 1 **g** – 3 **h** – 5

4 a *were* **b** *are* **c** *had been* **d** *'ll be/will be* **e** *'d be/would be* **f** *'d have been/would have been*

in

1 a Do you take sugar *in* your coffee?; **b** The train gets *in* at 6.55… **c** Do you want to stay *in* or … **d** …Why don't you ask her *in*? **e** Eating foods high *in* fat can result *in* obesity. **f** The government should step *in* and… **g** It's lovely here *in* spring … **h** Will you be *in* this evening?… **i** He's *in* pain but he doesn't believe *in* going to see a doctor. **j** She's *in* a good mood, *in* spite of the fact she's *in* hospital.

2 a *midnight* **b** *March* **c** *her birthday* **d** *night* **e** *five minutes* **f** *Wednesday morning* **g** *the 16th century* **h** *a day or two*

3 a *break* **b** *take* **c** *let* **d** *join* **e** *invite* **f** *settle* **g** *jump* **h** *phase*

4 a *in tears* **b** *In fact* **c** *in love* **d** *in particular* **e** *in hospital* **f** *in case* **g** *in trouble* **h** *in prison* **i** *in luck*

it

1 *It* was getting dark and the road was wet. *It* seemed to go on forever. 'It is another fifty miles,' said Tom. 'Will we make *it* before nightfall?' Debbie asked. 'I hate *it* when you keep asking that,' Tom said. 'I'm sorry,' she said. 'I can't help *it*. It worries me to think of the children, alone in the house. *It* is not fair.' *It* was then that her phone rang. She picked *it* up and switched *it* on. 'Who is *it*?' she asked. 'It is me, Jimmy,' said a little voice. 'It is late. Where are you?' 'We're nearly home,' said Debbie. 'It won't be long now. Are you OK?' 'Yes, but *it* is a bit scary. *It* is lucky that Mr McOnion is here.' 'Mr who?' Debbie whispered, turning pale.

2 a *It's unfair to blame the students.* b *It doesn't matter what you think.* c *It irritates me the way she talks to herself.* d *It must be awful not to be appreciated.* e *It worries me that you have no job.* f *It's unbelievable how much I've spent.* g *It doesn't surprise me that he has no friends.* h *It's nice being read to.* i *It's a pity that Alex didn't bring Victor to the party.* j *It's a joy not having to cook.*

3 a *wonder* b *hard* c *fault* d *shame* e *relief* f *aim* g *obvious* h *funny* i *unlucky* j *guess*

4 a *It was Elsie who went to Rome, not Brenda.* b *It was their daughter who got married, not their son.* c *It's my brother who's a vegetarian, not me.* d *It's Canberra that's the capital of Australia, not Sydney.* e *It's guns that are dangerous, not people.* f *It was the noise that kept me awake, not the coffee.* g *It was the police who were to blame, not the protestors.* h *It's what you eat that makes you fat, not your genes.*

just

1 a *I'm just so tired.* b *The bus has just left.* c *We're just about to go out.* d *Brian is just as tall as Martin.* e *There*

was *just* one check-in desk … f I was *just* getting in the shower when … g These shoes only *just* fit me …. h That's *just* the thing that Carol …

2 a – 2 b – 1 c – 5 d – 7
e – 4 f – 3 g – 8 h – 6

3 a *Sheila has just phoned.* b *I've just seen a great film.* c *We've just come back from holiday …* d *Maurice has just written to me.* e *I've just driven a hundred miles.* f *The film has just begun.* g *I've just eaten, thanks.* h *Jo and Kim have just gone.*

4 a – 3 b – 6 c – 7 d – 1
e – 4 f – 2 g – 8 h – 5

keep

1 b *The musicians on the* Titanic *kept playing.* c *Even when he was deaf, Beethoven kept composing.* d *Columbus kept looking for a western route to India.* e *Borges went blind but kept writing.* f *John Huston kept making movies in his old age.* g *Ann Frank kept writing her diary, until the day she was captured.*

2 Dear Mabs,
I am 14. My older sister, who is 16, is driving me crazy. She's always picking on me. She *keeps* telling me I am fat and useless, and she *keeps* calling me names. If I lend her things, she *keeps* them, and doesn't give them back. I try to *keep* myself to myself, but she won't leave me alone. My mother made her promise to be nice to me, but she didn't *keep* her promise. Also, she can't *keep* secrets: she tells everybody everything. I *keep* hoping things will change, as we get older, but they don't. What can I do, to *keep* from going crazy?
Desperate.

3 a *up* b *off* c *up with* d *to* e *down* f *away* g *on* h *in*

4 a *you posted* (keep you posted = keep you informed) b *it under your hat* (keep

something under one's hat = keep it a secret) c *your eyes peeled* (keep one's eyes peeled = be vigilant) d *your fingers crossed* (keep one's fingers crossed = hope for good luck)
e *an eye on things* (keep an eye on things = look after things during someone's absence) f *an open mind* (keep an open mind = consider all sides of the case) g *a straight face* (keep a straight face = refrain from laughing) h *your wits about you* (keep one's wits about one = be very alert and prepared)

know

1 1: h, j 2: c, l 3: f, k 4: d, g 5: b, i 6: a, e

2 A: I'd like to enrol in the French class.
B: OK. Are you a beginner?
A: I don't *know* exactly. I *know* a lot of vocabulary, but my grammar is terrible. You *know* what I mean.
B: Well, try Level 2. How does that sound?
A: You *know* best. Where is it?
B: It's in Room 13. Do you *know* where that is?
A: Yes. Who's the teacher?
B: Corinne.
A: Ah, Corinne.
B: Do you *know* her?
A: No, not personally, but I *know* of her. Is she Canadian?
B: Not that I *know* of. But, you *know*, I'm new here.
A: Oh really? I didn't *know*.

3 *Do you know …* a *… what the time is?* b *… where the bathroom is?* c *… who the person in charge is?* d *… when the next bus is?* e *… where the next bus leaves from?* f *… how much a ticket costs?* g *… when the plane arrived?* h *… where the check-in desk is?*

4 a *certain* b *about* c *full* d *never* e *get* f *how* g *let* h *well*

let

1 a *Could you let me see the ruins?* **b** *They won't let you use your mobile phone on the plane.* **c** *I asked to borrow the car but my father wouldn't let me.* **d** *(Can you) let me have your autograph?* **e** *Let me ask you a personal question.* **f** *The landlady wouldn't let me have guests.* **g** *Let's hire a car for the weekend.* **h** *Let's not/Don't let's invite the neighbours.* **i** *Let the dog go!* **j** *Let go of the dog!*

2 a didn't let *off* ➤ didn't let *up* **b** don't let *down* ➤ don't let *on* **c** let me *on* ➤ let me *out* **d** let *in* work ➤ let *off* work **e** let the kids *up* ➤ let the kids *down* **f** let you *out* ➤ let you *in*

3 a *the side down* (= not maintain the group standard) **b** *off the hook* (= released from a responsibility) **c** *it get you down* (= depress you) **d** *the cat out of the bag* (= revealed the secret) **e** *off steam* (= release anger, frustration) **f** *yourself go* (= stop caring for yourself) **g** *sleeping dogs lie* (= don't make unnecessary trouble) **h** *your hair down* (= behave in an uninhibited way).

4 a *be* **b** *go* **c** *fall in love* **d** *night together* **e** *drums* **f** *play* **g** *twist* **h** *roll*

like

1 1: d, h, j, n   2: c, k   3: i, m   4: a, f   5: b, e, g, l

2 a *How do you like your coffee?* **b** *What would you like to do tomorrow?* **c** *I don't like horror movies very much.* **d** *I feel like a sandwich.* **e** *I like the way she laughs.* **f** *He doesn't like it when you interrupt him.* **g** *Hilary looks like her mother.* **h** *Jean really likes listening to classical music.* **i** *He likes her a lot.* **j** *She likes him to make her breakfast.* **k** *Would you like me to do it like this?* **l** *What was LA like?*

3 a *to do* **b** *to do* **c** *to go out/going out* **d** *to do* **e** *to play/playing* **f** *to watch* **g** *to be* **h** *dancing* **i** *to dance* **j** *to dance*

4 a – 6 **b** – 2 **c** – 3 **d** – 1 **e** – 5 **f** – 4

little

1 a There is a *little* soup left … **b** There is *little* point in saving money … **c** … I'll open the window a *little*. **d** There is *little* or no hope … **e** … It's a *little* bit bigger than yours. **f** The village has changed very *little* …

2 a *Italian words* **b** *while* **c** *problems* **d** *butter* **e** *coins* **f** *crackers* **g** *furniture* **h** *salami*

3 a *few* **b** *a little* **c** *a little, a few* **d** *few* **e** *little* **f** *a few* **g** *little* **h** *a little*

4 a *little* **b** *small* **c** *little* **d** *little* **e** *little* **f** *small*

long

1 a *high* **b** *far* **c** *tall* **d** *long* **e** *far* **f** *high* **g** *tall* **h** *far* **i** *long* **j** *long*

2 a *wide* **b** *long* **c** *deep* **d** *high* **e** *long* **f** *old*

3 a Crocodiles can grow up to four metres *long*. **b** Have you been working here *long*? **c** How *long* did it take you to paint the kitchen? **d** The new bridge is finished, at *long* last. **e** This plant has flowers all year *long*. **f** Will the operation take *long*? **g** You can use the phone so *long* as you don't make international calls. **h** You've had the windsurfer *long* enough. Now it's my turn.

4 a – 5 **b** – 3 **c** – 1 **d** – 2 **e** – 6 **f** – 4.

look

1 a What are you looking *at*? **b** … looking *for* my glasses. **c** You look *as* though … **d** It looks *like* it's going to be … **e** I look forward *to* going home … **f** She wouldn't let *me* look at the letter. **g** The rain looks *set* to continue … **h** It *looks* unlikely that … **i** Can you look *after* my things … **j** I'll look *out* for you … **k** … What does he look *like*?

2 a *around* **b** *into* **c** *up* **d** *forward to* **e** *out for* **f** *after* **g** *up to* **h** *up*

3 a *watch* **b** *look at* **c** *Look at* **d** *see* **e** *watch* **f** *see* **g** *look at* **h** *see*

4 a – 5 **b** – 6 **c** – 1 **d** – 3 **e** – 2 **f** – 4

make

1 a *Gary always makes breakfast.* **b** *Shall I make you some coffee?* **c** *Who made this table?* **d** *What is it made of?* **e** *Exercise makes me sleep better.* **f** *It makes me sad to see homeless children.* **g** *The tourists were made to get off the bus.* **h** *Hemingway made Paris his home.*

2 a *up* **b** *up for* **c** *out* **d** *for* **e** *out up* **f** *up*

3 a – 6 **b** – 2 **c** – 4 **d** – 5 **e** – 1 **f** – 3

4 Across: 2 choice 4 decision 7 trip 8 noise 10 enquiry/inquiry 11 date **Down:** 1 visit 3 journey 5 speech 6 point 9 sound

may

1 Instructions:
The examination takes three hours. You *may* not begin until instructed. You *may* use calculators but you *may* not use any other electronic aid, such as portable computers. You *may* not smoke or talk during the examination. You *may* leave when you have finished. All papers must be handed in prior to leaving the room. Anyone found breaking these rules *may* be asked to leave.

2 a *must* **b** *may not* **c** *can't* **d** *may, may* **e** *may not* **f** *must, may* **g** *can't* **h** *may*

3 a *may have been looking* **b** *may not have found* **c** *may have surprised them* **d** *may have been shot* **e** *may have thrown the gun* **f** *may have driven off* **g** *may have done it*

4 a *The meeting may have been cancelled.* **b** *It may be a nice day tomorrow.* **c** *She*

may have lost the address. **d** *Mary may phone.* **e** *The film may well not have started yet.* **f** *Terry may well have been lying.* **g** *They may well be having lunch now.* **h** *Their plane may well have been delayed.*

mean

1 1: c, g, k 2: e, i, m 3: d, f, l 4: a, h, o 5: b, j, n

2 *Number 2 means 'don't wash'.*
Number 3 means 'danger: radioactivity'.
Number 4 means 'this way'.
Number 5 means 'just joking'.
Number 6 means 'no cycling'.
Number 7 means 'peace'.
Number 8 means 'wheelchair access'.

3 **a** *Did you mean to let the bird out?* **b** *I'm sorry, I meant to phone you, but I was so busy.* **c** *You were not meant to read the letter.* **d** *You are not meant to sit in those seats.* **e** *She was meant to be here by now.* **f** *I've been meaning to e-mail you.*

4 **a** *What do you mean?* **b** *I mean* **c** *I mean* **d** *You mean* **e** *I mean* **f** *Do you know what I mean?* **g** *You mean* **h** *I mean* **i** *Do you know what I mean?* **j** *I mean*

more

1 **a** *The soup needs more salt.* **b** *… three more cups of coffee, please.* **c** *How many more of those chocolates …* **d** *… need less water not more.* **e** *Do we need any more ice …* **f** *… Can you buy three more?* **g** *… is bigger and more crowded than …* **h** *… but James is a bit more independent.* **i** *… and much more expensive.* **j** *… can you repeat that more slowly?* **k** *… where I could travel more.* **l** *The more dangerous the sport, the more she likes it.*

2 **a** *taller, heavier, larger* **b** *smaller, more aggressive* **c** *better, more dangerous* **d** *more intelligent, more active, further/farther*

3 **a** *The train is more comfortable than the bus.* **b** *The train station is more convenient than the bus station.* **c** *The train leaves more often than the bus.* **d** *The train stops more frequently than the bus.* **e** *The train is safer than the bus.* **f** *The bus goes faster than the train.* **g** *The train takes more time than the bus.* **h** *The bus is cheaper than the train.*

4 **a** true **b** false: *People live a bit/a little longer.* **c** true **d** true **e** false: *There are a few more people per doctor.* **f** false: *People earn a lot more.*

most

1 **a** *I like most vegetables but …* **b** *Most of the people at the party …* **c** *Like most people, I spend …* **d** *…produces the most oil.* **e** *Which is the most expensive city …* **f** *…but Andreas is the most hardworking.* **g** *That was by far the most delicious meal …* **h** *… do you like most?* **i** *… the most expensive movie ever.* **j** *…, so make the most of it.* **k** *… you've ever seen?*

2 *What is …* **a** *the longest river in the world?* **b** *the heaviest animal in the world?* **c** *the largest lake in the world?* **d** *the highest waterfall in the world?* **e** *the brightest star (in the sky)?* **f** *the most ancient city in the world?* **g** *the smallest bird in the world?* **h** *the deadliest snake in the world?*

3 **a** *It's the most boring film I've ever seen.* **b** *It's the most amazing book I've ever read.* **c** *This is the most expensive hotel I've ever stayed in.* **d** *She is the most interesting person I've ever met.* **e** *It is the most boring conference I've ever been to.* **f** *They are the most peculiar couple I've ever known.* **g** *That was the most delicious meal I've ever had.* **h** *It was the most exciting game I've ever watched.*

4 **a** more **b** more **c** most **d** Most **e** most **f** more **g** Most **h** more **i** more **j** most

much

1 **a** *I don't know how much …* **b** *They have so much money …* **c** *… as much salad as you like.* **d** *… very much time left.* **e** *Do you spend much on clothes?* **f** *… eat too much sugar and fat.* **g** *… much more comfortable than …* **h** *…, or we'll arrive much too early.* **i** *… much too expensive.* **j** *I don't like olives very much.* **k** *… doesn't go out much.* **l** *… are much the same.*

2 **a** much **b** many **c** much **d** many **e** much **f** many **g** much **h** much **i** many **j** much

3 **a** *Has she got much money?* **b** *Nigeria is much bigger than Ghana.* **d** *I don't have much time.* **f** *There isn't much difference between white and black rhinos.* **g** *Does Bilbao get much rain?* **i** *Will there be a lot of traffic?* **j** *Does it snow a lot in winter?* **k** *You don't get a lot of exercise, do you?*

my

1 **a** *nephew* **b** *village* **c** *belt* **d** *chin* **e** *flat* **f** *aunt* **g** *ankle* **h** *slippers* **i** *elbow* **j** *flatmate* **k** *bedroom* **l** *scarf*

2 **a** *his* **b** *your* **c** *her* **d** *its* **e** *their* **f** *our* **g** *your* **h** *her* **i** *its* **j** *their*

3 **a** *All ~~the~~ my three children …* **b** *A ~~A~~ my room mate …* **c** *… to ~~the~~ my place …* **d** *… married ~~his~~ my school friends.* **e** *… and cut ~~the~~ my knee.* **f** *My sister and ~~his~~ brother …* **g** *In ~~the~~ my opinion …* **h** *… stole all ~~the~~ my belongings.*

4 **a** *his* **b** *mine* **c** *your* **d** *hers* **e** *ours* **f** *theirs* **g** *hers* **h** *my* **i** *his* **j** *her*

need

1 1: d, g 2: a, l 3: e, i 4: b, f 5: j, k 6: c, h

2 **a** *You don't need to worry. There's no need for you to worry.* **b** *You don't need to shout! You needn't shout!* **c** *Do we need to*

book a table? Need we book a table? **d** *Do I need to stay? Is there any need for me to stay?* **e** *She didn't need to buy a ticket. There was no need for her to buy a ticket.* **f** *You didn't need to tell your mother. You needn't have told your mother.*

3 a *mustn't* **b** *needn't/don't need to* **c** *mustn't* **d** *needn't/don't need to* **e** *mustn't* **f** *needn't/don't need to* **g** *mustn't* **h** *needn't/don't need to*

4 Nicky,
Thanks so much for offering to keep an eye on things while we are away. Just a few things you *need* to remember: the plants *need* watering every two or three days, especially if it's hot. There's no *need* to water the cactus, though. The cat and the dog *need* feeding every day: there are some tins of pet food in the kitchen. If you *need* more, they sell it in the supermarket. You will *need* to take the dog for a walk at least once a day. You don't *need* to feed the snake, because it is asleep! If you *need* something to read, there are lots of books in the study. In case you *need* to contact us, the phone number in Milan is 39 025094736. (You *need* to dial 00 to get an international line).

never

1 a The baby *never* cries …. **b** … are *never* at home. **c** … have *never* been overseas. **d** It *always* rains in October. **e** … is *often* late for work. **f** I *usually* have cereal … **g** … and *never* come back here again! … **h** Never *have* I been so happy. **I** They never *ever* say thank you. **j** I *never* really enjoyed … **k** Never once did *he* do the washing up.

2 a *No, there's never any coffee left.* **b** *No, there's never anybody at reception.* **c** *No, we never go anywhere nice.* **d** *No, we never have fun (any more).* **e** *No, there's never (very) much mail.* **f** *No, you never bring me anything.*

3 a *She's never failed an exam before.* **b** *We've never been to the opera before.* **c** *You've never called me 'Darling' before.* **d** *I've never flown first class before.* **e** *Neil's never been late before.* **f** *It's never snowed here before.*

4 a – 7 **b** – 5 **c** – 2 **d** – 1 **e** – 4 **f** – 8 **g** – 3 **h** – 6

no

1 a *There's no coffee left.* **b** *There were no parents at the meeting.* **c** *Is there no sugar?* **d** *They have won no games this season.* **e** *I've got no cousins.* **f** *Do you have no money at all?* **g** *They gave us no information.* **h** *I've heard no news from Paul.*

2 a *no* **b** *None* **c** *not* **d** *not* **e** *no* **f** *no* **g** *none* **h** *not* **i** *no* **j** *none*

3 a *Not really,* **b** *I don't think so,* **c** *Yes, but* **d** *I'm afraid not,* **e** *Of course not,/ Certainly not,* **f** *I'd love to but* **g** *Certainly not,* **h** *Not at all*

4 a *no knowing* (there's no knowing = you can never predict or be certain about anything) **b** *No problem* **c** *No sooner* (= as soon as) **d** *No wonder* (= it's no surprise) **e** *No way* (= certainly not) **f** *no longer* (= not any more)

not

1 b The sun does *not* go round the earth. **c** Penguins can*not* fly. **d** Astronauts have *not* been to Mars. **e** Fish do *not* have lungs. **f** Shakespeare did *not* write novels. **g** The Pyramids could *not* have been built by aliens. **h** The continents are *not* moving closer together.

2 a *isn't it* **b** *aren't you* **c** *isn't he* **d** *don't they* **e** *hasn't she* **f** *wasn't it* **g** *didn't he* **h** *shouldn't I* **i** *didn't you* **j** *won't it*

3 a Not *'have'* – *'am'* **b** Not *'no'* – *'don't'* **c** Not *'your'* – *'my'* **d** Not *'don't'* – *'doesn't'* **e** Not *'too'* – *'very'* **f** Not *'do you live'* – *'have you lived'* **g** Not *'never'* – *'ever'* **h** Not *'went'* – *'go'*

4 a *Not many/Not a lot of people came to the meeting.* **b** *Not much/Not a lot of money was spent on publicity.* **c** *Not enough money is spent on education.* **d** *Not all birds can fly.* **e** *Not enough help is given to the elderly.* **f** *Not all Swedes have fair hair and blue eyes.*

now

1 a 1 **b** 2 **c** 1 **d** 2 **e** 1 **f** 2 **g** 1 **h** 2

2 a – 5 **b** – 1 **c** – 6 **d** – 3 **e** – 2 **f** – 4.

3 a *currently* **b** *nowadays* **c** *to date* **d** *already* **e** *today* **f** *at the moment* **g** *yet* **h** *presently*

4 a *hour* **b** *never* **c** *Altogether* **d** *over* **e** *Go* **f** *friends* **g** *know*

of

1 Most *of* the world's water – 97 per cent *of* it – is found in the oceans. The oceans also receive most *of* the rain that falls. The rest falls on the land, where some *of* it evaporates back into the atmosphere. Some water is returned to the atmosphere from plants. As the water in the atmosphere cools, it condenses to form clouds *of* water vapour. Some *of* this water falls to the Earth again as rain. If this process *of* evaporation stopped, there would only be enough rain in the atmosphere to last for a couple *of* weeks.

2 a *pair of shoes* **b** *slice of bread* **c** *shortage of water* **d** *middle of the square* **e** *gang of youths* **f** *beginning of the movie* **g** *loads of food* **h** *sort of books*

3 a *the discovery of penicillin* **b** correct **c** *the history of art* **d e** correct **f** *the bottom of the tower* **g** *the top of the fridge* **h** correct **i** *the colour of your hair* **j** correct

4 *Lord of the Rings* •*Planet of the Apes*
Return of the Jedi •*Raiders of the Lost Ark*
Night of the Living Dead •*Lawrence of*
Arabia •*The Importance of being Earnest*
The Hunchback of Notre Dame •*The*
Silence of the Lambs •*Father of the Bride*
•*Invasion of the Body Snatchers* •*Close*
Encounters of the Third Kind

on

1 1: a, e, f, 2: g 3: d 4: c 5: b

2 I've had a lot *on* lately, so I've been
depending *on* Ron to keep an eye *on* the
children while I'm away *on* business. *On*
Monday evening I came home to find
Ron asleep *on* the couch, the television
on, and the baby crawling around *on* the
floor with nothing *on*. 'What's going *on*?!'
I shouted. 'Come *on*, Ron,' I said. 'This is
not *on*. I'm relying *on* you.' From then *on*
things have improved … a bit.

3 a *congratulate* b *catch* c *have* d *blame*
e *take* f *carry* g *survive* h *get*

4 **Across:** 1 purpose 4 board 6 ice
7 sale 9 time 10 Eve 11 alert 13 strike
Down: 2 side 3 diet 4 business 5 film
8 line 9 track 12 tap

one

1

A: Can I help you?

B: Yes, I'm looking for a sweater.

A: These *ones* here are quite nice. They're
reduced.

B: Do you have *one* in grey?

A: What size?

B: Small. It's not for me: it's for *one* of my
grandchildren.

A: There are no grey *ones* left. I've got *one*
in charcoal.

B: I quite like this blue *one*.

A: That *one* is medium.

B: Ok, I'll take the charcoal *one*.

A: OK. Would you like *one* of our catalogues?

B: I've got *one*, thanks all the same.

2 a *an* b *one* c a d *one* e a f *A* g *one*
h *One* i *one* j *one*

3 a *it* b *one* c *ones* d *them* e *it* f *one, it*
g *ones, them* h *one* i *it, one* j *them* k *one*

4 a *unique* b *only* c *single* d *once* e *sole*
f *first* g *individual* h *solitary*

or

1 a … left here *or* right? b … any bread,
butter, milk, *or* cheese. c … the dog goes
or I go. d … *or* shall I serve it for you?
e … whether she eats meat *or* not?
f … whether *or* not to pack my swimsuit.
g Shakespeare wrote forty *or* so plays …
h … *or* you'll get soaked. i … *or* else
she's lying. j … ~ More *or* less.

2 a – 7 b – 4 c – 1 d – 3
e – 6 f – 8 g – 5 h - 2

3 a *I haven't got the time or the money.*
b *She hasn't been to Rome or to Florence.*
c *It isn't your business or anyone's*
business, how I live my life. d *They don't*
have clean water, or shelter, or medicine.
e *Stop shouting or you'll wake the*
neighbours. f *Don't drink any more or*
you won't be able to drive. g *Be careful*
or you'll hurt yourself. h *Don't be naughty,*
or I'll tell your mother.

4 a *and* b *or* c *or* d *and* e *or* f *or* g *and*
h *and*

other

1 a … Have you got *another* one? b All
the *other* students … c … but *others* are
impossible. d Can you make *another*
hundred copies … e … and *the* other is
out of work. f … while I order *another*.
g The children seem to like each *other* …
h … , *the* others will want one, too.

2 a *more* b *other* c *another* d *others/*
more e *other* f *others* g *another*
h *other/more* i *other* j *another*

3 a *one way or another* (= by trying

different ways) b *this, that, and the other*
(= nothing special) c *one after the other*
(= happening in quick succession)
d *someone or other* e *one another* (=
reciprocally) f *among other things* (when
you mention just one of several things of
a kind) g *on the other hand* h *the other*
way round (= the reverse) i *in other words*

own

1 a … all their *own* design. b … and
make our *own* bread. c … I'd rather
have my *own* room. d This is a test, so
work on your *own* … e … and its *own*
bathroom. f … their very *own* box of
chocolates. g … to leave the house on
her *own* yet. h … does the prince *own*?

2 a *her* b *their* c *your* d *its* e *my, my*
f *our* g *your* h *its*

3 a *My father owned these paintings.*
b *Who owns this car?* c *The company*
belongs to the workers. d *Does this*
apartment belong to you? e *I don't like*
living by myself. f *Can you get home by*
yourself? g *We don't like leaving the*
children on their own. h *Delia prefers to*
work on her own.

4 *an own coffee* should be *our own coffee*

place

1 a – 6 b – 5 c – 4 d – 2 e – 8 f – 3 g – 1
(or possibly, 2) h – 7 i – 5 j – 8 k – 2

2

A: This is my *place*. Come in. Sorry about
the mess. Things are all over the *place*.

B: It's nice. It must be nice to have a *place*
of your own. How did you find it?

A: It wasn't easy. I looked at a lot of *places*.
I was looking for a *place* to work and to
live at the same time.

B: I know what you mean. You've seen my
place, haven't you? It's a wonderful
place to live, but it's not big enough.
There's simply no *place* to work.

A: Yes, I was happy in the *place* where I

was living before. But now I wouldn't change *places* for the world.

3 a *best* **b** *safe* **c** *wrong* **d** *quiet*
e *strange* **f** *public* **g** *change* **h** *get*
i *save* **j** *take* **k** *lose* **l** *take*

put

1 a Where did you *put* … **b** I put *it* on the shelf … **c** … so please put *it* out. **d** … I can put the water *in*? **e** … got some ice I can put *in* the water? **f** She really put herself *out* … **g** I don't know how to put *it*: … **h** … put *it* in writing? **I** Put *it* back before … **j** … what I have to put *up* with!

2 a *put you through.* **b** *put you up* **c** *put up the rent/put the rent up.* **d** *put out your cigarettes/put your cigarettes out.* **e** *put this bookcase together?* **f** *You are putting off the players/putting the players off.* **g** *Put back all the books/Put all the books back* **h** *put my knee out*

3 a – 5 **b** – 1 **c** – 2 **d** – 6 **e** – 4 **f** - 3
a *I put two and two together.* **b** *I'm going to put my foot down.* **c** *I really put my foot in it.* **d** *I wouldn't put money on it.* **e** *Don't put all your eggs in one basket.* **f** *I can't put my finger on it.*

4 HEALTH TIPS FOR OUR PASSENGERS:
Here are few tips for your safety and comfort.
    To sleep more comfortably: take off your shoes and *put* on the sleeping socks we have provided. *Put* the footrest down and *put* your feet on it. *Put* the seat back. *Put* the eye mask on and *put* the ear plugs in. Don't forget to *put* out the overhead light. If you don't want to be disturbed during the flight, *put* the 'Don't disturb' sticker on your head rest.
    We recommend regular exercise. For example, *put* your feet flat on the floor and press down firmly ten times. *Put* your arms above your head and stretch.
    Now, sit back and enjoy the flight!

say

1 a … I said *to* her. **b** 'It's getting late,' *she said.* **c** … say *what* she had been doing. **d** … doesn't say what the soup *is*. **e** … and I said *so*. **f** It *is* sometimes said that … **g** … is said *to* have fallen into a crevass. **h** … what I was *about* to say. **i** … said Arthur *cheerfully*. **j** What did you say *about* me …?

2 a *She said she was hungry.* **b** *Susan said she would be late.* **c** *The sailor said he had been robbed.* **d** *He said the bus hadn't stopped.* **e** *Donald said it might rain.* **f** *Lydia said she could hear voices.* **g** *Mrs Adams said she was going to complain.* **h** *They said they had to work.*

3 a *say* **b** *said* **c** *was saying* **d** *says* **e** *says, says* **f** *said*

4 a *Who says?* **b** *You can say that again.* **c** *That goes without saying.* **d** *Easier said than done.* **e** *I wouldn't say no.* **f** *I'd rather not say.* **g** *Whatever you say.*

see

1 1: b, f 2: h, j 3: a, l 4: d, g 5: i, m 6: c, e, k

2 I think I may have *seen* a UFO. Last night the dog was barking so I went out to *see* what was disturbing it. It was a clear night. You could *see* the stars. Suddenly I *saw* an object above me, travelling at high speed. At first I thought it was a plane. But I was amazed to *see* it change direction sharply, before it disappeared. That was all I *saw*. It was like nothing I have ever *seen* before. I don't believe in aliens, but how else can I explain what I *saw*?

3 I saw **a** … *the sun set.* **b** … *the lights coming on, one by one.* **c** … *people coming and going.* **d** … *a car stop suddenly.* **e** … *a man get out.* **f** … *him pointing a gun at someone.* **g** … *him shouting something.* **h** … *him pull the trigger.*

4 a *you see* **b** *I see* **c** *let me see* **d** *we'll see* **e** *you'll see* **f** *see you*

seem

1 1: a, g 2: c, j 3: f, l 4: e, m 5: h, i 6: b, d, k

2 a *He seems like a nice guy.* **b** *It seemed as if the crowd was going to riot.* **c** *It doesn't seem possible that Ben could fail.* **d** *They seemed to have been arguing.* **e** *It seemed to be a good idea at the time.* **f** *It seems that the doctor has called.* **g** *It seems as if his heart had stopped.* **h** *It seems unlikely that Catherine will marry.* **i** *It seems as if/as though you are enjoying yourselves.* **j** *Bronwyn seems (to me) to be lying.*

3 a *The television seems to be broken.* **b** *The phone doesn't seem to work.* **c** *The towels seem to be dirty.* **d** *I seem to have broken the toilet seat.* (OR: *It seems as if/as though/that I've broken the toilet seat*). **e** *There doesn't seem to be any hot water in our room.* (OR: *It seems as if/as though/that there's no …*) **f** *I seem to have lost my key.* **g** *There seems to be nothing in the mini-bar.* (OR: *There doesn't seem to be anything …*) **h** *The room doesn't seem to have been cleaned.* (OR: *It doesn't seem as if/as though/that the room has been cleaned*).

4 My friend Max has opened a restaurant, so I went to eat there. At first sight, the restaurant *looked/seemed* promising: well decorated and nicely lit. But when Max greeted us, he *seemed/looked* worried and his hand *felt* damp when I shook it. I soon realized why. From the kitchen I could hear the cook: he *sounded* drunk. Sure enough, when the first course arrived, it *tasted* disgusting: undercooked and oversalted. And when the cook came out to say hello, his breath *smelled* strongly of cheap wine. Not a good beginning ….

should

1 a *She should be there by now.* **b** *They shouldn't drink.* **c** *Should the boys wear jackets?* **d** *I should go tomorrow.* **e** *I should've gone yesterday.* **f** *I shouldn't have gone yesterday.* **g** *He shouldn't have gone yesterday.* **h** *Shouldn't he do something?* **i** *He should've done something yesterday.* **j** *Shouldn't he have done something yesterday?*

2 a *I must/should get a haircut.* **b** *You must/should read this book.* **c** *Dennis must have been delayed.* **d** *You should've apologized.* **e** *I must've left my wallet in the supermarket.* **f** *You should/ must eat more fresh fruit.* **g** *You should've eaten more fresh fruit.* **h** *You shouldn't have lost your temper.*

3 a *They should've taken a map.* **b** *They shouldn't have taken a short-cut.* **c** *They should've followed the signs.* **d** *They shouldn't have lit a fire.* **e** *They should've taken a first-aid kit.* **f** *They should've taken food and water.* **g** *They should've told someone where they were going.* **h** *They should've stayed together.*

so

1 a – 5 b – 7 c – 1 d – 8 e – 6 f – 2 g – 3 h – 4

2 a *so* **b** *such* **c** *so, such* **d** *such* **e** *such* **f** *so, such*

3 a *… and so do I* **b** *It was so pretty that …* **c** *… so that you don't get wet.* **d** *… so we phoned him.* **e** *… are so friendly. …* **f** *… but I'm not so sure.* **g** *… , but I don't think so.* **h** *… , it was so heavy.* **I** *I'm so glad you could come …* **j** *… As I was doing so, I heard a strange noise.*

4 a *So do I* **b** *So am I* **c** *Nor/Neither do I* **d** *So have I* **e** *Nor/Neither have I* **f** *So can I* **g** *So do I/So have I* **h** *Nor/Neither will I*

5 a *So long* **b** *so-so* **c** *Is that so?* **d** *so they say* **e** *So it is.* **f** *ever so* **g** *I told you so.* **h** *so be it*

some

1 a *… but I've got some orange.* **b** *… but I bought some anyway.* **c** *There are some more eggs in the fridge, …* **d** *Katie ate some of her vegetables…* **e** *… if you'd like some more.* **f** *I think there must be some mistake …* **g** *Harry spent some time in Africa, …* **h** *We need some bread …*

2 a *some* **b** *some* **c** *a* **d** *an* **e** *a* **f** *some* **g** *an* **h** *some* **i** *a* **j** *some*

3 a *'zero'* **b** *some* **c** *'zero'* **d** *some* **e** *'zero'* **f** *some* **g** *some* **g** *'zero'*

4 a *something like* (= approximately) **b** *something of* (= to a large degree) **c** *something about* **d** *something to do with* (= concerned in some way with) **e** *something wrong with* **f** *quite something* (= quite an achievement)

5 a *Some day* **b** *Some* **c** *something* **d** *Someone* **e** *someone* **f** *Something* **g** *Somebody* **h** *Somewhere*

sort

1 a type: b, g, j, k **b** not exactly/pause filler: a, c, e, i **c** verb: d, f, h

2 a *Sort of blueish-green, I think.* **b** *I sort of know it…* **c** *Well, he sort of apologized.* **d** *Sort of like my father …* **e** *I can sort of speak it …* **f** *Yes, sort of.*

3 a *model* **b** *make* (also: *sort, type, kind*) **c** *type* **d** *breed* (also: *sort, type, kind*) **e** *brand* **f** *kind* (also: *sort, type*) **g** *type* (also: *sort*) **h** *type* (also: *kind, sort*)

4 *any sort of children of my own:* when talking about whether you have children or not, you don't classify them

start

1 1: g, i 2: c, k 3: b, h 4: a, d 5: f, l 6: e, j

2 In these sentences *begin* would be unusual: c, d, e, h.

3 a *life* **b** *early* **c** *a rumour* **d** *fresh* **e** *up* **f** *flying* **g** *an argument* **h** *school* **i** *a fire* **j** *on*

4 To *start* the dryer, press the green button (A). If the dryer does not *start* immediately, check that the door is closed properly, then *start* it again. If it still won't *start*, check that it is not overloaded. Remove some items if necessary.

Occasionally the dryer may *start* to vibrate. If this happens, stop it, reload it, and *start* it again.

Warning: do not *start* the dryer if the red light (B) is flashing; this means the machine has overheated. If the red light *starts* flashing during a cycle, stop the dryer, and wait until the light stops flashing before re-starting it.

still

1 a *I am still learning …* **b** *They still won't answer …* **c** *… it is still dark.* **d** *I can still remember …* **e** *Is it still raining?* **f** *…, I still dream of Milford Sound.* **g** *It was still not summer.* **h** *I still can't drive.* **I** *Do you still live in …* **j** *… should still be hot.*

2 a *he is still lazy* **b** *I'm still waiting* **c** *it still hurts* **d** *he's still watching it/TV* **e** *they're still learning it/English* **f** *I still feel ill* **g** *she still loves it/horse riding* **h** *it's still dripping*

3 a *Have you done it yet? I am still doing it.* **b** *Have you had lunch already?* (OR: *Have you already had lunch?*) **c** *I still haven't passed my driving test.* (OR: *I haven't passed my driving test yet*). **d** *I haven't seen the Pyramids yet.* **e** *I still haven't seen the Pyramids.* **f** *I've already read it.*

(OR: *I've read it already*) **g** *He's still only 19, he's already graduated* (OR: *he's graduated already*). **h** *I'm not ready yet. I'm still getting dressed.*

stop

1 1: b, d 2: f, l 3: c, g 4: e, j 5: i, k 6: a, h

2 a. *playing* **b** *to change* **c** *smoking* **d** *to smoke* **e** *thinking* **f** *to change*

3 a *No, it just broke.* **b** *No, it just cracked.* **c** *No, they just shut.* **d** *No, they just burnt.* **e** *No, it just started.* **f** *No, they just opened.*

4 a *end/finish* **b** *stop* **c** *end/finish* **d** *stop* **e** *finish* **f** *end* **g** *stop* **h** *finish*

take

1 a *bring* **b** *take* **c** *take* **d** *bring* **e** *take* **f** *take* **g** *bring* **h** *Bring*

2 a *take part in* **b** *take pride in* **c** *took power* **d** *take place* **e** *took pity on* **f** *took pleasure in*

3 a *take it back* **b** *taken in* **c** *taken up* **d** *take after* **e** *took up* **f** *taken on* **g** *Take off* **h** *take over* **i** *taken to* **j** *took off*

4 a – 6 (*take your hat off to her* = congratulate her), **b** – 2 **c** – 5 (*taken as read* = accepted as true without any further proof) **d** – 3 (*take this lying down* = accept it without a fight) **e** – 8 **f** – 1 (*take the bull by the horns* = commit yourself to a necessary but risky action) **g** – 4 (*taken for a ride* = tricked or cheated) **h** – 7 (*take my word for it* = believe me).

tell

1 1: c, g 2: h, m 3: e, i 4: b, j 5: d, k 6: a, n 7: f, l

2 a … *to tell* you *a story?* **b** … ~ *Tell* it *to us.* **c** *She told her boyfriend* that *she* … **d** *I told* myself *to be brave* … **e** … *told him* to *go home.* **f** … *tell* one *from another?* **g** … *Matthew* told *me.*

h *Can you tell me* how *to* … **i** … *when we get* to *the turn-off.* **j** *I tell you* what: *let's* …

3 a *tell* **b** *said* **c** *Tell* **d** *said* **e** *was telling* **f** *tell* **g** *says* **h** *told* **i** *tell* **j** *say*

4 a *told* **b** *says* **c** *says* **d** *says* **e** *telling* **f** *says* **g** *tells* **h** *tells* **i** *says* **j** *says*

than

1 a … *more work than I* do. **b** … *by more* than *two thousand fans.* **c** *He can write* much *more correctly than* … **d** … *less peaceful* than *before.* **e** … *less often than I used* to. **f** *I'd* rather *eat in than* … **g** … other *than her immediate family.* **h** *More often than* not …

2 a – 5 b – 2 c – 7 d – 1 e – 4 f – 6 g – 8 h – 3

3 a *Blanc-o is more expensive than White-o.* **b** *I am older than my brother.* **c** *He's more intelligent than me.* **d** *It rains more on the coast than it does here.* **e** *Madonna can sing better than she can dance.* **f** *It was colder yesterday than it is today.* **g** *Spanish is harder than I expected.* **h** *The milkman used to pass by more often than he does now.*

4 a – 5 b – 4 c – 1 d – 6 e – 2 f – 3

that

1 Not possible to omit *that*: a, c, e, h
Possible to omit *that*: b, d, f, g

2 1: c, l 2: h, k 3: a, e
4: b, m 5: f, j 6: i, n 7: d, g

3 (Optional instances of *that* are in brackets):
The stethoscope is an instrument *that* is used to listen to a patient's breathing and heart beat. It was an invention *that* changed medical practice. It enabled doctors to diagnose diseases *that* were concealed until then, such as tuberculosis.

But it should not be assumed (*that*) all doctors and patients were enthusiastic about the invention. When they saw the doctor with his stethoscope some patients thought (*that*) they were going to be operated on, because, at *that* time, it was only surgeons *that* used medical instruments. The idea *that* people were afraid of stethoscopes now seems ridiculous.

4 a *agreement* **b** *impression* **c** *believe* **d** *suggested* **e** *seems* **f** *fact* **g** *doubt* **h** *news* **i** *realize* **j** *evidence*

the

1 Neil Armstrong was the (**d**) first person to set foot on the (**d**) surface of the (**b**) moon. In the (**a**) picture you can see him stepping out of the (**d**) spacecraft *Eagle*. The (**d**) words that he then said are famous: 'That's one small step for a man, one giant leap for mankind'. He and his co-pilot Buzz Aldrin then planted a flag and collected rocks. The (**c**) flag is probably still there. The (**c**) rocks have helped scientists understand the (**d**) history of the (**b**) solar system.

2 a … *and is learning* the *violin.* **b** *What is* the *best restaurant* … **c** … *is* the *kitchen.* **d** … *and* the *man was carrying a big bunch of flowers.* **e** … *but I don't like* the *ones with bones.* **f** … *One is next to* the *Town Hall.* **g** … *except* the *red one: it's mine.* **h** … *and* the *beauty of its women.* **i** … ~ *Not* the *Michael Douglas?* **j** … *The taxi drove off.*

3 DODO: *The dodo is an extinct bird, belonging to* the *pigeon family. Dodos lived on islands and couldn't fly. In the seventeenth century, sailors started visiting* the *islands, looking for food and water. The sailors hunted* the *dodos and ate them. The last dodo died in 1790.*

then

1 **a** *First* **b** *Then* **c** *before that* **d** *next/then*
e *Then/Next* **f** *eventually* **g** *finally*

2 **a** – 4 **b** – 8 **c** – 1 **d** – 6
e – 2 **f** – 5 **g** – 3 **h** – 7

3 **a** *Back* **b** *Since* **c** *From* **d** *Just* **e** *by*
f *Until*

4 The waiter refilled their glasses. It was *then* that Albert produced the ring. She stared at it for a minute or so and *then* she put it on. 'You do love me *then*?' she breathed. 'Passionately.' 'I've always loved you, too, Al,' she murmured. '*Then* will you marry me? (OR: Will you marry me *then*?)' he asked. 'Yes, but I'll have to ask daddy. Only *then* can I give you a firm answer.' 'When will you see him?' 'Next summer. Not before *then*.' 'But I can't wait until *then*,' Albert sobbed. 'By *then* it will be too late.' '*Then* take the ring back. (OR: Take the ring back *then*),' she sighed. 'If you cannot wait, *then* you do not truly love me.'

there

1 **a** pronoun **b** pronoun **c** adverb
d pronoun **e** adverb **f** pronoun
g adverb **h** adverb **i** pronoun

2
A: Excuse me. Is *there* a cashpoint near here?
B: Well, *there* used to be one over *there*. But it seems to have gone. Let me think: I think *there* is another one in the Ellis Arcade.
A: Where is that?
B: Do you see that tall building over *there*?
A: Yes.
B: Turn right *there* and keep going for two blocks. *There* is a cinema and next to that *there* is a shopping centre. It's called Ellis Arcade. *There* is a cashpoint in *there*.
A: Thanks very much.

3 **a** *There* **b** *it* **c** *it* **d** *There* **e** *There* **f** *there*
g *They* **h** *it* **i** *there* **j** *it*

4 **a** *then and there* (= immediately) **b** *so there!* (= I don't care what you think) **c** *there you go* (= there you are) **d** *so there I was* (a phrase used to summarize the situation in a story) **e** *there and back* (= from here to the destination, and back again) **f** *There you are, you see* (= I told you so) **g** *here and there* (= in or to different places) **h** *There, there* (a phrase to comfort someone, especially children)

thing

1 1: c, f 1a: e, h 2: a, g 2a: b, i 2b: d, j

2 **a** – 6 **b** – 5 **c** – 8 **d** – 3
e – 2 **f** – 1 **g** – 4 **h** – 7

3 **a** *whole* **b** *important* **c** *main* **d** *worst*
e *odd* **f** *first* **g** *best* **h** *strange*

4 **a** *the thing with him* (= the problem with him) **b** *of all things* (to emphasize how surprising or shocking something is) **c** *all things considered* (= when you take everything into account) **d** *no bad thing* (= despite being unfortunate, the situation is positive) **e** *the latest thing* (= the most fashionable thing) **f** *just one of those things* (= a situation that you can't prevent) **g** *no such thing* (to emphasize that something does not exist) **h** *a thing of the past* (= something that no longer exists)

think

1 1: e, i 2: d, j 3: b, h 4: a, k 5: g, l 6: c, f

2 **a** *I don't think it will …* **b** *… are you thinking about?* **c** *We can't think of a good name …* **d** *… but I don't think so.* **e** *Do you think he will get … ?* **f** *Do you honestly think …?* **g** *… is thought to have been destroyed by fire.* **h** *I would think long and hard before …* **i** *… you should think it over.* **j** *Who would have thought … !*

3 **a** *do you think* **b** *are thinking* **c** *are you thinking* **d** *don't think* **e** *have you been thinking* **f** *are you thinking*

4 **a** *Just think* **b** *Who would have thought?* **c** *I was thinking* **d** *Do you think so?* **e** *I think* **f** *Come to think of it* (= I now remember that …) **g** *You'd think* (= my expectation is …) **h** *Do you think you could* (= would you …)

this

1 **a** *this* **b** *that* **c** *those* **d** *This* **e** *that* **f** *that* **g** *this* **h** *These* **i** *This, that* **j** *This* **k** *that* **l** *these* **m** *that* **n** *that* **o** *this, this*

2 **a** *It* **b** *It* **c** *this* **d** *That* **e** *it* **f** *This* **g** *It* **h** *This* **i** *It* **j** *that*

3 *This* ➤ [the picture] is a picture of my family.
As you can see, we were a big family. *This* ➤ 'we were a big family' meant that, as a child, I always had company and never felt alone. I sometimes miss *this* ➤ 'I always had company and never felt alone', now that I am living on my own. But I don't miss the noise. *This* ➤ 'I don't miss the noise' is because I am a quiet person by nature. If you don't believe me, how about *this*: ➤ 'when I left college I spent three months alone living in a lighthouse!' *I think that this* ➤ 'when I left college I spent three months alone living in a lighthouse!' was probably the happiest period of my life.

time

1
A: Did you have a good *time* in Mexico?
B: We had a great *time*, apart from Jack, who was sick the whole *time*. It's the first *time* I've been there. So we spent most of the *time* in Mexico City, which is nice at this *time* of year: not too hot, and clear blue skies. We didn't have *time* to go to Yucatan and we didn't want to waste *time* on buses and

things, so we mainly stayed around the capital. There's so much to see, although at *times* you get a bit overwhelmed by the size of the place. But, at the same *time*, it's actually quite easy to get around: we took the metro all the *time*. You can get around in no *time*. And most of the *time* it's not too crowded. Yes, it was fantastic. I'd like to go back some *time*.

2 **a** *spend* **b** *have* **c** *waste* **d** *find* **e** *pass* **f** *take* **g** *save* **h** *take*

3 **a** *on* **b** *By* **c** *at* **d** *For* **e** *in* **f** *in* **g** *for* **h** *At*

4 **a** *lifetime* **b** *free time* **c** *lunchtime* **d** *time zone* **e** *time bomb* **f** *timetable* **g** *part-time* **h** *time limit*

5 **a** – 5 **b** – 2 **c** – 4 **d** – 1 **e** – 6 **f** – 3

to¹

1 **a** *She threatened to call the police.* **b** *The teacher permitted the class to leave.* **c** *Julia promised to be home before midnight.* **d** *Brad warned the boy not to go near the dog.* **e** *Anna invited me to come to dinner.* **f** *Ian reminded the others to turn out the lights.* **g** *Tom agreed to sign the contract.* **h** *I advised Ellie to take some painkillers.*

2 **a** *same* **b** *different* (If you *remember to do* something, you remember and then you do it; if you *remember doing* something, you do it, and then you remember the experience) **c** *different* (If you *stop to do* something, you stop what you are doing in order to do something else; if you *stop doing* something, you stop what you are currently doing) **d** *same* **e** *different* (If you *go on to do* something, you proceed to that activity; if you *go on doing* something, you continue doing the same thing) **f** *same*

3 *To book a holiday, you should go to a travel agency.* •*To borrow a book, you should go to a library.* •*To buy a magazine, you should go to a bookshop.* •*To send a parcel, you should go to the post office.* •*To keep fit, you*

should go to a gym. •*To have a key made, you should go to a hardware store.*

4 Dear Babs,
I am 16 and I have a problem. I have decided *to* be a singer and I want *to* leave school so I can follow this dream. But my parents won't allow me *to* leave. They have ordered me *to* stay at school and told me *to* keep studying until I am 18. I have begged them *to* let me leave, but it's no use. What should I do? It's impossible *to* stay at school when I have this burning desire *to* be a singer. Is there no way *to* convince them *to* give me my freedom? Please advise me what *to* do. I hope *to* hear from you soon.

to²

1 Dear Mrs Brennan,
Here is my report on your ex-husband's activities yesterday.

He left the house at 8.04 and walked *to* the station, where he took a train *to* the city centre. On the train he read a newspaper and listened *to* music on his portable stereo. He didn't talk *to* anyone, apart from giving directions *to* a passing *tourist*. He then walked *to* work, arriving there at 8.37. He came out at 12.31 and went *to* a café opposite his office, where he had lunch, alone, until 13.29. He then went back *to* the office, and was there from 13.30 *to*18.00. I followed him home. He got there at 18.43, and he did not come out again that evening.
As I explained *to* you in my last report, I do not believe that Mr Brennan is concealing anything. I will send you an invoice at the end of the month, as usual. I will also enclose the photo that belongs *to* you. Looking forward *to* hearing from you,
Monty Dagg (Private Detective)

2 **a** *Send the boss an e-mail.* **b** *The teacher taught the children the alphabet.*

c *A friend of mine sold me a painting.* **d** *Show the doctor your arm.* **e** *I told the neighbours the bad news.* **f** *Can you take Mrs Lowe this letter?* **g** *We gave Tom a skateboard and Josh a football.* **h** *Read me the article.*

3 **a** – 6 **b** – 4 **c** – 5 **d** – 1 **e** – 3 **f** – 7 **g** – 8 **h** – 2

4 **infinitive marker:** a, d, e, i, k, l, m, o
preposition: b (follows adjective), c (follows noun), f (follows noun), g (follows verb), h (follows adjective), j (follows verb), n (follows adverb)

too

1 **a** It's far *too* expensive for me. … **b** Is it *too* late to phone for a pizza? … **c** … the music was rather *too* loud. **d** I'm much *too* busy … **e** … That's far *too* far to walk. **f** … but the fish was *too* salty. **g** … got much *too* much money. **h** You're making *too* much noise … **i** … I'll have some sugar *too*. **j** … Can I come *too*?

2 **a** *The ceilings are not high enough.* **b** *The kitchen is not big enough.* **c** *The rooms are not light enough.* **d** *The apartment is not cheap enough.* **e** *There are not enough balconies.* **f** *There is not enough ventilation.* **g** *The train station is too far.* **h** *The apartment is too dirty.* **i** *There are too few bedrooms.* **j** *There is too little light.* **k** *It's too small for our family.* **l** *It's too old-fashioned for our tastes.*

3 **a** *very* **b** *too* **c** *very* **d** *too* **e** *too* **f** *very* **g** *very* **h** *very, very*

4 **a** *Far* **b** *Much* **c** *Heaven* **d** *Hot* **e** Busy **f** Big **g** Hot **h** Easily

up

1 cut *up* the cake: *into pieces* blow *up* the balloons: *to a bigger size* put them *up*: *to a higher position* climb *up*: *to a higher*

position wrap <u>up</u> the presents: _to_
completion bring <u>up</u> some firewood: _to_
a higher position chop it <u>up</u>: _into pieces_
tidy <u>up</u>: _to completion_

2 a _preposition_ **b** _adverb:_ Please pick your
clothes up off the floor **c** _adverb:_ Can
you bring the mail up when you come?
d _adverb:_ The thieves blew the safe up
and stole the diamonds **e** _preposition_
f _adverb:_ Eat your vegetables up.
g _adverb:_ Where shall I hang my jacket
up? **h** _preposition_

3 a _get up_ **b** _make up_ **c** _do up_ **d** _take up_
e _look up_ **f** _set up_ **g** _pick up_ **h** _bring up_
i _give up_ **j** _put up_

4 a _time is up_ (= time has expired)
b _what's up_ **c** _up to something_ (= doing
something they shouldn't be doing)
d _up to you_ (= your decision) **e** _up and
about_ (= living a normal active life)
f _up-and-coming_ (= likely to be
successful) **g** _up to my ears_ **h** _ups and
downs_ **i** _up to scratch_ (= at the required
standard) **j** _right way up_

used

1 1: f, h, j 1a: a, d 2: c, e, i 2a: b, g

2 a … _she reads all the time._ **b** _They never
used to argue_ … **c** … _you worry all the
time._ **d** _I never used to swim_ … **e** … _but
now he smokes all the time._ **f** … _we get it
(junk mail) all the time._

3 a, c, d, h: _would_ is not possible

4 a _We're getting used to the noise._
b _I'm getting used to/I've got used to the
humidity._ **c** _We're getting used to the
pace of life._ **d** _Derrin hasn't got used to
getting up early._ **e** _I haven't got used to
going to work on the underground._
f _I'm getting used to sharing a room._

very

1 a _wasn't very helpful_ **b** _isn't very realistic_
c _didn't seem very interested_ **d** _weren't_

very attractive **e** _aren't very significant_
f _not feeling very well_ **g** _isn't very legible_
h _weren't very polite_

2 a _absolutely_ **b** _very_ **c** _absolutely_
d _extremely_ **e** _Totally_ **f** _very_ **g** _very_
h _completely_

3 a _It was really freezing._ **b** … _it's really
cold._ **c** _This salad is really delicious._
d … _it's really tasty._

4 a correct **b** incorrect: … _has been much
criticized_ **c** incorrect: … _was much
warmer_ **d** **e** correct **f** incorrect: … _was
much more expensive_ **g** incorrect: …
greatly/ much improved **h** incorrect: …
greatly/ much loved **i** correct
j incorrect: … _very much influenced
/greatly influenced._

want

1 1: d, g, i 2: a, f, h 3: b, c, k 4: e, j, l

2 a I want you _to_ marry me. **b** Do _you_
want to… **c** I _never_ wanted to …
d They wanted _her_ to … **e** I want the
books _put_ back … **f** What we _don't_ want
is… **g** I _just_ want you … **h** Jamie
always wanted to … **i** What _I_ really want
is… **j** We wanted the chairs _painted_ …

3 a incorrect: _I want you to return my
money._ **b** incorrect: _What do you want
to eat?_ **c** incorrect: _I don't want them to
wear their shoes in the house._ **d** correct
e incorrect: _The police don't want you to
park here._ **f** incorrect: _The boys want a
sandwich._ **g** incorrect: _I don't want you
to smoke in here._ **h** incorrect: _What do
you want me to do?_

4 a 'I want love.' **b** 'I want to tell you.'
c 'I wanna be your man.' **d** 'I want to
hold your hand.' **e** 'Do you want to
dance?' **f** 'All I really want to do.'
g 'I'm a fool to want you.' **h** 'I want to
take you higher.' **i** 'I only want to be
with you.' **j** 'Do you want to know a
secret?' **k** 'Doesn't somebody want to
be wanted?'

was/were

1 1: c, h, k 2: a, e, f, 3: b, d, i 4: g, j, l

2 a _were playing, started_ **b** _rang, was getting_
c _got, was leaving_ **d** _was riding, fell off_
e _was working, crashed_ **f** _met, was
working_ **g** _was coming down, went out_
h _woke up, was snowing, went_

3 a The Mona Lisa _was painted in 1506._
b Shakespeare's Hamlet _was written in
1603._ **c** The electric battery _was invented
in 1800._ **d** Beethoven's Ninth Symphony
was composed in 1824. **e** The Eiffel Tower
was built in 1889. **f** Pluto _was discovered
in 1930._ **g** Gone With the Wind _was
made in 1939._ **h** Mount Everest _was
climbed in 1953._

4 a _am_ **b** _was_ **c** _is_ **d** _was_ **e** _is_ **f** _is_ **g** _were_
h _were_ **i** _Is_ **j** _was_ **k** _are, are_

way

1 1: d, e, k 2: a, h, l 3: f, i, m 4: b, g, n 5: c, j, o

2
Q: What's the best _way_ of cooking
artichokes?
A: One _way_ is to cut off the leaves and boil
the hearts (or 'chokes'), and toss them
into a salad. That's the _way_ they eat them
in Spain. That _way_, you don't have to
bother with the leaves. Another _way_ is to
deep-fry the baby ones in oil, the same
way you fry chips. I had them done that
way in Rome and it's the _way_ I prefer.
Either _way_, artichokes are delicious, and
very good for you. There's no _way_ you
are going to get fat, eating artichokes!

3 a _wrong_ **b** _own_ **c** _find_ **d** _ask_ **e** _possible_
f _clear_ **g** _lead_ **h** _hard_ **i** _make_ **j** _funny_

4 a _by way of_ **b** _In a way_ **c** _out of the way_
d _out of your way_ **e** _on the way/on your
way_ **f** _in the way_

well

1 **a** *Fiona plays the piano well.* **b** *How well can you type?* **c** *The children were not very well behaved.* **d** *He can read well but his writing is terrible.* **e** *They may well have taken the bus.* **f** *You don't look very well.* **g** *The castle is well worth a visit.* **h** *It was just as well we took a taxi.*

2 **a** *fast* (adverb) **b** *hard* (adjective) **c** *late* (adverb) **d** *well* (adverb) **e** *early* (adverb) **f** *early* (adjective) **g** *hard* (adverb) **h** *late* (adjective) **i** *well* (adjective) **j** *fast* (adjective)

3 **a** – 3 **b** – 6 **c** – 1 **d** – 5 **e** – 2 **f** – 4

4 **a** – 2 **b** – 3 **c** – 5 **d** – 1 **e** – 6 **f** – 4

what

1 Dear Belinda,
I don't know *what* to do about my parents. I am sixteen, and, *what's* more, I'm very grown up for my age. But my mum and dad won't let me do *what* I want. They tell me *what* to wear and *what* to do, and even *what* to think! Do you know *what* I mean? And, *what* really drives me mad is that they ask me *what* I want to do but they never listen to *what* I tell them. *What* a disaster! Tell me *what* you think I should do.
Desperate.

2 **a** *size* **b** *time* **c** *type* **d** *colour* **e** *make* **f** *breed* **g** *nationality* **h** *model*

3 *What do you think …* **a** *that black thing is?* **b** *you are doing?* **c** *the weather will be like?* **d** *we can do to help?* **e** *spiders eat?* **f** *Jack does?* **g** *the teacher said?* **h** *the police would have done?*

4 **a** *thing* **b** *morning* **c** *fool* **d** *wonderful* **e** *found* **f** *deserve* **g** *friends* **h** *want* **i** *world* **j** *love*

when

1 **a** When *are* you leaving for … **b** … when they *are* arriving? **c** 'When *does* the bank open?'… **d** … asked when the bank *opened*. **e** … find out when *to* check-in. **f** When you arrive *will* you phone? **g** Turn the lights off *when* you … **h** … the time *when* I lost my keys? **I** Since *when* did you … **j** I don't like *it* when you …

2 **a** *'When do the shops open?'* **b** *'When does the last bus leave?'* **c** *'When will the next course start?'* **d** *'When are you going on holiday?'* **e** *'When was the bridge destroyed?'* **f** *'When can I see the doctor?'* **g** *'When do I have to pay?'* **h** *'When will I know the results?'*

3 **a** – 3 **b** – 2 **c** – 7 **d** – 1 **e** – 5 **f** – 4 **g** – 6

4 **a** *had started* **b** *played* **c** *was working* **d** *were going* **e** *got off* **f** *hadn't read* **g** *had studied* **h** *left* **i** *had rained* **j** *was having*

who

1 **a** *Who phoned Jenny?* **b** *Who did Andy and Bill phone?* **c** *Who did Jenny phone?* **d** *Who did Dawn phone?* **e** *Who phoned Andy?* **f** *Who phoned Bill?*

2 **a** Who *is* my teacher? **b** Can you tell me who my teacher *is*? **c** Who *was* that woman I saw you with last night? **d** I wonder who that *was*. **e** Guess who is coming to dinner! **f** Do you know who Marion *is* seeing? **g** I don't care who you *are*! **h** … or who your father *is*!

3 *That* can replace *who* in these instances: he's that chap who (OR: *that*) did the quiz show; I was one of the many thousands of people who (OR: *that*) took part in that show; I was the spotty teenager who (OR: *that*) … answered: 'Was it Brahms?'

4 **a** Jane Arnold, *who* lives in Seville, … **b** …of that actor *who* was in *Gladiator*?

c That woman you met … **d** The waiter *who* served us … **e** The children I taught … **f** … of the man *who* did your kitchen? **g** My herbalist, *who* is Chinese, … **h** That writer you like, *who* wrote *Emma*, …

why

1 **a** *Why have you moved the sofa?* **b** *Do you know why the TV doesn't work?* **c** *Tell me why you are crying.* **d** *There must be a reason why they are late.* **e** *I don't understand why she needs an operation.* **f** *Why is it that theme parks are so popular?* **g** *Why don't we invite the neighbours?* **h** *Your eyes are why I love you.*

2 **a** – 7 **b** – 6 **c** – 2 (pickled = drunk) **d** – 4 **e** – 1 **f** – 3 **g** – 5 **h** – 8

3 **a** *Why are you wearing a tie?* **b** *Why is the road blocked?* **c** *Do you know why the car won't start?* **d** *Why haven't you done your homework?* **e** *Why won't you sing in English?* **f** *Why did you park your car on the lawn?* **g** *Do you know why the lights have gone out?* **h** *Why don't you vote Labour?*

4

Dad: Alan, *why* don't you help your brother with his homework?

Alan: *Why* me?

Dad: Because you are good at history.

Alan: Well, all right. But I don't know *why* you can't help him.

Dad: Because I'm cooking dinner, that's *why*.

Alan: So, what's the question?

Gerry: '*Why* were the pharaohs buried in tombs?'. Explain in one hundred words.

Alan: They want to know *why* the pharaohs were buried in tombs? That's easy. Because they were dead.

Gerry: That can't be right.

Alan: *Why* not?

Gerry: Because it's not a hundred words.

Alan: Look, I don't know *why* you asked me in the first place.

will

1 a … it *will* rain tomorrow. **b** A lion *won't* attack … **c** Who *will* be … **d** When *will* you have finished … **e** I *will* have to talk … **f** … you *won't* be late. **g** … you *will* be able to go to work soon. **h** When *will* you be … **i** You *will* need to go on-line … **j** We *won't* start eating …

2 a – 1 **b** – 1 and 2* **c** – 1 **d** – 1 and 2* **e** – 2 **f** – 1 **g** – 2 **h** – 2

3 a *What'll it be?* **b** *I guess I'll* **c** *We'll see.* **d** *Will it?* **e** *That'll do.* **f** *You're sure you won't?*

with

1 a … go home *with*? **b** It's a house *with* two bedrooms … **c** ~ What *with*? **d** … helps *with* the garden. **e** I'm having problems *with* the computer … **f** … I can't keep up *with* you. **g** I'm not going to argue *with* you … **h** She's fed up *with* her job …

2 *You use…* **a** *a cheese grater to grate cheese with.* **b** *a hairdryer to dry your hair with.* **c** *a bottle-opener to open bottles with.* **d** *a potato peeler to peel potatoes with.* **e** *nail clippers to clip your nails with.* **f** *a fire extinguisher to extinguish fires with.* **g** *a rice cooker to cook rice with.* **h** *a coffee grinder to grind coffee with.*

3 a *reference* **b** *pleasure* **c** *practice* **d** *view* **e** *feeling* **f** *care* **g** *ease* **h** *help*

4 a *Interview* **b** *Sleeping* **c** *Dances* **d** *A Room* **e** *The Man* **f** *Travels* **g** *To Sir* **h** *From Russia* **i** *The Trouble* **j** *Gone*

work

1

A: How was *work*?
B: Up and down. I got to *work* late, and found that the photocopier wouldn't *work*. By the time we had *work*ed out what was wrong with it and got it *work*ing again, it was practically lunchtime. So I didn't get much *work* done in the morning.
A: And in the afternoon?
B: Well, you know James (he's been *work*ing on that Beech-Reeds contract), well, he's decided to quit *work* and become a musician. So they've asked me to take over his *work* . That might mean a pay increase.
A: Nice *work!*

2 a *get done* **b** *light* **c** *steady* **d** *get down to* **e** *shoddy* **f** *going* **g** *take on* **h** *your own* **i** *tedious* **j** *heavy*

3 a *bodywork* **b** *worksheet* **c** *metalwork* **d** *coursework* **e** *workload* **f** *workmate* **g** *spadework* **h** *workforce*

would

1 1: c, f, m 2: d, j, l 3: a, e, h
4: b, g, i 5: k, n, o

2 a … *if you could afford to?* **b** If I *had* my own car, … **c** … you *would* be a good tennis player. **d** … I would *have* prepared your room. **e** … he would *be* home in time for dinner. **f** Would you *mind* turning the TV down? … **g** … if I *were* you. **h** … we would *often* go swimming in the canal … **i** Would you *rather* have tea or coffee? **j** Wouldn't you prefer *to* have …

3 a *If it was/were a nice day, we'd go/we would go to the beach.* **b** *If it had been a nice day, we would've gone to the beach.* **c** *If Elvis was/were alive, he'd be/he would be in his seventies now.* **d** *If Martha spoke French, she'd go/ she would go to France.* **e** *If I was/were in your position, I'd start/I would start looking for a job.* **f** *If we'd changed money at the airport, we would've had money for the taxi.* **g** *If Suzy had studied hard for her exams, she would've passed.* **h** *If my uncle had written his life story, he would've been famous.*

4 a – 5 **b** – 4 **c** – 1 **d** – 6 **e** – 7 **f** – 8 **g** – 2 **h** – 3

you

1 a *I, you* **b** *him, He* **c** *you, me, them, they* **d** *you, it, it* **e** *you, You* **f** *she, her* **g** *you, we, us, we* **h** *it, it, her*

2 a *personal subject, singular* **b** *personal object, plural* **c** *impersonal subject* **d** *impersonal subject* **e** *impersonal object* **f** *personal object, singular (probably)* **g** *personal object, singular* **h** *personal subject, singular* **i** *personal object, singular* **j** *impersonal object* **k** *personal subject, plural* **l** *personal object, plural* **m** *personal subject, singular (probably)*

3
Dermot: Hi, Natasha.
Natasha: Dermot! How are *you*?
Dermot: Fine, and *you*?
Natasha: Very well, thanks.
Dermot: What are *you* doing here?
Natasha: I'm looking for the Polish Consulate. Dermot, *you* are from around here, aren't *you*? Do *you* know where the Polish Consulate is?
Dermot: It's best if *you* take the next street on the right, and go down two blocks. *You* can't miss it. But why are *you* looking for the Polish Consulate?
Natasha: I need a visa.
Dermot: But *you* don't need a visa to go to Poland!
Natasha: *You* forget I'm from New Zealand. Not like *you*. New Zealanders need visas.
Dermot: Oh, yes. Right *you* are. Well, good luck.
Natasha: Thank *you*.

4 a 'All *you* need is love.' **b** 'Baby, *you're* a rich man.' **c** 'Do *you* want to know a secret?' **d** 'Got to get *you* into my life.' **e** 'Within *you*, without *you*.' **f** '*You* never give me *your* love.' **g** '*You've* got to hide *your* love away.' **h** 'I'm gonna sit right down and cry over *you*.' **i** 'I'm happy just to dance with *you*.' **j** '*You're* going to lose that girl.'